NARRATING HUMANITY

Narrating Humanity

LIFE WRITING AND MOVEMENT POLITICS
FROM PALESTINE TO MAUNA KEA

Cynthia G. Franklin

FORDHAM UNIVERSITY PRESS   NEW YORK   2023

Copyright © 2023 Fordham University Press

All rights reserved. No part of this publication may be reproduced, stored in a
retrieval system, or transmitted in any form or by any means—electronic,
mechanical, photocopy, recording, or any other—except for brief quotations
in printed reviews, without the prior permission of the publisher.

Fordham University Press has no responsibility for the persistence or accuracy
of URLs for external or third-party Internet websites referred to in this
publication and does not guarantee that any content on such websites is, or
will remain, accurate or appropriate.

Fordham University Press also publishes its books in a variety of electronic
formats. Some content that appears in print may not be available in electronic books.

Visit us online at www.fordhampress.com.

Library of Congress Cataloging-in-Publication Data available online at
https://catalog.loc.gov.

Printed in the United States of America

25 24 23   5 4 3 2 1

First edition

To my companions in story and struggle, from Hawaiʻi to Turtle Island to Palestine, who teach me new and better ways to be human

Contents

While working on these acknowledgments, I've been driving back and forth from the Ko'a. On July 1, 2022, a kāhea went out to gather at that shrine, set up outside the gate to the US Pacific Fleet Command Headquarters on O'ahu for an 'Anahulu (ten-day period) starting on July 2. This call went out in response to the state and military's failure to address an ongoing water crisis caused by the US Navy's leaks from its Red Hill fuel tanks into an aquifer that sits 100 feet directly below the tanks. In 2021, over 15,000 gallons poisoned thousands; since 1943, the tank has leaked at least 180,000 gallons of fuel. The contaminated aquifer serves as the primary drinking water source for the island, and the tanks have yet to be drained. The kāhea was also issued to protest the start of RIMPAC. In this biannual event, nations (twenty-six in 2022) bring their naval fleets to the waters in and around the Hawaiian Islands, to engage in what the US Navy boasts to be the world's largest military exercise, done in the name of fostering "safety," "security," and "cooperative relationships." The call also followed a week of devastating SCOTUS rulings that support climate catastrophe and guns, and that (continue to) declare war against women, children, Indigenous people, poor people, and pretty much everyone (human, other-than-human) trying to live and breathe on this endangered planet.

On July 2, as we pulled into a military parking lot with its view of the frigates and destroyer ships homing into the harbor, I felt weighed down by SCOTUS, RIMPAC, and a military that continues with impunity to poison our drinking water. I also just had read that the Ko'a, the circular piles of stone built by kia'i (protectors) as an ahu or sacred altar, had been vandalized. As we crossed the highway from the parking lot and entered the space of the Ko'a,

I felt a lifting. I could see that the ahu already had been restored, and at the Orientation tent I recognized the same women who welcomed visitors to the Puʻuhonua (place of refuge) set up at the base of the Mauna Kea Access Road in 2019. While waiting for a debriefing session on the Red Hill water crisis, I talked to friends running the information tables on Red Hill, or Kapūkakī. That morning, there were a few dozen people, a few tents, tables, and banners, some coolers, water, and, by midday, several trays of Chinese food. Within the next few days, the space grew into a vibrant hub of activist organizing and community building. By the time I arrived on July 4, more than one hundred people were gathered, circled together on mats and camping chairs, ready for the full day and evening of programming. Near the ahu, crates of donated water were stacked high for families most impacted by the petroleum poisoning. Tables were loaded with food enough to feed us all. In a tent off to the side, children were learning chants. The main-event tent housed a movie screen, a sound system, a disco ball(!), and supplies for workshops and art builds. Sessions included poetry in commemoration of Haunani-Kay Trask, a regalia-making workshop, artivism activities, a workshop on true security, and presentations on demilitarization, and on waterback and landback initiatives. Evenings featured film screenings and live music. In a few days, organizers had reclaimed a space made ugly and unsafe by military occupation and transformed it into one of mutual aid, in which people could come together in safety and make art, share food and music and poetry, study and learn together, plot resistance, and dream decolonial and abolitionist dreams into existence.

Many of those at the helm of this organizing are featured in the pages of this book. Some were working with well-established groups (HULI, Women's Voices Women Speak, Hawaiʻi Peace and Justice, the Sierra Club); others, with newer or re-emergent organizations (the Koa Futures initiative, Hui Aloha Aina o Honolulu, Oʻahu Water Protectors, Oʻahu Mutual Aid). The speed with which these organizers were able to establish an infrastructure to bring people together to stand for the land, waters, and one another owed to the ongoing life and lessons of the movement for Mauna Kea—and to that movement's predecessors. What was unfolding at the Koʻa evidenced the way older movements give rise, sure as breath, to new movements.

I begin these acknowledgments with the Koʻa because in the face of militarized, heteropatriarchal, racist, capitalist and colonial violence (including July Fourth "Independence" celebrations that put all this violence on loud, proud display), it is these movements in the making—and the people who bring them into being—that animate this book and give it purpose.

To write this book and find its purpose has been a journey full of zigs and zags. Over the past twelve years, at times I have abandoned it to pursue other projects—coediting "Life in Occupied Palestine: A Special *Biography* Issue," building Students and Faculty for Justice in Palestine at the University of Hawai'i (SFJP@UH), participating in the US Campaign for the Academic and Cultural Boycott of Israel (USACBI) and in Mauna Kea Protectors at UH. I also was having trouble finding the story I wanted to tell and figuring out how to tell it. I did not know how all the pathways that took me away from *Narrating Humanity* would lead me back to it. Just as this book concerns ways life writing can emerge out of and offer a way to participate in political organizing, so too can scholarship.

At every stage of its writing, comrades, friends, and colleagues have played an integral part in this book's vision, and shaped all that is right about it, even as any errors are my own. Working collectively is not only the subject of much of this book; it is a practice that has made writing it possible and sometimes even joyful.

In a writing group with Betsy Colwill, Monisha Das Gupta, Candace Fujikane, Linda Lierheimer, Laura Lyons, Kieko Matteson, Naoko Shibusawa, and Mari Yoshihara, I received comments on the earliest drafts that have continued to guide me, just as their friendship has been sustaining. Monisha, Candace, and Naoko continued to nurture this project through all its iterations, by way of detailed feedback, check-ins, and pomodoro sessions as our books have taken shape in conversation with one another.

Participation in a writing group with Rana Barakat, Ebony Coletu, Sami Hermez, and Sherene Seikaly has been paradigm-shifting. Sherene, Ebony, Rana, and Sami challenged me not only to more fully center theoretical frameworks offered by Black and Palestinian scholars but, in doing so, to rethink my whole approach to the story this book attempts to tell. I am still aspiring to put into practice all they have taught me.

Two UH English Department Research Outcomes Grants gave me an opportunity to strengthen this book's arguments and direction. In a 2020 book publishing workshop with Richard Morrison, I was able to share proposals and exchange ideas with my colleagues and friends: Derrick Higginbotham, No'u Revilla, Pua Warren, and Emily West. This workshop also was the starting point for the privilege of working with Richard Morrison, editor extraordinaire. Then in spring 2022, together with wonderful grad students and colleagues, I participated in a "Liberate Your Research!" workshop led by the brilliant and badass Nadine Naber. This experience, together with Nadine's feedback as we hiked and swam together, enabled me to more fully claim this book's theories and methodologies.

Other students and colleagues have been generous in reading and responding to different chapters or specific portions of this book. My thanks go to

Lauren Berlant, Tim Brennan, Vrinda Dalmiya, Sierra Dew, Bryan Kamaoli Kuwada, Salah Hassan, Ali Musleh, Andre Perez, Noʻu Revilla, Juliana Spahr, Jack Taylor, and John Zuern. I especially appreciate the willingness of those featured in chapters 4 and 5 and the Postscript to share photos included in this book, and to review what I wrote; there is no audience to whom I feel more responsible.

Thank you to Bill Mullen and Kandice Chuh, for readers' reports that enabled me to raise this book's stakes and clarify its aims.

Thank you to Susanne Rostock for not only granting permission to include a still from her Dream Defenders video, but also sharing stories about the video's making.

This book also has been shaped by giving talks for different audiences. At the ACLA, ASA, ASQ, IABA, and MLA conferences, I received valuable feedback, including from my fellow panelists. So, too, I learned from discussions following presentations given at the University of Hawaiʻi (I'm especially grateful to Kathy Ferguson for encouraging me to rethink my key terms), and at universities in Spain, England, India, and Palestine. Thank you to my hosts for making these opportunities possible: at University of Navarra, Rocío Davis; at King's College, Clare Brant; at EFL University, Hyderabad, Nikhila H.; at Delhi University and Jawaharlal Nehru University, Charu Gupta and Subarno Chattarji; at IIT Madras, Mathangi Krishnamurthy; at Al-Quds University, Ahmad Ayyad and Shaira Vadasaria.

I am lucky to have close friends who are brilliant and generous critics. Cristina Bacchilega, Monisha Das Gupta, and Hannah Manshel not only read drafts. They quite literally walked me through some of the stuck places. Years of Sundays spent walking the oceanside stretch from Kaimana Beach to Kahala with Cristina have been not only restorative, but ways to work through manuscript knots. Weekly Mānoa Valley walks with Monisha were problem-solving sessions that kept me grounded—and that also lifted me up, thanks to the company of our favorite tiny human, Aila Kahakauwila, who (from snugli to stroller to our running in her wake) is a source of unadulterated joy. During the pandemic, hiking along the Waʻahila Ridge with Hannah and Lucy was not only tree therapy, but a place to test out ideas.

J. Kēhaulani Kauanui has been a treasured friend whose insights, rigorous feedback, and advice inform every chapter in ways small and large. Through writing sprints, phone calls, daily check-ins, and lānai hangouts, Kēhaulani also gave me faith that this project was worth pursuing, and kept me writing.

My gratitude also goes to friends who have passed. Even when she disagreed with my positions, Miriam Fuchs was unstinting in her support and astute insights. Paul Lyons's writings in the margins unfailingly made points of central importance. Barbara Harlow, Fred Ho, and Haunani-Kay Trask, all larger than life, continue to inspire me with their bravery and brilliance. Conversations with Patrick Wolfe were unforgettable events that provided structure to my thinking. His comments on early drafts were sharply insightful, bighearted, and often hilarious. One register of his astonishing mind is that I cannot imagine the ways this book would have been better had he been here to keep me company through the last years of writing it—I just know it is so, and I miss him hugely.

It has been my great fortune to have been able to work with students from whom I have learned so much about radical forms of human becoming and belonging. Some I am now lucky enough to have as colleagues; all continue to do transformative work in the world as educators and organizers. Ali Musleh merits particular mention: even as I have had the privilege of being on his dissertation committee and of continually learning from his scholarly brilliance, he has come to be a cherished comrade who, together with Sheika and Karam, is family to me. My love and gratitude go as well to other participants in SFJP@UH and related inter/national struggles for ea (sovereignty, life, breath, rising): Katherine Achacoso, Māhea Ahia, Eliah Aoina, Kim Compoc, Lilly Fisher, Ikaika Gleisberg, Janet Graham, Sarah Hamid, Sam Ikehara, Kawena Kapahua, Akta Kaushal, Lee Kava, RaeDeen Keahiolalo, ʻIhilani Lasconia, Kauwila Mahi, Rajiv Mohabir, Leilani Portillo, Noʻu Revilla, Anjoli Roy, Stephanie Sang, Lamiaa Soliman, Gabriel Verduzco, Quynh Vo, Rain Wright, Aiko Yamashiro, and Ida Yoshinaga. I was revising this book while teaching a "Genres of Protest" graduate class, and this work was energized by all that Lilly, Ryan Gapelu, Kawena, Nina Gibson, Kauwila, Bre Riddick, and Lamiaa taught me. Under the leadership of Katherine and Māhea, working on the Mauna Kea Syllabus Project as a faculty advisor and cocurator of the "Allies" section was a learning experience in forging solidarities that informs this book.

Narrating Humanity attempts to honor what I've learned from those I've already named, along with other students, colleagues, community members, and friends who are part of the movement for Mauna Kea, SFJP@UH, and related forms of organizing. Thank you to Barbara Altemus, Imani Altemus-Williams, Ibrahim Aoude, Cristina Bacchilega, Tuti and the rest of the Baker ohana, Reem Bassous, Alohalani Brown, Ellen-Rae Cachola, Kū Ching, Anna Chua, Waleed Doany, Joy Lehuanani Enomoto, Konia Freitas, Candace Fujikane, Rebecca Goldschmidt, Vernadette Gonzalez, Monisha Das Gupta, Tina and Lisa Grandinetti, Hilary Hacker, Carolyn Hadfield, Sue Haglund, Joseph Han, Clare Hanusz, kuʻualoha hoʻomanawani, Bianca Isaki, Kahala Johnson, Kaleikoa Kaʻeo, Kyle Kajihiro, Camille Kalama, Puna Kalipi, Hatim and Dolores Kanaaneh, Noe Goodyear-Kaʻōpua, Terrilee Kekoʻolani, Gwen

Kim, Sophie Kim, Ciara Lacy, Vivien Lee, Nanea Lo, ʻIlima Long, Brandy Nālani McDougall, Laurel Mei-Singh, Shelley Muneoka, Carol Murry, Nicole Naone, the Osorio ohana, Maen Owda, Andre Perez, Kekai Perry, Punahele, Rich Rath, Charlie Reppun, Noʻu Revilla, Walter Ritte, Dean Saranillio, Keahi Setareh, S. Shankar, Mimi Sharma, Kahikina de Silva, Noenoe Silva, Healani Sonoda-Pale, Ty Kāwika Tengan, Ann Wright, Risa Yamamoto, and Kalaniʻōpua Young. Through relationships deepened by standing together on the Mauna, giving testimony at too many UH Board of Regents Meetings, participating in ʻaha on Wise Field, holding press conferences at Campus Center, protesting at the State Capitol, inching along the H1 as part of an airport caravan, sharing food at solidarity gatherings, marching, sign waving, meeting up for film and reading groups, attending planning meetings, or hanging out on the lānai, being in relationship with these makers of movements has informed this book's belief that we can create ways to be human that are based not on violence and separation but on love and radical reciprocity.

Decolonial Novembers and other events SFJP@UH and Sabeel-Hawaiʻi have participated in have served as important ways to build solidarity, from Hawaiʻi to Palestine. In ways the second half of this book can only begin to capture, I have learned from the brilliant, visionary, and radical scholars, poets, and activists who have spent time here. Thank you to Rabab Abdulhadi, Yousef Aljamal, Hala Alyan, Sumaya Awad, Rana Barakat, Ramzy Baroud, Noor Daghlas, Angela Davis, Noura Erakat, Mai Hassan, Stefano Harney, Sarah Ihmoud, Nour Joudah, Remi Kanazi, J. Kēhaulani Kauanui, Tariq Luthun, Fred Moten, Steve Salaita, Nadera Shalhoub, and Robert Warrior.

Thank you as well to my USACBI comrades, to others I worked with on MLA and ASA boycott resolutions, and to the amazing folks at EI, JVP, Palestine Legal, NSJP, and USCPR who are part of the Campus BDS Support Network—you exemplify the liberation that comes with speaking truth to power, and this book is a better one because of all I have learned from you: Tony Alessandrini, Dena Al-Adeeb, Dina Al-Kassim, Sumaya Awad, Kristian Davis Bailey, Anna Baltzer, Omar Barghouti, Nora Barrows-Friedman, Tallie Ben Daniel, Ebony Coletu, Rebecca Comay, Roua Daas, Lisa Duggan, Falastine Dwikat, Maya Edery, Nada Elia, Noura Erakat, Richard Falk, Keith Feldman, Terri Ginsberg, Lenora Hanson, Barbara Harlow, Salah Hassan, Sami Hermez, Sarah Ihmoud, Liz Jackson, Remi Kanazi, Persis Karim, Charlotte Kates, J. Kēhaulani Kauanui, Tanya Keilani, Alex Kerry, Zoha Khalili, John King, Michael Letwin, David Lloyd, Ben Lorber, Alex Lubin, Sunaina Maira, Curtis Marez, Adam Miyashiro, Fred Moten, Bill Mullen, Leah Muskin-Pierret, Rima Najjar, David Palumbo-Liu, Loubna Qutami, Noam Perry, Jasbir Puar, Julie Rak, Tim Reiss, Jordy Rosenberg,

Andrew Ross, Bob Ross, Steve Salaita, Malini Johar Schueller, Heike Schotten, Dan Segal, Stephen Sheehi, Magid Shihade, Rajini Srikanth, Neferti Tadiar, Robert Warrior, and Omar Zahzah.

Many other communities and individuals have supported this book in not always tangible but significant ways: the UH *Biography* team (Miriam Fuchs, Craig Howes, Paige Rasmussen, Anjoli Roy, Stan Schab, John Zuern); the people with PARC, especially Penny Mitchell; my coeditors Ibrahim Aoude and Morgan Cooper, and all the contributors to "Life in Occupied Palestine"; my Sabeel-Hawai'i coconspirators (Beverly Davis Amjadi, Mary Carpenter, Christopher Golding, Brian Grieves, George Hudes, Noel Kent, and Neal MacPherson); the Solidarity Forever Gang (Hosam Aboul-Ela, Karen Fang, Persis Karim, Shankar and Yumna Siddiqi); UC Berkeley friends and mentors (Kim Drake, Lauren Muller, Francesca Royster, Sue Schweik, John and Kimball Wilkins); friends and colleagues at UH (Sarah Allen, Laurel Fantauzzo, Anna Feuerstein, Pat Penn Hilden, Tiana Kahakauwila, Njoroge Njoroge, Georganne Nordstrom, Robert Perkinson, Suzanna Reiss, John Rieder, Shawna Yang Ryan, Danielle Seid, David Stannard, Val Wayne). (As a side note, Danielle Seid, who has kept me LOLing throughout the pandemic, has put me on notice that acknowledgments are where an academic's astrological makeup truly comes out. I await her reading with trepidation.)

Thank you as well to everyone at Fordham University Press. Working with Richard Morrison was a dream come true, and I am especially grateful to him for his generative feedback and his vision, including his insistence that I transform a postscript on Mauna Kea into a chapter. My appreciation also goes to Nancy Basmajian for her meticulous copyediting and for insightful observations that helped me sharpen my analysis.

And thank you to Joy Enomoto for designing a cover image that is arrestingly beautiful and generative; I only hope the book can live up to it.

This book has as its foundation the love and support of my family. Thank you to the Franklin-Pitts: my brother, Bob, Jessica, Ivan, and Avery. Thank you to the Franklin-Follansbees: my sister, Julie, Mark, Ayla, and Jasper. Thank you to my son, Jesse Franklin-Murdock, and Alice Ahn (and Paigey!). Thank you to my Aunt Diane and the rest of the Leon family. Thank you to UDPPN and the rest of the Landys. A special thank-you to my mother, Elaine Franklin. My father, Shel Franklin, died during the writing of this book, but I think of him and my grandparents daily, and with gratitude. Thank you to everyone in Chennai (Amma, Shekar, Lakshmi, Sumita, Kumar), Hyderabad (Girija, Anusha, Rohit, Raman, Zara, Zephyr), Uganda (Abishek, Dharini), and the Bay Area (Sumanth, Sukanya, Ujay!) who during the writing of this book cheered me on, in-person and during our biweekly Zoom calls.

My biggest, deepest thanks go to S. Shankar, my life companion. I have taken every step in the writing of this book in his most excellent company, which only got better during the pandemic. Shankar has talked through the big ideas, helped give shape to messes I've made, edited drafts I thought were done, come up with titles, and been a source of unwavering support and encouragement. Shankar, I have more gratitude than I can translate into words for your patience, formidable intelligence, kindness, creativity, political commitments, passion for ideas, compassion, cooking, and love. You helped me to write the best book I can. More importantly, even in times of crisis, you make me a happier and better human.

NARRATING HUMANITY

Introduction

The Human in Crisis

Narrating Humanity: Life Writing and Movement Politics from Palestine to Mauna Kea explores life writing texts that have catalyzed or respond to contemporary crises in the United States concerning the status of the human. Despite thoroughgoing critiques by scholars, activists, and the many groups of people excluded from its domain, "the human" continues to be a concept we cannot theorize away. Rather, it remains one that we need to wrestle with. After all, understandings of who and what count as human continue to determine who lives and dies, who has the right to breathe freely and fully, who has airways that can be choked or crushed. As well, new—or a resurgence of old— formulations of the human can enable ways of being and becoming that are necessary for not only surviving but thriving during a time of accelerating crises brought on by the intersecting effects of racial capitalism, imperialism, heteropatriarchy, and climate change. Through analysis of high-profile case studies focused on Hurricane Katrina, Black Lives Matter, Palestine solidarity, and Native Hawaiian sovereignty, and featuring life narratives that expose civil society's dependence upon dehumanization, this project explores how life writing can be mobilized to do more than perpetuate forms of dehumanization that underwrite state violence. I contend that life narratives that participate in liberatory political movements can counter hegemonic forms of dehumanization and help us envision ways of being human based on queer kinship, inter/national solidarity, abolitionist care, and decolonial connectivity among humans, more-than-humans, land, and waters.

I approach the life writing texts under consideration in this book through the analytic of "narrative humanity," by which I mean the established narrative genres and conventions that define the human. As well, in the second part of this book, through the lens of a concept I have named "narrated humanity," I look to how life writing texts can serve to narrate into being understandings of the human inspired by contemporary political movements that are based on radical care and connectivity. In the third and final part, I continue this exploration as I introduce the term "grounded narrative humanity" and consider decolonial formulations of the human that emerge from Indigenous-led movements, that are premised on deep and respectful relationality with the more-than-human. In the progression through *Narrating Humanity*, I learn from the writers and activists in this study and come to write side by side with them in my own acts of narrated humanity, refusing the boundaries between autobiography, community-based activism, and literary and cultural criticism. As I do so, I hope that those reading this book will keep company with them, and with me, in a journey toward materializing more just, capacious, and joyful ways of human being and belonging.

It is my contention in *Narrating Humanity* that the present moment is not only one of horrific violence and brutal inequalities that depend on new and ongoing forms of dehumanization, but also one in which we see creative and visionary rethinkings of the human replete with possibilities. During the post–World War II era through the Civil Rights era, struggles over the human largely were pitched within what Hannah Arendt, with her outraged awareness that being accorded human status depended on being a citizen of a nation-state, called "the right to have rights" (*The Origins of Totalitarianism*). Arendt is not alone in perceiving the problems with this exclusionary conceptualization of the human. Groups and movements engaged in Black, Third World, Indigenous, women's, trans, queer, workers', refugee and migrant, prisoners', environmental, and disability-related struggles have worked within and against this ideology that upholds the power of nation-states and the ruling classes at the expense of those deemed noncitizens and, in circular logic, not human or deserving of rights.

Today, the terrain has shifted, in large part thanks to a long genealogy of struggle and resistance, and also owing to spectacularly failed democracies and accelerating threats to planetary survival. As David Palumbo-Liu observes, "between the precarity of our devastated planet and a political system that lies in tatters, we stand at a decisive point in history" (4). At this juncture, it is not just those on the far left who believe that nation-states, judiciaries, and international NGOs cannot provide solutions to climate crisis, to rising fascism, to poverty, to racism, to migrant and refugee crises, to sexual and gender violence, to unmet needs for health care. Instead, there is a widening awareness that governmental entities and their corporate offspring in fact *cause* human and more-than-human suffering, violence, and premature death. Building on previous revolutionary movements and social justice organizing, then, those collectively engaged in what Joy Lehuanani Enomoto names "The Struggle for Ea" in her breathtaking image featured on the cover of this book are achieving a teleological break with liberal individualist and rights-based conceptions of the human, and refusing dependency on nation-states as givers of rights or arbiters of the human. Through these articulated movements, and stories of the human that support and emerge out of this political organizing, what is on the rise is a nonstatist form of human becoming and belonging based on a living, breathing, loving interdependence and political solidarity not only with other humans, starting with those who are most vulnerable and besieged, but also with land, waters, elemental forces, and our more-than-human relations. As captured in Enomoto's image that intertwines lungs and tree roots, and as Leanne Betasamosake Simpson puts this in her love song "The Oldest Tree in the World," "I breathe it in, you breathe it out."

To set the stage for this book's investigation, I begin with the Eichmann trial and Hannah Arendt's *Eichmann in Jerusalem: A Report on the Banality of Evil*—a work that has had enormous impact on modern understandings of the human, by a philosopher whose insights into the interrelations of being human, being a citizen, and being accorded the most basic of rights are essential to *Narrating Humanity*. Attention to the trial and its narratives establish this book's broad historical and geopolitical relevance. So, too, controversies sparked by often competing representations of Adolf Eichmann, the Israeli state, the prosecution, and the trial's witnesses introduce this book's focus on the important role life narratives can play in exposing the slippery status of the human and in participating in high-stakes contestations over who counts as human. So, too, a reckoning with Arendt's bleak vision of the human and the banality of evil—which includes the need to hold ourselves accountable for human suffering and cruelty—is a necessary pathway toward imagining the more hope-filled ways of human being and belonging afforded by political movement building in our contemporary and still-violent moment.

The Human on Trial

In 1961, the Israeli state put Eichmann on trial. After kidnapping him from Argentina in 1960, Israel charged him with fifteen counts of war crimes, crimes against the Jewish people, and crimes against humanity. Hannah Arendt, a Jew who fled Germany to escape the Nazis, and who eventually assumed US citizenship in 1950, went to Jerusalem to provide serial coverage for the *New Yorker* of this internationally broadcast trial. *Eichmann in Jerusalem* was then published in 1963. Arendt's trial narrative occasioned what Anson Rabinbach described as "the most bitter public dispute among intellectuals and scholars concerning the Holocaust that has ever taken place" (97). In representing Eichmann as banally human, Arendt broke with hegemonic narratives about the Holocaust and the SS officer widely known as its architect. The critical eye she cast on the trial's political purposes also proved incendiary. As historians have noted, the Eichmann trial played a crucial role in consolidating Israel's identity as a Jewish nation. Held thirteen years after the founding of Israel, the trial is sometimes referred to as Israel's coming-of-age event, or bar mitzvah. Arendt vigorously objected to Israel's first prime minister, David Ben-Gurion, and the leading prosecutor, Gideon Hausner, using the trial as political theater. Her blistering critique came at a time when Israel's nation-building efforts and US support for Zionism were being mobilized through this trial that conflated being Jewish and being Zionist, and that also helped cover over the Nakba, or Israel's catastrophic expulsion in 1948 of 750,000 Palestinians from Palestine. Out of step with the times, Arendt not only disrupted this state-building narrative; she also initiated a bitter battle over modern understandings of the human.

Attention to Arendt's character study of Eichmann and to her account of the trial's witnesses provides insights into the role life narratives play in constituting who and what counts as human—and the extent to which hegemonic formulations of the human are attended by, and depend on, violent processes of human unmaking. In particular, *Eichmann in Jerusalem* and responses to it illuminate the narratives of humanization and dehumanization required to uphold the colonial myth of Israel as a "land without a people for a people without a land." As well, *Eichmann in Jerusalem* suggests how life narratives (broadly defined to include not only texts but also, as in this case, performative events such as trials) can challenge as well as reinforce the human-inhuman binaries that legitimate, naturalize, and invisibilize the Holocaust, as well as the colonial violence on which Zionism and other settler states depend. The struggles waged over Eichmann's humanity indicate the power as well as the historical variability of these human-inhuman binaries and the need to resist dehumanization on political as well as ethical grounds.

Before I get underway, an acknowledgment: although a work of continuing importance when it comes to understanding the human, *Eichmann in Jerusalem* is far from the only way to begin what is an American studies book. I begin here because *Eichmann in Jerusalem* initiated my entry into this project. As I was delivering a conference paper on Arendt's Eichmann at a 2010 life writing conference, the panel chair cut me off after ten minutes and shut me out of the Q&A. The next day, a conference organizer hesitated to accept my contribution to a graduate student travel fund. He explained that word had spread that I had given a paper that was "scandalous" and "inappropriate." The reason? I had likened the anger *Eichmann in Jerusalem* aroused in the 1960s to contemporary responses to anti-Zionism in the academy. This conference experience surely validated my argument. It also moved me as a white Jew to go beyond engaging in anti-Zionist critique. If reading *Eichmann in Jerusalem* sharpened my criticisms of the Israeli state, my colleagues' reactions provided an impetus to become involved in sustained Palestine solidarity work as they confirmed for me the power of *Eichmann in Jerusalem* and, more generally, works of life writing. These encounters also suggested the limits of challenging Zionism through denouncing formulations of the human that make colonial violence possible. Crucial as her insights into the human are, staying as Arendt does within a mode of life writing—or, in my case, life writing studies—premised on castigation and critique did not seem sufficient. I began thinking more about the importance of not simply taking "anti" positions in which those who have been dehumanized remain abstractions, or not (fully) human. The works of life writing in this study refuse such an approach. And in my own engagement with these works, which informs and is informed by political activism and by relationships of solidarity and love, so too do I. But first, before turning to these works, a return to the Eichmann trial, and the crises and controversies Arendt's analysis occasioned.

At issue in the rancorous disputes concerning Eichmann was his status as human. During the trial, whereas Eichmann strove to establish his ordinary humanity, the prosecution was intent on disproving it. Positioning him in a glass box as a sealed-off specimen of evil, they cast him as a monster who embodied a long history of antisemitism. Arendt's representation of him as all too human disrupted the human-inhuman binaries that Eichmann and Ben-Gurion attempted, from opposing sides, to occupy. Whereas Eichmann attempted to exonerate himself by explaining that he was just doing his job and following his superiors' orders, for Arendt this conformity made Eichmann "terribly and terrifyingly normal" (276). Arendt's Eichmann emerges as a petty bureaucrat, whose actions overseeing the evacuation and execution of millions of people derive from his investments in advancing his career and from his unquestioning belief in the law of the land. Arendt's Eichmann, unboxed, exists within even as he unsettles the category of the human.

Readers of Arendt took umbrage at not only her insistence on Eichmann's ordinary humanness but also her perceived dismissal of antisemitism and dehumanization of Jewish Holocaust survivors. To bolster international support for Israel as a Zionist state, and to establish identification between Israelis and Jews in Europe who had experienced the Holocaust, the trial architects focused on Eichmann as a stand-in for Nazi Germany and what Hausner described as "'anti-Semitism throughout history'" (qtd. in Arendt, 19). Arendt condemned this use of the trial as "bad history and bad rhetoric; worse, it was clearly at cross-purposes with putting Eichmann on trial" (285). She was equally critical of Hausner's extralegal purposes in featuring testimony from 112 Holocaust survivors, all Ashkenazi, Jewish and European. Chronologically arranged to convey the history of the Holocaust and, as the prosecution put it, "to introduce tension and to elevate the trial out of dull routine" (qtd. in Yablonka, 99), this testimony, broadcast daily to an international audience, played a critical role in dramatizing its horror. A high point occurred when Yehiel Dinur (a.k.a. KZ-nik) collapsed on the witness stand. In the few passages she devotes to witnesses' testimony, Arendt wrote about it with irony, even flippancy, drawing fire from readers who charged her with heartlessness and antisemitism.

Arendt's analysis also upset the Zionist narrative the Eichmann trial helped solidify—a narrative that, in conflating Zionist and Jewish identity, perpetuates an understanding of the human that erases and dehumanizes Palestinians. Historians have made the case that Israel held the Eichmann trial not only to justify the need for a Zionist state, but also to position anyone contesting this as aligned with Nazis. In the context of the new state of Israel, Palestinians were cast either as akin to Nazis in the alleged threat they posed to Jewish existence, or as nonexistent—two contradictory but complementary forms of dehumanization that served simultaneously to legitimate and deny Israel's ongoing practices of ethnic cleansing (Zertal, 115). With keen awareness of the extent to which human rights depend on national belonging, Arendt objected to how the trial supported the very conditions of statelessness that brought so many Jews to Israel following World War II.

Arendt's challenges to the Eichmann trial illuminate its larger historical and political stakes, and how crucial—and difficult to pin down—definitions of the human and humanity are. The Nazi genocide instigated a crisis in the category of the human—one connected to anxieties about the fragility of empathy and the strength of human cruelty and indifference. Through the Eichmann trial, Ben-Gurion and the prosecution responded to this crisis by asserting the inhumanity of Eichmann—and of Nazis and antisemites—and the humanity of Jewish survivors/victims and, by extension, all Jews. Through Jewish survivors' testimonies, the trial also helped make hegemonic the narrative justifying Israel as a Zionist state and a homeland that serves all Jews as a refuge and bulwark against future threats of genocide. As it aligns Jews, Zionists, and being human, this narrative depends on the dehumanization not only of Nazis but also of Palestinians. Through her representations of Eichmann, Hausner, Ben-Gurion, and the Jewish witnesses, Arendt upsets the human-inhuman binaries and the righteousness of the Zionist project that this trial was helping enshrine.

As I will be exploring through the course of this book, life narratives—and what I will be defining as forms of narrative and narrated humanity—play an important role in shaping understandings of the human. As I hope this brief reading of *Eichmann in Jerusalem* and the trial suggests, life narratives help form, expose, and disrupt the norms that, in constituting who counts as human and who does not, determine who lives and who dies; who receives protection from legal and other institutions; and who is expendable not only when it comes to war but also within systems of justice and the structuring of civil society. As Arendt enters into a contestation over Eichmann's status as human, she challenges her readers to confront our own complicities in all-too-human acts of inhumanity and in processes of dehumanization that are foundational not only to Nazis and states of war, but also to the everyday functioning of nation-states. She crucially calls on us to claim responsibility for our actions, to not take refuge in platitudes, and to be willing to refuse compliance with authority and break with governing norms. However, as Arendt focuses on Eichmann to exemplify the banality of evil, and how states and their institutions normalize acts of inhumanity, she makes no attempt to represent the humanity of those whom the Eichmanns of this world and nation-states dehumanize. Because she does not attend to the humanity of those whom states instrumentalize and more violently dehumanize, she accounts only partially for the significance of life narratives.

The strengths as well as deficiencies of Arendt's approach to the human come into focus when compared to Shoshana Felman's (much less astute) assessment of the Eichmann trial. In an analysis of the trial that also recognizes its ideological power, albeit to dramatically different ends, Felman extols the Holocaust survivors' testimony. She celebrates how the trial, "through its monumental legal chorus of the testimonies of the persecuted, unwittingly became creative of a canonical or *sacred narrative*" (236). As Felman endows the witnesses with an exalted agency that is at once their own and God-given, the Israeli state and its role in cannily conducting this "legal chorus" go entirely unacknowledged. Focusing exclusively on how the trial, as it radically transforms victims into historical agents, creates "the privileged text of a modern *folktale of justice*" (238), Felman need not distinguish between the significance that witnesses' testimony held for them and other survivors, and that which it held for the Israeli state. As she ignores the trial's state-building purposes, she participates in its erasure of Palestinian humanity.

In her discussion of the witness testimony, Arendt moves in the opposite direction from Felman, one designed to strip away claims to justice and appeals to religion or the sacred. This approach, however, comes at a cost. Crucial as it is, Arendt's focus on the state's use of witnesses' testimony is unaccompanied by any consideration of what it meant to them to share their trauma. As she berates Ben-Gurion and the prosecution for politicizing the trial, these witnesses become so much collateral damage, and in dismissing their trauma and dehumanization, Arendt contributes to it. And though she calls attention to how the trial puts in place a narrative that shores up the Israeli state, including its dispossession of Palestinians, her own counternarrative includes no mention of Palestinian lives. In short, even as *Eichmann in Jerusalem* intervenes in the formation of a narrative that supports state violence and dehumanization, what Arendt does *not* do is make use of life writing to assert the humanity of those excluded from the domain of the human. Nor does she employ life writing to narrate new and better ways of being human.

The Politics of Narrating Public Lives

This book attends to life narratives that, like *Eichmann in Jerusalem*, enter into ideological struggles over the human and, unlike it, posit alternative ways of being human. The narratives that are the focus of *Narrating Humanity* all counter processes of dehumanization that hegemonic formulations of the human legitimate, gloss over, and naturalize. In distinction to *Eichmann in Jerusalem*, as these narratives expose and contest human-inhuman binaries and forms of dehumanization and oppression on which civil society depends, they simultaneously draw on life narratives' possibilities for imagining more just and liberating ways of being human. Each chapter centers on life writing texts that have either catalyzed a public controversy or intervened in an existing crisis over the human. These texts take up the Katrina Complex and the war on terror (chapter 1); antiblack police violence and the Black Lives Matter movement (chapters 2–3); the New McCarthyism on college campuses and the Palestinian-led Boycott, Divestment and Sanctions (BDS) campaign (chapter 4); and the movement to protect Native Hawaiians' sacred mountain and ancestor Mauna a Wākea (chapter 5). The book is divided into three parts. Part 1, "Narrative Humanity," considers texts that work within established literary forms and conventions. Part 2, "Narrated Humanity," takes up life narratives that, as they participate in movement politics, inspire new ways to narrate the human. Part 3, "Narrated Humanity and Grounded Narrative Humanity," continues this exploration as it also moves beyond a focus on the human through attention to Indigenous activism and ways of knowing. At issue throughout are ways life writing texts can mediate between political movements, theory, and history to make space for freer and more radically inclusive and caring ways of being human.

I approach this study as a scholar of life writing who comes at the field sideways. Even as this project takes as its premise the importance of analyzing representations of lives and complements my work coediting the journal *Biography*,[1] my main concern is not with debates and directions in life writing studies. Rather, I see this primarily as an American studies project with a two-fold orientation toward movement politics and literary criticism. At the same time, this book is informed and invigorated by, and I hope contributes to, other intersecting fields of study. These include not only life writing studies but also critical ethnic studies, Indigenous and decolonial studies, settler colonial studies, university studies, Black studies, Palestine studies, feminist studies, queer studies, literary and film studies, and cultural studies. With this transdisciplinary approach, I build on my first two books, *Writing Women's Lives: The Politics and Poetics of Multi-genre Anthologies* and *Academic Lives: Memoir, Cultural Theory, and the University Today*, which also take up the relationship between genres of life writing and participation in political movements, and which also investigate interrelations between academic work and activism in and beyond the university. I bring these books' commitments to engaged scholarship here as I draw upon, and I hope extend, my support for BLM and my participation in solidarity work for Palestinian liberation (as a white, Jewish anti-Zionist American) and for a decolonial Hawai'i (as a settler ally). These allegiances along with my situatedness in American studies have determined my concentrated areas of focus.

Although I intend for my approach and arguments to extend beyond the struggles I take up, this book does not of course even begin to "cover" the many contestations over the human that have occurred in the contemporary United States, let alone across time and place. To make its arguments about how narratives shape our understandings of the human in highly consequential ways, this book just as productively could have addressed works of life writing and political movements that center prisoners, queer and trans people (and in fact this book is informed by an article I cowrote with Laura E. Lyons on the Gwen Araujo case), immigrants and refugees, those with disabilities, old people, young people, poor people, Indigenous peoples, and the list goes on, in a way that substantiates the violent exclusions that make up the seemingly broad and universal category of the human.

So, too, of course, it is not only life narratives that give representation to the human, and although I concentrate on life writing for reasons I address below, this book's analytic can apply to texts of any genre that, through the stories they tell, engage in the processes of human making and unmaking. This includes novels, poems, short stories, films, songs, dance performances, and also genre-defying works that blur the lines between fiction and non-fiction as they shape our understandings of the human. So, too, I believe this book's approach can provide an optic to analyze scholarship (autoethnographies, cultural anthropology, histories, cultural theory, etc.) that employs elements of personal and/or collective auto/biography to theorize the human. Even as *Narrating Humanity* offers a possible approach to reading such academic writing, much of this scholarship deeply and sometimes directly informs this book, as well as my overall commitment to making use of my tenured position to work within as well as against university structures and scholarly conventions. The body of work that I am thinking of includes writings by Māhealani Ahia and Kahala Johnson, Gloria Anzaldúa, Rana Barakat, adrienne maree brown, Hazel Carby, Ebony Coletu, Brittney Cooper, Ann Cvetkovich, Monisha Das Gupta, Angela Davis, Nick Estes, Candace Fujikane, Noelani Goodyear-Kaʻōpua, Stefano Harney and Fred Moten, Saidiya Hartman, Sami Hermez, bell hooks, Sarah Ihmoud, Michelle Jones, June Jordan, Daniel Heath Justice, Robin D. G. Kelley, Naomi Klein, Bryan Kamaoli Kuwada, Audre Lorde, Sari Makdisi, Cherríe Moraga, Nadine Naber, Derecka Purnell, Claudia Rankine, Barbara Ransby, Jordy Rosenberg, Francesca Royster, Steven Salaita, Eve Kosofsky Sedgwick, Sherene Seikaly, Nadera Shalhoub, Christina Sharpe, Leanne Betasamosake Simpson, Neferti X. M. Tadiar, Ty Kāwika Tengan, and Rhaisa Williams. Along with many others, their work has shaped my methodology and this book's understandings and arguments regarding genres of the human. Their transdisciplinary and genre-crossing work provides models for how to create scholarship that, as it challenges academic conventions, comes out of and draws on participation in movement building. Over the course of the book, as I engage texts and movements that I am personally and politically connected to, I take inspiration from these scholars who, as they envision new ways to be human, transgress the boundaries between scholarship, life writing, and activism.

I approach the university, then, as a site of political disobedience and of community making with students, faculty, and staff who are not out to reform or restore it, but rather to organize together to make movements and create narratives that remake what counts as knowledge, what counts as being human. Such aims involve taking from the university the privileges and freedoms it affords, particularly for those of us in tenured positions (and without "executive" management ambitions!), while also resisting its practices and refusing its ideologies that leave those most vulnerable as less than human, as unable to breathe. In "The University and the Undercommons: Seven Theses," Fred Moten and Stefano Harney proclaim that in the United States, "it cannot be denied that the university is a place of refuge, and it cannot be accepted that the university is a place of enlightenment. In the face of these conditions one can only sneak into the university and steal what one can. To abuse its hospitality, to spite its mission, to join its refugee colony, its gypsy encampment, to be in but not of—this is the path of the subversive intellectual in the modern university" (101). As I will be exploring in chapter 4, which concerns the firing of Steven Salaita, subversion can result in expulsion. This is an indicator of just how dangerous knowledge production is, and also of just how necessary it is to organize collectively within and against the university as a corporate and state power, while also staying connected to those outside the university, who while taking to the streets, while occupying mountains, while creating abolitionist communities of care that put people over property, breathe life into resurgent and fugitive ways to be human.

"Towards the Human"

In its hegemonic uses, "human" is a Western term the roots of which make clear its limits and exclusions. Etymologically, "human" as an adjective and noun in English traces back to the 1500s from Old French, Latin, and Greek (*Online Etymology Dictionary*). The earliest adjectival meanings are "(of) man," "earthly" (as opposed to the gods), "male," and also "humane, philanthropic, kind, gentle, polite; learned, refined, civilized." "Human rights" came into usage in the 1680s. In its noun form, the term "a human being" emerged in the 1530s from the adjective "human," and as one interchangeable with "man." As derived from Greek, Latin, and European languages, "man" denotes "human being, person." In its foundational meanings, then, "the human" at once lays claim to universality and delineates a "civilized" (i.e., imperial) subject of European origins who is white, male, and in possession of money and land. These contradictions and inconsistencies are anything but arbitrary. Moreover, although there are other pathways to understanding the human, and although definitions change over time and place, the human's claims to universality and its oppressive exclusions persist into the present.

Because understandings of who and what counts as human play a crucial role in distributing and withholding rights, and in sustaining state-sanctioned structures of domination, debates over "the human" are fierce, consequential, and thoroughly political. Scholarship grappling with the concept of the human ranges across disciplines, just as determinations of the human exceed any one disciplinary formation or discursive field. In ways explored by a range of scholars, the terms human, humane, civilized, civil subject, man, citizen, and person are often related or conflated, and sometimes disarticulated. As Mitchum Huelhs observes in his engagement with the work of Jacques Rancière, Wendy Brown, and Judith Butler, the "referential value" of the human is one of "ongoing interpretation" (18). That human making and unmaking are constructed and unstable does not make the process less material. If defining the human is like trying to contain a moving target, those designated "inhuman" are likewise moving targets who regularly suffer violent ends.

The intention of this book is neither to settle on a definition of the human nor to rehabilitate dominant understandings of the human. Nor is it to remain within frameworks of human recognition and rights. At the same time, I do not believe we can dispense with the human. Even as I approach the human as "a shifting mode of being" (Whitlock, vii), my intent is not to leave "the human" behind, as too often happens in scholarship on the posthuman. Theorists in these areas of study draw on the natural sciences or environmental studies to question anthropocentrism or the special status given to the human. They also challenge, from a variety of approaches (including animal, digital, or disability studies), distinctions between humans and other animals, life forms, objects, and machines. These approaches are at times noncomplementary, and at other times overlapping. They also often, as some posthuman scholars themselves have noted, skip over the profound inequities among different groups of people, some of whom must fight for the most basic human rights even while recognizing the limits and harms of rights-based frameworks. As I write this introduction, Israel is once more escalating its violence against Palestinians from Sheikh Jarrah to Gaza, and in the United States, even as the Derek Chauvin trial has ended with a rare verdict that finds him guilty of murdering George Floyd, police are still killing Black people. These are but two of too many possible reminders that approaching "the human" as a universal category in order to then critique it and posit a "posthuman" present or future can serve reactionary purposes. With such an approach, theorists become complicit in the violence that inheres in the very category they seek to deconstruct or jump over. Not all posthuman critiques fall into this trap, although, as summarized by Walter D. Mignolo and Catherine E. Walsh, "Posthuman is a Eurocentric critique of European humanism" (171). So, too, critics including Tiffany Lethabo King have traced the colonialism retained by "posthuman" projects based on Western nonrepresentational (subjectless and nonidentitarian) theories (*Black Shoals*).

In approaching the human, then, I instead look to contemporary scholarship from various and sometimes intersecting perspectives that come out of queer, feminist, postcolonial, settler colonial, Indigenous, and Black studies. This diverse body of work challenges the inhumanity on which liberal Eurocentric formulations of the human and human rights discourse are premised. As David Lloyd has noted, "liberal conceptions of the human as a universal value prove to have little to offer beyond defensive appeals. Increasingly it becomes apparent that the concept of the human and the terms that congregate around it—freedom, self-determination, rights, property—do not transcend difference and division. Rather, they constitute the very lines of demarcation that separate human subjects from subjected humans" (*Under Representation*, 2). Lloyd's trenchant critique of Eurocentric understandings of the human is one articulated in various ways by a range of theorists whose work informs my own; these include Giorgio Agamben, Hannah Arendt, Wendy Brown, Judith Butler, Lennard Davis, Sami Hermez, Daniel Heath Justice, Walter Mignolo, Edward Said, Leanne Betasamosake Simpson, Neferti X. M. Tadiar, Rosemarie Garland-Thomson, and Gillian Whitlock.

Rather than "prove" or "recognize" the humanity of those who have been dehumanized as a solution to political violence, many of these scholars challenge such approaches (Hermez) and engage with other origin stories and envision new genres of the human (Justice, Simpson). To take one example, in "Life-Times," Neferti X. M. Tadiar analyzes how thoroughly what she calls "the war to be human" is an "imperial project to secure and further aggrandize the privileges and powers enjoyed as well as bequeathed by the already human within a capitalist order" (2). Rather than partaking in this war to be human, or working within the hegemonic humanism that serves as "the ethicopolitical arbiter of rights and responsibilities, privileges and burdens, value and non-value" (2), Tadiar instead argues for the creation of "other genres of being human" (17). She urges participating in alternative ways of "becoming human in a time of war" that "consist of tangential, fugitive, and insurrectionary creative social capacities that, despite being continuously diminished, impeded, and made illegible by dominant ways of being human, are exercised and invented by those slipping beyond the bounds of valued humanity in their very effort of living, in their making of forms of viable life" (7). Of particular relevance to this study—which considers interrelations among life writing texts and political events and movements—are abolitionist, anticolonial, and decolonial theories that range beyond Western bourgeois formulations of the human.[2]

When it comes to thinking and rethinking the human, Jamaican philosopher Sylvia Wynter has been a pathbreaking scholar, and with her critical approach to questions of genre, her work holds particular pertinence for my project. As Wynter makes room for what Katherine McKittrick calls an "emancipatory breach" ("Yours in Intellectual Struggle," 3), and practices what Mignolo calls "epistemic disobedience" ("Sylvia Wynter," 106), Wynter challenges her readers to move away from culturally specific Western European understandings—or what she calls "genres"—of the human that are integral to Western bourgeois imperialism. Wynter historicizes how, as systems of knowledge have represented these genres as universal, they have served to support imperial conquest and colonial violence ("Unsettling," 213–14). For Wynter, from the sixteenth century, the genre Man1 was defined as a rational, political subject and a settler of

European descent; then, in the nineteenth century, Man2's logics define the human within "dually biogenetic and economic notions of freedom" (317). Situating the contemporary moment in relation to this history of a falsely universalized Man-as-Human, Wynter contends, "all our present struggles with respect to race, class, gender, sexual orientation, ethnicity, struggles over the environment, global warming, severe climate change, the sharply unequal distribution of the earth resources . . . —these are all differing facets of the central ethnoclass Man vs. Human struggle" (260–61). To engage in this struggle, Wynter urges what Mignolo describes as "the decolonial option" as she advocates for "a practice of rethinking and unraveling dominant worldviews that have been opened up by Indigenous and black and Caribbean thinkers since the sixteenth century in América (with accent) and the Caribbean" ("Sylvia Wynter," 107). For Wynter, culture plays a crucial role in this political project: "Cultural conceptions, encoded in language and other signifying systems, shape the development of political structures and are also shaped by them" (qtd. in Mignolo, "Sylvia Wynter," 112). Rather than simply exposing how cultural narratives of the Human work to secure and universalize a racist, capitalist, patriarchal and colonial order, Wynter calls for the invention of an entirely new modality of being human—a process of "rehumanization" (Kamugisha) that, through Black art, culture, and poesis will bring into being a decolonial future that comes after Man. After all, as Wynter makes clear, being human is a praxis (Wynter and McKittrick).

In ways that often engage Wynter's formulations of the Human, as well as her call to move "Towards the Human, after Man," Black studies serves as one of the most fertile sites for theorizing the human—and for understanding the "being" in "human being" as a verb. To sometimes significantly different ends, as contemporary Black scholars build on Wynter, and intellectuals including Frantz Fanon, Aimé Césaire, Hortense Spillers, and Saidiya Hartman, they explore the human as a formation that is colonial and antiblack, and they often pose radical alternative ways of human being. For example, in her exploration of how Black life is lived in the wake of slavery, Christina Sharpe both investigates "Black exclusion from social, political, and cultural belonging; our abjection from the realm of the human" (*In the Wake*, 14) and looks to how Black people, against all odds, have been able to "reimagine and transform spaces for and practices of an ethics of care (as in repair, maintenance, attention), an ethics of seeing, and of *being* in the wake of consciousness" (130). Or, as Alexander Weheliye calls attention to how "Man represents the western configuration of the human as synonymous with the heteromasculine, white, propertied, and liberal subject that renders all those who do not conform to these characteristics as exploitable nonhumans, literal legal nobodies" (135),

he explores a decolonial process he calls "habeas viscus." A liberatory corrective to Agamben's and Foucault's conceptions of bare life and biopolitics that
draws on Spillers, Wynter, and Hartman, habeas viscus enables "an originating
leap in the imagining of future anterior freedoms and new genres of humanity" (136). In *Becoming Human*, a work that brings together Black studies, animal studies, and feminist studies, Zakiyyah Iman Jackson challenges "Universal humanity" as an ontologically fixed, antiblack genre (23), while also reading
key African diasporic theoretical and cultural texts to consider other more
fluid, disordering ways of being. In different ways, these theorists are conceiving decolonial and abolitionist ways to challenge and remake the human. This
politically engaged work often feeds as it is also fed by the liberatory movements and literary cultural texts that are the subject of *Narrating Humanity*.

However, as I draw extensively on Black theorizing to understand how
political moments and movements participate in processes of human being, becoming, and belonging, I also part ways with Afro-pessimism, one of the most
influential contemporary directions in Black studies, and especially relevant to
me for its confrontation with the human and humanism as foundationally racist
formations. Even as Afro-pessimism also theorizes the human as an antiblack
formation (or what I will be referring to as an "anti-Black" one, when referencing
Afro-pessimism's essentializing perspective), it is a singularly focused analytic that
sees anti-Blackness as omnipresent and ontological. As Frank Wilderson puts this,
"Human Life is dependent on Black death for its existence and for its conceptual
coherence. There is no World without Blacks, yet there are no Blacks who are in
the World" ("Afro-Pessimism & the End of Redemption"). For Afro-pessimism's
proponents, because there are no solutions short of annihilation, the source of a
radical politics can lie only in understanding this anti-Blackness. As Wilderson
contends, "There is no epistemological way to think 'solution' and 'Blackness'
together—unless you call for the end of the world" ("I am Frank Wilderson").
Or, as Calvin Warren states in *Ontological Terror*, "Black freedom . . . would constitute a form of world destruction" (6). Afro-pessimism's antihumanist analytic
not only precludes possibilities for any profound political transformation in who
counts as human; it also positions Black people as *singularly* outside the human.
This means that "the coalition is, from the jump, an anti-Black formation"
("'We're Trying to Destroy the World,'" 18).[3] For Wilderson and others, including
Jared Sexton and Nicolas Brady, coalition work therefore requires guarding
against "genuine bonding with people who are really, primarily, using Black
energy to catalyze and energize their struggle" ("'We're Trying to Destroy the
World,'" 13). In short, Afro-pessimists exhibit a determined pessimism when it
comes to reconstituting the human or participating in political movements that
are coalitional, intersectional, Indigenous, decolonial, and abolitionist.

Black studies' ontological and political positions are complicated, and I have not included in this brief account scholars who, although they in many ways align with Afro-pessimists, find ways to think beyond, outside, or in excess of anti-Blackness, often in ways that my study is indebted to. I am thinking here, for example, of Tiffany Lethabo King, who writes to support Black-Indigenous solidarities in opposing what she calls "conquistador humanism" (*Black Shoals*); or Denise Ferreira da Silva, who looks to Black cultural production to imagine "the end of the world as we *know* it" (Leeb and Stakemeier); or Fred Moten, who positions his optimism as "apposite" to Afro-pessimism and follows Wynter and da Silva in exploring liberatory ways of nonbeing that can destroy anti-blackness ("Blackness and Nothingness"). Nor am I including as Afro-pessimists Hortense Spillers, Lewis Gordon, Fanon, Hartman, or other theorists cited by Afro-pessimists who imagine ways of being beyond antiblackness, and who in some cases have sharply differentiated their work from Afro-pessimism.[4]

As Afro-pessimism has gained purchase not only in the academy, but also in more mainstream circles, several Black cultural critics have issued insightful and often devastating critiques of it, and of the political purposes to which it is being put. Especially following the publication of Wilderson's second memoir, *Afropessimism* (2020), by a subsidiary of W. W. Norton, Afro-pessimism has received attention in venues including the *New Yorker*, *The Nation*, the *New Republic*, and the *New York Times*, as well as an increasingly critical reception by many Black public intellectuals on the left who oppose its ahistoricism, Eurocentrism, and American exceptionalism; its lack of intersectionality (particularly its inattention to class); and the political dead ends and debilitating nihilism that come with its reification or fetishization of Blackness (Spillers and Gordon). Lewis R. Gordon, Nick Mitchell, Annie Olaloku-Teriba, Kevin Ochieng Okoth, Adolph Reed, Hortense Spillers, Greg Thomas, and Vinson Cunningham are among those who have taken issue with how, to quote Cunningham, Afro-pessimism overwrites history "with the darkest, most permanent marker."[5] These critics all object to how Afro-pessimism, in defining Black people as singularly oppressed, as always already and forever slaves, forecloses not only Black political agency but also solidarity with other colonized or otherwise oppressed peoples. For reasons that these theorists and cultural critics have so carefully delineated, the Afro-pessimist approach to the human is at odds with mine in *Narrating Humanity*; my focus is instead on possibilities for liberatory forms of human becoming and belonging, and on the role that life narratives and political movements can play in these processes.

The criticisms of Afro-pessimism that are particularly pertinent to *Narrating Humanity* concern how the literary, the autobiographical, the theoretical, and the political work together in Afro-pessimism—and in *Afropessimism*, the life narrative that stands in for this body of thought. In his review of *Afropessimism*, Nick Mitchell analyzes how the details of Wilderson's life serve as the evidence that supports his claim that Afro-pessimism is a "meta theory." Mitchell observes how this move sets any "would-be critic up for the charge of an ad hominem attack" (113), and casts anyone in disagreement with its claims as "a symptom of the problem it is diagnosing" (118). Mitchell also explores the way *Afropessimism*'s intermixing of autobiography and theory presents Wilderson's story as "metanarrative" that, like Afro-pessimism as "meta theory," presents itself as coming from a transcendent view from nowhere. This means that Wilderson's privileged upbringing and his situatedness in the US academy as a tenured faculty member disappear from view, even though "that class-related specificity organizes the entire itinerary of the book" (117). Mitchell concludes that

> in the end, Afropessimism is a view from somewhere, and that somewhere is, perhaps all too obviously, the university. The place where all roads in Afropessimism ultimately lead, that place where theorizing is a valued mode of practice in and of itself, and where it does not need to be justified on any other terms. . . . Afropessimism claims to offer no sanctuary while its practitioner is in fact modeled on the privileged subject of Enlightenment humanism, which sought to liberate knowing from being judged by the actions it did or did not enable. (120)

In their conversation about Afro-pessimism, Lewis Gordon and Hortense Spillers also consider Afro-pessimists' investments in Enlightenment humanism in relation to their location in the academy, observing how they substitute imagination for history and ontology for theory. Questioning whether Afro-pessimists are suffering from a Eurocentric exhaustion, Spillers contrasts this stance to her own interest in creativity and generativity, in "torque" movements that say "yes and no" to the terrifying force of antiblackness. What Spillers, Gordon, and Mitchell all ponder are the powerful interplays of autobiography, literature, history, theory, and political movements—and in the case of *Afropessimism*/Afro-pessimism, how this mix can obfuscate privilege and disable political engagement. As I explore these interrelations, like Spillers my commitment is to the creative and political movements that can emerge from these dynamic interrelations, which I approach through the study of life narratives that attempt to wrestle with, resist, revise, and leave behind the Human as Man.

Life Writing

Centered as they are on human lives and relationships, life writing texts (broadly defined to include testimony, social media postings, journals, diaries,

documentaries, bio-pics, or any generally nonfictive narratives that represent
people's lives) constitute a particularly important terrain for understanding—
and participating in—human making and unmaking as differential, historically
variable processes. Saidiya Hartman has called attention to how "the autobiographical example" "is not a personal story that folds onto itself; it's not about
navel gazing, it's really about trying to look at historical and social process
and one's own formation as a window onto social and historical processes, as
an example of them" (Saunders, 5). In *Lose Your Mother*, as Hartman's own
brilliant forays into life writing demonstrate, the process of telling life stories
provides a way not only to understand but also to challenge and provide alternatives to ongoing forms of dehumanization that justify what she calls "the
afterlife of slavery" (4) as well as other forms of dehumanization. Life narratives not only can partake in but, with their grounding in perceived and often
verifiable truths, also can serve as crucial supplements to and critiques of the
legal justice system: they can account for crimes that are societal and historical, but nonetheless depend upon individual agency. And they constitute sites
to interrogate conceptualizations of justice, even as they themselves may investigate but a single life. They also offer a way to demand accountability from
individual readers without forgoing an exploration of ethical questions, and
structural analysis and critique.

It is precisely because life narratives have this power, if not singularly so,
that life writing critics have devoted considerable attention to exploring ways
these narratives have been and continue to be at the center of resisting dehumanization and participating in human rights struggles. For the past decades,
scholars have looked to how individuals or groups tell their stories to contest
in legal and extralegal ways myriad forms of dehumanization that justify violence, and to assert their humanness. Such work challenges not only dominant
ideas of the human, but also understandings of literature exalted by humanist
critics (for example, Harold Bloom's *Shakespeare: The Invention of the Human*).
And yet, even as life writing scholars often approach life writing as an invaluable domain for understanding and—at its best—revisioning conceptions of
the human, and for achieving human rights, life writing can also be and often simultaneously is a source of dehumanization. I make this point not simply because the need to prove one's humanness is inherently dehumanizing,
though it surely is. In addition, counterhegemonic life narratives that aim to
humanize can end up reinforcing or simply reversing or redistributing processes of dehumanization, because interconnected yet differential forms of dehumanization often divide rather than unite those subjected to them.

In ways that often complement Black studies scholars' interrogations of the
human, Indigenous studies scholars have offered particularly keen insights into

the double-edged power that stories hold in shaping formulations of the human. Their work informs my approach. As Daniel Heath Justice (Cherokee) has aptly observed in *Why Indigenous Literatures Matter*, some stories "do far more harm than good. And the stories of how we become and remain human are some of the most dangerous of all" (36). He further contends, "If 'human' is a learned process rather than simply a state of being, so, too, is kinship—moreso, even. Relationships are storied, imagined things; they set the scope for our experience of being and belonging" (73). While part 3, the final chapter of *Narrating Humanity*, explores how, in Indigenous decolonial life narratives, kinship and personhood extend beyond the human, my analysis in previous chapters also is animated by Indigenous understandings of the power stories hold when it comes to understanding human being, becoming, and belonging. Throughout, I attend to how life narratives challenge as well as advance genres of the human that come before, and after, those encapsulated by what Wynter calls Man1 and Man2. This book is premised on the conviction that to challenge disciplinary—and punishing—genres of the human, we need not only the new modes and methods of research Wynter calls for, but also the kinds of life stories that, today, we see emerging from decolonial, Indigenous, and abolitionist movements.

In making this argument, I take inspiration from Barbara Harlow's theorization of resistance literature. Harlow's pathbreaking *Resistance Literature* is itself indebted to Ghassan Kanafani's 1966 *Resistance Literature in Occupied Palestine: 1948–1966*. As Harlow builds on Kanafani's theorization of Palestinian resistance literature, she explores how resistance literature both reflects and participates in Third World liberation movements and, as it does so, "also presents a serious challenge to the codes and canons of both the theory and the practice of literature and its criticism as these have been developed in the West" (xvi). Following Ngugi wa Thiong'o, Harlow divides literature into two categories: that "which is 'participatory' in the historical processes of hegemony," and that which is written in "resistance to domination" (9). She argues, "No more than common law or criminal prisoners can be separated from political detainees can literary genres be isolated from their political and ideological context and consequences" (137). Although the distinctions I make in this book are less sharp—the texts in part 1 of this study are, to quote Eve Sedgwick, "kinda subversive, kinda hegemonic" (15), whereas those in part 2 fall more firmly into the category of resistance literature even as they might retain uses of familiar literary genres and narrative conventions—I follow Harlow as I analyze the imbrication of these literary genres, codes, and conventions in maintaining or resisting domination and hegemony.

From Juridical to Narrative and Narrated Humanity

The concepts "narrative humanity" and "narrated humanity" that I introduce in this book are inspired by Samera Esmeir's work on juridical humanity. In *Juridical Humanity*, Esmeir details how during the colonial history of Egypt, the human assumed, in the Foucauldian sense, a disciplinary status (location 1718) as it came to be defined as a juridical category rather than "a condition of birth" (loc. 163). Via Fanon, Esmeir determines how, with this advent of juridical humanity, "the operations of colonial power unleashed by the negotiability of the human" established a situation in which "the human is also a nonhuman" (loc. 262). As a technology of colonial control, humanity came to be thought of as something that could be "confiscated or allocated" (loc. 258), with law laying "claim to a monopoly over the power to declare the presence of the human" (loc. 214). Moreover, as Esmeir brilliantly contends, under juridical humanity, the law came to serve as the instrument not simply for restoring a violated humanity, but also for setting the terms and conditions that made some violations legitimate. In other words, within the logics of juridical humanity, some practices of dehumanization are claimed as just and humane. Esmeir further traces how, "with its claims of overcoming a despotic past," juridical humanity legislated what counted as unproductive, disproportionate violence, and what "types of violence became figured as 'humane'" (loc. 362). With this power, juridical humanity "was from start to finish a concept productive of subjugation to the state and its law" (loc. 428).

Esmeir's interest lies not only in understanding juridical humanity as a process for maintaining colonial power; she is also interested in other, liberatory concepts of the human. She states her intent "to clear a space beyond the juridical to think about both the human and politics" (loc. 434). Although she contends that "struggles and rebellions may only end up reproducing the sovereignty of the state and its positive law," she also claims that "some rebellions and struggles carry the potential to introduce new texts and practices for losing the human in politics, or articulating other concepts of the human, while challenging the texts and practices of state law" (loc. 428). In concluding the epilogue to her book, she upholds the way the revolutionary protests in Egypt "affirm a subject who rejects the system of bondage with the state and its law" (loc. 5495). For Esmeir, juridical humanity serves as "both the subject of critique and the tool of critique" (loc. 5462): it perpetuates violence and dehumanization and as such, is to be resisted, even as it also can and must be used to lay claim to violated rights. At the same time, her work supports the need for a way of being human that is not subject to the law.

Narrating Humanity proposes "narrative humanity" as a companion to Esmeir's "juridical humanity." I further posit "narrated humanity" as a lens through which to study how narratives participate in struggles to conceive human being beyond juridical and narrative humanity. As I build on Esmeir's work, in employing these concepts, like Esmeir, I do so from a position of political engagement—of alliance with and often participation in the struggles the life narratives included in this study take up.

I use the term narrative humanity to describe the range of historically variable but persistently ideological generic and narrative conventions and codes that, emerging from Western colonial contexts, create understandings of the human and, within the human, the inhuman. As critics including Lauren Berlant and Ann Cvetkovich have insightfully argued, genres and aesthetic forms powerfully convey ideologies and "evidence of historical processes" (Berlant, 16). This includes establishing historically variable normative ways of being human. As these norms get encoded in narratives, these narratives also exclude and render as illegible, inhuman, or less-than-human those who do not conform to them. In this way, what I am calling narrative humanity can and most often does uphold norms that justify violent exclusionary practices and forms of repression and exclusion as it works in tandem with juridical humanity to justify and universalize what Billy-Ray Belcourt (Cree) calls "the cannibalistic genre of the human inaugurated in the laboratories of the New World" (116). And just as subjects appealing for human recognition in courts of law must work within the very system of juridical humanity that has designated them as inhuman, so too those countering dehumanization often must lay claim to the very genres or narrative conventions that, in their time and place, have come to constitute hallmarks of the human.

This book scrutinizes forms of narrative humanity that, over the past several decades, have been dominant in the United States, paying particular attention to their ongoing relevance in processes of dehumanization that are at once differential, multifaceted, and interlinked. More importantly, however, I attend to ways narrative humanity can productively challenge understandings of the human. Because critical engagements with narrative humanity can defy, if not in wholesale ways, already-existing genres and conventions, narrative humanity differs from a juridical humanity that measures the human in accordance with more formally established (though also and importantly subject-to-change) institutionalized legal definitions. Narrative humanity is the stuff of ideology, but also of imagination: it enables those without state power to transgress if not wholly escape established parameters—and cultural institutions such as publishing houses and the film industry—to define the human more capaciously. In other words, narrative humanity bespeaks a set of conventions that can be used toward repressive *or* counter-hegemonic if not revolutionary purposes.

In part 1 of this study ("Narrative Humanity"), I analyze life writing texts that mobilize forms of narrative humanity to challenge the dehumanization on which state violence depends. In the contexts of the contemporary United States, I investigate the central role narratives of family, citizenship, career, religion, self-making, and exploration play in determining who counts as human, and how these narratives maintain interlocking systems of heteropatriarchy, racial capitalism, and settlerism (a term I prefer to settler colonialism, in keeping with Kaleikoa Kaʻeo and Kekailoa Perry's insight in "Hawaiian Place of Yearning" that it bespeaks a colonial ideology rather than simply describing a type of colonialism). I argue that relying uncritically on these forms of narrative humanity results in perpetuating hegemonic, and therefore often liberal and/or invisible, forms of oppression. If, as Audre Lorde stated in her challenge to white feminists, the master's tools cannot dismantle the master's house, so too, this book contends that the familiar narrative codes and conventions that make up narrative humanity cannot *wholly* unwrite or envision alternatives to hegemonic understandings of who and what counts as human. However, even as narrative humanity consists of historically sedimented forms that convey cultural norms, I also contend that engaging critically with these forms can result in life writing texts that revise and expand parameters of the human in ways that contribute to conditions for greater freedom and justice.

In part 2 ("Narrated Humanity"), I focus on life narratives that, rather than relying on established forms of narrative humanity, instead engage in acts of what I call "narrated humanity." By "narrated humanity," I mean narrative forms and genres that have not yet been codified in literature, and that emerge out of and advance political movements in the making. Whereas narrative humanity describes forms with entrenched literary structures, narrated humanity demarcates acts of narrating humanity that break with these structures and the ideologies about the human that they support. As acts of narrative in the making—and here the shift from the noun "narrative" to the verb "narrated" is indicative—narrated humanity offers formulations of the human that are still in process and (not-yet) established, though over time they might well be. What is at issue, then, is not a distinction between a "bad" or repressive narrative humanity and a "good" subaltern narrated humanity, but rather different narrative modalities: those that are convention-bound (narrative humanity), and those still in formation (narrated humanity).

The acts of narrated humanity explored in parts 2 and 3 emerge out of a specific new set of historical conditions that have given rise to liberatory political movements that are deliberately intersectional, community-oriented, and committed to acting in solidarity with other struggles. These contemporary movements, all of which refuse the violences of settlerism, racial capitalism, and heteropatriarchy, cross-fertilize, interconnect, and converge. As they do so, they break with established narratives founded on capitalist and colonial extraction and disposability, criminalization, and incarceration, and they bring into being a new and urgently needed understanding of the human that is in-ter/national, decolonial, abolitionist, queer, and premised on a respect for and kinship with the more-than-human (including water, trees, and mountains). This profoundly difficult political and epistemological work, reliant as it is on stories, necessitates the creation of new genres, narratives, narrative conven-tions and forms. Acts of narrated humanity that bring into being aesthetic forms and narratives therefore are not ancillary, but central to movements. My argument in parts 2 and 3, then, concerns ways political movements shape and are shaped by acts of narrated humanity. The texts I take up explore the specific possibilities afforded by the Black Lives Matter movement, the Boy-cott, Divestment and Sanctions movement, and, in part 3, the Indigenous-led movement to protect Native Hawaiians' sacred mountain and ancestor, Mauna a Wākea. With their attention to solidarity and intersectionality, these move-ments depend on and inspire decolonial and abolitionist stories about being and becoming human. As they create forms of queer kinship, non-statist be-longing, and community, these stories depart from those that dominant modes of narrative humanity naturalize to sustain articulated forms of institutional violence.

Part 3 ("Narrated Humanity and Grounded Narrative Humanity") intro-duces the term "grounded narrative humanity" to accompany the exploration of narrated humanity. I conceive this term, which is inspired by Yellowknives Dene scholar Glen Sean Coulthard, to describe a system of narrative humanity that emerges from understandings of the human that are normative within In-digenous worldviews, or what Coulthard theorizes as "grounded normativity."[6] As stories based in grounded narrative humanity posit humans in time im-memorial relationships to land and more-than-humans, they also show human making to be part of an ongoing creation story. As such, they also often simul-taneously constitute acts of narrated humanity, ones that at times work be-yond but not against grounded narrative humanity's understandings of the human to realize a decolonial future.

As part 3 makes particularly clear, there is no firm line between narrative and narrated humanity. Forms of narrative humanity often introduce elements of what I am calling narrated humanity, and vice versa. So, too, when they gain institutional acceptance and narrative features become legible as literary

codes and conventions, narratives that in their time and place might be instances of narrated humanity can instead be considered examples of narrative
humanity. Relatedly, ideas of who or what the human is or can be change over
time—as with culture, human becoming is necessarily always in process. Moreover, as Antonio Gramsci has taught us so well, because hegemony is on the
move, those engaged in counterhegemonic resistance must continually change
tactics.

By critically engaging formal constraints and contradictions of the texts
under consideration with attention to their historical and political contexts,
and also by putting the texts from the book's three parts in dialogue with one
another, I hope to participate in the necessary and always unfinished work of
expanding understandings of who counts as human. More specifically, I seek
to challenge interlocking and debilitating forms of capitalism, racism, Islamophobia, antisemitism, settlerism, and heteropatriarchy. Even as these forms of
oppression are, for scholars of US literature and culture, all too familiar, I hope
that approaching them through the lenses of "narrative humanity," "grounded
narrative humanity," and "narrated humanity" enables sharpened attention to
the powerful possibilities of life writing's narrative codes and conventions as
we engage in high-stakes contestations over who counts as human.

Organization of the Argument

Chapter 1, "Love and Terror: Formulas of Citizenship in *Zeitoun* and *Trouble
the Water*," focuses on two life writing texts that address Hurricane Katrina and
the intersections of this unnatural disaster with the war on terror, antiblack
racism, Islamophobia, climate catastrophe, governmental incompetence, and
disaster capitalism. Through analysis of Dave Eggers's biographical narrative
Zeitoun (2009) and Carl Deal and Tia Lessin's documentary *Trouble the Water*
(2008), this chapter explores linkages among processes of dehumanization at
work during the Katrina Complex that pertain to race, religion, gender, class,
and nation. It also considers possibilities and limitations of countering these
interconnected forms of dehumanization by engaging the formulas of narrative humanity that normalize them.

In his celebrated narrative, Eggers chronicles the Zeitoun family's experiences of Hurricane Katrina by mobilizing textbook articulations of the marriage
plot, the self-made man narrative, the narrative of conquest/discovery, and
the immigrant success story. Eggers employs these forms of narrative humanity, which present Zeitoun as an exemplary American, to condemn how the
convergence of post-9/11 conditions during Katrina resulted in Zeitoun's detention. However, after *Zeitoun*'s publication, when Abdulrahman Zeitoun is

charged with domestic violence, media responses illuminate how readily Zeitoun's story converts into the familiar narrative wherein patriotism and the protection of (white) women justify US imperialism. As I examine how easily Eggers's narrative can be flipped, turning Zeitoun from a "good" to a "bad" Muslim, I also explore how casting Zeitoun as an ideal American sustains dominant (neo)liberal formulations of heteronormativity, multiculturalism, settlerism, and racial capitalism.

To consider how narrative humanity, if employed in more unruly ways, can trouble and transform the logics that define the human, I turn to *Trouble the Water*. This award-winning documentary follows the journey of Scott and Kimberly Roberts, a couple who filmed their experience of Katrina while trapped in a Ninth Ward attic. As *Trouble the Water* riffs off the genre of the slave narrative, it updates and at other times departs from this Christian, abolitionist form of narrative humanity. As a counterpoint to *Zeitoun*, this documentary suggests the need to create genres wherein "upward mobility," marriage and family, citizenship, and masculine individualism are neither markers of humanity nor a cover story for antiblack racism and gendered processes of dehumanization that sustain an ongoing history of imperial violence in the United States and abroad.

To continue part 1's exploration of the politics and poetics of narrative humanity, chapter 2 focuses on two texts that have been lauded as works of art and as foundational to Black Lives Matter, one of the defining social justice movements of our time. In "Criminals and Kinship: *Fruitvale Station*, *Between the World and Me*, and Black Selfhood in the Age of BLM," I analyze how forms of narrative humanity in Ryan Coogler's 2014 *Fruitvale Station* and Ta-Nehisi Coates's 2015 *Between the World and Me* (BTWAM) at once contribute to and coincide with, as they also depart from, BLM in their highlighting of BLM's concerns with self-making, kinship, and criminality.

The release of Coogler's 2014 docudrama coincided with an almost all-white jury exonerating Trayvon Martin's killer, George Zimmerman. Noted by BLM organizers as a catalyst for BLM, *Fruitvale Station* complements the movement's aims, even as—indeed because—its modes of narrative humanity not only resist the police's criminalization of Oscar Grant, but also his conversion into a political symbol after his death. As *Fruitvale Station* dwells on Oscar Grant's final twenty-four hours as a struggling young father and son, through reworking narratives of self-help, family, and criminality, the film reaches out to a broad audience and conveys that his ordinary life and its everyday particularities matter.

BTWAM also contests the racist system that criminalizes and renders Black life disposable. Widely hailed as a BLM anthem, this memoir dwells upon the anti-Blackness that fueled the killings of Trayvon Martin, Michael Brown, and Eric Garner. Structuring his memoir as a letter to his son, Coates instructs Samori to engage in struggle, however futile, against a cosmologically anti-Black necropolitical order. In ways that uphold familiar forms of masculine individualism and liberal humanism, and that exist in tension with the memoir's Afro-pessimist critique of anti-Blackness, this father-son narrative also chronicles Coates's journey to becoming a writer. Coates's investments in the Künstlerroman and a father-son narrative run counter to his accounts of a world premised on white criminality and the plunder of Black lives. The memoir's oscillating and competing beliefs in a distinctly literary humanism and a world defined by anti-Black necropolitics issue a powerful protest that resonates with BLM. At the same time, BTWAM diminishes BLM's grounding in collective organizing and solidarity, and its investments in fighting for transformative justice. As I explore BTWAM's points of connection and divergence with BLM, I consider the challenges of using literary humanism to denounce an antiblackness that its logics reproduce, and the incompatibilities that exist between intersectional movement politics, Afro-pessimism, and narrative humanity.

Chapter 3, "From Movement to Memoir: When They Call You a Terrorist and the Power of Queer Black Kinship," continues an investigation of life narratives that articulate with BLM, while transitioning to part 2's investigation of narrated humanity that emerges out of and participates in abolitionist and decolonial movements. In When They Call You a Terrorist: A Black Lives Matter Memoir (2017), BLM cofounder Patrisse Cullors and her coauthor asha bandele engage in acts of narrated humanity that overturn antiblack representations of terror and dehumanization that are features of narrative humanity and white supremacist violence. By way of narrative forms that exceed the terrorist/citizen binary that itself serves to terrorize Cullors and her kin, this memoir also represents and partakes in the collective life story and life-giving aims of the BLM movement. At its center is a queer, Black, feminist account of love, kinship, and community, one in which Black people help one another not only heal and survive, but also breathe freely and thrive.

As Cullors and bandele put their loved ones at the center of their address, they give a sustained narrative form to the focus, tropes, turns of phrase, conventions, and storylines that animate BLM. Rather than "prove" that Black lives matter, this memoir takes that mattering as a starting point in narrating into being a better world, one that predates centuries of racism, while also drawing on BLM to envision an abolitionist future that is queer, feminist, and rooted in communities of care. Their memoir thus demonstrates the political possibilities of narratives that grow out of, and help imagine and materialize, movement politics.

Chapter 4, "'Nursing Visions of the Unimagined': BDS and Steven Salaita's World-Making Narratives of Fatherhood, Affiliation, and Freedom," focuses on Steven Salaita's 2015 *Uncivil Rites: Palestine and the Limits of Academic Freedom*. This memoir was occasioned by attacks on Salaita for tweets that sparked a national controversy and enabled administrators to fire him from a tenured position at the University of Illinois Urbana-Champaign. In ways that reverberate with the writings of Edward Said, Salaita responds in his memoir to issues relevant to his firing—most notably, Israel's 2014 assault on Gaza and the criminalization of the Palestinian-led international Boycott, Divestment and Sanctions (BDS) movement, but also the clampdown on free speech, the increasing corporatization, and the undermining of Indigenous studies and solidarities in the US academy. Salaita interweaves this account with stories about parenting that extend his love for his son to all children, including those in besieged Gaza. As he mobilizes liberal tenets of narrative humanity through stories of family, Salaita supports BDS as a movement that, like his memoir, is liberal in its demands but radical in its implications and intersectional commitments. Acts of narrated humanity that further contribute to BDS and his visions for it as an "inter/national" movement accompany these contextually radical instances of narrative humanity. Through this mix, *Uncivil Rites* challenges distinctions between scholarly and political writing—and life writing and activism—that I also take inspiration from, as in this chapter I engage in my own experimentations with life writing that are based on my involvement with BDS organizing.

I next turn to the website Salaita started in 2019, after he left academe and began working as a school bus driver. Whereas Salaita writes *Uncivil Rites* in a largely reactive mode that refutes Zionist narratives and exposes civility as a colonial regime, his website's long-form essays take Salaita deeper into freer forms of narrated humanity. Through stories about fatherhood and education, he imagines what it means to be free, and envisions forms of security based on communities of love and care rather than on capitalist accumulation and settler violence. Writing during the era of BDS, Standing Rock, and BLM, Salaita draws on understandings of security and freedom that resonate with and strengthen these inter/national, intersectional struggles for justice. Through the resulting experiments with narrated humanity, his website provides glimpses of what a decolonial mode of life writing can look like.

Chapter 5, "'E Hū ē' (Rising Like a Mighty Wave): Mauna Kea and the Movement beyond the Human," serves as both conclusion and aperture. In the final section of this book, through attention to the movement for Mauna Kea led by Kanaka Maoli kiaʻi (Native Hawaiian protectors), I reflect on the implications of my arguments concerning the interrelations between cultural genres and political movements when it comes to rethinking the human. I also consider what happens if we broaden our perspective to think about the human not as a bounded category, but as one related to all living entities. Attention to the movement for Mauna Kea evidences the limits of focusing on the human. The stories emerging from and as part of this movement pose necessary challenges to assumptions that the human is a distinct category. These stories, based in grounded narrative humanity, also often simultaneously constitute acts of narrated humanity that exist in dynamic relationship to other movements including BLM and BDS. As they counter forms of dehumanization that are the subject of *Narrating Humanity*, they help create ways of being human based on radical and resurgent relations of care, connection, and love.

Whereas previous chapters focus on stories that take part in public controversies and crises concerning the human, here I work largely from my experiences as a settler ally supporting the movement for Mauna Kea. With this fuller move into a life writing mode, I consider the significance of the small acts of grounded narrative and narrated humanity that go into the making of movements that are in conversation with one another. I conclude by wondering how the refusal of boundaries between different movements, and also between humans and nonhuman beings, land, water, and skies, suggests pathways for future scholarship that build on even as they go beyond parts 1 and 2's engagements with narrative and narrated humanity, and their structuring concern with the politics that attend being human.

I conclude with "Hope, Joy, and 'The Struggle for Ea.'" In this postscript, through a reading of Enomoto's cover image and a song by Kauwila Mahi and 'Ihilani Lasconia, I consider this book's through lines, and how, in the face of crushing violence, humans continue to rise, together, and breathe into being old and new stories of human and more-than-human becoming and belonging.

About Time

To write about contemporary movements and moments is to write against time—to produce work that can read as dated rather than historical. In the past year alone, the contexts in which I have been situating this study have been shifting, sometimes dramatically. A global pandemic and climate catastrophes are accelerating all existing inequities and creating challenges yet to be grasped. I also have been revising during new waves of antiblack, anti-immigrant, gendered, and colonial violence, and while participating in emerging or renewed movements that respond to this violence. A second wave of BLM has sharpened and popularized the movement's abolitionist demands; Palestinians are rising up throughout Palestine and across the world, joined by allies in the Unity Intifada; Indigenous peoples engaged in decolonial struggle have created the Red Deal as "a manifesto and movement . . . to liberate all peoples and save our planet"; and in Hawai'i, Kanaka Maoli kia'i and settler allies have come together to stop legislation (HB499) that extends leases on seized Native Hawaiian land and, in the fight to shut down Red Hill, to contest military occupation and the poisoning of O'ahu's water supply. These movements directly relate to this book's concerns and impact its analyses in ways I cannot satisfactorily account for. When writing about the present there is no catching up. At the same time, I hope that this book's contributions do not depend on doing so: after all, one of its most basic premises is that the human is on the move—that human making is unfinished and in process. So, too, this book is motivated by my belief in the power of liberatory movements and imagination to combat the dehumanization on which colonialism, racial capitalism, and heteropatriarchy depend. This belief is bigger than my ambition to remain timely or to come to hard and fast conclusions about what the human is or can be.

My more modest hope, then, is that as *Narrating Humanity* studies a slice of history in the making, it also offers an approach that proves helpful to understanding ways of being human that pre- and postdate the texts and movements considered here. At the outset of this introduction, we looked to how Arendt unseals Eichmann as a lone specimen in a glass box to insist on the all-too-human "banality of evil" that sustains nation-states and makes it necessary and possible to render some humans as disposable, inhuman. My hope in writing this book is that as I work to understand the lives and movements it details, I can keep good and contributive company with those who have made—and those in the process of making as well as those who are yet to make—the journey away from Wynter's Man, as through acts of narrated humanity we create ongoing stories of human becoming and belonging.

PART I
Narrative Humanity

1

Love and Terror

Formulas of Citizenship in Zeitoun *and*
Trouble the Water

Over the past decade, the conjunctures of climate crisis, colonialism, and racial capitalism have come ever more sharply into focus. Along with melting glaciers, rising sea levels, increased temperatures, and other signs of global warming, the accelerating force and frequency of fires, floods, hurricanes, and other extreme weather events have brought home the pervasiveness of this planetary crisis and its catastrophic impact on lands, waters, skies, and all living beings. At the same time, the impact of climate change has only exacerbated existing inequalities, with those most vulnerable to it cast aside by their governments and regularly represented in the mainstream media as noncitizens, as less than human. While coverage of the suffering kangaroos in the Australian bush or the burning redwood trees in California has rightly sparked a collective mourning, humans in the most precarious positions are often (further) criminalized, dehumanized, and disregarded. Think back to POTUS Donald Trump in 2017, pitching rolls of paper towels to people gathered in Calvary Chapel, San Juan, during his one day in Puerto Rico after Hurricane María decimated its infrastructure and left people without power, water, food, or housing. The resulting three thousand deaths, which Trump denied, and the devastation to the island were attributable not only to the weather, but also to what some have called "the coloniality of disaster" (Bonilla and LeBron, 11). This includes the Trump administration's participation in a continuing dismissal of the US citizens who make up Puerto Rico, the world's oldest colony that still has the status of an "unincorporated territory."[1] Although media coverage of Trump's paper towel tossing was far from favorable, the people of Puerto Rico quickly dropped from the news cycle. Because of US governmental ineptitude and disregard for people possessing only "the illusion of US citizenship"

(Morales, 3), and in combination with disaster capitalism (the privatizing of the electrical system, the Department of Homeland Security's slowness to waive the Jones Act[2]), Puerto Ricans continued to struggle for months with a mounting death toll and without a functioning infrastructure (Morales; Bonilla and LeBron; Klein).

As indicated in the response to Hurricane María, and in ways this chapter will be exploring through attention to Hurricane Katrina, the dehumanization and denial of the rights of citizenship that accompany climate crisis are, like climate change itself, part of ongoing histories of colonialism and racial capitalism. A wake-up call regarding the arrival of climate crisis, Katrina looms large in the US imaginary. Life narratives that cover over while perpetuating—and those that expose and resist—the state and institutionalized forms of violence behind this "natural" disaster have played a critical role in Katrina's afterlife. Through analysis of two Katrina texts—Dave Eggers's biographical narrative Zeitoun (2009), and Carl Deal and Tia Lessin's documentary Trouble the Water (2008)—this chapter explores linkages among forms of dehumanization at work during the Katrina Complex that pertain to race, religion, gender, class, and nation. I first examine how Eggers asserts the humanity of his Muslim protagonist caught within Katrina's convergence of forces by inserting him into highly codified forms of narrative humanity, arguing that uncritical reliance on these narrative formulas achieves (limited) inclusion at the cost of reproducing intersecting forms of dehumanization. With the understanding that cultural narratives and genres can materially trouble and transform as well as simply expand while reinforcing the logics that define the human, I then turn to Trouble the Water. As it follows the journey of Kimberly Rivers-Roberts and Scott Roberts, a couple who filmed Katrina while trapped in a Ninth Ward attic, this documentary presents more unruly and possibility-filled ways to work within and against the confines of narrative humanity.

One of the five deadliest hurricanes ever to hit the United States, when it slammed into Southeast Louisiana on August 29, 2005, Katrina was a perfect storm not only of wind and water, but also of governmental bureaucracy and ineptitude; post-9/11 militarization and Islamophobia; antiblack racism; neoliberal profiteering; and disregard for poor, old, and otherwise vulnerable people. A display of nature's power, Katrina also scandalously exposed new and persisting structures of racial capitalism, heteropatriarchy, and colonialism that inform understandings of who counts not only as a citizen, but also as human.

An apt illustration of these processes of dehumanization that sustained the US government's disregard for citizens most vulnerable to Katrina—and a companion piece to Trump's paper towel tossing—occurred on September 5, 2005, when former first lady Barbara Bush and George H. W. Bush toured Hous-

ton's Astrodome. Crammed with cots, the complex provided makeshift housing for fifteen thousand of the million people displaced from their homes when
Katrina struck and the shoddily built levees broke, leaving 80 percent of New
Orleans under water. The senior Bushes, joined by former president Bill Clinton and senators Hillary Rodham Clinton and Barack Obama, were there to
display bipartisan support for Katrina victims. Among those packed into the
Astrodome, people awaited news of missing loved ones. Many required medical attention; were among the hundreds of thousands left suddenly jobless; or
soon would find their homes opportunistically demolished and then be sold
out yet again by insurance companies; a few would be "lucky" enough to receive
often uninhabitable trailers provided by the Federal Emergency Management
Agency (FEMA). After her visit, Barbara Bush appeared on the National Public
Radio show *Marketplace* to chat about her visit. "What I'm hearing," she
said, "which is sort of scary, is they all want to stay in Texas." Remarking on how
"everyone is so overwhelmed by the hospitality," she continued, "And so many
of the people in the arena here, you know, were underprivileged anyway, so
this is working very well for them" ("Barbara Bush Calls Evacuees Better Off").
With this remark, Barbara Bush represented the economically disenfranchised and predominantly African American New Orleans residents—many,
especially from the Ninth Ward, direct descendants of US slavery—as at once
on-the-take noncitizens and grateful recipients of charity; as unsettling threats,
uninvited guests, and agentless victims; as without attachments, homes, emotions, or intelligence.

Barbara Bush's commentary for *Marketplace*, a show focused on business,
was one of many that, rather than foregrounding the disaster's underlying economic conditions, instead deflected blame onto its victims. Pundits joined
politicians in casting those hit hardest by Katrina as needy, resource-draining
refugees, or as thugs, looters, and rapists—distinct but complementary representations (Sommers et al.; Bouie, "Where Black Lives Matter"). Media stories played a key role in how people, predominantly Black, were deemed
lacking in civility and even human status and stripped of their civil and
human rights as New Orleans was made "secure" by the National Guard and
federal troops. Through intersecting discourses of class, race, gender, ability,
age, region, and nation, affect-laden life narratives asserted the humanity of
those with most privilege over against the humanity of people struggling for
their survival.

Katrina's critics have analyzed how such responses crucially facilitated what
Naomi Klein calls disaster capitalism—the government-corporate collusions
that exploit large-scale trauma to push forward neoliberal agendas resulting
in gentrification of poor neighborhoods, privatization of public services, and

the permanent displacement of Black and other disenfranchised people (Ben-Porath and Shaker; Fleetwood, "Failing Narratives"; Žižek). As suggested by Barbara Bush's remark, this societal reengineering happened not only through neglecting but also through telling stories about those impacted by Katrina. Even when, as with Barbara Bush's infamous account, such narratives back-fire, too often the focus remains on castigating a few powerful individuals for their lack of humanity, without disrupting the human-inhuman binaries their narratives put into place.

In the wake of Katrina, people of the Gulf Coast have powerfully combated the assault on their humanity and citizenship by telling their stories. Their life narratives not only expose the systemic dehumanization they have experienced, but also in many cases link failures of civil society to the war on terror and the post-9/11 convergence of FEMA with the Department of Homeland Security (DHS). As well, these personal narratives contest how the mainstream media, in labeling New Orleans as "Third World," represents poor Black people as non-US citizens and as not fully civilized.

These Katrina stories exist in a variety of genres and styles: fiction, including Jesmyn Ward's *Salvage the Bones*; biographical narratives including *Zeitoun* and Sheri Fink's *Five Days at Memorial: Life and Death in a Storm-Ravaged Hospital*; first-person accounts such as Chris Rose's *1 Dead in Attic: After Katrina* and Natasha Trethewey's *Beyond Katrina: A Meditation on the Mississippi Gulf Coast*; oral histories such as *Voices from the Storm* and *Alive in Truth: The New Orleans Disaster Oral History and Memory Project*; songs and poems; and documentary films including Spike Lee's *When the Levees Break: A Requiem in Four Acts* and *Trouble the Water*.[3] As climate crisis becomes increasingly palpable, these Katrina narratives continue to hold urgency, suggesting as they do how forms of narrative humanity can bolster (as does *Zeitoun*, however inadvertently, in significant ways) or break with (as does *Trouble the Water*) the stories that sustain the same man-made structures and practices of racial capitalism and colonialism that contribute to the frequency and force of extreme weather events.

From "Bad" to "Good" Muslim and Back Again: Zeitoun on and off the Page

Of the substantial body of Katrina literature, *Zeitoun* is among the most critically and popularly acclaimed. Winner of the American Book Award, and on *Entertainment Weekly*'s "best-of" "end-of-the-decade" list, Eggers's narrative affords insights into the complex yet patterned processes of dehumanization that constitute Katrina as catastrophe. Through this chapter's reading of it, as

I elaborate the concept of narrative humanity and the costs of relying on it, I pay particular attention to how the humanity of *Zeitoun*'s eponymous hero is "proven" by inserting him into the marriage plot, the narrative of discovery and conquest, and the self-made man and model minority narratives. As *Zeitoun*'s mobilization of these forms of narrative humanity challenges the post-9/11 Islamophobia that Zeitoun experienced during Hurricane Katrina, reliance on these very forms simultaneously imbricates *Zeitoun* in long-standing structures of dehumanization.

In making this argument, my objective is not to denounce Eggers, nor to issue a wholesale dismissal of inhabiting such narratives to contest the violence that comes with dehumanization. Rather, I am interested in exploring what happens when they are uncritically relied on to include an individual or group that these narratives regularly exclude in their formulations of the human. *Zeitoun* constitutes a particularly good case study because of the exactitude with which Eggers utilizes familiar formulas of narrative humanity. He implements these formulas with precision and fullness, rather than remixing them to expose their contradictions, or to provide critical angles into them, as do the other texts in this study. *Zeitoun* is, then, an especially apt text through which to launch an investigation of narrative humanity. As I will be contending, through attention to *Zeitoun*'s implications in processes of human unmaking that inhere in narrative humanity, opposition to dehumanization cannot be partial or compromising. This is not only because solidarity or concern for others' struggles is ethical, but also because fractions and divisions are integral to the calculus of dehumanization. To strive to include only one cast-out group into the fold of the human does little to disrupt—and indeed can provide a liberal varnish that glosses over—the very formulations of the human at work in Trump's towel throwing, or in Barbara Bush's "this is working very well for them." As I go on to argue in subsequent chapters, even as I believe it necessary to move beyond existing forms of narrative humanity, critically engaging with their constraints and contradictions, especially with a commitment to intersectionality and solidarity, can importantly contribute to the necessary and always unfinished work of expanding understandings of who counts as human, and imagining ways of life free from interconnected forms of racism, Islamophobia, carcerality, class oppression, colonialism, and heteropatriarchy.

Eggers sets out not to perpetuate, but rather to oppose at least some of these manifestations in the post-9/11 United States. In linking the war on terror to Islamophobia and to the US government's inhumane and inept response to Hurricane Katrina, Eggers relies on his ability to issue structural criticisms affectively through a simply told story of one man and his family. Eggers's interest in the Zeitouns' story is precisely because it encapsulates conditions post-9/11. As he explained in a 2010 interview, "There have been so many polemics about the war on terror, but [individual] stories illustrate these things much better. . . . I was angry about the war on terror and the suspension of all sense of decency. This seemed like the absolute nadir of all the Bush policies and here was this family squeezed between all these distorted priorities" (Cooke). Eggers learned of the Zeitouns' story through its inclusion in the 2005 *Voices from the Storm* compilation, part of McSweeney's nonprofit Voice of Witness series, which Eggers cofounded in 2004 to provide "empathy-based understanding" (Voice of Witness website) about human rights crises through oral histories. For an author known for walking the line between fiction and nonfiction, it is unsurprising that the Zeitouns' story caught Eggers's attention. It came ready-made with narrative hooks and details easily adaptable to hegemonic narratives about US multiculturalism; love, marriage and family; adventure, exploration, and mishap; and upward mobility.

Through Eggers's omniscient telling, we learn how Zeitoun grew up in Syria as part of a large, overachieving Muslim family; moved to the United States; and married Kathy, a white American who years before meeting Zeitoun had converted from Christianity to Islam, drawn to its "bent towards social justice" and its teachings "to be more patient and forgiving" (67). Together Kathy and Zeitoun were bringing up four children and running a painting and contracting business when the hurricane hit. Zeitoun stayed behind to look after his home and job sites while his family fled to Kathy's brother's home in Baton Rouge. Zeitoun, who grew up in the coastal town of Jableh with a "passion for the sea," is surreally at home when the levees break. He serenely paddles through the flooded city in a canoe, rescuing stranded people and abandoned pets. When a police and military crew descend upon one of his rental properties, they arrest him and three others as Al Qaeda suspects. The men are detained without due process, first in the makeshift Camp Greyhound prison (pre-Katrina, the New Orleans Union Passenger Terminal), then in Elayn Hunt, a maximum security prison. Eggers chronicles the abuses Zeitoun undergoes while incarcerated for twenty-three days; Kathy's desperate and resourceful efforts to locate her husband; their post-Katrina entanglements with government bureaucracy; and the family's only partial recovery from this trauma that leaves them with an assortment of health problems.

Eggers, who shared multiple drafts with the Zeitouns and spent three years interviewing family members in the US, Spain, and Syria, presents their story through omniscient access to Zeitoun and Kathy. As he occupies their points of view, he renders Abdulraman Zeitoun as transparently knowable and heroically American. Eggers refutes stereotypes of the Islamic terrorist by showing

Zeitoun to be a model family man, businessman, and citizen whose Syrian origins and Muslim faith add to his American status. The presentation of Zeitoun as idealized yet wholly accessible to a mainstream American reader-ship is key to the book's denunciation of post-9/11 Islamophobia. The vantage point, while crystal clear, remains exterior; Eggers presents Zeitoun as if viewed through a pane of glass. This lack of depth is integral to characterizing Zeitoun as a "what-you-see-is-what-you-get" man who is smart, but simple in his good-ness. The first edition's cover portrays him as a cartoon figure, canoeing through the city. Once the narrative is underway, Zeitoun springs to life, but remains persistently two-dimensional. Through this narrative strategy, Egg-ers's access to Zeitoun appears unpresumptuous and noninvasive, but also hon-est and complete. Zeitoun appears devoid of a complexity that would render him foreign, opaque, or in any way deserving of suspicion. Eggers's surface ap-proach turns the stereotyping of Muslim men on its head. Whereas the US military literally cannot see what is right before their eyes—namely, Zeitoun's acts of good citizenship—as anything other than Islamic terrorist activity, Eggers challenges this racist and Islamophobic stereotyping by portraying Zeitoun's uncomplicated innocence. As a family man and businessman, Zeitoun breaks from the ordinary American only because his actions show him to be unusually enterprising, independent, and decent. As Eggers states, "The Zeitouns stand for everything that we consider all-American values: hard work, community, family, personal responsibility . . . he's an example to us all" (Cooke). In his analysis of Eggers's *What Is the What*, Brian Yost contends that Eggers fulfills biography's purposes in representing his subject "as a model for ideal development while simultaneously fostering the imagined bond Bene-dict Anderson theorizes between the subject, a community, and the reader" (151). So, too, in *Zeitoun*, Eggers establishes Zeitoun as an exemplary US citizen.[4]

This approach has been successful in exposing the inhumanity of Bush's America, and in countering the dehumanization of Muslims—or, as these groups have become increasingly interchangeable, Arabs and Middle Eastern-ers (Volpp)—in a climate that demands prototypical and assimilable Ameri-can "goodness," especially for men, who are otherwise (or sometimes anyway) presumed to be terrorists. As Sunaina Maira and Magid Shihade observe, "'Good' Muslim and Arab Americans, in the imperial state's view, . . . are will-ing to propagate the belief that the U.S. is indeed the exemplar of 'freedom' and 'democracy' and strive for inclusion in the nation. 'Bad' Muslim and Arab Americans . . . oppose the basic premise of the War on Terrorism and reject the cloak of 'human rights' and 'liberation' that is worn by U.S. imperial in-terventions" (122). This perception of the "bad" Muslim American works in tandem with casting "foreign" or "un-American" Muslims as terrorists who are guilty until proven otherwise. This is particularly true during extreme weather events. In the US war on terror, the DHS, warning that terrorists can seize on hurricanes as events to exploit, establishes hurricane-devastated cities as war zones. As Jung-Suk Hwang notes in the essay "Post-9/11-Disaster Katrina: Reenacting American Innocence in Dave Eggers's *Zeitoun*," the DHS report, "Information Analysis and Infrastructure Protection," subtitled "Strategic Red Cell: How Terrorists Might Exploit a Hurricane," proposes that any city substantially hit by a hurricane should be approached as "a potential battlefield in the war against terrorism." He explains how "the DHS responded to Katrina using this playbook, magnifying an already-devastating storm into a post-9/11 disaster by fueling anxieties about the Arab or Muslim Other" (34). What this report makes clear is how, in the name of "security," the state creates for those it is obligated to protect not structures of safety and care, but conditions of war and dehumanization.

By making his hero a "good" Muslim American mistaken for a "bad" un-American Muslim, Eggers is able to denounce the war on terror *and* espouse a belief in American freedom and democracy disrupted by 9/11 and Bush-era policies. This viewpoint, which ignores what Erica Edwards calls "the long war on terror," appeals to a broad liberal readership. Eggers has achieved celebrity status and a reputation as a "one man zeitgeist" (Hamilton, 5) through his attention to paratexts and epitexts. Through McSweeney's and together with his publisher, he has marketed *Zeitoun* not simply as a book but also as a teaching tool and as a vehicle for supporting entrepreneurial human rights efforts. The book has been required reading in high schools and colleges. Zeitoun's story was featured on *Democracy Now* to mark Katrina's five-year anniversary. Eggers has directed his royalties to the Zeitoun Foundation, for distribution to organizations that rebuild New Orleans and promote religious tolerance. Jonathan Demme optioned the book for an animated feature film—a way to extend Eggers's vision and to further the story's success in countering, for a mainstream audience, common tenets of Islamophobia and the war on terror.

Yet Eggers's approach has dangerous limitations. Postpublication circulation of stories of the "real" Zeitoun expose the perils of resting a structural critique on an individual life, particularly if the author has represented that life as exemplary and fully known. In March 2011, police were called to the Zeitoun home because Zeitoun was punching his wife in the head in front of their children. He pled guilty to negligent injury charges and was sentenced to anger management classes. In February 2012, the Zeitouns divorced. That July, Zeitoun was jailed for smashing his ex-wife's windshield with a tire iron and beating and choking her until stopped by a witness. In August 2012, while awaiting trial, he was charged with soliciting another soon-to-be released inmate, Donald Pugh, to murder his ex-wife, a man she was seeing, and her son from her first marriage. The judge, Frank Marullo, found Pugh not credible due to his criminal record, and Zeitoun received a not-guilty verdict on the murder-related and earlier assault and battery charges. The media headlined these events as an extension of Eggers's narrative. The *New York Times* described Zeitoun's arrest as "a jarring twist for the main character" (Brown); another story had as its lead, "Abdulrahman Zeitoun used to be known as the hero of a best-selling nonfiction book. . . . More recently, Zeitoun has been cast as a villain . . . , repeatedly accused of either beating or stalking his ex-wife" (DeBerry, "Zeitoun's Latest Arrest"). *Salon* announced that "a far more complex Zeitoun has walked off the page, without a political and moral agenda, borderless and uncontainable" (Patterson). Charges against Zeitoun have continued to mount, and when he was found guilty in 2016 of violating a protective order and engaging in a "campaign of menace" that left Kathy Zeitoun fearing for her life, *The Advocate* headline proclaimed, "Literary Hero Abdulrahman Zeitoun Convicted of Felony Stalking" (Simerman). Zeitoun's actions along with such coverage have not only put Eggers's credibility into question; they have also upset Eggers's objectives in telling Zeitoun's story.[5]

As I proceed to examine how readily Eggers's narrative can be flipped, turning Zeitoun from a "good" to a "bad" Muslim when Zeitoun upends his status as ideal American, I argue that this is owing not only to post-9/11 Islamophobia, but also to how Eggers's narrative upholds dominant formulations of masculine individualism, multiculturalism, settlerism, neoliberalism, and American exceptionalism that predate 9/11. Each of these contributes to Eggers's idealization of ways Zeitoun exerts dominance over his wife, and they also obscure ways Zeitoun values property over people, exploits migrant labor, and acts in complicity with antiblack racism and Indigenous dispossession. I contend that Eggers's uncritical rendering of these dehumanizing practices are embedded in, even as they are covered over by, forms of narrative humanity that assert Zeitoun's value. So, too, by keeping the focus on the Zeitoun family and the incompetence and Islamophobia of Bush's America, *Zeitoun*'s modes of narrative humanity obscure and romanticize the ongoing story of US imperialism in the Middle East and its interconnections with the antiblack and settler violence that is integral to the United States (Edwards; Jamal and Naber).

To explain Zeitoun's domestic violence, media accounts turn not to Katrina and the US government's detention and abuse of Zeitoun, but rather to his increasingly "radical" belief in Islam. Arun Kundnani analyzes the emergence in 2004 of a "'new terrorism,' seen as originating in Islamist theology, and the 'old terrorism' of nationalist or Leftist political violence, for which the question of radicalisation is far less often posed" (5).[6] This ideology that depoliticizes terrorist violence and understands "radicalization" as "a psychological or theological process by which Muslims move towards extremist views" (Kundnani, 7) is at work in the media's representation of Zeitoun. Reporters misrepresent Kathy Zeitoun's remark connecting Zeitoun's domestic violence to the adoption of "a radical religious philosophy" that she emphasizes "does not reflect true Muslim beliefs" (Gorman). They also largely ignore how, when accounting for his abuse, she explains that during Katrina, the US government "took his control away; he took mine and my children's" (Gorman). Instead, media accounts align Zeitoun's Muslim beliefs with his abuse. For example, even as the *New York Daily News* reports on how Kathy Zeitoun differentiates her husband's radicalism from her understanding of Islam, the story's very next page features a photo (fig. 1) captioned "Kathryn Zeitoun sits next to her then husband Abdulrahman Zeitoun. . . . She claims his more radical Muslim views have led him to a 'darker place'" (Gorman). Like a badly played game of telephone, this misrepresentation gets reproduced and recirculates in statements such as the following, published in *Salon*: "Ms. Zeitoun claimed in one interview that Eggers's depiction was accurate at the time, but that her husband had subsequently become angrier and more violent, and his Islamic views more radical" (Patterson). Or, as reported in the *New York Times* and then reprinted in the *Los Angeles Times*, "In an interview with *The New Orleans Times-Picayune*, Ms. Zeitoun said the book had accurately portrayed their relationship at the time. But she said her ex-husband had since grown angrier and more violent and his Islamic views had become more 'radical'" (Brown). As these distorted accounts link Zeitoun's domestic violence to his turn to a radicalized Islam, they serve to justify the war on terror. The charges against Zeitoun also result in the first attention to his not being a US citizen; when jailed in 2013 on an immigration hold, media coverage conflates his domestic violence and his Syrian citizenship (Simerman, "Katrina Literary Hero"). Rather than exploring Kathy Zeitoun's postulation that trauma caused by the US government's baseless detention triggered his violence at home, media accounts— which regularly include photos of Kathy Zeitoun post-divorce, without her hijab—reinforce the dominant narrative that Muslim women are victims who need saving from Muslim men, in a way that upholds the legitimacy of Zeitoun's initial incarceration for terrorism. That Kathy Zeitoun is being endangered not only as a Muslim wife, but also as a white American, further leaves Zeitoun open to the stereotypes that Eggers sets out to oppose, associating Islam with repression of women, foreignness, and violence.[7]

Figure 1. This *SMUDailyMustang* image appears in the *Daily News*, with the caption "Kathryn Zeitoun sits next to her then husband Abdulrahman Zeitoun during an interview. She claims his more radical Muslim views have led him to a 'darker place.'" (Photo credit: *SMUDaily Mustang*)

White Women Saving Brown Men: Replotting *Pride and Prejudice*

Owing in large part to *Zeitoun*'s reliance on marriage plot conventions, these recent events have undermined Eggers's condemnation of the post-9/11 era. Zeitoun's acts of domestic violence need not have discredited the criticism Eggers wishes to make. As Kathy Zeitoun suggests, domestic violence perpetrated by men against women and children is a patterned response from some men who have been subjected to violence and a loss of power outside their homes.[8] Indicting the war on terror need not be incompatible with Zeitoun's abuse; it might instead accompany an exploration of articulations between domestic and US state violence.

In fact, attention to Zeitoun's domestic violence potentially contributes to understanding the spread of dehumanizing practices connected to the war on terror *and* exposes the systemic nature of violence against women. The latter is borne out by a look at the judge who acquitted Zeitoun of his initial charges. With a record of disrespect for domestic violence cases, shortly before ruling on Zeitoun's charges, Frank Marullo had dismissed a case that included videotaped evidence of a twenty-two-year-old woman being punched in the face by her boyfriend. Marullo accompanied his dismissal of the case with a complaint about the Municipal Court sending him such cases "when we have cases where people get shot and things like that" (DeBerry, "Trayvon Martin").[9] Marullo made this statement a month after two men fighting domestic abuse charges were arrested for murder. In one case, a man acquitted of punching his wife killed her days after his release. The other was a quadruple homicide by a man on probation for attacking his girlfriend. This man also was fighting another domestic violence charge in Municipal Court and had three convictions against three different women (DeBerry, "Trayvon Martin"; Filosa, "Domestic Violence Defendant"). The murders these two men committed catalyzed the decision Marullo protested, to move domestic violence cases out of Municipal Court. Prior to this change, of the region's approximately three thousand domestic violence cases annually, 93 percent shared the docket with violations such as public urination; over half were dismissed; few saw trial (Filosa, "Recent Domestic Violence Tragedies"). As these data indicate, Marullo's response is no more aberrant than the violence itself. When Marullo's son was charged with domestic abuse that involved strangulation, twelve sitting criminal court judges recused themselves because Frank Marullo was their long-time colleague (Daley, "Judge Frank Marullo's Son"). Marullo also had company in trivializing Zeitoun's violence against Kathy Zeitoun. The New Orleans Police Department failed to respond with appropriate urgency to her repeated calls expressing fear of her ex-husband (DeBerry, "Trayvon Martin"). In 2014, despite having violated four protective orders when out on bail for another felony stalking charge, Zeitoun was inexplicably released from the state's monitoring program (Daley, "Zeitoun Arrested Again"). These cases, including Zeitoun's, suggest the pervasiveness of violence against women, and institutional negligence bordering on acceptance of this violence—true nationwide as well as regionally.[10]

Eggers's narrative does not, however, lend itself to insights into the gendered violence that structures US society, including how state violence intensifies it. Instead, Eggers's critique of the war on terror rests on idealizing the heteronormativity that defines the Zeitouns' relationship, which he encodes through an update of the traditional marriage plot. When we first meet the Zeitoun family, Kathy is making school lunches while her three daughters sit at the breakfast table, reciting lines from the movie *Pride and Prejudice*, which they watch nightly with Kathy. This scene helps introduce the Zeitouns' story as a contemporary American version of *Pride and Prejudice*—one in which the dashing Mr. Darcy figure is not landed English gentry, but a landlord who is a self-made immigrant. The story of the Zeitouns' courtship and marriage resonates with *Pride and Prejudice*'s: *Zeitoun*'s Katrina story is intertwined with this marriage plot that the hurricane—and Bush's America—endangers. In the lead-up to the storm, readers learn of Zeitoun's pursuit of Kathy after a friend match-makes them. We read about their prolonged courtship, and of how Zeitoun persistently overcomes Kathy's rebuffs and hesitations (34). As the storm sets in, they are married, living in a big house, and running a business together, enjoying prosperous family life.

Significantly, this story of courtship, marriage, and children makes no room for Kathy's son from her previous marriage. Zachary, fifteen at the time Katrina strikes, is barely mentioned in descriptions of the family's life together, and nowhere does Zeitoun claim him as a son. His disavowal happens between the lines of the book—when, for example, Zeitoun refuses to pay $10,000 in bail, because "that money would be better spent elsewhere—in [the girls'] college trusts for example" (282). In the last of the rare mentions of Zachary, he is eighteen and living with friends in his own apartment (318).[11] Donald Pugh, the man who reported Zeitoun's commissioning of Kathy's murder, alleged that he "was instructed to kill her and two men who might accompany her—one of them Kathy Zeitoun's son—as long as the couple's four children weren't present" (Maggi). As Pugh's account indicates, Zeitoun's understanding of family does not allow for children who are not biologically his own. It also suggests that Zachary exists as a threat to Zeitoun's singular possession of Kathy, and to his role as paterfamilias. Rather than explore these or whatever other tensions the relationship between Zachary and Abdulraham introduces into the Zeitoun family, Eggers participates in Zachary's erasure, and the naturalization and romanticization of a traditional family.

As Eggers suggests that it is post-9/11 America that endangers the Zeitouns' wellbeing, he glosses over the foundational fractures that first appear in their courtship, and then in their marriage and family life. Despite Eggers's idealized representation, starting with the account of their courtship, we can see Zeitoun's need for control over Kathy. When a mutual friend, knowing Zeitoun is looking to be married, recommends Kathy to him, Zeitoun determines his interest in her by planning a "stakeout" (33), observing Kathy at her workplace from his car. When he discovers she is parked next to him, he takes cover, "crouching below his dashboard" (33). Rendered as a humorous exploit, this scene that comes from wanting "no confusion, no hurt feelings" (32) is an ominous precursor in light of Zeitoun's later convictions for stalking.

Once married to Kathy, Zeitoun is clearly the reigning boss and patriarch. He makes the major decisions, and Kathy acts as office manager from home, while doing the housework and childcare. A "distracted" father (10), Zeitoun acts as protector to his daughters and wife. Although he calmly handles racist clients who object to his Latino painting crew or his last name, on learning of a client's rudeness to Kathy, he storms off the job, saying "no one talked that way to his wife" (39–40)—an act Eggers represents as admirably chivalrous. Eggers also uncritically reveals how Zeitoun asserts his autonomy at Kathy's expense. When Mayor Nagin mandates a hurricane evacuation, Zeitoun disregards Kathy's pleas that he leave with the rest of the family, and her increasing anxiety as he remains in New Orleans until few besides abandoned dogs remain. The dogs index Zeitoun's humanity—Eggers contrasts the FEMA and DHS crews' cruel indifference to Zeitoun's kindness as he makes sure the dogs have fresh water and feeds them steak from his freezer. Eggers presents Zeitoun's imperviousness to his family's panic as he remains in the deserted city as an endearing mark of his independence and strong will, with his care for the abandoned dogs distracting from his neglect of his family. As Kathy's worry overtakes her, literally turning a swath of her hair white, she recalls a "totemic memory" (196) of Zeitoun. The memory involves a beach day in Malaga that, despite Kathy's objections, turns into a 15-mile walk as Zeitoun is driven to touch a distant rock. Relaying this incident from Kathy's vantage point, Eggers writes, "She had married a bullheaded man, a sometimes ridiculously stubborn man. . . . Whatever he set his mind to, even a crackpot idea of touching some random rock miles in the distance, she knew he would not rest until he had done it. It was maddening. It was strange, even. But then again, she thought, it gave their marriage a certain epic scope" (199). *Zeitoun's* narrative structure precludes knowing whether to attribute this memory's placement entirely to Eggers's artistry, or Kathy's chain of associations. Either way, together with the dogs, this ordering manages a difficult moment in the narrative—when Zeitoun's stubbornness affects his family's health—by having Kathy recount a memory in which she casts her husband's relentless single-mindedness as comically heroic.

The narrative does not invite, and arguably works to stave off, any indication that, powerless and angry in the grip of racist state violence, Zeitoun might shore up his masculinity and regain his sense of agency by exerting violent control over his wife and her son from her previous marriage, instantiating what Rachel Luft calls "disaster patriarchy." Luft explains "disaster patriarchy" as a return to and concentrated reanimation of "the most regressive elements of gender that are still embedded in social life. . . . Disaster patriarchy . . . reveals . . . the way in which racialized patriarchy has been the underlying logic all along" (7). Rather than exposing and denouncing this logic, Eggers celebrates the patriarchal characteristics that make Zeitoun both a model American husband and a devout Muslim. In a 2013 interview, Kathy Zeitoun discloses having hidden from Eggers her husband's pre-Katrina abuse, stating that although their relationship worsened after Katrina, from the beginning, "we didn't have a fairytale marriage" (Martin). That the marriage appears as such is not entirely thanks to what the Zeitouns hid. The fairytale elements that Eggers celebrates via the marriage plot (Zeitoun's dominance) have abuse as their underbelly; as Kathy Zeitoun discloses, after Katrina, "It was as if he blamed me for everything that had happened to him. Every anger, every hatred that he had for anybody else, he focused it on me" (Martin). In other words, Zeitoun's violence toward Kathy is not a break from the marriage plot; rather, the marriage plot justifies, romanticizes, and masks a heteropatriarchy that, at its foundation, depends on subjugation. Relying on the marriage plot as a vehicle to humanize Zeitoun imbricates Eggers and Zeitoun in the gendered violence encoded in, and disavowed by, this form of narrative humanity. The coverage of Zeitoun's arrest makes visible the intersecting forms of racism and Islamophobia that underwrite the marriage plot—and other forms of narrative humanity—and that enable the displacement and erasure of domestic violence, in this case onto Zeitoun as a violent Middle Eastern Muslim.

The case of Zeitoun serves not only to expose the marriage plot's implications in romanticizing patriarchal violence. So, too, a consideration of *Zeitoun* reveals how, with its liberal color-blind approach to love, the marriage plot disavows ways race impacts romance. From the time Zeitoun first spies her and notes her hijab, jeans, youth, and "fresh-faced" beauty (33), Kathy's whiteness goes unmarked by Zeitoun. Zeitoun's racial identification also remains unclear: we learn only of Kathy's initial attraction to his "handsome gold-skinned face" (34). This description supports both Syrian Americans' provisional whiteness (see Gualtieri) and the marriage plot's racial politics. If the marriage plot constrains *Zeitoun*'s insights into the dynamics of romantic love, as Zeitoun's postpublication abusiveness surfaces, Eggers's uncritical reproduction of this form of narrative humanity threatens to undo *Zeitoun*'s condemnation of the Islamophobic war on terror, which rests on the government's wrongful arrest of the eponymous hero. Moreover, this narrative's "color-blindness" obscures how Kathy's whiteness might function for Zeitoun, both in his attraction to her, and later in the rage he directs toward her—this inattention is not a byproduct of but foundational to the heteronorms of the marriage plot that centralize, invisibilize, and naturalize whiteness.

A New World, Charted

Zeitoun's marriage plot overlaps with its narrative of conquest and discovery—another form of narrative humanity that privileges masculine individualism and dominance, and positively codes settlerism as adventure and exploration. Zeitoun's single-minded quest to touch a rock, which threatens but ultimately conforms to the marriage plot, also serves to support Eggers's celebration of

Zeitoun as a man of conquest. So, too, Zeitoun's pursuit of Kathy corresponds both to the marriage plot and also in a submerged way to the narrative of discovery and conquest—conjunctures Kim TallBear illuminates in her analysis of the ways "biologically reproductive heterosexual marriage . . . was crucial to settler colonial nation building" (146). Tracking how these narratives at times strain against one another, and at times coalesce in *Zeitoun*, we can see how the valorization of masculine individualism and colonialism at work in each narrative uncritically positions woman either as object to be conquered, or as impediment to adventure and exploration. When the levees fail, Zeitoun's time in the city is a voyage of discovery and a break from the constraints of family life; as he rows across New Orleans in a secondhand canoe he bought because "it seemed to speak of exploration, of escape" (73), he revels in the role of lone seafaring pioneer laying claim to "his city" (95). To capture Zeitoun's experience, Eggers draws on language borrowed from narratives of conquest and discovery, perpetuating the romanticization of colonialism that inheres in this form of narrative humanity: "This was a new world, uncharted. He could be an explorer. He could see things first" (95). Eggers adapts this narrative formula of exploration to idealize and render assimilable, for his US audience, Zeitoun's status as a Syrian immigrant. Zeitoun's racial ambiguity also plays a role in this process, bracketing from consideration, and therefore leaving intact and unchallenged, the colonialism and racism that structure narratives of discovery.

Zeitoun's expert navigation in the water flowing through the narrative consolidates his identity as explorer/conqueror who lays claim not only to New Orleans but also to a masculine heroism that is at once distinctly American and unbounded by race or place. His facility in water traces back to his Syrian childhood and to his youthful experience working on a cargo ship where "he was always testing himself, seeing how much his body could endure" (145). In ways that harken back to *Zeitoun*'s opening fishing scene when the men and boys of Jableh practice the Italian art of lampara, Zeitoun's relationship to water evidences, quite literally, his ability to traverse boundaries of race, nation, and culture; his powers of mobility enable his rise in and belonging to US society as they enrich his adopted city and country. Zeitoun's adeptness in water comes increasingly to demonstrate his transcendent individualism and extraordinary determination that he derives from his Syrian past. When the levees break, memories of his brother Mohammed, the world's best long-distance swimmer before he died in a car crash at age twenty-four, flood Zeitoun's mind and inspire him as he assists those in need. With Zeitoun's agile and enterprising individual navigation across the flooded city contrasting to the US government's rigidity and ineptitude, Zeitoun's immigrant identity and border-crossing masculinity are crucial to the book's narrative of discovery and conquest as these qualities also make Zeitoun a model American. This identity and the claim it gives him to America articulates with his role as a man who pursues and then possesses a woman who is at once Muslim and a white American.

As part of the work of positioning Zeitoun as a border-crossing adventurer/ explorer who is also quintessentially and ideally American, *Zeitoun*'s depiction of Syria as a place of serenity and Christian and Muslim coexistence, as a mix of a quaint, untouched-by-time seaside life and Mediterranean-inflected cosmopolitanism, serves not only to counter Islamophobia. This representation of Zeitoun also perpetuates a view of American innocence, pre-9/11—a well-charted one that glosses over long and ongoing histories of US Islamophobia and imperialism in the Middle East. Nowhere does *Zeitoun* include mention that Syria has been on the US list of state sponsors of terrorism since the list's inception in 1979, or that Syria has been subject to US economic sanctions since 2004, or that the US has spent decades treating Syria as a site of terror on the basis of its being pro-Soviet and anti-Israel ("U.S. Relations with Syria"). In short, with his focus on the Zeitouns' humanity, Eggers omits how the US has a long history of imperialism in Syria and the Middle East more generally, fomenting violence and suffering as different administrations that pre- and postdate George W. Bush, both Democrat and Republican, have pursued extractive economic and empire-building political interests.

In "Post-9/11-Disaster Katrina," Hwang provides an insightful discussion of how the focus on the Zeitouns' humanity obscures this history of US–Middle East relations and renders Zeitoun "politically voiceless" in the interest of presenting Zeitoun as "a faithful believer in America." As Hwang observes, "Syria constantly features in the story but only as a pastoral setting in Zeitoun's memory in relation to the familiar, universal sentiments of a nostalgic childhood, his family, and the sea, devoid of any political, religious, or critical elements." Hwang goes on to establish how, by remaining within Kathy's touristic vantage point, Eggers counters negative stereotypes of Syria and instead "celebrates the region's unanticipated astonishing view and delightful, quintessential Mediterranean atmosphere." Hwang notes how Kathy's appreciation of the harmonious coexistence of mosques and churches is uninterrupted by any discussion of how in 2003, when the Zeitouns visited Syria, the US invasion of Iraq resulted in tens of thousands of Syrian Christians fleeing from Islamist rebels in cities including Aleppo, Homs, and Qusayr. And when Eggers mentions that Zeitoun's Syrian family cannot obtain visas to visit him (201), Hwang notes that *Zeitoun* includes no mention of how this relates to Syria's presence on the US's list of state sponsors of terrorism. He also looks to how Eggers, in keeping his focus on Zeitoun's brother Mohammed's accomplishments as a swimmer, avoids discussion of the United Arab Republic (UAR)–US involvement in the Syria crisis that destabilized the region and consolidated US-Israeli relations—imperialist activity Eggers references simply as "growing American influence in the region." Hwang establishes how Eggers similarly depoliticizes the Iran-Iraq War, omitting any mention of the US's role in it, or of how it presaged the war on terror. Instead, Eggers's reference to this "long and crippling war" is folded into a story about how Zeitoun decides to stop working at sea so he can start a family. After the tanker he is on, which is transporting Kuwaiti oil to Japan, is attacked by Iranian torpedoes while passing through the Gulf of Oman, Zeitoun exits the tanker when it stops in Houston, so he can settle down and "find a woman to marry" (263).

In ways Hwang's analysis helps illuminate, the intersections of oil interests, logistical capitalism, Middle Eastern religious and national conflict, and US imperialism are obscured by and subsumed into the marriage plot and the narrative of exploration and adventure. Through Eggers's mobilization of these forms of narrative humanity, he is able to represent Zeitoun's pre-9/11 move to the US as seamless with his earlier life of adventure, a fluid crossing from Syria to America born of his ease with navigating waterways, and one that serves him well as he discovers and traverses "his" city of New Orleans. The romanticized view of Zeitoun on the water holds at bay what is in the water of the flooded city: the oil, the toxins, and the abandoned bodies of Black and poor people. In this way, Eggers erases the racial capitalism, Islamophobia, and imperialism that are not post-9/11 aberrations but saturate US history and the forms of narrative humanity that uphold this hegemonic narrative of American exceptionalism.

So, too, in romanticizing colonial conquest, Eggers's account of Zeitoun perpetuates settlerism's ongoing erasures, including any account of the approximately 4,500 Indigenous people living along the southeast Louisiana coast, who, as reported by tribal leaders and state officials, lost everything to Hurricane Katrina, only to have 5,000–6,000 more people lose their homes when Hurricane Rita hit four weeks later. Those most affected by the hurricanes—the United Houma Nation, the Pointe-au-Chien Tribe, the Isle de Jean Charles Indian Band of Biloxi-Chitimasha, the Grand Caillou-Dulac Band, and the Biloxi-Chitimasha Confederation of Muskogees—experienced wholesale neglect by the media, relief organizations, and the federal government ("Indian Tribes and Hurricane Katrina").[12] As Indigenous peoples lost their homes, livelihood, and lives, and, while working together to survive and address the devastation of the storms (including, for example, having to turn a nearby high school into a morgue), their material losses and trauma were exacerbated by being

treated as if they were an already vanished people.[13] Not only through Indigenous absence in *Zeitoun*, but more actively through celebration of Zeitoun as
quintessential American citizen/explorer/immigrant, we can see how forms of
narrative humanity play an integral role in perpetuating while erasing ongoing
practices and effects of US colonialism, at "home" as well as abroad.

At the same time, it is possible to find critical ruptures in *Zeitoun* that
disrupt narrative humanity's erasures and legitimations of colonial violence
and dehumanization. One such passage appears as Kathy, attempting to find
Zeitoun after he goes missing, engages in research, and reads about the armed
mercenaries who have descended on New Orleans:

> Immediately after the storm, wealthy businesses and individuals had
> called in private-security firms from all over the world. At least five
> different organizations had sent soldiers-for-hire into the city, including
> Israeli mercenaries from a firm called Instinctive Shooting International.
> Kathy took in a quick breath. Israeli commandos in New Orleans?
> That was it, she realized. Her husband was an Arab, and there were
> Israeli paramilitaries on the ground in the city. (194)

Having learned of the presence of Instinctive Shooting International, an organization composed of former Israeli military officers, Kathy goes on to worry, too,
about the Blackwater soldiers also providing "security" who are "responsible
to no one" (195), and she considers with alarm that there must be about 28,000
guns circulating in the city. She attempts to calm herself by recalling that US
troops also have been deployed to New Orleans. But then her panic resur-
faces: because "these were vets coming straight from Afghanistan and Iraq,"
this "could not bode well for her husband" (195). As she struggles to account
for Zeitoun's disappearance, formulas of narrative humanity that have been at
work throughout *Zeitoun* to support its protagonist, even as we closely follow
his detention and incarceration, fail. At this moment, as Kathy grapples with
how Zeitoun will have appeared to US and Israeli "security" forces, what
comes to the fore is how he is positioned against dominant imaginings of the
human and citizen: as noncitizen, as terrorist, as not human.

As Kathy considers how Zeitoun's disappearance might be due to anti-Arab,
Islamophobic mercenaries and soldiers, she comes up against the material consequences of narratives that, as they conjoin Israel and America, dehumanize
Zeitoun. In this moment that dramatizes the conjunctures of imperialism, neoliberalism, racism, Islamophobia, militarization, "natural" disaster, and "security," we see that as Zeitoun is caught in the web of these forces, his character,
however good or bad, is beside the point. Simply on the basis of being Syrian,
or Arab, or Muslim (identities that in US contexts are largely interchangeable),

he can be detained and subjected to torture, incarceration, or execution. However fleetingly, this moment in *Zeitoun* makes evident the limited power of laying claim to the conventions of narrative humanity in order to counter dehumanization, since to do so is to leave these conventions in place while burying their deep structure and the ways their processes of making and unmaking humans are central to the workings of civil society. What flashes into focus here is how narrative humanity sustains the Islamophobia, nationalism, and racism that underwrite the US government's (long) war on terror, Israel's settler colonial project, US-Israel ties, and the state's capture of Zeitoun. Although Eggers moves quickly past this moment—and without contextualizing how Zeitoun might be particularly suspect given Syria's standing as an anti-Israel country being monitored by the US in its war on terror—this moment is nonetheless a splinter in the narrative.

"The Eyes of an Entrepreneur": The Antiblackness of Race-Blind Narratives of Self-Making

Once he is released from prison and post-Katrina, as Zeitoun reclaims "his" "new city" by buying up property and rebuilding homes, *Zeitoun*'s narrative of conquest merges with the immigrant success or model minority / self-made man narrative. Through *Zeitoun*'s reliance on these articulated forms of narrative humanity that perpetuate the interstitial workings of colonialism, racism, sexism, and class exploitation, those who disappear from the plot line are those whose lives Katrina showed to be most disposable—in addition to Indigenous peoples, the millions of people, poor and disproportionately African American, who are displaced when the levees break and destroy their homes and their livelihoods. Patrick Wolfe succinctly observes, "settler colonialism destroys to replace" ("Settler Colonialism," 388). A similar dynamic characterizes disaster capitalism, companion to settlerism (and here it is worth noting how often for Indigenous people dams have served, as Nick Estes puts it, to turn "life giving waters into life taking waters"). With disaster capitalism (as with capitalism more generally), along with Indigenous peoples, other vulnerable populations—including descendants of slaves—occupying land or property worth more than their labor are conveniently expelled or expunged, and their homes destroyed and replaced. As Zeitoun profits from the wreckage wrought by the compromised levees, his upward mobility as a self-made man shows the articulations between heteropatriarchy, antiblack racism, settlerism, and capitalism, and how the dominant narratives that make up narrative humanity at this time and place participate in similarly interconnected forms of dehumanization.

In telling Zeitoun's story, Eggers shows him to have been an immigrant to America who goes from "rags to riches"—a narrative with a trajectory that overlaps with the marriage plot's and establishes Zeitoun as a model businessman. Kathy first falls for Zeitoun because he has "the eyes of an entrepreneur" (11). He not only wins over Kathy, but also becomes a builder and a property owner owing to his masculine individualism, resourcefulness, intelligence, and work ethic. Once under way with his own business, he succeeds due to his acumen and open-minded pragmatism. His "niche" market consists of gay men who like the rainbow logo that Zeitoun painted onto his van, oblivious to its significance. After becoming aware of its symbolism, he maintains the logo because changing it would be costly and because "anyone who had a problem with rainbows, he said, would surely have trouble with Islam" (12). The book's culminating statement focuses on Zeitoun's identity as a builder as the consummate indicator of his humanity: "There is no better way to prove to God and neighbor that you were there, that you are there, that you are human, than to build. Who could ever again deny he belonged here? If he needs to restore every home in this city, he will, to prove he is part of this place" (325). In an interview, Eggers asserts his identification with Zeitoun, explaining that they are both "very practical" men who "build things" and "make things happen" (Cooke). In the book's conclusion, as Zeitoun's and Eggers's voices converge, *Zeitoun* upholds the settler colonial narrative of pioneering. *Zeitoun* reproduces the connections this form of narrative humanity sustains between conquering, accumulating property, and capitalist success, and the equation of these market-driven values and practices with dreaming, creating, building, belonging, and being human.

Zeitoun's optimism in chronicling the ills of post-9/11 America rests on the embrace of an immigrant success narrative that Eggers suggests is only temporarily derailed when the Bush administration poses a significant but surmountable challenge to it. The first-person plural of the book's final incantatory lines continues the merger between Eggers, Zeitoun, and all Americans: "Progress is being made. We have removed the rot, we are strengthening the foundations. There is much work to do, and we all know what needs to be done. . . . So let us get up early and stay late, and, brick by brick and block by block, let us get that work done" (325). As this building metaphor suggests, *Zeitoun* posits a secular narrative of progress, in which the events of 9/11 and all their corrosive consequences were a setback that can be overcome through the hard work, entrepreneurial vision, resourcefulness, and strength of individual men. When Barack Obama delivered his November 5, 2008, victory speech, he promised "to join in the work of remaking this nation the only way it's been done in America for 221 years—block by block, brick by brick,

callused hand by callused hand." As Zeitoun's concluding words echo with
Obama's promise to get the nation back on track, Eggers reinforces an idea of
America in which the Bushes' corrupt and undemocratic reign was an aberra-
tion, an interruption of the American narrative of progress, democracy, decency
and self-making.

As *Zeitoun* perpetuates this American dream, what requires further attention is what, and who, it represents as "the rot" that needs removing. Just as
Eggers identifies Islamophobia as mostly a post-9/11 phenomenon, he also min-
imizes, in large part through the narrative's striking inattention to African
Americans, antiblack and other foundational forms of US racism.[14] The absence of African Americans can be attributed partly to Eggers expecting readers to know that they were hit hardest by the disaster. But *Zeitoun's* inattention
also owes to Eggers's and the Zeitouns' investments in the self-made man narrative. This narrative, along with the marriage plot, encodes the multicultural
or "race-blind" liberalism so central to narrative humanity and to *Zeitoun*—
up until Zeitoun's detention, although the Zeitouns express appreciation
for people from diverse backgrounds, references to race occur almost entirely
when narrating the Zeitouns' occasional encounters with racist individuals,
not in relation to institutionalized structures.

As *Zeitoun* portrays Muslims' diversity (Kathy's best friend, Yuko, is a Japa-
nese American convert to Islam), it successfully counters stereotypes that
equate Muslims with Arabs, South Asians, or Middle Easterners, but at the
expense of exploring how Islamophobia and racism interrelate. Before Zeitoun's
incarceration, most incidents of Islamophobia are occasioned by Kathy's hijab. For example, post-9/11, Kathy is attacked by teenagers in a parking lot while
her Iraqi companion, whose hair is uncovered, is left alone. Not until the storm
hits and the military moves in and profiles Zeitoun as Al Qaeda do the connections between racism and Islamophobia, and the slippages between being
Muslim, Arab, and a terrorist, become evident. As Eggers's vantage point
merges with the Zeitouns', the narrative presents a vision of a mostly harmonious US multiculturalism where hard-working immigrants achieve material
success, regardless of race or ethnicity. In this way, *Zeitoun* merges the self-
made man and the model minority narratives, and extends model minority
status to Muslims, or immigrants from the Middle East.[15] In other words, rather
than explore the way these forms of narrative humanity contour the human
in accordance with white and American norms, Eggers suggests their capacity to encompass Zeitoun as Muslim and Middle Eastern. Investing in these
narratives and the capaciousness of their formulations of the human, Eggers
suggests that it is the ruptures of post-9/11 America that disrupt them, and in
ways that a return to these long-standing narratives can help rectify.

One of *Zeitoun*'s few breaks with the immigrant success story pre-9/11 occurs in Camp Greyhound, when Zeitoun, newly detained, notices for the first time the mural there that captures in its sweep Native genocide, chattel slavery, and anti-immigrant racism. The mural also contextualizes the storm and the broken levees as part of a history of capitalist greed and destruction: "In one segment, oil derricks stood below a flooded landscape, water engulfing a city" (214). This image situates the Katrina disaster in relation to corporate capitalism. As Greg Palast notes, the canal that "drowned New Orleans" during Katrina "was like a rifle barrel pointed right at the city," and it was constructed to circumvent the winding Mississippi River because "oil companies wanted to save time" (Desvarieux). Zeitoun's moment before the mural constitutes a significant but rare break that places his struggles in relation to a violent US history. Just as quickly as this disruption occurs, however, it is recuperated into the immigrant success story. Zeitoun realizes he has an infection in his foot, and recalls seeing "his workers, most of whom were uninsured and afraid to register at a hospital, ignore their injuries. Broken fingers went unset, horrible cuts went untreated" (237). This recollection prompts him to break a Tabasco bottle and fashion an instrument to extract the splinter. As Zeitoun both relates to and avoids through a highly masculine ingenuity the fate of his undocumented workers, he—and Eggers—dodge an exploration of Zeitoun's and the construction industry's responsibility for the abysmal labor conditions of undocumented immigrants. Instead, *Zeitoun* reinscribes the self-made man narrative and the myth of the model minority that reinforces contemporary versions of it.

This is not the only time *Zeitoun*'s adherence to an immigrant success narrative denies the sexism, racism, colonialism, and capitalist exploitation that bedevil narrative humanity and its current investments in neoliberalism. In the celebration of Zeitoun as a builder, Zeitoun and Eggers overlook the destructiveness that characterizes construction when it is part of a capitalist enterprise tied to the uprooting, displacement, dispossession, and rise in houselessness of the city's most vulnerable residents. Eliding the inequalities of racial capitalism and patriarchy, the narrative moves seamlessly between language in which Zeitoun positions himself as a landlord and a concerned and religiously observant father figure. When Eggers describes how "somewhere along the line they [he and Kathy] started buying buildings, apartments, and houses, and now they had six properties with eighteen tenants," he narrates Zeitoun describing each tenant as "another dependent, another soul to worry about" (14). However, when the rent goes unpaid, these tenant-turned-dependents become for Zeitoun troublesome "clients." Even as the slippage of terms obscures Zeitoun's role as landlord, the shift from Kathy and Zeitoun's

joint ownership to his paternalistic control foregrounds the persisting nature
of the heteropatriarchy of landownership. Toward the conclusion, the Zeitouns'
recovery is indexed by their accumulation of property: "Zeitoun and Kathy began to buy houses in their neighborhood. Their next-door neighbor had fled
the storm and hadn't returned. She put the house on the market and the
Zeitouns made an offer. It was half the value of the house before the hurricane, but she accepted. This was the most satisfying of all the transactions they
made" (299). What this success story omits is the stories of those who sell their
homes at rock-bottom prices. Along with these stories, and those of their
tenants unable to pay their rents, would surely come accounts of capitalist
extraction, lost jobs, exploited labor, insurance companies' swindles, and
homelessness—and the dehumanization that accompanies conditions of
"downward mobility" in a market-driven economy.

When it comes to antiblack racism and its intersections with capitalism, the
problem in *Zeitoun* is not simply one of omission, but one of implication. A
return to its building metaphor brings this into relief. In the book's conclusion, the "rot" removed to strengthen foundations is not only the government's
incompetence and Islamophobia that resulted in Zeitoun's incarceration. In
light of the properties the Zeitouns buy up to fix and rent "block by block" (at
the time of their divorce, they owned eleven [Martin]), this metaphor, in failing to account for those routed out of New Orleans when their homes were
ruined, suggests that those displaced—who are disproportionately Black—are
disposable, are not part of the foundation. Instead, as Ansfield Bench notes in
his analysis of Katrina's aftermath, the language of reconstruction is "readily
collapsed into the project of geo-racial purification" (137). In lauding *Zeitoun*
as a builder and acquirer of property who is removing "rot," Eggers reinforces
what Nicole Fleetwood identifies as the government's narrative of progress and
its justification of and dependence on rendering Black citizens as marginalized and disposable: "On policy and urban development levels, Hurricane Katrina was the panacea that wiped the city clean of its disease, that is, lawless,
lazy, and premodern blacks in large numbers. The framing of displaced black
residents, instead of Katrina or the years of social and structural neglect, as
the cause of the city's destruction allows for developers to begin the process of
reshaping the city without regard for the majority of the city's population prior
to the hurricane" ("Failing Narratives," 785). The transformation Fleetwood
anticipated in 2006 indeed occurred, with conditions proving no better under
Obama than under Bush. Although New Orleans is back to about 80 percent
of its preflood population, half of the Black population lacked the money or
means to return, including in the Lower Ninth Ward, which until Katrina was
over 98 percent Black, and had the highest concentration of African American

homeownership in the United States (Fussell). Five years after Katrina, African American unemployment in the city remained at almost 50 percent, with Black households earning 50 percent less than white ones. Public education and housing have been largely privatized or demolished. Ten years after Katrina, occupancy in the Ninth Ward was at 12 percent, with many of its residents coming from outside New Orleans (Karoliszyn). And by contrast to New Orleans, where homeowners received little to no compensation, when the Westhampton Beach area of New York was wiped out twice by hurricanes, the federal government rebuilt every single beach mansion. In addition, almost all post-Katrina reconstruction has been done by radically underpaid laborers from El Salvador and other Latin America countries (Desvarieux).

The lives of these builders, along with the people drowned, displaced, and abandoned by the US government in conjunction with corporate violence are rendered disposable in *Zeitoun* as, to "humanize" Zeitoun, Eggers uncritically employs forms of narrative humanity to tell familiar stories of immigrant self-making, marriage, and discovery and conquest in multicultural America. Sarah Gualtieri notes that by the 1920s in the US South, Syrians (mostly Christians) were able to use their provisional whiteness to "find places in the local economy where they could function and blacks could not. . . . Their arrival in many areas was in fact viewed by native middle and upper class whites as a way to deprive blacks of potential economic opportunity" (69). In its assessment of how to strengthen America's foundations, *Zeitoun* supports this ongoing history and the foundational racism, nationalist imperialism, and settlerism that a focus on Bush's America or narratives of multiculturalism and immigrant success mask. While humanizing its hero in the face of post-9/11 Islamophobia through these and other assimilative narratives, *Zeitoun* participates in forms of narrative humanity that sustain and obscure intersecting forms of violence.

Zeitoun illuminates how life writing, which, like literature more generally, is often considered an invaluable domain for understanding and, at its best, expanding our conception of the human, can also be, and often simultaneously is, a domain of dehumanization. The same goes for narrative humanity. I have dwelled so long, and so critically, on *Zeitoun* because I think it has much to teach us, both through its textbook deployments of forms of narrative humanity that feature characters who are transparent and relatable and through complexities and contradictions that become apparent when Zeitoun "walks off the page" and media accounts convert his story into dominant narratives that Eggers strives to resist. Taken together, *Zeitoun* and the Zeitouns' ongoing story evidence the need to tell alternative narratives about becoming human, the need to create genres of the human wherein "upward mobility," national belonging, and masculine individualism are neither markers of humanity nor a cover story for the empire building, settler colonial violence, lost lives and livelihood, and gendered processes of dehumanization upon which many forms of narrative humanity and the ongoing history of the United States depend. If, as happens in *Zeitoun*, genres remain purely reiterative of received conventions—that is, are used in a conventional way to humanize those subjects usually excluded from narrative humanity—then, even when such efforts do not slide into incoherence or backfire, the resulting "successful" narratives nonetheless can reproduce, enforce, and obscure structures of dehumanization. As this chapter's next section indicates, however, and as I go on to argue in the rest of this book, even as genres are historically sedimented forms that perpetuate cultural norms, they also can be engaged in subversion, toward more progressive ends.

Troubling the Water

To transition to this book's exploration of how life writing texts can partake in—or oppose—narrative humanity in more critical, unruly, and revisionary ways, I close this chapter with a reading of *Trouble the Water*. This Zeitgeist Films documentary, an Oscar nominee that won the Sundance 2008 Grand Jury Prize for Best Documentary along with several other awards, follows the story of Kimberly Rivers-Roberts and Scott Roberts, who were among the 100,000 who lacked transportation to evacuate New Orleans before Katrina made landfall. Stranded in the attic of their Lower Ninth Ward home when the levees broke, Rivers-Roberts recorded their experience with a $20 camcorder. Hindered rather than helped by the National Guard, after the Robertses finally escape the flooded city, they meet and join forces with producers and directors Carl Deal and Tia Lessin in a Red Cross shelter. Best known for their work with Michael Moore on *Fahrenheit 9/11*, Deal and Lessin had intended to shoot a documentary about National Guard soldiers returning from Baghdad to respond to Katrina.[16] When the National Guard public relations team shut them out, citing *Fahrenheit 9/11* as the reason, they changed directions. The resulting collaboratively made documentary suggests how forms of narrative humanity can be utilized not simply in additive but also in more radically challenging ways. As the documentary revises and at times upends the forms it engages, creating openings for more foundationally just and free ways to understand the human, it illuminates how narrative humanity is not always easily distinguished from narrated humanity. If my reading of *Zeitoun* enables an analysis of "textbook" forms of narrative humanity, then my analysis of *Trouble the Water* foreshadows later engagements with narrated humanity while also contending with ways works of life writing (and literature, more broadly speaking) rarely adhere to such strict patterns, creating ruptures and ripples that productively open spaces for new ways of being human.

In chronicling the Robertses' Katrina journey, *Trouble the Water* draws on the genre of the slave narrative. At its inception the slave narrative constituted an example of narrated humanity, one that grew out of and participated in an abolitionist political agenda. Over time, the slave narrative has evolved into a recognized literary genre—into, in other words, a form of narrative humanity— that writers and artists continue to take up, often to contend with what Said-iya Hartman calls the "afterlife of slavery" and its ongoing dehumanization of Black people.[17] In their engagement with this genre, Deal and Lessin estab- lish lines of continuity between Confederate and post-9/11 America as the story they and the Robertses tell also anticipates the political commitments out of which BLM and its accompanying narratives emerge (some, as in chapter 2, engaging with forms of narrative humanity; others, as in chapter 3, constituting abolitionist acts of narrated humanity). Jamelle Bouie asserts, "Black collec- tive memory of Hurricane Katrina, as much as anything else, informs the pre- sent movement against police violence, 'Black Lives Matter'" ("Where Black Lives Matter"). Not only Black collective memory but also the community ac- tivism that came out of Katrina inform BLM. As a story that captures grassroots organizing to survive the United States' indifference to Black life, *Trouble the Water* thus serves as a counterpoint to the formulaic literariness of *Zeitoun*, as it also provides a way to shift attention to the concerns of the chapters that follow: narrative humanity's possibilities (the subject of the next chapter), and in parts 2 and 3, its dynamic relationship to narrated humanity and the mak- ing of political movements.

Trouble the Water riffs off the slave narrative genre, updating while employ- ing hallmarks of this Christian, abolitionist form of narrative humanity.[18] Starting with its title, taken from the spiritual "Wade in the Water," the docu- mentary signals this influence. Stories about "Wade in the Water" tell of how those fleeing the South via the Underground Railroad used its lyrics to com- municate coded messages to elude capture. The song's verses that urge escape through water, and that include the line "God's going to trouble the water," resonate with the Old and New Testaments—with the Israelites' escape from Egypt, and with the promise of healing found in John 5:4: "For an angel went down at a certain season into the pool, and troubled the water: whosoever then first after the troubling of the water stepped in was made whole of whatsoever disease he had." *Trouble the Water*, which includes two contemporary renditions of "Wade in the Water," revises and at times challenges this story of redemp- tion and the familiar and familial forms of narrative humanity that pertain to self-making, kinship, and Christianity that are encoded within it and the slave narrative genre.

The relationship between the Robertses and Deal and Lessin evokes while reconfiguring the usual power dynamics of the slave narrative. In ways that resonate with the genre, the Robertses' story is an "as-told-to," produced and directed by award-winning white filmmakers who contextualize, edit, and otherwise shape the Robertses' story into a film that protests how the US government treats those in New Orleans who are Black, poor, disabled, old, or otherwise vulnerable as if they are noncitizens, or, to draw on Orlando Patterson's phrase, socially dead. However, the Robertses do not relinquish to Deal and Lessin the role of authenticating and authorizing their story.[19] Instead, they insist both within the film and in numerous interviews that a condition of sharing their story be that Deal and Lessin keep the documentary "real." We also see Kimberly Rivers-Roberts take command as a storyteller, both in her own footage and as Deal and Lessin film her. Roger Ebert remarks on the power of her presence, noting that although her footage "is surrounded by professionally filmed material that deepens and explains what happened," not only does it have "a desperate urgency that surpasses any other news and doc footage I have seen," but also Rivers-Roberts takes command of the film with a keen awareness of genre conventions: "Using lessons learned from TV news, she interviews her family, friends and neighbors, does voiceovers while making shots, even signs off with her stage name as a rapper." Kimberly's direct address makes no appeal to her audience to recognize her humanity: she seeks not to convert viewers so much as to assert her sovereignty, over herself and as part of a Black New Orleans community that, having been denied rights of citizenship, can rely only on itself and God. This approach is powerfully encapsulated when she performs her song "Amazing," with its proclamation, "I don't need you to tell me that I'm amazing."

As it engages the slave narrative, *Trouble the Water* also challenges registers of narrative humanity that are integral to but go beyond the slave narrative: the documentary represents the Robertses' journey through troubled waters as part abolitionist struggle, part capitalist venture, part assertion of Black pride, and part journey to Christian redemption. In telling stories of self-making, family, community, and God, the film at times embraces or revises and at other times critiques or refuses these forms of narrative humanity. This is a documentary that repudiates political purity. In its unapologetic contradictions, it respects the ideological messiness that is part of being human, while also confronting viewers with unsettling questions about how to be human when the world, at every turn, denies your humanity. While insisting on the need to abolish foundational and ongoing conditions of antiblack state violence, *Trouble the Water* leaves viewers to wrestle with whether those whom the state dehumanizes can become human in the terms set by the slave narrative and other narratives that would determine who counts as human: Can African Americans and others abandoned by the state become rights-bearing individuals? And, should possession of these rights dictate human being, and what counts as freedom? Kimberly Rivers-Roberts's stage name, Queen Black Kold Madina—with its mix of Black-centered cultural assertion (including its nod to Tone-Lōc's song "Funky Cold Medina"), toughness (the Urban Dictionary defines "kold" as "cold-blooded, not afraid to kill"),[20] political resistance, and religious faith ("Madina" denotes both the Islamic holy site of the Prophet Muhammad's tomb and also the ancient quarter of many North African cities)—captures her and the documentary's complex and sometimes competing engagements with these questions and concerns.

In its central narrative, the film casts the Robertses' story as a journey of Christian redemption, self-making, and community uplift. This story line emerges organically as it follows the Robertses. In a way that resonates with "Wade in the Water," the Robertses and their friends greet the hurricane as an opportunity God provides them to escape suffering and experience healing. At the Red Cross shelter, Larry, doing what Kimberly affectionately calls his "saving people dance," explains that he thanks God for the storm, "because I never thought God could use a man like me." When Kim leaves Louisiana for Memphis, for a music career and to find a church, she is wearing a "Jesus is Lord" T-shirt, singing along with "God's gonna trouble the water," and greeting Katrina as the bringer of new possibilities. In her TED talk "Triumph over Tragedy," Kimberly highlights this understanding that Katrina has enabled a cleansing of sins and a spiritual rebirth when she states that Katrina survivors are "relatives by baptism." Through the film's title, soundtrack, camera work, and editing, Deal and Lessin shape the film in accordance with this narrative arc, as does Zeitgeist Films in its marketing synopsis: "*Trouble the Water* is a redemptive tale of self-described street hustlers who become heroes—two unforgettable people who survive the storm and then seize a chance for a new beginning." Through foregrounding this story of redemption, one that draws on the most mainstream of narrative humanity's forms and conventions, the film establishes its appeal to a wide audience.

At the same time, *Trouble the Water* remixes and updates this Christian narrative to tell a story of self-making that also, in following the Robertses' journey as "self-described street hustlers," engages the particularities of their Black, urban poor, and capitalist contexts. Kimberly and Scott move from a life of hustling for survival, a life riven with violence, addiction, drug dealing, and poverty, to another form of hustling by which, through street smarts and hard work, they uplift themselves and their community. Scott describes how before Katrina, he hated his life and his lack of options, and states that he was on his way to ending up "in jail or under the ground." Once Katrina strikes, he scavenges a boat, and then gets hold of a truck, using both to rescue his neighbors. By the end of the documentary, he is earning money and (in striking contrast to the Zeitouns) working to restore his community, rebuilding homes in the Ninth Ward. Kimberly follows a similar trajectory. She describes having to steal food and soap to survive a childhood with a mother who, addicted to drugs, could not take care of her and who died of HIV/AIDS when Kimberly was thirteen. When Katrina approaches, Kimberly is broke, and still struggling. As Kimberly films the storm, she lets viewers know of her plans to sell the footage to the news, to "make money off of white people." As she elaborates in a YouTube interview: "You know I was thinking about a come-up. I'm in the hood you know, trying to make a few quick dollars" ("Trouble the Water Pt. 1"). Through quick thinking and resourcefulness, she saves herself and her neighbors. As she puts this in her TED talk titled "Triumph + Adversity," "If you're not thinking, then your ship is sinking." Her success establishes that she is not, as she puts it in another TED talk, titled "Triumph over Tragedy," "a poor me-er." The film enables her and Scott to start the record label Born Hustler that features her music, and she goes on to direct a documentary of her own, *Fear No Gumbo (stop stealing our sh*t!)*. In short, the Robertses' story is distinctly Black and at the same time conforms roughly to redemptive and rags-to-riches formulas for self-making.

At the same time, the documentary challenges these forms of narrative humanity through sharp reminders of the dehumanization Black Americans continue to experience. As Deal and Lessin follow the Robertses in the months after the storm, Kimberly and Scott comment on how Katrina remains with them, and we witness how they must contend with a government that has left them with a devastated infrastructure, a neighborhood full of unlivable and foreclosed homes, unobtainable FEMA checks, and other conditions of state violence that outlast the storm and extend beyond Louisiana (they are unable to make it in nearly all-white Memphis). Meanwhile the film documents how the government, at their expense and in combination with corporations, invests in tourists and its wealthiest citizens—a scenario of disaster capitalism that in her follow-up documentary Rivers-Roberts continues to contest (stop stealing out sh*t!).

To expose and condemn the afterlives of Katrina and of slavery, the film stays within its Christian framework, while also troubling its accompanying narrative of redemption. The Robertses and their friends express keen awareness of the government's failure to protect them as they instead turn to God for protection.[21] We see this when Brian meets a soldier in the streets of New Orleans. Expecting neither harm nor help from him, he offers him prayers that he need not return to Iraq, telling him, "That's not our war. This is the war right here." As Kimberly and Scott head back to New Orleans having survived the storm, Kimberly says, "Thank God, I got no one else to thank." When, post-Katrina, Kimberly finally if only briefly has running water, she attributes this not to the government officials she distrusts, but to "a blessing from God." Their faith in Christianity does not legitimate or encourage passivity in the face of white supremacist institutions, but instead transcends and enables survival of them.

In a way that respects the Robertses' faith while also extending critiques of Christianity found in the slave narrative, Deal and Lessin juxtapose the hypocrisy of an institutionalized or duplicitous Christianity that maintains systems of oppression to faith in a God who is on the side of freedom and equality. Toward these ends, the film includes a newsclip of President George W. Bush, who, after urging residents to take precautions and listen to the authorities, proclaims, "In the meantime America will pray." Deal and Lessin cut from this cynically deployed Christianity to an abandoned city drowning in water from the broken levees, and then to footage from Kimberly, who is left with nothing but her Christian faith: "We under siege. Everybody lost everything around here. We barely living up here but the Lord with us." Throughout, the film's composition, including its breaks with chronology, complicate the slave narrative's Christian abolitionism in a way that at once respects the Robertses' faith and disrupts the narrative arc of a progression from captivity or entrapment to redemption and freedom.[22] Its disorienting jumps back and forth in time, between the lead-up to the storm, the storm itself, and its aftermath, capture the experience of PTSD, and also the enduring nature of the dehumanizing societal structures that Hurricane Katrina exacerbates. As Deal and Lessin make space for without themselves endorsing the Robertses' religious faith, they depart from the slave narrative and its reliance on true Christianity as an index of humanity. At the same time, their film conforms to the genre's condemnation of how, as an institution, Christianity serves to hypocritically deny the humanity of those who are Black and poor.

Throughout, the Robertses' individual successes and salvation—and their failures and disappointments—are tied to stories of family and community that, as with its narratives of self-making and redemption, articulate with the slave narrative genre. As connections among family members evidence their humanity, they also—as in slave narratives—evidence the inhumanity of a society structured to rupture them. In contrast to Eggers's idealized depictions that establish the Zeitouns as model citizens and family members, *Trouble the Water* shows Black families to be under siege, and rather than apologize for or contest their non-conformity to good citizenship, the documentary upholds their bonds and condemns the society that has dehumanized and declared war upon them. One of the documentary's most powerful moments is when Kimberly returns to her storm-destroyed home to rescue a photo of her mother. Cradling it close, she looks into the camera, and directly addresses the audience: "This is a picture of my mom, y'all. I was waiting to get it. I didn't know how I was going to do without it." In valuing people over property and showing the strength of Kimberly's bond to her mother despite her mother's inability to parent her, the documentary provides an alternative to narratives of family that prop up racial capitalism and that are coterminous with dominant modes of good citizenship.

When other family members are left to die in the storm, the film represents these deaths not as a rupture, but as in keeping with a social order that renders Black life disposable. We see this when Kimberly's grandmother dies during Katrina, neglected in a hospital. We also witness this through the treatment of Kimberly's brother, Wink, incarcerated for a misdemeanor when Katrina strikes. After Kimberly and Scott work their way through layers of prison bureaucracy, an operator informs Kimberly that Wink "doesn't have telephone privileges anymore," and when she finally succeeds in bailing him out so he can attend his beloved grandmother's funeral, he describes how inmates are treated like "animals" and "slaves." Wink expresses his shock over how the incarcerated men were abandoned, left without food or water when Katrina descended, with some so desperate they jumped from windows. Wink speaks to this injustice, saying, "We got families," and asking, "Why they do us like that? We humans just like them." In each of these instances, the humanity of the family members we meet is established through their love for one another as they work to survive carceral, bureaucratic, militarized state violence and the dehumanizing societal conditions that pre- and postdate Katrina.

The story of the Robertses' marriage also testifies to their humanity without idealizing their relationship and without its serving to make a case for their good citizenship or "all-Americanness." Toward the documentary's conclusion, having witnessed the solidity of the Robertses' partnership and the consistency of their respect and care for one another, we learn how hard won these practices are: in her song "Amazing" Kimberly reveals that when they first met, as a sixteen-year-old she made front-page news for slashing Scott's face with a razor, and that the two have survived a history of drug addiction and dealing. As Kimberly raps this story, the camera cuts back and forth from her to close-ups of Scott's scarred face, as he watches his wife with an expression of tenderness, love, and pride. Throughout the documentary, the Robertses' experiences of violence, incarceration, poverty, drug use, and drug dealing do not confirm dehumanizing antiblack stereotypes. Without disavowing their responsibility for or romanticizing their past, accounts of these experiences do not criminalize them. Instead, the film incriminates a society with an ongoing history of treating Black people as not human, while engendering appreciation and respect for the strength, resilience, and love that enable the Robertses to survive with their humanity intact. If stories of family regularly serve to support ideological state apparatuses, and, as in *Zeitoun*, are integral to hegemonic genres of the human and the citizen, in *Trouble the Water* stories of family are markers of the human as they also challenge the state structures designed to criminalize Black people, and to destroy their bonds of kinship.

Instead of making family coterminous with good citizenship, *Trouble the Water* represents the Robertses' familial bonds as seamless with those of community, and as a way to survive a state that denies them their rights as citizens and as humans. In this way, the documentary critiques and reworks forms of narrative humanity that align the family, citizenship, and national belonging, and that posit them as central to formulations of the human. Throughout *Trouble the Water*, the Robertses protect, work with, and struggle alongside other Black Americans whom they introduce as their brothers, sisters, mothers, cousins, and uncles. Only as the documentary progresses do we learn that only some of these community members are relations by birth or marriage. Despite their lack of money, the Robertses shelter in their attic and feed neighbors the state has abandoned. We see Scott with his "brothers" Larry Simms and Brian Noble brave the water (Larry uses an old punching bag, then once they meet up with Brian, an old boat) to save elderly neighbors and children. In contrast to Zeitoun's prowess in the water, Scott's inability to swim adds to the heroism of his actions. At one point, Kimberly turns down rescue to care for five children and a neighbor with a disability. When Scott states, of those he and Kimberly met during the storm, "Everything we did, we did as a family," he encapsulates one of the documentary's primary narrative lines. He reinforces this position in a YouTube interview, explaining that the film "is about look out for your neighbor. Everybody needs someone. It is about humans" ("Trouble the Water Pt. 1"). Formulated in accord with conventions of narrative humanity that are Christian and humanitarian, *Trouble the Water* asserts that whether it be the "uncle" who awaited Katrina passed out on his doorstep, or those who risked their lives to save their neighbors, everyone is part of the same human community and is worthy of being treated with a care and respect that run counter to the state's dehumanizing violence. As it redefines family to encompass community, the documentary values as human the kinship among community members and the forms of mutual aid that they practice to survive their status as noncitizens in an antiblack America.

What remains unresolved is whether the documentary—and the Robertses themselves—engage forms of narrative humanity to make the case for being recognized as citizens, or whether their stories of kinship and community upend formulations of narrative humanity that premise being human on national belonging, and refuse such understandings of belonging altogether. One example of how the film oscillates between these two positions occurs when the National Guard refuses the Robertses and community members shelter in a closed US Navy base with 500 evacuated rooms and 200 empty family units. After soldiers tell Scott, "We can't help you, you're on your own," he describes how, when he questions this, more troops arrive and point loaded M16s at them. With nowhere to stay, Scott manages to rent a moving truck and transport more than twenty-five people to safety. His account of the voyage out of the flooded city is intercut with the song "Hurricane Water." As Citizen Cope sings, "See I will carry you, through the hurricane water . . . until the city and country ain't divided, until then," the camera homes in on the faces of men, women, and children suffering in the sweltering Superdome. As the camera cuts to a mural of Martin Luther King Jr., Scott explains, "I had a dream that I was going to get me some transportation no matter what it took to get my people out of New Orleans." This sequencing, as with the Robertses' multifaceted positioning, at once makes an appeal to struggles for civil and human rights as it also, in its exposure of the state's horrific abandonment in what is the afterlife of slavery, refuses this liberal approach and the values and assumptions about being human that are embedded in familiar forms of narrative humanity.

A strength of *Trouble the Water* is its ability to activate and orchestrate different and sometimes competing forms of narrative humanity—of spiritual regeneration, family and community, capitalist self-making—in ways that adhere to and challenge their formulations of the human. In the ways it brings these narratives into a productively precarious balance, the documentary represents the Robertses as humans replete with human contradictions and complexities, while also issuing a wholesale indictment of a society whose profits depend on their dehumanization. So, too, the film's narrative remixings raise questions about whether rights-based narratives serve as the best pathways to being human, as they also create apertures through which to consider alternatives for human flourishing, and, in a time of climate crisis, planetary survival. As the film documents Kimberly and Scott's struggle for their own and their community's survival in the wake of Hurricane Katrina, it captures their emergence as community organizers, a role that comes more sharply into focus in the film's conclusion. More than a year after Katrina, Queen Black Kold Madina's "Trouble the Water"—a song calling for the government's accountability in the massive destruction that came with the hurricane—plays as the documentary cuts to slow sweeping shots of decimated New Orleans neighborhoods, marked off with the yellow tape of a crime scene. Superimposed by the editors, the crimes written across the tape are those that comprise the everyday workings of US civil society: doubled rates of rents and houselessness, skyrocketing incarceration, undisbursed moneys for rebuilding, still-flawed levees. The film cuts from there to a march that is part celebration, part protest, which culminates in front of New Orleans City Hall. Kimberly is part of a crowd in which people hold signs that say, "From Outrage to Action"; "Stop the Killing of Black People"; and "Unite Black People." Stating that "here in New Orleans it's like they are preparing us for prison," she explains she is present for those who cannot represent themselves.

In the aftermath of *Trouble the Water*, Rivers-Roberts uses the platform the documentary gives her to engage in acts of representation and in community organizing. We learn from the credits and from the many interviews, talks, and projects she undertakes that she has gone on to become an activist and artist, fundraising for the New Orleans Women's Shelter to aid homeless women and children; making records for her label Born Hustler and selling merchandise as Queen Black Kold Madina; and directing the film *Fear No Gumbo*. This documentary, which shows "that Katrina is still alive and well" (Karoliszyn), extends the work of *Trouble the Water*. In this film, however, Deal and Lessin appear as cast members, and Kimberly is clearly in charge, as we follow her and community members as they fearlessly oppose big money and gentrification, zoning laws, tourism, and artistic and cultural appropriation. As Kimberly / Queen Black Kold Madina puts this in one of the film's many scenes of confrontation with men in power, "You don't control me, motherfucker, you're trippin."

Trouble the Water works within as it also revises and challenges forms of narrative humanity, in order to counter stories that, as they naturalize man-made disasters, perpetuate existing inequities and a system that does not protect against but creates and—as Rivers-Roberts goes on to demonstrate in *Fear No Gumbo*—profits from these disasters. *Trouble the Water* does so less to appeal to a liberal audience, as happens in *Zeitoun*, and more in the spirit of provocation and challenge—and as an expression of love for the people of New Orleans, especially the Black Americans who make up the Lower Ninth Ward. Also in counterpoint to *Zeitoun*, *Trouble the Water*'s story line shows how forms of narrative humanity can be employed, reworked, and overturned in the service of uplifting communities that value practices of love and kinship, rather than sustaining nation-states that perpetuate masculine individualism, imperial violence, racial capitalism, and climate catastrophe. In this way, as this modern-day slave narrative presages contemporary abolitionist calls to invest not in corporations, police, and prisons, but rather in communities of mutual aid and care, *Trouble the Water* also anticipates BLM-inspired forms of narrative and narrated humanity that are the topic of this book's next two chapters.

2

Criminals and Kinship

Fruitvale Station, Between the World and Me,
and Black Selfhood in the Age of BLM

The first Black Lives Matter march in Honolulu took place on August 15, 2014. The event was organized to protest the acquittal of Federal Agent Christopher Deedy, who killed Kollin Elderts, a twenty-three-year-old Kanaka Maoli (Native Hawaiian) man, while in Honolulu in 2011 to provide security for the Asia Pacific Economic Conference (APEC). For the second time, Deedy had been found not guilty of the murder of Elderts when, off-duty and after a night of barhopping, he picked a fight with Elderts in a McDonald's and then shot him dead (Mendoza). Only days before Deedy's acquittal, Police Officer Darin Wilson had shot Michael Brown in Ferguson, Missouri, where the governor had then declared a state of emergency as Black people in Ferguson rose up and faced heavily militarized police forces to protest his murder, turning Black Lives Matter from a hashtag into a movement. Dozens of us converged to march through Waikiki to protest Deedy's acquittal and to support Elderts's family and the movement for Black lives. As we joined together in a circle before heading down Kalākaua Avenue, organizers and Kollin Elderts's cousin and legal team shared their grief as they connected the long history of Kanaka Maoli criminalization and premature death to antiblack police violence.

Before beginning the march to the Waikiki police station, I sorted through an array of signs, finally opting for one that read "No justice, no peace, no racist police!" Many signs linked Elderts to Black people also killed by police violence: Michael Brown, Renisha McBride, Eric Garner, and Trayvon Martin. Others proclaimed, "I can't breathe," "I am Trayvon Martin," "We are all Oscar Grant," "Hands up, Don't shoot!," and "Black Lives Matter!" As I looked at these signs, spread out on the grass, I remember feeling overcome—with sadness, anger, and also, questions. What did it mean for those of us who had not experienced the fear of having our air supply cut off by the police, for those of us who were not Trayvon Martin or Oscar Grant and/or part of a collective "we" who live with a target on our backs, to carry such signs? Then there was the outrage of having to assert that Black lives matter. And the power but also the complexities of connecting Black and Kanaka Maoli struggles. These concerns seemed indispensable, but so too did the necessity of asserting a common humanity that brought people—Black, Indigenous, and those of us present as non-Black settler allies—to gather in a circle, and then to take to the streets on that hot, humid August day.

As we made our way down Kalākaua Avenue, we demanded justice for Elderts and chanted "Hands up, don't shoot!" and "Black lives matter!" Sunburned tourists shopping for designer clothing and cheap souvenirs or in pursuit of late afternoon lattes or mai tais for the most part ignored us. Some young white men singled out and heckled the Black marchers, shouting into their faces "All lives matter!" In the face of this disregard and aggression, one thing was clear: the urgent need for non-Black people to stand with Black people to proclaim "Black lives matter." So, too, responses from this site of heightened racial capitalism and tourism brought home the importance of linking without conflating different forms of racist and settler violence, and of creating new ways of being in relation to one another.

Since 2014, BLM's necessity and radical potential have come ever more sharply into focus as BLM has continued to gather power and build communities of care at the grassroots level, while also strengthening its solidarity with other struggles for transformative justice, and achieving mainstream impact to become what *Time* magazine describes as "one of the most influential social-justice groups in the world" (Chan) in its March 2020 issue featuring BLM's cofounders on the cover.[1] In accounting for BLM's significance while also continuing to explore possibilities and limitations of narrative humanity, this chapter examines the interrelations of the movement's humanist appeal that Black lives matter; its exposure of a necropolitical order in which Black lives do not matter; its commitments to intersectionality, community building, and solidarity; and ways narrative humanity is and is not positioned to support these sometimes competing emphases.[2]

Even as the BLM movement pulls in both liberal and radical directions, it is a movement that uniformly contests a necropolitical order that marks Black bodies for death (Threadcraft), and one that derives power from stories about the premature deaths of Black lives that matter. In its abolitionist rather than reformist iterations—explored in the chapter that follows this one—BLM does not seek rights or recognition within existing structures of a police state that operates by surveilling, criminalizing, and incarcerating Black bodies. Instead,

BLM organizers engage in creating, including through acts of narrated humanity, new ways of human being and belonging premised on care and community. Other articulations of BLM—my focus in this chapter—contest the human as an antiblack construct, often through inhabiting forms of narrative humanity that "humanize" Black individuals, while also exposing the injustice of a world that systemically devalues Black lives.

Through analyses of Ryan Coogler's 2013 *Fruitvale Station* and Ta-Nehisi Coates's 2015 *Between the World and Me*, I argue that to address antiblack dehumanization while also adopting forms of narrative humanity to value Black life involves productive as well as compromising or entrapping contradictions. To refuse narrative humanity is to leave in place a significant means of sustaining white supremacy. And yet, to take up in order to take over forms of narrative humanity too often requires replicating liberal humanism's omissions and hierarchies and covering over its antiblackness. This ultimately means making only (some) Black lives matter, and—as happens with Black Americans in *Zeitoun*—leaving behind people these narratives structurally exclude.

As I analyze how *Fruitvale Station* and *Between the World and Me* (hereafter, following Coates's own abbreviation, *BTWAM*) contribute to and coincide with, as they also depart from, BLM, this chapter augments the previous chapter's investigations of narrative humanity's capacity to challenge the dehumanization that sustains the inequitable workings of civil society. I focus on *Fruitvale Station* and *BTWAM* because these texts have been so widely received as foundational to BLM, and because their engagements with narrative humanity allow for an exploration of concerns with self-making, kinship, and criminality that are central to BLM.

Coogler's 2013 docudrama was released to theaters at the same time as an almost all-white jury exonerated Trayvon Martin's killer, George Zimmerman. Noted by BLM organizers, including cofounder Alicia Garza, as a catalyst for #BLM, *Fruitvale Station* complements the movement's aims, even as—indeed because—its modes of narrative humanity resist not only the police's criminalization of Oscar Grant, but also his conversion into a political symbol after his death. Nicole Fleetwood's observation regarding Trayvon Martin's image, which "circulates as material object, viral transmission, traumatic wound, and historical fact" (*On Racial Icons*, 30), holds true for Grant as well, fueling the BLM movement by insisting that his life matters while also abstracting it. A complement and counter to Grant's status as political icon, *Fruitvale Station* dwells on his last day as a struggling family member determined to improve himself. The film reaches out to a broad audience to convey the significance of his everyday life and its particularities.

Arguably the most widely known BLM text, *BTWAM* also contests the racist system that criminalizes Black men and robs them of their lives. This memoir, which appeared for sixty-six weeks on the *New York Times* nonfiction bestseller list, also topped the *NYT* monthly "Race and Civil Rights" bestseller list in December 2015. The book was adapted for stage at the Apollo Theater in 2018, and in 2020, it was made into an HBO special. A text that sounds BLM's keynotes, *BTWAM* meditates on the anti-Blackness[3] that fueled the killings of Trayvon Martin, Mike Brown, and Eric Garner. In *BTWAM*, structured as a letter to his son, and modeled on James Baldwin's address to his nephew in *The Fire Next Time*, Coates instructs Samori to engage in struggle, however futile, against the pervasive plundering of Black bodies in a white supremacist world. Drawing on the literary genre of the Künstlerroman, this father-son narrative simultaneously chronicles Coates's development as a writer of literature. Exploring *BTWAM*'s relationship to BLM, as I explore their points of connection and divergence, I also consider ways *BTWAM* illuminates the challenges of using literary humanism to denounce a relentless anti-Blackness (and I employ this term here, in differentiation from "antiblackness," to underline an essentialism that articulates with an Afro-pessimist analytic) that its logics reproduce, and the incompatibilities that exist among social justice movements, an Afro-pessimist analytic, and narrative humanity.

Perhaps the most powerfully prevalent narratives that underwrite the devaluation of Black lives are those that define the human—as individual, as family member, as citizen—against Black criminality. Such forms of narrative humanity deny Black people positive forms of agency or belonging, while assigning them hyperagency for acts of violence and criminality (see da Silva, "No-bodies"). As Robin Kelley explains, the transformation of the Black community from citizens to "thugs" "works to both criminalize and dehumanize the dispossessed while masking the violent operations of the state and capital"; in this way, "Black people are also made to pay for the very system that renders them non-persons" ("Thug Nation"). Both elastic and continuous, narratives that define the human against Black criminality in the US date back to the nation's formation and continue into the present, or what Saidiya Hartman and Christina Sharpe describe as the afterlife of slavery, and what Michelle Alexander calls "the New Jim Crow."[4] As Colin Dayan notes, "The ghost of slavery is built into our legal language and holds our prison system in its grip. To the extent that slaves were allowed personalities before the law, they were regarded chiefly—almost solely—as potential criminals." In *The New Jim Crow*, Alexander looks to how today's prison industrial complex not only partakes in an ongoing system of legalized discrimination, but also, in large part through its "war on drugs," constitutes a modern-day form of slavery, one that particularly targets African Americans, who are five times as likely as white people to be imprisoned for drug charges. As well, police and lawmakers target Black people for a whole range of petty misdemeanors—broken taillights, unpaid parking tickets, truancy from school—to the point that in some US cities, 80 percent of Black men have done time in prison. The pervasive and long-standing criminalization and incarceration of Black people, and the corresponding assault on Black kinship structures and citizenship rights, affect every aspect of Black life—housing, voting rights, education, public benefits, employment, and health.[5] This violence, both systemic and individual, is enabled by—and takes forms that include—narratives that, in sustaining white supremacist structures of power, deny Black people their status as human, as citizens, and as family members, by equating Blackness with criminality.

BLM's formation has centrally involved contesting or refusing narratives of Black criminality. Cofounded in July 2013 by Alicia Garza, Patrisse Cullors, and Ayo (formerly Opal) Tometi in a Facebook response to a jury acquitting George Zimmerman for the 2012 killing of seventeen-year-old Trayvon Martin, BLM grew from an online hashtag campaign to a full-blown, "leaderful" grassroots movement in 2014 catalyzed by the police killings of Eric Garner and Michael Brown. In July 2014, New York City police officer Daniel Pantaleo put Garner in an illegal chokehold in the process of arresting him for selling loose cigarettes, with Garner repeating, eleven times, "I can't breathe" before he died.[6] Then, in Ferguson, police officer Darren Wilson detained eighteen-year-old Michael Brown for jaywalking. Within ninety seconds of encountering him, Wilson shot Brown six times, twice in the head, with Brown reportedly holding his hands up, saying "Don't Shoot." Captured on camera and blasted out over Black Twitter and other social media sites, these murders showed the world the expendability of Black lives.

Exonerating police perpetuating antiblack violence depends upon a reversal of the existing power dynamics, one in which the police defend themselves against superhuman agents of violence. "Phobic fantasies of demonized monstrous black criminality," George Lipsitz observes, "stand at the center of the national political imaginary." In accounting for these fantasies, Ta-Nehisi Coates explains that "to plunder a people of everything" requires representing Black people as "demonic, unnatural, inhuman" ("Ta-Nehisi Coates on *Vanity Fair*'s September Issue"). In his grand jury testimony, 6'4" officer Darren Wilson described feeling like a five-year-old grasping the arm of 6'5" Brown, whom Wilson likened to "Hulk Hogan," and a bullet-defying "demon." This language, which draws on superhero comics to cast Black men and boys as inhuman and in possession of terrifying superpowers, resonates with descriptions of Rodney King, Trayvon Martin, and Jordan Davis (Bouie, "Michael

Brown"), or with Hillary Clinton's typecasting of Black urban youth as "super-predators" (Ransby, 33). (And here it bears noting that both Coogler and Coates counter antiblackness not only through realist genres of life writing, but also through Black Panther, Marvel's first Black superhero comic. Through Black Panther narratives, they celebrate rather than demonize the power of Black men and boys—Coates through writing for Marvel *Black Panther: A Nation under Our Feet* in 2016; Coogler, inspired by "his favorite writer" Coates [Riesman], through making the 2018 blockbuster Marvel Cinematic Universe film *Black Panther*.)

The BLM movement has sparked outrage over how narratives that represent Black men in possession of monstrous agency and superhuman strength work to justify the inability of Black people to exercise the most basic of rights—to walk freely, to breathe, and also to grieve. Denying family members the right to grieve those lost to police violence has served as an important catalyst for BLM. Horrific as the police shooting of Michael Brown was, the protests that coalesced BLM into a movement also resulted from the police leaving Brown's body lying facedown in the street for over four hours, as they kept his parents away at gunpoint and with dogs. Brittney Cooper calls this "a moment of rupture, a white supremacist prophecy about the value of the lives of Black folks."[7] Lipsitz observes that the disrespect not only for Brown's body, but for Brown's friends and family, "encapsulated in microcosm the degrading, demeaning, and debilitating forms of institutionalized racism that black people face every day"—ones Lipsitz dates back to *Plessy v. Ferguson*. Claudia Rankine notes of this cruel disregard, "Whatever their reasoning, by not moving Brown's corpse for four hours after his shooting, the police made mourning his death part of what it meant to take in the details of his story. No one could consider the facts of Michael Brown's interaction with the Ferguson police officer Darren Wilson without also thinking of the bullet-riddled body bleeding on the asphalt" ("The Condition"). As this image spread over social media, Patrisse Cullors, together with writer/activist Darnell Moore, organized the first in-person national BLM protest, a "Black Lives Matter Freedom Ride" to Ferguson, where, as the organizers announced, people "came together in Mike Brown's name, but our roots are also in the flooded streets of New Orleans and the bloodied BART stations of Oakland. We are connected online and in the streets. We are decentralized, but coordinated. Most importantly, we are organized" (qtd. in Taylor, *From #BlackLivesMatter*).

Neither these high-profile and widely publicized murders nor the protests over them have slowed down police executions of Black people—in 2016, the US police killed 1,129 people, 25 percent of them Black. In 99 percent of the cases, officers, including Wilson and Pantaleo, have not been convicted of a crime. Nicholas Mirzoeff notes that "the appearance of due process is in fact the production of immunity for police as part of a social order where the police produce and supervise a racialized hierarchy" (71). This social order approximates a caste system—one that, as I discuss in the next chapter, we see being pressured to change in 2020, as BLM returns in full force, in a way that realizes BLM's and a longer history of movement building and Black organizing.

If broadcasting acts of state terrorism caught on camera has not put an end to antiblack violence, the circulation of these videos, together with family members' grief-filled stories—what Laura E. Lyons and I elsewhere have called "relational witnessing and testimony" ("'I Have a Family'")—spurred the growth of BLM into a network that extends across the US and internationally. Perhaps more crucially than circulating these images, which can perpetuate as well as evidence antiblack violence (Mowatt), BLM has created a space for family members to tell stories in which they grieve their loved ones. Drawing on forebears that include the Black Panthers, Malcolm X, Assata Shakur, Angela Davis, Audre Lorde, and others representative of the Black Radical Tradition and Third World movements, BLM has intensified attention to familial grief. Even as BLM's stories and signage appeal to non-Black people to recognize Black people's humanity, this emphasis on the human first and foremost comes from the movement's commitment to hold space for Black people to mourn, and to care for themselves and one another.

In its broadest impact, BLM has brought a humanist but contextually radical political position (Black lives matter) into the mainstream of US culture. Celebrities, sports teams, artists, writers, and musicians have taken up and amplified BLM in films, music, and scholarly and popular books that celebrate and advance the movement—in a way that both foregrounds its humanism and also exposes, often through backlash, the reality of US society's antiblackness. Some BLM organizers have become involved in shaping electoral politics and proposing legislative reform, even as others call for an uncompromising abolitionism.

Its successes as it works within and between both liberal and radical frameworks have led to reactionary formations (#AllLivesMatter, #BlueLivesMatter), job loss (Colin Kaepernick), and charges of antisemitism (leveled at M4BL for its endorsement of BDS). As well, the movement has been accompanied by increasing repression on college campuses (see chapter 4); state violence (teargassing, kettling, arrests, kidnapping and assault by Federal agents, and killing of protesters); an uptick in incidents of antiblack racism by white nationalist groups and individuals; cooptation by politicians, corporations, and university presidents in the form of glib "solidarity" statements and BLM endorsements;

and so on. The intensified backlash has resulted from BLM gathering in force starting in 2014. It also constitutes a racist reaction to America's first Black president, Barack Obama; and with the election of Donald Trump, from the impact of having an openly white supremacist administration in power during a time of increasing international racism, ethnonationalism, fascism, and, starting in 2020, a global pandemic that has exacerbated racism, poverty, and other such preexisting conditions.

Narratives focused on law and order or criminalization, self-making, and family play a key role in upholding systemic racism as they define the (white) human subject, and the American citizen, over against Black life. As Julius Bailey and David Leonard explain, "To say 'Black Lives Matter' is to challenge the cultural equation of Blackness with criminality" (24). As part of this work of asserting that Black lives matter, BLM activists seek to take control of, or to overturn entirely, master narratives that render Black people as criminals—or as perpetual children—while denying Black children their right to a childhood, and while killing and incarcerating Black men and denying them rights to paternity and citizenship. BLM narratives also counter those that, as they pathologize Black mothers, fathers, and families, cover over a history of having torn apart Black families. Whereas the next chapter takes up BLM as a movement that, rather than focusing on "proving" the humanity of Black people, instead engages in abolitionist world making that begins with the valuing of Black lives, this chapter's texts work within the more liberal strains of BLM.[8] As they assert that Black lives matter, *Fruitvale Station* and *BTWAM* provide a way to think more broadly about the power of life writing and narrative humanity as they expose and then refuse or revise forms of narrative humanity. In both their differences and their convergences, the forms of narrative humanity in these two texts provide ways to explore the significance of BLM's sometimes complementary and at other times competing mix of liberal humanism, Afro-pessimism, and radicalism.

The Making of the Future Life of Oscar Grant: *Fruitvale Station* and BLM

When he was killed on New Year's Day of 2009, Oscar Grant III was only twenty-two years old. Johannes Mehserle, a white San Francisco Bay Area Rapid Transit police officer, shot Grant at the Fruitvale BART station. The BART police had pulled Grant and his friends off the train for rowdy behavior. Mehserle, after positioning Grant facedown on the ground, shot him in the back as he lay pinned to the ground with a knee to his neck, surrounded by BART police officers. Mehserle later claimed he mistook his gun for his

Taser. Grant died seven hours later. The events at Fruitvale Station, captured on private cell phone cameras, reached millions of viewers, sparking uprisings throughout the San Francisco Bay Area and beyond. The footage included not only Mehserle's shooting of Grant, but also BART officer Tony Pirone hurling racist and sexist epitaphs at Grant. It took BART officials more than a week to offer apologies to the Grant family, and in their legal response they described the death as "a tragic accident," caused in part by Grant's alleged combativeness. Over a year later, Mehserle was charged with murder. He resigned his BART position and pleaded not guilty. Less than one month after the trial began, Mehserle was found guilty only of involuntary manslaughter. Sentenced to two years minus time served, he was paroled after eleven months. The trial's outcome led to nonviolent protests as well as looting; arson, including the burning of an Oakland police car; and destruction of property, including the Oakland Police Internal Affairs office.[9] The police, wearing gas masks and approaching protesters by helicopter, used tear gas and roadblocks, and issued over 120 arrests.

Although this set of events preceded BLM, Oscar Grant is cited as one of the Black people killed by the police whose deaths gave rise to this movement, and the film version of his life on the day the BART police shot him, as told in the award-winning docudrama *Fruitvale Station*, is part of the story of #BLM's beginnings. A film student at the University of Southern California at the time of Grant's murder, Ryan Coogler was moved to make his first film about Grant who, like Coogler, was twenty-two years old and from the Bay Area. In directing *Fruitvale Station*, Coogler received mentoring from Forest Whitaker's production company and funding from the Sundance festival and the San Francisco Film Society. After a bidding war with Fox Searchlight, Paramount Pictures, Focus Features, and CBS Films, the Weinstein Company acquired the movie for two million dollars (Xan Brooks). This critically acclaimed film put Coogler and Michael B. Jordan, who plays Grant, on *Time*'s 2013 list of "30 People under 30 Changing the World" (Begley). *Fruitvale Station* premiered in Oakland on July 12, 2013. Ayo Tometi describes #BLM's birth by giving an account of exiting a screening of the film in an Oakland theater on July 13 and receiving a flood of messages concerning George Zimmerman's acquittal in the slaying of Trayvon Martin. She explains how, sitting curbside outside the Grand Lake theater, she realized the need for a collective movement against police violence, one with its own social media platform (Craven).

As described by Alicia Garza in *The Purpose of Power* (104–22), Grant's story is also part of the movement's genesis, just as his death is one BLM continues to organize around. In interviews, she tells of her intimate involvement in the campaign for justice for Grant that was spearheaded by her spouse Malachi

Garza. Drawing connections between Grant's death and Michael Brown's, Garza tells of her decision to make BART a site for BLM protests. On "Black Friday," in November 2014, in a radical disruption and brilliant repurposing of this consumer capitalist holiday that has been tagged onto a colonial one, Garza organized a protest designed to shut down BART for four and a half hours—the amount of time police left Michael Brown's body in the street.[10] This linking of Grant's and Brown's deaths indicates Grant's iconic significance for BLM. Grant's image on T-shirts, protest signs, and city murals, and slogans such as "I am Oscar Grant," have served as models for how BLM commemorates Black people murdered by the police.

Oscar Grant's importance to BLM derives at least in part from how *Fruitvale Station* sounds BLM's keynotes as it elicits mourning for, identification with, and remembrance of the dead that is also a demand for respect and recognition for the living. As Claudia Rankine notes, "Unlike earlier black-power movements that tried to fight or segregate for self-preservation, Black Lives Matter aligns with the dead, continues the mourning and refuses the forgetting in front of all of us" ("The Condition"). *Fruitvale Station* sets the stage for BLM's concentration on recognizing the value of individual Black lives through attention to themes of self-making, family relations, and citizenship as it focuses on the life of Oscar Grant and his everyday relationships with his family members, friends, and coworkers. As we watch Oscar sneak snacks to his daughter, text birthday wishes to his mother, banter with a coworker, and dance with friends on the BART train, the film attaches viewers to Oscar and conveys that his life mattered, not because he was extraordinary or exemplary, but because he was a human being, with relations to other human beings that deserve respect and recognition. In this way, the film powerfully counters genres of the human that oppose "human" and "citizen" to "criminal" and "Black."

Divergent responses to the film differently demonstrate the power of these binaries, the need for BLM, and the ways in which BLM encompasses a politics that at once works within and disrupts liberal humanism. While some critics acclaimed the film for its politics and artistry, others lambasted it for being artistically compromised because of its political agenda. On the one hand, we find laudatory reviews such as those by *Village Voice* writer Stephanie Zacharek, who praises the film for capturing "the texture and detail of one human life" and by *Guardian* critic Peter Bradshaw, who finds "what is so potent about Grant's story, . . . is its apolitical, or non-political aspect." For these critics, that Oscar Grant emerges "as a human being" might, as reviewer Steven Boone puts it, "sound like a silly project to undertake," but in the context of pervasive antiblack racism—including in the US film industry, which overwhelmingly depicts Black men, when they appear at all, as criminals or buffoons—the film packs a powerful political punch. On the other hand, detractors denounce the film for being too politically motivated. Geoff Berkshire, for example, criticizes how the film's depiction of Grant "forgoes nuanced drama for heart-tugging, head-shaking and rabble-rousing." Kyle Smith goes further, claiming that Grant is idealized (presumably because he appears as a human being?) in order to "place a heavy hand on the scales of justice" ("Fruitvale Station Is Loose"). In two different reviews, Smith refers to the "real" Grant as "this criminal" or "a low-level criminal" ("'Fruitvale Station' Is Loose"; "'Fruitvale Station' Tells"). He rebukes Coogler for making up the scene where Oscar tries to rescue a dog, and for "fabricating" the scene where Grant throws away the bag of marijuana. He finds it even more egregious that Coogler omits Grant's former conviction for illegal possession of a handgun, and that Grant fled when tasered by a cop during a 2006 traffic stop, as if these experiences justify Mehserle's actions. And he finds the decision to leave out details about the BART shooting a manipulative attempt to "create a strong impression Grant was a victim of a racist cop" ("'Fruitvale Station' Tells Some").[11]

If the positive reviewers recognize the need for a Black Lives Matter movement, the negative reviewers demonstrate this with even greater urgency, as they assert that representing Grant as anything other than a criminal is "rabble-rousing," and as they turn to Grant's prior criminal record (which the movie neither covers over nor elaborates) as proof that his death was not wrongful. Such reviews, like the claim that "All Lives Matter," engage in zero sum logic according to which the humanity of white people depends on the exclusion of Black people—a logic Sylvia Wynter captures brilliantly when she theorizes "the human" as a genre defined to uphold the white liberal subject as universal.

The film opens with eyewitness cell phone footage of the shooting, and the closing features a brief shot of Oscar Grant's daughter Tatiana Grant at a protest one year later, but the film otherwise focuses on Grant's everyday life. Far from "rabble-rousing," it makes no explicit political demands of its viewers. As underlined by Coogler in interviews, his intent was to get viewers to feel as if they knew Grant on a personal level: "I wanted the audience to get to know this guy, to get attached, so that when the situation that happens to him happens, it's not just like you read it in the paper, you know what I mean? When you know somebody as a human being, you know that life means something" (Rhodes; see also Bloomenthal). Artist Ron English reports (critically) on Coogler's decision to focus on Oscar's humanity rather than on police violence. One of three artists hired by the Weinstein Co. to advertise the movie in the form of city street murals of Grant, English's initial concept was for "a version of a Norman Rockwell painting, in which he depicted a little African American boy with a target on his back. He was told, however, that the image was 'too aggressive.'" English reported that Coogler said the mural could not "'be anything negative, or about the police or guns'" ("Street Artists"). And yet, precisely because we live in a world where the genre of "the human" excludes Black people, *Fruitvale Station*'s humanist approach is irrevocably political. By virtue of highlighting Oscar Grant's humanity and his life rather than his death, the movie is contextually not simply liberal, or a form of "selling out," but rather challenges the existing order in which the dominant cultural narratives and the US police state determine "the conditions of possibility for being human" (King, "Humans Involved," 180).[12]

Coogler's decision to zoom in on what would have been an ordinary day in Grant's life were it not also to be his last is a refusal to instrumentalize Grant. The film represents Grant not as the household name and political symbol he became; it focuses on his day-to-day life and everyday struggles and pleasures, with work, family, and friends. It is after all Grant's death that enters him into the realm of politics. Paradoxically, then, in becoming part of a movement for Black lives, Oscar Grant in his particularity disappears, as can the importance of his life in narratives that concentrate only on his premature death. As Brittney Cooper and Treva Lindsey observe, "The peril of collectivity is that the magic, importance, and particularity of a single Black life can get lost" (739). It is Oscar Grant's full and complex life that *Fruitvale Station* restores to him, in a way that attracts the market-driven liberalism of a company such as Weinstein and a more mainstream audience, while also anticipating and helping instigate BLM in a way that simultaneously, and productively, counters and complements Grant's conversion into an icon of victimage, or as evidence of police violence.

To enable audience members to get to know Grant "as a human being," Coogler takes up—often in revisionary ways—different forms of narrative humanity. Those most relevant to *Fruitvale Station* are the self-improvement or conversion narrative (via Oprah Winfrey), and the story of family (with a focus on Black kinship). The film also employs a "whodunnit" or law and order narrative that it subverts to expose the criminality not of Grant or Black men, but of white supremacy. Taken together, these narratives work to assert Grant's humanity, and to insist that Black lives matter.

Self-Making, via Oprah

Even before the first image of *Fruitvale Station* appears, the film introduces the theme of self-making. As the screen is still completely dark, we hear two voices we come to know as Oscar's and Sophina's. The audience thus enters into their private conversation—the kind couples have late at night while lying

in bed as they await a new year. Oscar asks Sophina what her New Year's resolution is. Sophina says, "I am going to cut carbs." When Oscar protests that
she is Mexican and won't be able to eat her grandma's food, Sophina explains
that according to Oprah, it only takes thirty days to form a habit, and then it
becomes second nature. Oscar says his resolution is to stop selling trees. With
this opening, the film asserts that race and culture are not defining, as, taking
us into his and Sophina's bedroom, it also introduces Oscar to us as a young
man with whom we establish an immediate intimacy as we listen in on how
he wants to change his life. And Coogler shows us that his desire for change
might have been possible. Oscar faces economic pressures and has lost his job,
and nonetheless, we see him decide to dump a full bag of weed. While waiting for the buyer, he looks at a photo of his daughter, then exits his car to sit
by the San Francisco Bay. As the ocean laps the rocks, in the film's only flash-
back, we move back in time with him to San Quentin Prison, on New Year's
Eve 2007, as he is getting strip-searched before being allowed a visit with his
mother, Wanda. Perceiving the trouble Oscar is getting into in prison, she
leaves abruptly, sharply reminding him his poor choices are hurting his
daughter. The film then cuts back to the bay and Oscar tosses the weed into
the ocean. When, later that day, he tells Sophina he lost his job, and also about
dumping the weed, she says to him, you threw a whole zip of weed out and
you don't have a job? He says he wants to start fresh, and do something legal
if he can avoid messing up for thirty days.

Allusions to Oprah are woven throughout the film as codes that advance a
story line of self-transformation, or self-making. A dominant form of narrative
humanity in the US dating back at least to Ben Franklin's *Autobiography*, the
self-made man narrative defines the human as an individual with the power
to pull himself up by his bootstraps. Coogler mobilizes this narrative to establish Oscar Grant as a human who wants the chance to learn from his mistakes
and improve himself. Coogler updates this narrative by using Oprah Winfrey
as a shorthand, presenting a version of self-making that is contemporary, distinctly women-centered, and African American. Winfrey, sometimes called the
"queen of self-made glory," was born into poverty, and transformed herself into
arguably the most successful Black entrepreneur and philanthropist in US history (Finn). Much of her career has been devoted to creating TV shows, magazines, diets, and movies that extend the self-made man narrative to include
Black folks and women. Even as it remains firmly rooted within a capitalist
framework in which wealth is a marker of success, the Oprah Winfrey version
of self-making breaks with this narrative's masculine individualism which
obscures human interdependencies, especially Black women's unpaid labor
(emotional and material), and the obstacles to self-making that result from

societally created raced and gendered traumas and inequities. For Oprah, self-making happens with community support and social structures that engender "self-help." So, too, Oprah decenters the white cis-male subject as she foregrounds the lives of Black women who have survived sexual trauma and domestic violence or triumphed over addiction. Grant, following Oprah's roadmap to change via Sophina's example and with direction offered by her and his mother, is derailed neither by substance abuse, engagement in illegal activities, nor a lack of hard work and initiative-taking, but by a system of policing that casts him as criminal, as fungible, as not (fully) human. With Oscar's inability to follow the expected trajectory to success, the film subverts and critiques the narrative of self-making, as Coogler conveys how self-transformation is denied to Oscar Grant.

In other words, even as Coogler employs this familiar genre of narrative humanity in its Black popular-culture version to establish Oscar's humanity in terms that will enlist a mainstream audience's support for him, the film also shows us how, as a Black man, Oscar is denied the opportunity to make himself into the person he wishes to become. Coogler in this way, without offering a thoroughgoing critique of capitalism, nonetheless challenges a narrative that Eggers uncritically upholds (see chapter 1), as he conveys achieving success and self-making as antiblack processes. Part of the film's power is that viewers know this from the outset, and see its injustice. Through the documentary footage that ruptures the opening dialogue about Oscar and Sophina's dreams for the future, *Fruitvale Station* forecloses any expectations of the usual triumphant "self-made man" arc, or its updated one of a self-help success story. Then, as the film progresses and we see Oscar making the right choices—he stops lying and resolves to stop cheating on Sophina, he desists from selling drugs, he avoids driving when drinking, he resolves to be a better employee—we await the death we know is coming, and the self-made man narrative turns into a tragedy, one that is owing not to Grant's fatal flaws, bad judgment, or criminal actions, but to politically constructed and deeply embedded narratives that define society—and the genres of the human and the citizen—over against Black life. When they shoot Oscar Grant, all that the BART police see is what critic Kyle Smith sees: Blackness as criminality. Through his deployment of the self-made man narrative, Coogler insists that Oscar Grant's life, so full of everyday forms of potential, matters even as, through the way this narrative falls apart, *Fruitvale Station* demonstrates how the mattering of Black lives exists in a future tense that Oscar Grant is denied. The film's commemoration and mourning, together with its insistence on the past, present, and future value of all Black lives, capture the affective politics that structures the Black Lives Matter movement at the moment of its making.

Papa's Baby

So, too, the film's focus on Black kinship—including its emphasis on those who will grieve the premature death of their family member—articulates with BLM's. Oscar's desire to remake himself into a better person, breaking as it does via Oprah from the masculine individualism that attends the self-made man narrative, is tied in the film to his relationships with his mother, daughter, and Sophina. The story of family and especially fatherhood is key to *Fruitvale Station*'s insistence on why and how Oscar Grant's life matters, and in a way that establishes what becomes a central focus of BLM. As I have been arguing throughout this book, stories of family figure centrally in narrative humanity, just as what Orlando Patterson has called "natal alienation," or the denial to Black people of familial relations, plays a key role in the processes of dehumanization so crucial to slavery and its aftermath. As Ruha Benjamin notes, "For those whose ancestors were enslaved, the assault on black kinship is ever-present and pernicious. This is not simply a *byproduct* but a central tenet of maintaining white social order." Slavery was particularly effective in severing the relations of fathers from their children—a formulation brilliantly summed up by Hortense Spillers as "Mama's Baby, Papa's Maybe: An American Grammar Book." As Spillers discusses, the legacy of denying paternity to Black men extends into the present, often also serving to pathologize Black women. The 1965 Moynihan Report offers a particularly egregious example of this in linking the contemporary social and economic problems of African Americans to an allegedly matriarchal family structure responsible for stripping Black men of their power. In her trenchant analysis of this influential government report, Angela Davis finds that Moynihan's thesis is that "the source of oppression was deeper than the racial discrimination that produced unemployment, shoddy housing, inadequate education and substandard medical care. The root of oppression was described as a 'tangle of pathology' created by the absence of male authority among Black people! The controversial finale of the Moynihan Report was a call to introduce male authority (meaning male supremacy of course!) into the Black family and community at large" (*Women, Race and Class*, 13). Charles Murray demonstrates the persistence of the Moynihan Report's white supremacist and heteropatriarchal logic when, in a 1993 article, he perpetuates a fantasy of white middle-class fatherhood by defining it against the "underclass" fatherless Black family.

Rather than pathologizing Black women and men or supporting male supremacy, *Fruitvale Station* honors Black women's strength while confirming a pattern of women-headed households. Oscar, the film's only father, has no male role models—absences that garner no attention in the film. *Fruitvale*

Station includes no mention of Grant's father, Oscar Grant II, who was incarcerated for most of his son's life and up until his son's death. Oscar Grant II is one of Oscar Grant's family members who mobilized to demand justice for Oscar Grant, along with his uncle, Cephus "Uncle Bobby X" Johnson, now known as "the People's Uncle," who also served as an adviser for *Fruitvale Station*. Rather than tell the story of the men in Oscar's life, the film stresses Oscar's closeness to the women, and his efforts to be a father without male role models. Oscar's mother, Rev. Wanda Johnson; his grandmother, Bonnie Johnson; his sister, Chantay Moore; and Sophina's mother all appear as single mothers.[13] That the film does not provide their or Sophina Mesa's full names supports the film's commitment to maintaining a vantage point of familial intimacy. As Oscar parents Tatiana, we see him struggling with how to be a father, and often acting more as her playmate and coconspirator. By contrast, we see the mothers juggling too much work and caring for their own children as they also serve as what Black feminist critic Patricia Hill Collins calls "other mothers" and help each other out. *Fruitvale Station* affirms these mothers while countering any sense that it is their strength let alone matriarchal power that leads to the lack of fathers in the film. To the contrary, we see these women's powers as limited. Oscar's mother, for example, struggles in her efforts to keep her son safe while encouraging him to be a good father. As is true for Tatiana and for Oscar Grant, one in seven Black children in the US have had a parent behind bars, with incarceration serving, as Benjamin notes, as "an ongoing regime of social control and containment" and a new form of "natal alienation." As the film gives us a glimpse into this condition, Wanda, appealing to Oscar's parental responsibilities, can only urge him to get himself out of trouble. And although the criminalization that comes with being a young Black man proves stronger than his individual actions, including his struggle to be present for Tatiana, as the film represents women-centered Black family structures with loving respect, it simultaneously foregrounds Oscar's potential and commitments as a father.

Through allowing viewers into Oscar Grant's intimate domestic spaces, Coogler attaches audience members to Oscar and his family. By placing Oscar's relationships with his mother, his girlfriend, and their daughter at the heart of the film, *Fruitvale Station* counters ways Black men are dehumanized in film. As Uncle Bobby X observed, the movie enables its viewers to understand that Oscar could be "their brother, their father, their friend" (Palestinian Youth Movement). Coogler's consciousness of the power of family relations to establish a person's more general relatability or humanness is dramatized in the film via Katie, who serves as a stand-in for white liberal audience members. In the grocery store scene, Katie moves from a racialized and gendered distrust and fear of Oscar to warmth when he goes from being a Black male stranger whom she shies away from as a possible threat, to a Black employee from whom she expects service, to a friend she can greet on the BART train, and one whose brutalization by the police she protests—a transformation that hinges on seeing him as someone's grandson. It also bears remarking that Katie's friendliness to Oscar when she loudly hails him on the BART train inadvertently sets in motion the events that lead to Oscar's death—a kind of parable of the dangers of white liberalism's good intentions—and it is also worth noting that the BART police ignore her outrage in a way that underlines both her white privilege and her gendered insignificance. Along with Katie, viewers get to know Oscar as a beloved grandson, as we also come to appreciate him as a son who treats his mother with devotion and respect. As well, via the affluent white couple he befriends, we see him as a loving if fallible father and as a future husband. As reportedly happened in real life, Oscar's final words in the film—"You shot me bro. You shot me and I got a daughter"—register the extent to which our value as humans is tied to our family relationships. Furthermore, when he addresses the police as "bro," the police's failure to reciprocate underscores his and not Grant's inhumanity. While differentiating the families of color we come to know from the stock image of the white nuclear family in the birthday card Oscar buys his mother as a joke, *Fruitvale Station* upholds the value of family, even as it centers family members who are Black, Brown, and poor. By the film's end, when Oscar's family and friends hold vigil in the hospital after Oscar is shot, we as audience members wait with them and feel sorrow over their impending loss as we also grieve for Oscar Grant. In this way and throughout, the film counters denials of Black kinship that support antiblack state violence

Drawing on forms of narrative humanity that center familial relations, *Fruitvale Station* anticipates appeals that are central to BLM. What BLM calls for, in the face of racist police violence, is acknowledgment of Black humanity, the grievability of Black lives that end prematurely, and the dignity and suffering of the family members whose rights, too, are violated when their loved ones are killed. BLM does this grief work by featuring the organization Mothers of the Movement and their stories; through posters and protests that represent those killed by police violence as family members; and through the words and photos of grieving children, fathers, sisters, and brothers. "My son is your son," Trayvon Martin's mother, Sybrina Fulton, repeatedly asserted at rallies and press conferences (Ransby, 30). As Claudia Rankine says of the movement and its attention to the grief of those who lost their kin, "National mourning, as advocated by Black Lives Matter, is a mode of intervention and interruption that might . . . align some of us, for the first time, with the living" ("The Condition"). From our last glimpse of Katie, who got to know Oscar Grant so fleet-ingly; to Oscar, whose last words are those of a father; to his grieving family members and friends, the film, like the movement, works to align at least some of us with the living as it also puts at its center a love for Black life and an insistence that Black lives matter. At the same time as *Fruitvale Station* tethers the mourning of Oscar Grant to his family and his desire for change, Coogler also arguably poses an implicit challenge to viewers, one that suggests conditions for mourning should be much simpler: Oscar Grant was a person and he was killed.

True Crime with Heart

As it chronicles the events and conversations that make up an ordinary day, *Fruitvale Station* achieves its narrative tension through use of conventions of a crime narrative, one wherein the culprit is not Mehserle, but the United States as a white supremacist society. The shots fired at the start of the film let us know how Oscar Grant's day will end. By opening with the shooting, and then moving back in time, the film's setup is that of the "whodunnit" or crime narrative. This opening functions less to introduce a form of narrative human-ity than to create the expectation for a suspenseful and action-oriented narra-tive directed at discovering who committed a crime and why. With his deploy-ment of this opening, Coogler flips the usual script, presenting the police as the perpetrators. Coogler then abandons the crime narrative and the crimi-nal/citizen binary it supports. Oscar, who has a criminal record and who has dealt drugs, is not defined as a criminal, though the police cast him as such when they shoot him. Nor does the film pursue a story line in which the shooter (or the police) is pinpointed as the criminal. Instead, the police drop from the frame until the film's final moments. *Fruitvale Station* takes no interest in the individuals directly responsible for Grant's death—they have no backstory or motives, nor do we learn even the most basic details about them, nor does the camera go to their faces to register their responses after they shoot Oscar. The camera instead closes in on the faces of Grant, Sophina, his friends, and Black bystanders. The film also resists naming the police involved, even though we watch Grant and his friends take photos of their names and badge numbers; even though the credits that roll at the end reference Mehserle's sentencing; and even though many audience members will know his and the other officers' names. As the film refuses the usual conventions of the crime narrative, it suggests that there is no mystery to the shooting, nor any particular motives to assign to the individual police officers. This absence of backstory or con-text is, in effect (and here is the source of Kyle Smith's outrage), a refusal to re-center whiteness or to complicate or otherwise individualize the actions of those who took Grant's life.

Abandoning the usual plotline of a film that begins with a murder, *Fruitvale Station* substitutes for suspense and the revelation of motive the tension and fear that come with awaiting a death that both is senseless and conforms to the necropolitical logics that govern a society that is foundationally antiblack. Coogler does not depict Oscar's death as resulting from an under-slept officer having a bad day, or from one or two "bad apples." Nor does Oscar Grant's past or his behavior explain why the police deny him standing as a citizen or as human. Instead, the antiblack violence, though embodied in the police, is without individual motive, in ways that resonate with commentaries about the need for BLM. As Keeanga-Yamahtta Taylor notes, "The racism of the police is not the product of vitriol; it flows from their role as armed agents of the state" (*From #BlackLivesMatter*). Or, as Rinaldo Walcott succinctly puts this, "The law is violence" (Simpson, Walcott, and Coulthard, 87).

Coogler's systemic indictment of civil society derails what begins as a crime story. The narrative tension comes not from a suspenseful reveal of whodunnit, but instead from the discomfort and fear of the devastation viewers know will inexorably arrive. One of the promotional stills from the film, a close-up of Oscar with his daughter, her arms around his neck, is captioned "True crime with heart?" (Xan Brooks). In ways this captioned photo captures well, the film reworks a crime narrative. Oscar appears not as the perpetrator but as the victim of a true crime, and one of these crimes is the heart-wrenching severing of his relationship with his daughter. As viewers await the ending we know is coming, there is a haunting quality to the film—Oscar is alive in the scenes that unfold, and yet viewers know him to be dead and await the coming violence with an anxiety born of having come to care about the lives soon to be shattered. In the film's final scene, Sophina is in the shower with Tatiana, who asks where her father is. As the camera closes in on Sophina and her daughter looking at one another, Sophina is without words as the screen goes black. If in crime and horror films, shower settings regularly serve as violently traumatic and often opening scenes where women, at their most vulnerable, are assaulted by male intimates or intruders, in this one, the horrific crime, the violent severing of kinship ties, has no identifiable perpetrator, and in the place of sensationalist violence, there is raw grief.

To convey the structural nature of white supremacist violence in a film largely devoid of white people (and this absent presence is part of its eeriness and impact), Coogler features the BART train as the conveyor of crime. The haunting soundscape derived from these trains, which sometimes exists independently of the film's images of them speeding along the tracks, serves as a source of narrative tension. *Fruitvale Station*'s darkly ambient soundtrack comes from manipulating the sound of the BART train, and through adding layers of guitar so the effect is, as its composer Ludwig Göransson puts it, "almost like haunting pads" ("Fruitvale Station Soundtrack"). In this way, the BART train becomes a felt presence, and a sinister and foreboding one that conveys how BART, as part of the societal structure in which Oscar is situated, is responsible for the violence that is about to tear through his life and devastate his loved ones. When nondiegetic sounds of the train enter at the most ordinary of moments, they serve as a reminder of the ending that awaits Oscar Grant, and the ruin that awaits his loved ones. As Oscar goes to drop off his daughter at Sophina's sister's, as the camera zooms in on Tatiana's face in the quiet of the car ride that we know will be her last time with her father, the almost-musical, muted strains of the soundtrack play. It is this impending loss of the most ordinary moments of family intimacies that serves as the film's climax. Through the film's manipulation of genre and narrative codes, then, the focus goes to the Black lives that matter, and *Fruitvale Station* denounces the entire social structure in which BART and its police are embedded.

Like the slogan "I am Oscar Grant" or "We all are Oscar Grant" (or Trayvon Martin, or Eric Garner, or Michael Brown) that attended protests on behalf of Oscar Grant and appear in any number of BLM protests, *Fruitvale Station* invites identification with Grant and the way that his death haunts the lives of Black people, even as his life extends into theirs and animates a movement that foresees a future for Oscar Grant. *Fruitvale Station* does this by mobilizing, via Oprah, a contemporary Black women-centered version of the self-made man narrative that critiques this narrative even as it insists that Oscar Grant's life matters. The focus on family is another way the film utilizes a dominant form of narrative humanity to assert Oscar Grant's humanness—which antiblack racism denies. Finally, by deploying only to depopulate the crime narrative, the film issues an unsettling structural critique of white supremacy that accompanies its focus on Oscar's humanity. In representing Oscar Grant in this way, before his death made his life matter as a stand-in for all Black lives, *Fruitvale Station* asks us to mourn the haunting loss of this particular man. Brittney Cooper and Treva Lindsey insist on the importance of this particularity in describing the work of BLM:

> The insistence in the movement for Black Lives in calling the individual names of Black people lost to state violence demands of us an attention to the particularities of each Black life—that Trayvon Martin was watching the all-star game and loved talking on the phone to his homegirl Rachel Jeantel, that Sandra Bland graduated from Prairie

View A&M and was returning to start her dream job, and that Eric Garner was loved by a community of women, including his mom, his wife, and his daughter, Erica. We have lost so many Black lives to state violence that sometimes the details run together. But each of the details matters. (739)

That Oscar Grant's life matters and that all Black lives matter in all their particularities should be irrefutable. Through its deployment of forms of narrative humanity and as it anticipates BLM, *Fruitvale Station* helps create a future in which the BLM movement can be consigned to the past—one that, in undoing the binary between criminal/citizen and Black/human, makes it an everyday *and* radicalizing way of knowing that Oscar Grant's life matters.

At the same time, hovering just outside its frame, and haunting this film, is the question of why, for Oscar Grant's murder to matter to a mainstream audience, it must mobilize a narrative of uplift centered on a young man full of potential, and on his relations to his family members who love and miss him? Why, for his life to matter, must *Fruitvale Station* tell a story of "true crime with heart"? In the next section, on *Between the World and Me*, I continue to explore the limits as well as possibilities of using narrative humanity to further the aims of a movement like BLM that at once works within and against understandings of the human that inhere within its genres and forms.

Between the Cosmic and Coates: BLM and Literary Humanism

Whereas *Fruitvale Station* helped catalyze and sounds keynotes for BLM, Coates's *Between the World and Me* has been greeted by many cultural commentators as a BLM anthem, as it has catapulted Coates to fame. A sought-after lecturer who regularly writes for or is featured in prestigious literary as well as mainstream venues ranging from *Playboy* to the *Atlantic* to the *New York Times*, Coates won the National Book Award for *BTWAM*, was a finalist for a 2016 Pulitzer Prize for General Nonfiction, and received a MacArthur "genius grant" largely on its basis. *BTWAM* was ranked seventh by the *Guardian* on its list of the top 100 books of the twenty-first century. On its basis Toni Morrison hailed Coates as the present-day James Baldwin; George Packer named Coates "the most influential writer in America today" (Mishra); Barack Obama invited Coates to lunch after reading the galleys; Supreme Court Justice Sonia Sotomayor referenced *BTWAM* in one of her dissenting opinions (Cherry); and dozens of US colleges have selected *BTWAM* as their common reading book. The book also has been widely received as one of BLM's foun-

dational texts. As a register of its timeliness, in the wake of the church massacre in Charleston, South Carolina, and the founding of BLM, Penguin/Ran-
dom House moved up its publication date from September to July 2015
(Krotov). In the *New Yorker*, as Brit Bennett reflects on the start of BLM, she
singles out *BTWAM* as "a crucial book during this moment of generational
awakening." The Apollo Theater adapted the book for stage with one of its performances including Alicia Garza, who also, as part of an all-star cast, appears in the fall 2020 HBO special based on the memoir (Saad).

The ways in which Coates's memoir has met not only with acclaim but also with considerable
criticism, from BLM's opponents and supporters alike. Whereas some critics
condemn BLM and *BTWAM* as one and the same in one antiblack breath, as
Richard Cherry does when he calls *BTWAM* "the intellectual and emotional
voice of the Black Lives Matter movement," other Black intellectuals and activists have marked distance between the two, including BLM cofounders Tometi and Cullors. Cullors has remarked that Coates's work is "not definitive of
our communities or movements" ("Ta-Nehisi Coates & Cornel West"). Writing with Naomi Klein, Tometi commends Coates's brilliance while finding
that his work raises questions "about our relationship to empire and transnational capital . . . that every progressive movement and intellectual across
North America should urgently confront." Kibo Ngowi upholds Coates as "an
important voice for black resistance against systemic racism" and, as he reviews
critiques of the memoir, insists on the unfairness of assigning Coates the "unwanted status as 'the voice of black people.'" Others have more directly taken
the memoir to task, in particular for its lack of hope, internationalism, solidarity, and intersectionality. Some have done so with love and respect, as do Klein
and Tometi; or Michelle Alexander in the *New York Times*; or Zinzi Clemmons
in "Ta-Nehisi Coates Has Given #Black Lives Matter Its Foundational Text:
How to Love an Imperfect Genius, and Other Considerations." The memoir
also has been the subject of harder-hitting criticism. Cornel West has lambasted
Coates for being neoliberal and inattentive to global imperialism. Others have
critiqued Coates for his gender politics (bell hooks, Brit Bennett, Britni Danielle, Shani O. Hilton, Brittney Cooper); for mystifying racism and leaving no
room for resistance and class struggle (R. L. Stephens); or for "assuaging white
guilt" (Cedric Johnson, hooks). As this chapter assesses *BTWAM*'s articulations
with and divergences from BLM, I take up the range of responses to the memoir, and consider how they relate to its deployments of narrative humanity.

The ways in which Coates's memoir engages self-making, family, and crime
through its portrait of an artist, its father-son narrative, and its tropes of literary naturalism further arguments I have been making regarding whether and
how dominant forms of narrative humanity can be mobilized to challenge the

dehumanization on which (state) violence depends. The preceding section on *Fruitvale Station* examined the potential uses to which liberal appeals to the human, as encoded in forms of narrative humanity, can be put, and how they can support BLM's more reformist as well as contextually revolutionary directions. This section's discussion of Coates homes in on how such appeals, when they rely on dominant literary values and narratives, can establish a work's widespread reach, while also undermining commitments we see in BLM and other liberatory movements to an on-the-ground praxis that will transform who counts as human and how we live in relation to one another. As I argued in the previous chapter and for reasons I further develop here, relying uncritically on liberal forms of narrative humanity can result in reinforcing exclusionary understandings of the human. So, too, I contend that *BTWAM*'s oscillating and competing beliefs in a distinctly literary humanism and in a world defined by anti-Black necropolitics foreclose the collective organizing that defines BLM.

My objective here is not to castigate Coates for failing to give adequate voice to BLM, but instead to consider the significance of *BTWAM*'s widespread reception as an expression of BLM. As the memoir has catapulted him to fame, Coates has resisted the role of spokesperson for Black America, and he neither includes BLM references within the memoir nor claims to be part of BLM. His interview on *Democracy Now!* shortly after *BTWAM*'s publication indicates his stance. When asked for his reaction to a recent BLM action, he tells Amy Goodman, "It's very, very hard for me to respond to the protest, because—and this is the God's honest truth—I have been absorbed with like trying to keep up with this book" ("'Between the World and Me': Ta-Nehisi Coates Extended Interview"). As I investigate the widespread association between *BTWAM* and BLM despite the distance Coates maintains between his memoir and the movement, I am particularly interested in how forms of narrative humanity can powerfully and productively mainstream BLM's insistence that Black lives matter while simultaneously maintaining parameters for the human that many BLM organizers are intent on abolishing as they narrate into being ways of being human that foreground care, interdependency, internationalism, and intersectionality.

Life Sentences: Coates and the Künstlerroman

As does *Fruitvale Station*, *BTWAM* takes up the self-made man narrative and exposes not only its inapplicability to Black people but also the role it plays in sustaining an anti-Black world. Cautioning his son not to buy into the Dream that is part and parcel of the narratives of self-making, Coates explains this

Dream's delusionary and self-justifying foundations: "its adherents must not just believe in it but believe that it is just, believe that their possession of the Dream is the natural result of grit, honor, and good works" (98). Drawing on James Baldwin's formulation, Coates tells his son that the people living inside this Dream "who think they are white" are not inherently superior but have built their comfortable lives and their very sense of themselves as human on the lies and plunder of Black lives. Acutely conscious of the role that narrative humanity plays in enforcing the Dream and its accompanying ideology of self-making, he instructs Samori, "A society, almost necessarily, begins every success story with the chapter that most advantages itself, and in America, these precipitating chapters are almost always rendered as the singular action of exceptional individuals. 'It only takes one person to make a change,' you are often told. This is also a myth" (96). Coates's view of society as telling a story made up of chapters is not merely a metaphor: it exemplifies his belief in the material power of literature to determine the course of lives.

Throughout *BTWAM*, the narrative lines and turns of phrase that are the stuff of stories play a key role in capturing the truth of a world that denies Black people their humanity, as they also constitute a form of struggle against this brutality. When Coates describes to his son the madness of being "cast into a race in which the wind is always at your face and the hounds are always at your heels" (107), his references to "a race" and to "the hounds" function both as metaphors and literally, to describe how dogs have been used to surveil and terrorize Black people during slavery and in its afterlife.[14] Not merely stylistic flourishes, Coates's carefully wrought literary figures of speech constitute not only the very means to represent the unremitting racist assaults on Black bodies and existence, but also the only way to resist this violence.[15] He contrasts the Dream that is "gilded by novels and adventure stories" (102) to his own narration of an unending nightmarish reality in which the self-deluded Dreamers have placed a "noose around the neck of the earth" (151). Offering *BTWAM* as a counternarrative that conveys truth, he tells his son, "The struggle to understand is our only advantage over this madness" (106). Although *BTWAM* meditates on planetary destruction, its focus is the ongoing history of anti-Blackness to which this coming apocalypse connects—a history that Coates conveys largely through telling stories of Black lives that end in death, as he exposes the anti-Blackness that inheres in narratives of self-making.

Embedded in the stories Coates tells is an insistence that however dehumanized, Black lives matter. In a memoir that includes a litany of names and narratives of slain Black men and boys, Coates dwells in particular detail on the story of his college friend Prince Jones, who by all accounts should have "made it." He tells of his devastation when the police, acting "with great regularity, as though moved by some unseen cosmic clock" (76), shoot Prince dead. For Coates, if telling Prince's story cannot prevent the white supremacist violence, at once systemic and cosmic, that renders Black life disposable, and if his narrative cannot overturn those that—as they cast Prince as a criminal—support this necropolitical regime, his storytelling can assert that Black lives matter. As his stories about the fate of Prince Jones—and of Trayvon Martin, Michael Brown, Eric Garner, and others—indicate, especially when coupled with the exoneration of their killers, Black people's agency is limited to engagement in a struggle that "is all we have because the god of history is an atheist, and nothing about his world is meant to be" (71). To convey this cosmic injustice, Coates's memoir focuses on stories not of life, but of death.

Even as Coates exposes how narratives of self-making depend on criminalizing and dehumanizing Black men, his belief in the power and beauty of literature and the journey he undertakes to become a writer provide a current of hope, partially rehabilitating the individual humanist elements of such narratives. Indeed, Coates's account of coming into consciousness and power as a writer resonates with the Künstlerroman. A subgenre of the Bildungsroman—one of the key conveyors of the self-made man narrative—the Künstlerroman chronicles the coming of age of a sensitive youth who, in finding a place in society as a poet, artist, or musician, stands out for contributions to humanity. Künstlerroman narratives frequently reinforce dominant societal norms and often display what Leslie Hankins calls the "ethnocentrism, androcentrism, and class bias in their 'universal' norms"—these include a magical childhood, a journey or quest, evolution, then rites of passage (159). Coates represents his evolution as a writer in terms that are epic and secular, as well as individualist and masculine. His account preserves the Künstlerroman's liberal humanist beliefs in the writer's exceptional sensitivity and in his powers of expression, which are transcendently beautiful and uplifting for society and for humankind.

Coates revises as well as works within this form of narrative humanity to center his experiences as a Black man following a distinctly Black lineage. His account of becoming a writer involves a journey from a childhood of scarcity and violence to an adulthood of privilege, one in which he learns from the Black intellectuals who have come before him. His time as a student at Howard University importantly figures in his individual transformation. Nourished in that historically Black institution which, as an atheist, he claims as his "Mecca," Coates experiences an intellectual and artistic awakening, one that is a salve to the racism that defined his childhood and teen years. Although he values his peers, he attributes his most significant learning to a self-determined course of reading. As he explains to Samori, "The classroom was a jail of other people's interests. The library was open, unending, free. Slowly, I was discovering myself" (48). Cloistered in the library, he tells Samori, "My reclamation would be accomplished, like Malcolm's, through books, through my own study and exploration" (37). Even as Coates follows a distinctly Black lineage in coming into his own as a self-educated writer and intellectual, in his valuing of writing as an individual literary endeavor, he also parts ways with Malcolm X and other Black intellectuals for whom writing was a pathway to revolution.

Coates's journey of self-making is largely a literary one he undertakes unaccompanied by others. He notes the importance of "fellow travelers" such as his son's uncle Ben (49) and expresses gratitude to his mother for teaching him "the craft of writing as the art of thinking" (51). However, the Black artists and poets "who pulled their energy from the void" (50) are his main focus. Naming Greg Tate, Chairman Mao, dream hampton, Malcolm X, and others, he explains to Samori, "It is important that I tell you their names, that you know that I have never achieved anything alone" (50). Those he names, in other words, are authors, not intimates. He states that by studying in solitude, he achieves a sense of freedom, exercising his desire "to write as those black people [at Howard] danced, with control, power, joy, warmth" (62). As he links the collective act of Black dance and his writing, he also sets himself apart from the Howard community, with his most significant acts of communion taking place through texts.

Despite the genealogy of revolutionary Black writers he draws upon, in many ways Coates's Künstlerroman narrative maintains its understandings of literature and of the writer's role as exceptional individual. This is exemplified in Coates's account of his travel to Paris, which stands as a culmination of the success that has come with being a writer. In spending extended time there, Coates participates in a patterned exodus for alienated Black American writers including W. E. B. DuBois, James Baldwin, and Richard Wright. However, whereas his predecessors, while in Paris as disaffected Black Americans, broaden their understandings of interconnected imperialisms and forge Third World alliances, Coates notes that in going to Paris, he "did not think much about Baldwin or Wright" (122). The Wright in Coates's memoir is not Wright the internationalist, but the Wright who authored the 1935 poem "Between the World and Me." In this poem, a Black man becomes separated from the world when he comes upon the site of a lynching, the terror of which leaves him reduced by its end to "dry bones and my face a stony skull staring in yellow surprise at the sun" (Wright). It is this terror-filled world that Coates describes escaping in Paris, getting there by a "starship" that rockets him into "some other blue world" (121), one with "incredible" wine and "magnificent" food (123), with beautiful art and public gardens (124), a language he loves (125), and fashionable dress and luxury cars (127). Coates's Paris also brings relief from anti-Black racism that he particularly welcomes for his son, although he acknowledges that racism and colonialism are differently present in Paris, and also that "to be distanced, if only for a moment, from fear is not a passport out of the struggle" (127). In a departure from the unremittingly harsh reality of America, his time in Paris serves as an almost fantastic, otherworldly refuge from US racism, and as a locale of high culture that he enjoys as a writer and lover of language.

The Künstlerroman narrative in *BTWAM* exists in tension with its thoroughgoing critique of the self-made man narrative's anti-Blackness. Even as Coates expresses his painful awareness that, like all Black males, he is vulnerable to premature death, his journey to success as a writer and his beliefs in literature and study provide an exit of sorts from many of the exigencies of Black existence. He explains to his son that achieving recognition as a writer means, "I did not fail. I have my family. I have my work. I no longer feel it necessary to hang my head at parties and tell people that I am 'trying to be a writer.'" He continues, "And godless though I am, the fact of being human, the fact of possessing the gift of study, and thus being remarkable among all the matter floating through the cosmos, still awes me" (115). Stature as a writer, then, does not only grant Coates confidence and respectability in social circles, or access to Paris. Like Paris, writing and study offer an escape hatch from anti-Blackness, endowing him with a sense of his humanity and a cosmic claim to being exceptional.

Coates's speaking engagements and interviews in the wake of *BTWAM*'s publication reinforce his account of himself as, first and foremost, a writer. When addressing what it means to be Black in America, he resists what Kibo Ngowi refers to as his "unwanted status as 'the voice of black people,'" and claims a particularity of experience that counters the homogenization and dehumanization of Black life (its nod to Wright notwithstanding, his title underlines this first-person perspective). Brit Bennett tells of hearing Coates speak at the University of Michigan, where "the mostly white audience was insistent on asking him for a grand solution to racism, but Coates politely refused to answer those questions. He seemed uncomfortable with the expectation that he was the correspondent for Black America. What he knew, he kept saying, was writing." Coates elaborates on this position in a *Playboy* interview: "I'm a good writer. I think there are very few people who can do journalism, do history, form an argument, an argument with a brain, and then write in such a way that it gets at your heart also." This commitment to writing is everywhere evident in *BTWAM*, not only via the deployment of a Künstlerroman story line and the memoir's insistence on the importance of literature, but also in the beauty and power of its sentences.

Coates departs from his self-presentation as writer, not political actor, in his qualified endorsement of Obama and in his high-profile arguments for reparations. He has been credited for having "more or less single-handedly resurrected the conversation about reparations for black Americans" (Grady) in essays for *The Atlantic*, a magazine for which he long served as a national correspondent. As well, he has spoken before Congress in support of HR 40, a bill proposing a study regarding the effects of slavery and how to remedy them. Bracketing for now the complications that attend arguments for reparations—as critics including Cornel West and Cedric Johnson have noted, they often appear as a form of moralism or sloganeering rather than a real political demand, and as consonant with a neoliberalism and individualism that does not allow for solidarity-based politics—Coates's political advocacy strains against the totalizing and immobilizing pessimism of *BTWAM* and its belle lettres investments. In the interview "Ta-Nehisi Coates Is an Optimist Now," Coates's description of his decision to write Black Panther comic books as a pathway toward reparations marks a shift toward greater optimism and less compartmentalization between literature and politics: "Our politics occurs within the imagination of the citizen. If I don't believe that black people are human, it really doesn't matter what you say to me about policy. So the question is: How do we decide who gets to be human and who doesn't? . . . All of that is tied together in the stories we tell ourselves." He continues, "It's the imagination that sets the terms for what's possible in terms of policy" (Levitz).[16] This belief in the political possibilities afforded by the power of narrative—in this case by participating in the creation of a fantasy world populated by Black superheroes—marks a departure from the pessimism of *BTWAM*. Coates's pessimism and his distinction in *BTWAM* between literature and politics, in other words, are not fixed positions.

What Coates's optimism in Black Panther shares with the Künstlerroman narrative in *BTWAM* is that both strain against his contentions in *BTWAM* that to be Black is to be categorically denied human status. Coates's romanticism about art and literature disrupts the memoir's depiction of a world that entirely and necessarily devalues Black life. Although Coates critiques the self-made man narrative as anti-Black, his journey to becoming a writer reopens that pathway to narrative humanity. In *BTWAM*, Coates's humanity comes from his ability to give beautiful expression to the ugliness of anti-Black racism, setting him apart from as well as conjoining him with a collectivity of Black folks, and disrupting his analysis of a totalizing anti-Blackness.

As the memoir's narratives of self-making oscillate between an assertion of liberal humanism and ontological anti-Blackness, *BTWAM* both resonates with and departs from an Afro-pessimist analytic, and from BLM.[17] Writing from an Afro-pessimist perspective, Calvin Warren addresses the way BLM's declaration that "Black Lives Matter" "compels us to face the terrifying question, despite our desire to look away. The declaration presents a difficult syntax or an accretion of tensions and ambiguities within its organization: can blacks have life? What would such life mean within an antiblack world?" (1). Warren pursues this line of questioning: "can black(ness) ground itself in the *being* of the human? If it cannot, then on what bases can we assert the mattering of black existence? If it can, then why would the phrase need to be repeated and recited incessantly? Do the affirmative declaration and its insistence undermine this very ontological ground?" (1). *BTWAM* dramatizes these questions that are so central to both Afro-pessimism and BLM as Coates tells stories of Black death alongside those of his coming into being as a writer. The memoir also smooths over the unsettling contradictions Warren uncovers in a way that has liberal appeal, mainstreaming BLM's central premises, while also containing both its Afro-pessimism and its radical and visionary solutions. In combination with *BTWAM*'s insistence that Black self-making is ontologically impossible, its reliance on traditionally individual humanist elements of the Künstlerroman narrative to represent Coates's coming into his own as a writer means that the memoir poses no real challenge or alternative to the antiblackness that structures society.[18] By contrast, as I discuss in the next chapter, BLM organizers center not the plundering power of white "Dreamers" or an unchangeable anti-Blackness, but the life-affirming agency of Black people, who, by embracing joy, beauty, and creative expression as forms of political action, can narrate into being new ways to be human.

Between Father and Son

The memoir's father-son address works in tandem with the Künstlerroman narrative, and similarly contributes to the memoir's uneven relationship to BLM through the ways it serves to assert the meaning and value of Coates's fatherhood. Fatherhood is of course an important hegemonic marker of humanity and, as discussed in the previous section, one historically denied to Black men. Through Coates's letter to his son, the memoir counters this dehumanization. *BTWAM* derives beauty from the strength and eloquence of Coates's love for his son. In contrast to the emotional complexities and particularities involved in writing to or about a parent (for example, in "Notes from a Native Son," Baldwin explores his bitterness and hatred as well as his love for his father), a parental address is often heart-rending and universal in appeal, and Coates uses this form of narrative humanity with great power. The brutality of the world Coates describes is even more striking in its contrast to the purity of the love he expresses for his son—his own humanity shines through all the more, situated as it is in a world in which people view him and his precious son as criminal, as without value, as not human.

In a way that reverberates with BLM's insistence that the world hear from parents grieving the loss of beloved children, Coates's love letter to his son is urgent and moving because their relationship is haunted by a backdrop of violence and precariousness—by Coates's awareness that he and his son exist in a world that considers both of them disposable. We see this when Coates interviews Prince Jones's mother, Dr. Mabel Jones, and his voice comingles with hers in an intimate second-person address that is one of its most direct and powerful evocations of BLM. After telling Samori how Mabel Jones "would not forget the uniqueness of her son, his singular life" (113), Coates tells Samori how "the mother of the murdered boy [then] rose, turned to you, and said, 'You exist. You matter. You have value. You have every right to wear your hoodie, to play your music as loud as you want" (113). As this mother's words to Samori merge with Coates's, the pathos of the account derives from Coates's complex positioning as he mourns his friend and identifies both with Prince's/a slain boy's parent and with a young man who could have been him as well as his son—or Trayvon Martin; or Jordan Davis, the seventeen-year-old shot for playing his music too loudly; and the list goes on. If Samori and Coates himself are Prince, so too Coates here is Prince's mother. In writing a letter to his young son, Coates takes hold of a powerful form of narrative humanity, one whose second-person address possesses a direct and universalizing humanist appeal. He simultaneously carves out a space for Black fatherhood that at key moments such as this one channels a Black maternal voice into a narrative that, in establishing Black humanity, is distinctly masculine.

In *BTWAM*, Coates stands out as an exceptional father: fathers are otherwise absent or, having been scarred by white supremacist violence, abusive. He tells his son how Samori's mother "had never known her father, which put her in the company of the greater number of everyone I'd known" (65). Coates situates this absence in relation to the premature death that haunts Black men's existence, explaining to Samori, "I knew that my father's father was dead and that my uncle Oscar was dead and that my uncle David was dead and that each of these instances was unnatural" (15). He explains that these losses result in fear and violence; for his own father this entailed beating Coates into submission: "my father . . . beat me as if someone might steal me away because that is exactly what was happening all around us" (15–16). Surrounded by such representations that contextualize rather than overturn negative stereotypes of Black fatherhood, Coates provides an alternative narrative; he counters portrayals of violent or absent Black fathers with his own paternal presence, one full of tenderness, love, and instructions for survival.

The singularity of Coates's status as a Black father limits *BTWAM*'s ability to counter the erasure and demonization of Black fathers. bell hooks mercilessly homes in on this aspect of the memoir when she asks of Coates, "'Is it [*BTWAM*] a letter to your son, because you want him and other black boys to understand, or is it a letter to white people, so that you can let them know you're not like those other trifling negroes that don't have shit to say to their sons?'" (qtd. in Ngowi). I depart from hooks in concluding that Coates uses the epistolary father-son address to pander to, rather than simply to reach, an audience that includes white people. Moreover, the reception of the memoir suggests that Coates's memoir resonates for many Black as well as white and other non-Black readers. At the same time, drawing on this form of narrative humanity (one Coates himself describes in the *Democracy Now!* interview as "mostly . . . a literary technique") to connect with readers who might not otherwise see Black boys and men as human contributes to the memoir's white, liberal appeal and its masculine individualism. Coates's skill in reaching a wide audience through an address that will appeal to a (white) liberal readership helps account for the memoir's widespread success in declaring that "Black lives matter"; this narrative strategy also limits the memoir's participation in and representation of BLM as a movement that first and foremost establishes collective forms of love, care, and community for Black people.

Because BLM is a resolutely feminist and queer movement, one of its challenges is that the violence the state enacts against Black men and boys has more visibility than the violence it perpetrates against Black women and gender nonconforming people. Coates's memoir, with its status as a foundational BLM text, contributes to this lack of visibility. As Coates focuses on a father-son narrative that works within conventions of narrative humanity, his failure to question the masculine individualism that regularly characterizes such narratives results in an inattention to Black women, who, when they appear at all, serve primarily as conduits for Coates's own growth. Black feminist critics have widely and unfavorably remarked upon the memoir's gender dynamics. Brittni Danielle comments on how it "sidelines women" who are "satellites" or "footnotes" to Black men's stories; Bennett relates *BTWAM*'s disproportionate focus on Black men to the need for the SayHerName document and campaign that challenge BLM's focus on men and boys; Zinzi Clemmons critiques the memoir for not being intersectional, noting "its lack of real engagement with women's stories." In ways critics including these observe, and in contrast to *Fruitvale Station*, which provides loving attention to the women in Oscar Grant's life, *BTWAM* largely ignores Black women.

Not only is *BTWAM* a father-to-son address in which his son's mother's presence is muted, but so too are any references to Black women as intellectuals, activists, or shaping forces in Coates's life. The memoir thus supports Brittney Cooper's contention that Coates continues the pervasive tendency to overlook the rich contributions Black women have made as historical and political forces. Instead, in the memoir women exist mostly as ventriloquists for expressing parental love, as happens with Mabel Jones, the woman who receives the most attention. Or, as happens with Samori's mother (Kenyatta Matthews, to whom Coates dedicates the memoir, but who goes unnamed in it), women serve as bridges for Coates's own awakening, as background figures, or as others whose suffering is outside the scope of his imagination. In his account to his son of his romantic relationships (including with Samori's mother), he discloses in a telling if unintended evocation of the landmark anthology *This Bridge Called My Back* and its prefatory "The Bridge Poem" by Kate Rushin (both of which refuse the burden of continuing to serve as a bridge for the benefit of others), that "every girl I've ever loved was a bridge to somewhere else" (86). In one of the few discussions of Kenyatta Matthews, when he explains to Samori, "Your mother had to teach me how to love you. . . . That is because I am wounded" (125), he fails to consider how women, too, might be wounded. With his lack of a feminist or intersectional framework, Coates can only perceive that his shortcomings as a father result from racism, and not also from codes of masculine individualism and a naturalization of patriarchal structures in which women, when they appear at all, at best serve Coates as bridges.

Despite the power with which Coates's father-son narrative supports BLM's insistence that Black lives matter, and with the space the movement creates to grieve Black lives lost to police violence, *BTWAM*'s adherence to masculine individualism reproduces the liberal humanist exclusions that BLM opposes. To cast this memoir as an expression of BLM undercuts that movement's commitments to intersectionality and to standing for all Black lives. To uncritically uphold *BTWAM* as *the* memoir that gives voice to BLM serves to contain BLM within the liberal and masculine individualist framework that the memoir's deployments of narrative humanity reproduce.

Crime as Ontology

If its father-son and Künstlerroman narratives pull *BTWAM* in a liberal humanist direction, its focus on crime takes it in a distinctly antihumanist direction—one that intersects with BLM's profound challenge to the human as an antiblack formulation, while also straining against the BLM movement, unaccompanied as *BTWAM* is by any interest in political action. In *BTWAM*, the police state's plunder, dehumanization, and criminalization of Black bodies registers as a crime, but unlike BLM, one that is ontological, leaving no room for activism or collective organizing. Instead—and in contrast to Coates's fight for reparations in the political sphere—the struggle in *BTWAM* against plunder is at once necessary, futile, beautiful and noble, but tragic. The memoir's few mentions of protests against the crimes the state enacts on Black bodies concern either those by lone individuals—in Paris, Coates reminds Samori of a man they saw standing outside the subway, holding a French sign protesting Trayvon Martin's killer's acquittal (129)—or meditations on the futility of past movements. In the wake of Prince's death, as Coates considers "how we ultimately cannot save ourselves," he thinks back "on the sit-ins, the protestors with their stoic faces, the ones I'd once scorned for hurling their bodies at the worst things in life." He realizes with Prince's death, "Perhaps they had known something terrible about the world," but this recognition brings only a new respect for their knowledge, not faith in the power and possibilities of collective action. It is this defeatism that leads critics including R. L. Stephens to find that, "riddled with fear and futility, [*BTWAM*] begs us to retreat."

Throughout *BTWAM*, Coates represents the violence done to Black bodies not only as criminal, but also as cosmic, abstracted, inevitable, and entirely outside of Black control. As Stephens notes, in what is a brief book, the word "body" or "bodies" appears more than three hundred times. Coates regularly accompanies these references with descriptions of theft. Coates's rendering of the horrific crimes against Black bodies in a white supremacist world are so totalizing that Black life becomes entirely dehumanized, and bodies lose their materiality and, like the humans perpetuating this violence, become abstractions. In statements such as, "You cannot forget how much they took from us and how they transfigured our very bodies into sugar, tobacco, cotton, and gold," he portrays this dehumanization as complete. Through his letter to Samori, he conveys his understanding that "perhaps being named 'black' was just someone's name for being at the bottom, a human turned to object, object turned to pariah" (55). In the face of this totalizing system of criminal oppression, his relationship to his son becomes one of horizontality; he explains to him, "We are captured, brother, surrounded by the majoritarian bandits of America" (146). The focus on the theft of Black bodies means that even as Coates intimately addresses his son, Black people become indistinguishable, and the terrible crimes done to them become abstractions, with anti-Blackness as an ontological condition that can only be understood, not countered.

The force of this inevitable and omnipresent anti-Blackness gets figured in *BTWAM* through the weather, in ways that draw on tropes of literary naturalism that foreground the deterministic force of heredity and the environment. Coates's representations of the weather echo with Wright's depictions in *Native Son* of racism materialized as the blankets of snow that bury Chicago and entrap Bigger Thomas, though in *BTWAM*, naturalistic elements serve as resignation rather than, as with Wright and others working in the Black protest tradition, to sound an alarm and issue a warning to a White America.[19] Weather in *BTWAM* does not simply capture what it *feels* like to live in an anti-Black world, or even the pervasive atmospheric reality racism brings into being—or, as with Coogler's representation of BART, a materialization of structural racism. Rather, the weather in *BTWAM* stands in for/as racism itself, creating new ecologies that exceed human agency or comprehension. Coates likens the Middle Passage to "an earthquake, a tornado, or any other phenomenon that can be cast as beyond the handiwork of men" (7); anti-Black racism, which comprises "the elements of the world" (17), falls "random and relentless, like great sheets of rain" (19). Coates tells his son there is no system of justice to adjudicate the crimes done to Black bodies, casting them not like but *as* forces of nature: "The earthquake cannot be subpoenaed. The typhoon will not bend under indictment" (83). When he concludes the book, his repeated reference to sheets of rain reinforces the memoir's many descriptions of racism as bad weather: "Through the windshield I saw the mark of these ghettos—the abundance of beauty shops, churches, liquor stores, and crumbling housing—and I felt the old fear. Through the windshield I saw the rain coming down in sheets" (152). The fear these ghettos inspire—poverty that cannot be mitigated by self-care, God, or alcohol—reworks white racist stereotypes of ghettoes as dangerous spaces that breed Black criminality. Instead, this familiar fear is of a whiteness that criminalizes Black bodies, that condemns Black bodies to conditions of violence, death, delusions, and despair that can be mitigated only by the tragic beauty of bearing witness to necropolitical violence through words. With its elegiac anger, *BTWAM* leaves readers with little alternative to feeling grief and despair for a world doomed to anti-Black plunder and annihilation, with Coates's brilliant ways with words and his exceptional love for his son standing as moving testimony to this injustice.

In the (a)political ends to which its condemnations of white criminality and state violence point, the memoir parts ways with BLM. In contrast to BLM, there is no hope of abolishing and remaking an antiblack world through political organizing and acts of imagination; instead, Coates's better "other blue world," reached by way of a rocketing "starship" (121), is Paris, which he enjoys as a space of "high culture," and as an individual respite from a white supremacist world that is simultaneously distinctly American and cosmic (and therefore timeless and placeless). A number of Black writers have critically commented

on how *BTWAM* casts crimes against Black people as simultaneously planetary and provincially American, and as without solutions. R. L. Stephens contends, "To imbue race with an ontological meaning, to make it a reality all its
own, is to drain it of its place in history and its indelible roots in discrete
human action. To deny the role of life and people—*of politics*—is to also foreclose the possibility of liberation." So, too, Zinzi Clemmons has lamented the
memoir's "lack of connection to the rest of the world"; Cornel West has lambasted Coates for being inattentive to global contexts of imperialism; Tometi
and Naomi Klein, who criticize West's attack on Coates, also address how
Coates fails to place US experiences in a broader context of US imperial power.
This sets the memoir apart from a movement that foregrounds the power of
acts of narrated humanity and solidarity (the topic of chapter 3), and formulates new proposals, laws, and policies that extend from local communities to
the international level (as in the 2016 M4BL Vision Plan).

In 2020, Coates possesses more optimism about the efficacy of political protest than he does in *BTWAM*, but his representation of it continues to obscure the grassroots, collective organizing that has established BLM as a force
for transformation. In guest editing a set of essays for *Vanity Fair* in August 2020
that speaks to a shift in which for the first time he perceives that "a legitimate
anti-racist majority is emerging," he comments, "To clearly see what this country has done, what it is still doing, to construct itself is too much for any
human to take. So it was with the slave narrative. So it is with the cell phone.
The reaction of the beholder is physical. They double over in disgust. They
wail on the floor. They punch the air. They pace the room until they are at
last compelled out of their sanctuary, out of their privilege, out into the streets,
out into the diseased air, to face off with the legionaries who guard the power
implicit in their very names." With his focus on the elements (fire), techno-
logical innovation (the cell phone), and white protesters, what disappears are
BLM organizers. At the same time, other contributions he selects for this special issue situate themselves in a long history of Black resistance. Coates's
work thus continues to mainstream BLM productively, but also sometimes in
ways that mystify and erase it as a radical and collective Black movement.

Exploring the points of connection and departure between BLM and *BT-
WAM* provides insights into the political movement with which the memoir
is most commonly aligned, while also advancing this book's arguments concerning narrative humanity's possibilities and limitations when it comes to
imagining new genres of the human. Coates's investments in the Künstlerroman
and a father-son narrative mainstream BLM, but also curtail tenets central to
the movement as, in reproducing the masculine individualism and heteropatriarchal norms of these forms of narrative humanity, the memoir perpetuates

the liberal humanist exclusions that BLM opposes. Countering these humanist currents, his accounts of pervasive anti-Black dehumanization—conveyed through denouncements of narratives of self-making and representations of a timeless white criminality that is at once American and cosmic—similarly issue a protest that resonates with BLM, while diminishing the movement's grounding in collective organizing and solidarity.

From Narrative to Narrated: The Movement of BLM

If *Fruitvale Station* and *BTWAM* often receive recognition as life narratives that mark BLM's origins and register its foundational themes, in 2020, the story of this movement shifted dramatically: upon entering its second life, BLM has become more radical and more pervasively present. In ways I discuss in part 2, the resurgence in Black-Palestine solidarity has been especially remarkable, building most immediately but not exclusively on organizing in 2014 by BLM and Palestinian activists working against militarized state violence in both the US and Israel.

In part 1, I have been contending that Palestine often serves as a bellwether for assessing the limits of narrative humanity. To conclude part 1 and prepare for part 2, I turn to the question of Palestine, considering how, though Palestine figures in neither *Fruitvale Station* nor *BTWAM*, its presence and absence throughout Coogler's and Coates's bodies of work illuminate their uses of narrative humanity and relationships to BLM. Next, I look forward to part 2's shift to narrated humanity—a shift that emerges out of movements committed to solidarity, internationalism, and intersectionality, and out of memoirs connected to these movements. As I argue in part 2, Palestine constitutes an important issue in these movements and also an index for assessing the possibilities of narrated humanity.

Although Palestine has no place in *BTWAM*, it does enter the work for which, along with *BTWAM*, Coates is best known: his award-winning, debate-sparking 2014 *Atlantic* cover story on reparations for Black Americans. In that article, Coates posits Germany's reparations to Israel as a possible "road map for how a great civilization might make itself worthy of the name" ("The Case for Reparations"). In her critique of how Coates, in upholding Germany as a model, conflates Jews with Israel and Zionism, Rania Khalek points out how Coates also "accepts uncritically the ahistorical claim that Israel and Zionism were the victims of the Nazis." Khalek further notes that the billions Germany gave to Israel, which went to expanding Israel's military capacity, "were not used to repair but to destroy." Coates, who ignored criticisms he received on social media for legitimating Israel's practices of colonialism, occupation, and

ethnic cleansing, doubled down on his argument on *Democracy Now!*, a move
Khalek connects to Coates's patterned erasure of Palestinians.[20] As Pankaj
Mishra notes, it is no accident that Coates espoused Zionist positions as *The
Atlantic*'s national correspondent during the time that Jeffrey Goldberg served
as *Atlantic* editor: a former Israeli prison guard, Goldberg describes Coates as
"a dear friend" ("Coates Leaves *The Atlantic*") and he appeared with Coates
at a live event to promote Coates's argument for reparations.

The case Coates makes for reparations stands in marked contrast to the
M4BL's. An endorser of BDS, in its call for reparations, the M4BL instead calls
for a Universal Basic Income (UBI) in Finland and Switzerland. Remarking
on this distinction, Garrett Felber notes, "While the M4BL platform clearly
defines Israel as an 'apartheid state,' what remains glaringly absent from Coates's
analysis is the internationalism which provided the backbone for radical re-
jections of Zionism." Felber points out Coates's inattention to decades of
work by Black radicals who are also internationalists, and we see this as well in
BTWAM. I do not believe that this inattention can be understood apart from
Coates's approach to Palestine, or from the memoir's departures from BLM—
nor can it be separated from Coates's investments in narrative humanity. In
part 2, my interest will be in how practices of narrated humanity that emerge
out of engagement with solidarity-based movements such as BLM and BDS
enable breaks with established forms of narrative humanity and the violences
they encode.

Stories and representations of Oscar Grant are one way we can track the
movement from narrative to narrated humanity, as well as the increasing solidarity between the BLM movement and organizing for Palestine. Up until the
pandemic, just steps from BART's Fruitvale Station, at Reem's California, we
could find one example of renewed Black-Palestinian solidarity, and of how
Oscar Grant has become part of this story.[21] Community and labor organizer
Reem Assil, the daughter of a Palestinian refugee and a Syrian immigrant, describes her bakery/café as "a place of life, a place of nourishment and sustenance." This gathering space for community organizing features a 2017 mural
of Palestinian political prisoner and beloved Chicago activist Rasmea Odeh,
wearing an Oscar Grant pin.[22]

In 2020, with the advent of the COVID-19 pandemic, BLM-Palestine solidarity has been building not only in community spaces and on the streets, but
also in virtual spaces, including a proliferation of webinars hosted by social
justice organizations, left publishing venues, and progressive student and faculty groups. To consider the afterlife of *Fruitvale Station* and Oscar Grant's
importance to this solidarity, I close with attention to one such webinar: "Our
Fight for Liberation: A Conversation with the Families of Oscar Grant and

Eyad Hallaq," sponsored by the Palestinian Youth Movement (PYM) on June 20, 2020. During this conversation, cofounder Loubna Qutami noted that PYM came into existence with the conjuncture of Oscar Grant's murder and the attack on the Gaza Strip—events that mobilized Palestinian youth committed to joint struggles. With fifteen cosponsoring groups, "Our Fight for Liberation" featured Oscar Grant's Uncle Bobby X, and Diana Hallaq, the sister of Eyad Hallaq, the autistic man executed by Israeli soldiers on May 30, 2020, while on his way to his special needs school in Occupied East Jerusalem. During this event, Uncle Bobby X gave a presentation in which, in commemorating his nephew's life, he takes up but goes beyond the forms of narrative humanity discussed in this chapter, in ways that transition us to part 2 of this book and to how movements can shape, and be informed by, acts of narrated humanity.

The conversation begins with Raneen Abdelghani of PYM asking Uncle Bobby to give us a sense of Oscar Grant's "story, who he was, his dreams and aspirations" (16:30). Before answering, Uncle Bobby first expresses his family's condolences to the Hallaq family. He then provides remarks that contextualize his nephew's life and death. His focus is fourfold: (1) he outlines the historical and political conditions, including pervasive police killings and impunity, necessary for understanding Oscar Grant's murder; (2) he pays tribute to his nephew and his ability "to bring community [of color] together" to enjoy life (22:30); (3) he situates Oscar's death as "the seed" for what became BLM;[23] (4) he insists on the power of love to unify people internationally, not in abstract ways, but through kinship networks that can take down "the beast of white supremacy" (40). He thanks his "Palestinian brothers and sisters," and people across the globe, for supporting justice for Oscar, and "for loving on us as a family" (20:30). Describing the organization he cofounded, Families United for Justice, a network that connects families with murdered loved ones in the US to families in London, Uncle Bobby attributes the strength of these family members to how they are "bonded by blood but united in love" (1:30). Later, in the Q&A, Uncle Bobby addresses the need to stand for "our babies and grandbabies," to be "activated, so they can have joy in life, and not suffering and pain."

On Facebook, a lively stream of commentary accompanied this presentation. When Uncle Bobby paid tribute to Coogler's *Fruitvale Station* for how it "put a face on who we are" (24:00), Jontae Henry wrote in the chat box, "Uncle Bobby break down of what happened is way better than the movie Fruitvale Station, this break down should've been included."

The story that Uncle Bobby tells about Oscar Grant, contextually complex and wide in scope, does indeed provide an analysis Coogler does not, not only because Coogler works within established forms of narrative humanity, but also because he made his movie before the BLM movement put new narratives about being human in place. Uncle Bobby, representing his nephew as a beloved family member, connects Oscar's story not only to interconnected instances of state violence on a global scale but also to the story of BLM as a movement that activates grief and anger into a struggle for justice premised on kinship, love, and solidarity. In his presentation, as in the conversation more generally, he and the other contributors insist that being recognized as human is not enough, that it cannot serve as an endpoint. They attend to how processes of dehumanization must be understood structurally in terms of their embeddedness in the workings of civil society, and to how meaningful opposition to dehumanization requires bringing new worlds into being. When Uncle Bobby upholds the importance of joy for "our babies and grandbabies," it is because he sees himself engaged in a movement that is creating a future in which Black people and all humans can flourish. In conversation with PYM organizers and Diana Hallaq, Uncle Bobby departs from the individualist focus and pessimism regarding defeating the "beast of white supremacy" that we find in *Fruitvale Station* and *BTWAM*, even as these works make use of narrative humanity to powerfully assert that Black lives matter.

I began this chapter with an account of Honolulu's first, 2014 BLM march, also organized in support of justice for Kollin Elderts. Uncle Bobby's narrative in 2020 marks the progression, thanks to the work of BLM, PYM, and related movements, of ways to engage in solidarity and to carry forward stories of Oscar Grant, of Eyad Hallaq, of Kollin Elderts, and of all those slain by the state, in ways that end not with death, but with life—even as a necropolitical order persists. How urgently needed stories of love, life, and solidarity—and new pathways to practicing what it means to be human—can emerge from political movements is the focus of part 2 of this book.

PART II
Narrated Humanity

3

From Movement to Memoir

When They Call You a Terrorist *and the Power of Queer Black Kinship*

Let me be clear—every single day, people are dying, not being able to take another breath. We are in a state of emergency. . . . If you do not feel that emergency, then you are not human.

—PATRISSE CULLORS ("#BLACKLIVESMATTER ACTIVISTS
DISRUPT SANDERS AND O'MALLEY SPEECHES")

Freedom is a measure of breathability.

— BILLY-RAY BELCOURT, *A HISTORY OF MY BRIEF BODY*

In the previous chapter, I focused on how Ryan Coogler's 2013 *Fruitvale Station* anticipates and Ta-Nehisi Coates's 2015 *Between the World and Me* (*BTWAM*) sounds the keynotes for BLM's insistence that Black lives matter—a mattering established in these texts through forms of narrative humanity that powerfully refute Black criminality; that expose the systemic nature of anti-black violence;[1] and that uplift Black life through an assertion of love among family members and, in the case of Coates, literary brilliance and self-making. At the same time, I explored ways that their adherence to narrative humanity confines them to hegemonic parameters of the human. As this chapter continues chapter 2's investigation of life narratives that articulate with BLM, I turn from part 1's attention to *narrative* humanity to part 2's exploration of *narrated* humanity. Through a reading of BLM cofounder Patrisse Cullors and asha bandele's 2018 *When They Call You a Terrorist: A Black Lives Matter Memoir*, I look to how Cullors and bandele, in drawing on narratives that emerge from and contribute to the BLM movement, are formulating new ways of being human based on abolitionist, nonstatist, anticapitalist understandings of love, freedom, and justice. My analysis focuses on issues of intersectionality, solidarity, emotional well-being, and queer kinship that are integral to the collective and ongoing life of BLM in its struggle against state violence. This includes a militarized police that targets and then terrorizes Black people as the agents of terror. This chapter also follows one of this book's through lines: how in the United States today, solidarity with Palestine, or its absence, presents a significant means of testing the limits of narrative humanity, and of understanding how acts of narrated humanity can strengthen relationships between those engaged in seemingly distinct struggles against state violence.[2]

To situate my reading of *When They Call You a Terrorist* and the insights it provides into how acts of narrated humanity can articulate with movement politics, I begin with attention to the 2020 resurgence of BLM.

"Black Like We Never Left": The Return of Black Lives Matter

Chapter 2 opened with consideration of the first BLM march in Honolulu, partly occasioned by a not guilty verdict for Christopher Deedy, the off-duty federal agent who killed Kollin Elderts. That August 15, 2014, a few dozen of us marched through the streets of Waikīkī, led by veteran organizers and Elderts's defense team, who drew connections between antiblack and anti-Hawaiian racism and police violence. Six years later, on June 6, 2020, under conditions of COVID-19 lockdown, a core group of high school students organized via Zoom and group chats what turned out to be a massive march from Ala Moana Beach Park to a rally at the Hawai'i State Capitol. Mentored by seasoned activists, the teenagers formed Hawai'i for Black Lives. Heeding their call put out over social media, more than 10,000 (by some estimates 20,000) of us converged at the Capitol, masked and bearing signs insisting that Black Lives Matter in the Hawaiian Kingdom (fig. 2). Other islands held coordinated protests. When sixteen-year-old Nikkya Taliaferro, one of the leaders, took the mic before the multiracial crowd packed into the Capitol rotunda, she announced, "My humanity should not be a protest! My humanity should not be debated! I should not have to be up here telling people that Black lives matter, that Black people should not be killed" (Suevon Lee). Her speech served as an assertion of unity with the audience who raised their fists and cheered her on. It was also a provocation to address antiblack racism. Throughout the summer, people participated in protests, candlelight ceremonies, webinars, online roundtables, and open and closed meetings, confronting antiblack—and anti-Micronesian—racism in Hawai'i communities and move-

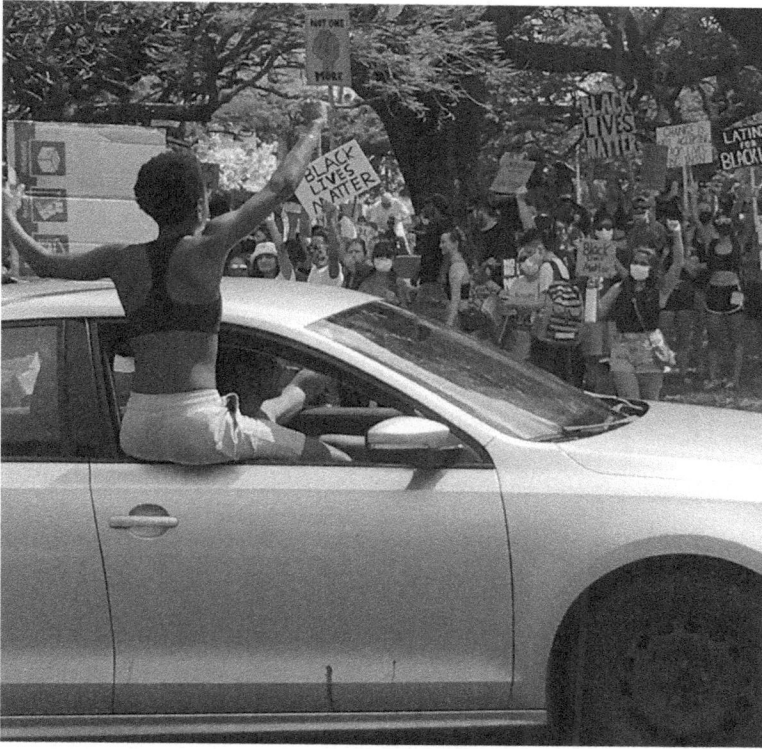

Figure 2. Photo of June 6, 2020, BLM March and Rally in Honolulu, taken just before reaching the Hawai'i State Capitol. (Photo taken by author)

ments, and foregrounding why Black lives matter in transformative justice work. The exponential growth of BLM since 2014 and its increasing power were on full display that summer, not least through the organizing efforts of fiercely articulate youth like Taliaferro, who were barely in their double-digits when the BLM movement started, and who situated themselves as part of a genealogy of Black and anticolonial activism.

The resurgence of BLM in Hawai'i was part of a global uprising catalyzed by the murder of George Floyd. On May 25, 2020, in Minneapolis, Minnesota, police officer Derek Chauvin cut off Floyd's air supply as he pinned this unarmed man to the ground and pressed his knee into his neck for more than nine minutes. Through documentation provided by Darnella Frazier, a seventeen-year-old Black girl who bravely filmed Floyd's murder on her cell phone, the world witnessed Floyd pleading for his life and calling out for his deceased mother for almost six minutes as he also, twelve times, echoed the

words of Oscar Grant, Eric Garner, Elijah McClain, and how many others?:
"I can't breathe." Floyd's murder closely followed other widely publicized police killings. In mid-March in Louisville, Kentucky, police stormed the home
of Breonna Taylor, an EMT in training to be a nurse. Entering with a "no
knock" warrant in the middle of the night, they shot her at least eight times,
after their suspect was already in custody. When people rose up for Floyd, they
also demanded justice for Taylor, and for other recently slain Black people,
including Ahmaud Arbery, Iyanna Dior, David McAtee, Tony McDade, Dreas-
jon "Sean" Reed, and McHale Rose. And they braved the streets as the virus
tore through the United States at one of the most rapid rates in the world and
the US COVID-19 death toll surpassed 100,000.

Although sparked by Floyd's death and other unchecked police murders,
the protests sweeping across the country were overdetermined. BLM's second wave was also fueled by how COVID-19's dramatically unequal impacts multiplied ways Black and other oppressed people living in America
cannot breathe. Even as this virus, often felt as a foot on one's chest, can
leave the healthiest susceptible to breathing troubles and organ damage, Black
people—along with other BIPOC, those who are elderly, disabled, trans, queer,
and/or poor—are disproportionately suffering and dying. So, too, as police violence ramped up under the pressures of the pandemic—with police outfitted
in military-grade gear as health care workers were left to wrap themselves in
garbage bags and don makeshift masks—the ways in which Black lives don't
matter intensified, even as all the deeply grooved forms of oppression were
deemed not newsworthy. The movement grew as a response to the racist prov-
ocations of Trump (with his tweet "when the looting starts the shooting starts,"
his invocation of the Insurrection Act, and his calling upon the military and
the Department of Homeland Security to "dominate" "domestic terrorists").
People rose up in resistance to the police kettling, arresting, beating, pepper-
spraying, tear-gassing, trampling, shooting, and killing nonviolent protesters
and journalists; and in defiance of white nationalists (including those identified
on Black Twitter as police) fomenting violence. Remarking on the significance
of these events in terms of their deep historical contexts—or what Erica Edwards
calls "the long war on terror"—Patrisse Cullors announced in a May 29, 2020,
Instagram posting, "When Black people uprise we must call it what it is. A
human reaction to a deeply unstable and dysfunctional relationship to a country
that has dehumanized us for centuries" ("For hundreds of years").

As discussed in the previous chapter, during its first five years, BLM morphed
into different hashtags, movements, and organizations no longer aggregated
under the Movement for Black Lives (M4BL) or BLM hashtags. The latest,
heightened instantiations of white supremacist violence catalyzed its return.

With renewed calls for concrete actions to end the war against Black people, the Movement for Black Lives (M4BL) announced on its website that it was "Black like we never left." In the *New Yorker*, one of the many venues to feature BLM's return, Keeanga-Yamahtta Taylor heralded this next wave of BLM for ways it built "on the incredible groundwork of a previous iteration of the Black Lives Matter movement" ("How Do We Change America?").[3] Actions included both peaceful demonstrations and property destruction, especially but not only of corporate-owned stores, police stations, statues honoring perpetrators of slavery and genocide, and other sites and monuments of institutional violence.

In addition to commemorating victims of police violence by "saying their names" and holding up their pictures, actions on the streets and in mainstream venues increasingly included calls to defund the police and other abolitionist demands: to end and create alternatives to institutions premised on surveillance, incarceration, policing, and punishment. On social media, BLM began putting out day-by-day agendas for people to follow. These ranged from engaging in self-reflection and education to participating in local, national, and global actions. As part of a chorus of writer/activists working in the tradition of radical Black feminist abolition (e.g., Charlene Carruthers, Angela Davis, Gina Dent, Alicia Garza, Prentis Hemphill, Mariame Kaba, Robin D. G. Kelley, Beth and Andrea Ritchie), Cullors highlighted BLM's decisive abolitionist turn: "Our demand is no longer about the accountability of law enforcement. . . . We must defund law enforcement and reimagine a world that relies on an economy of care versus an economy of punishment" (qtd. in Yes! Editors).

The state's response to the uprisings and to BLM's sharply defined abolitionist demands was a swift doubling down on the violent status quo, even as mainstream media and those with political power (government officials, university administrators, corporate entities) scrambled to make "solidarity" statements and promise reforms (some substantive, some cosmetic) to contain the power of this revolutionary moment. In the first ten days alone, state and federal governments deployed over 17,000 National Guard troops, arrested over 10,000 people, killed more than 12 (mostly Black men), and imposed curfews in at least 30 cities (Taylor, "How Do We Change America?"). In the article "Black Lives Matter May Be the Largest Protest Movement in U.S. History," the *New York Times* estimated that from late May to June 2020, 15–26 million people in the United States participated in protests over Floyd's death (Buchanan et al.). Because of disproportionate focus on the violence of the protests, in corporate media venues Black people were often further criminalized and state violence was sanitized or seen as a necessary response to Black protesters who were cast as "thugs," "looters," "terrorists," and COVID-19 super-spreaders. Simultaneously, there was a growing mainstream acknowledgment of systemic police brutality and antiblack racism, as well as a new receptivity to decades-long calls from Black activists to defund the police, with abolitionists such as Mariame Kaba being featured on the NBC news, and in *Good Housekeeping* and the *New York Times* (Kaba).

BLM's impact was also international. As Black organizers enacted intersectional forms of love and care for one another, allies and Black folks across the globe (Mexico City, Buenos Aires, Berlin, London, Cape Town, Tokyo, Ramallah, Accra, Karachi, Quezon, and more) asserted righteous rage and solidarity. Racial uprisings in the United States, coinciding as they did with Israel's announcements about annexing the West Bank, renewed solidarities between liberation movements in the United States and Palestine. So, too, those in the streets drew on the energies and lessons learned from the Third World Liberation Front and other radical left movements (Walcott).

This groundswell of support and grassroots organizing was accompanied by a huge influx of donor money and a renewed focus on BLM's cofounders that presented possibilities for building power. Within a year, the Black Lives Matter Global Network Foundation (BLMGNF) went from negligible to $90 million in holdings.[4] Much of this funding came from small donors. It also came from celebrities, such as the Korean pop band BTS, who inspired their fans, BTS ARMY, to match their million-dollar donation overnight. Corporate giants like Amazon, Airbnb, and Microsoft built their brands by making donations accompanied by "solidarity" statements. RITZ Crackers, for example, broadcast their $500,000 donation with a tweet announcing that they and their "sister brands" "stand in solidarity with the Black community." The mainstreaming of BLM also brought increased social media opportunities and influence (in addition to her 366,000 followers on Instagram, Cullors, for example, started a YouTube channel), book deals, and national tours for BLM cofounders and others in BLM leadership positions.

This media attention put those publicly at the front of BLM, perhaps especially Cullors as the BLMGN Foundation's executive director, under an intense spotlight. Separate from criticisms originating within the movement, Cullors became the target of a right-wing media campaign. An April 2021 "exposé" in the *New York Post* charged Cullors with appropriating and otherwise mishandling BLMGNF funds (Vincent).[5] Cullors took accountability for a lack of transparency in running the foundation, and for being ill-prepared in suddenly finding herself at the helm of a $90-million organization. While acknowledging the problems, as she put it, of "building the plane while flying it" (Morrison), Cullors categorically denied unsubstantiated right-wing claims insinuating that she had stolen money from the foundation to buy homes for her family and for other personal gain.[6] The highly publicized controversies swirling around Cullors, and also her partner Janaya Khan with Black Lives Matter–Canada, were mostly focused on real estate. In addition to Cullors's individual purchases of four homes, BLMGNF had transferred funds to BLM-Canada to establish a center for art and activism, or what her partner Janaya Khan described as the realization of "brick and mortar dreams" (Khan). These attacks from the media targeting the buying of real estate, and the flood of death threats they unleashed, reveal the deep-seated ways in which, in the afterlife of slavery, Black people continue to be criminalized for property ownership—a marker in the US imaginary for being human, and a constitutionally protected right of citizenship. Attacks on Cullors also speak to the challenges and vulnerabilities that come with being the face of a movement, particularly when that movement achieves mainstream success. In interviews and on social media Cullors shared her emotional distress, and her fear for her life in what was "not just a character assassination campaign, but a campaign to actually get me assassinated" (Malik). Attacks on Cullors also indicated how targeting movement leaders serves as a strategy to take down movements.

At this chapter's end, I return to the controversies surrounding the BLMGNF and Cullors. However, I dedicate most of the chapter to a reading of Cullors and bandele's BLM memoir. Written before the second wave of BLM and the eruption of the controversies, *When They Call You a Terrorist* focuses on the life of an individual and her chosen family as they bring into being revolutionary ways to breathe, to grieve, to heal, and to love. The memoir provides a way to explore what it might mean to lift up, and also to sustain, the life of a movement through acts of narrated humanity.

From Narrative to Narrated Humanity

When They Call You a Terrorist: A Black Lives Matter Memoir not only tells the story of BLM's coming to being; it also evidences how acts of narrated humanity packaged in the form of a memoir of one person's life can crucially contribute to BLM's future-oriented vision, and—as is the subject of part 2 of this book—to liberatory movements more generally. In comparison to the forms of narrative humanity explored in chapter 2, my subject here is a memoir that tells a story that is collective (rather than individual) and focused on life (rather than death). In *When They Call You a Terrorist* (hereafter, *WTCYAT*), as they engage in acts of narrated humanity that overturn the antiblack representations of terror and criminality that are features of narrative humanity and white supremacist violence, Cullors and bandele participate in the collective life story and life-giving aims of the BLM movement. Published five years into the movement, it evidences Cullors's and BLM's success, as it is also catalyzed by the continuing need to create a world in which Black lives matter. At the center of the memoir's chronicling of Cullors's life and that of the BLM movement is a queer, Black, feminist account of love, kinship, and intentional community. As Cullors and bandele join a chorus of other queer Black feminist abolitionists at the forefront of BLM, the memoir's mobilization of narrated humanity helps bring into being a world in which Black people not only help one another survive but also thrive.

Throughout this chapter, I use the term "narrated humanity" to distinguish how Cullors and bandele depart from established forms, codes, and conventions ("narrative humanity"), and instead draw on forms of expression that, emerging as they do out of a political movement in the making, have not yet been codified in literature. Whereas narrative humanity depends on entrenched literary structures, "narrated humanity" demarcates acts that break with these structures and with the ideologies about the human that they support. As WTCYAT engages critically with self-making (especially 12-stepping) and exposes how the state has criminalized and terrorized Cullors and her kin, leaving them unable to breathe, Cullors and bandele narrate ways of being human that arise out of and deepen the BLM movement. These include BLM's commitments to intersectionality, solidarity, self-care, and queer-inclusive forms of kinship and abolitionist community making. These practices constitute ways to effect transformative justice, a concept Charlene Carruthers defines as "a liberatory approach to violence that seeks safety and accountability without relying on alienation, punishment, or state or systemic violence, including incarceration or policing" (Carruthers). In focusing on Cullors and bandele's breaks with narrative humanity, this chapter explores possibilities narrated humanity offers in relation to political organizing. As Cullors and bandele dismantle given conventions and codes to represent Cullors, her kin, and Black people more generally not as terrorists but as humans whose Black lives matter, WTCYAT also participates in the BLM movement: WTCYAT is memoir as movement, and movement as memoir.

Part 1 of this book investigated narrative humanity's strengths and limits in challenging dehumanization; part 2 develops my contention that to effectively counter processes of dehumanization—that work in multiple historically specific but also articulated and systemic ways to justify the violence integral to civil society—we need narratives that imagine new ways to understand the human. As Audre Lorde memorably contended, the master's tools cannot dismantle the master's house. So too, *Narrating Humanity* maintains that forms of narrative humanity cannot wholly undo hegemonic understandings of who counts as human. Acts of narrated humanity that emerge out of contemporary movements committed to intersectionality, solidarity, and abolitionist and de-colonial forms of care and community offer pathways to being human that break with narratives of the human founded on capitalist and colonial extraction and human disposability, criminalization, and incarceration. The remainder of this book explores such acts of narrated humanity and how they participate in movement politics in imagining new ways of being (human). In Carruthers's words, "Our work today is about redefining humanity and transforming our relationships with each other and with the land" (*Unapologetic*, 136). Or, as Tiffany Lethabo King remarks, "If Black Lives Matter (BLM) is asking to be absorbed into the category of the human, then BLM's version of the human does not yet exist" ("Humans Involved," 180). This radically transformative work, I contend, requires engagement in acts of narrated humanity; it requires the creation of new genres, narrative conventions, and forms.

Stories, in other words, are not ancillary but central to movements. For BLM, this includes not only the stories activists tell in organizing spaces and at BLM gatherings to commemorate, grieve, and protest the loss of those whose lives have been taken prematurely, but also narratives transmitted in more recognizably literary genres and cultural forms. In a society whose police in their internal communications use the acronym "NHI" or "No Humans Involved," largely in reference to cases involving Black people, BLM has had as one of its primary aims the abolition of the police state as a way to dismantle "the social order and the scaffolding that upends and holds together the human" (King, "Humans Involved," 180). As Sylvia Wynter insists in her brilliant critique of "western humanism," narratives promulgated in academic discourse make possible the NHI designation, and scholars have a responsibility to "undo their [Black people's] narratively condemned status" ("No Humans Involved," 70). Critics can participate in this project by attending to the power of narrative. Like academic discourse, narrative humanity makes possible forms of systemic violence that refuse to grant Black people positive forms of agency and relationality while assigning them hyper-agency for acts of criminality. In the ways in which they criminalize and render Black people as less than or only fractionally human, forms of narrative humanity are both elastic and continuous (Alexander, Hartman, Kwate and Threadcraft, Sharpe).

However, narrative humanity can also serve more progressive purposes. As discussed in chapter 2, it can not only perpetuate, but also support BLM in countering, the criminalization of Black people and forms of social death that include a denial of citizenship and bonds of kinship. For a wide-ranging public, the texts studied in chapter 2, which employ conventions and genres that have come to delineate the human, convey how Black lives do not but should matter. This accounts for their importance to BLM, even as their forms of narrative humanity circumscribe their political interventions and the directness of their support for BLM as a collective movement committed to making *all* Black lives matter, to draw on Barbara Ransby's formulation.

If contesting and grieving Black deaths contributes to BLM, this heterogeneous political movement also issues challenges to radically rethink Black life that are crucially supported through acts of narrated humanity. In its radical iterations, including those put forth by the movement's unapologetically Black, feminist, and queer cofounders, BLM formulates new ways of (Black) human being and belonging that draw on the vocabulary, concepts, and values that have emerged out of BLM and related movements. This conception of the human takes as its starting point not the plea or demand that Black lives count as human, but the assumption that *all* Black lives matter, including the lives of those who are trans, queer, poor, disabled, undocumented, old, and young. From this foundation—and through its rallying calls, "None of us are free until all of us are free" and "We have nothing to lose but our chains"—BLM seeks to create communities that center Black lives. BLM organizers craft abolitionist and other transformative justice policies and programs, organize protests, disrupt electoral politics, participate in artistic and cultural production, and prioritize anticapitalist practices of self and community care and well-being.[7] This world making involves acts of imagination, or what Robin D. G. Kelley calls "Freedom Dreams," and new ways to narrate being human. It necessitates disregarding narrative forms and conventions that, as they make appeals for recognition of Black humanity, decenter Black people in terms of their presumed audience. Instead, BLM-inspired narratives put Black lives at their center, including as subjects of address.

To engage in such acts of writing and other forms of artistic expression is to engage in political work, or artivism. Cullors's activism involves performance art as well as organizing and writing. Trained in Theatre of the Oppressed and dance, Cullors explains on her website that her work for BLM includes "using theatre techniques, performance audio, and movement" to "render bare the narratives of state-induced trauma while lifting up a path towards healing" ("Artist"). Her projects range from cowriting episodes of the television show *Good Trouble* that feature Black activists (Petski), to placing 100 jail beds in downtown Los Angeles to protest the building of two $3.5-billion jails (Agrawal), to staging an Afrofuturist 2020 performance piece where she donned wings made from her brother Monte's clothes to mark her twenty years of activism on his behalf and as a way of "transforming trauma into literal flight" ("Performance Piece"). In a July 2020 project, Cullors had the words "Care, not cages" flown over L.A.'s Men's Central Jail. As Cullors explains of her artivism, "My work is about imagining worlds. Creating portals. Destroying and rebuilding systems! Making and creating community" ("Tonight I received the Durfee Stanton Fellowship"). After exiting her position as executive director of BLMGNF in 2021, she signed a production deal with Warner Brothers with the intent of continuing "to uplift Black stories, talent and creators that are transforming the world of art and culture" ("12 Steps to Changing Yourself"). In short, Cullors is keenly attuned to the transformative power of narrative, art, and acts of imagination.[8]

WTCYAT is part of this world making. Through their memoir, Cullors and bandele help realize BLM-inspired forms of queer self-making, kinship, and community. As they put their loved ones at the center of their address, they give a sustained narrative form to BLM's objectives, vocabulary, and reimagining of human being and belonging. Unlike the conventions of narrative humanity that govern Fruitvale Station and BTWAM, WTCYAT's forms of narrated humanity contribute to BLM's objective to hold space for all Black people to mourn, to experience joy, and to love one another and themselves. In this way, this BLM memoir breathes life into the BLM movement and its work in remaking an antiblack world while telling the movement's story. It also illuminates the dynamic relationship between BLM—and liberatory political movements more generally—and acts of narrated humanity.

"If We Can Imagine It, We Can Create It": Materializing the Movement for Black Lives

In WTCYAT, Cullors and bandele use the memoir genre not to claim Cullors as the face of BLM, but rather to tell a collective story of Cullors as a family and community member who has lived through—and found ways to thrive in the face of—state violence aimed at herself and her loved ones. In a memoir that tells a (not the) story of BLM while participating in it, Cullors and bandele do not revise and appropriate but instead show the inhumanity that inheres in dominant forms of narrative humanity. WTCYAT exposes the antiblack racism at the foundation of narratives of self-making and citizenship. It chronicles what it means to be Black and caught within binaristic narratives that define the human and the citizen against Black children and adults, who are cast as inhuman, and criminalized and incarcerated as terrorists. At the same time, WTCYAT imagines new narrative forms that exceed the terrorist/citizen binary that itself terrorizes Cullors and her kin. In their formulations of narrated humanity, Cullors and bandele draw on tropes, metaphors, turns of phrase, and concepts that animate BLM and the Black radical tradition, as well as other contemporary liberation movements. Cedric Robinson, in his work on the Black radical tradition, contends that Black radicals do not set out to critique antiblack racism, but rather to engage in a revolutionary "rejection of European slavery and a revulsion of racism in its totality" that is "internationalist, anti-colonial/anti-imperialist, and anti-capitalist" (310). WTCYAT, like BLM, shows Black radical thinking at its best also to be attentive to care-based economies and queer feminist forms of relationality.[9]

WTCYAT demonstrates the political possibilities of narratives that grow out of, and help imagine and materialize, movement politics. Rather than approaching who counts as human through a focus on the individual or the exclusions that structure forms of narrative humanity, WTCYAT embraces the expansiveness and connections that come with BLM's concentration on intersectionality, kinship, and community. Rather than "prove" that Black lives matter, this memoir takes that mattering as a starting point in narrating/dreaming/imagining into being a better world, one that predates centuries of racism by reminding us that humans all are made of stardust, while also envisioning a future that is queer, feminist, and rooted in a distinctly Black past. As bandele puts this in the memoir's Q&A, "if we can imagine it, we can create it" ("Q&A").

Cullors writes her memoir at a time when she has achieved widespread recognition for her BLM organizing. Since 2014, together with BLM's other cofounders Alicia Garza and Ayo (formerly Opal) Tometi, Cullors has regularly been called on to speak as the voice of BLM, and all three women have been prominently featured in venues ranging from mainstream news outlets, to fashion magazines, to Black media, to queer publications, to a panoply of progressive or left-leaning publications. When Time magazine selected women of the year for a 100-year span in their March 5, 2020, issue, they chose Cullors, Garza, and Tometi for the year 2013, and featured them on the cover. President Obama invited Cullors to the White House in 2015 in recognition of her leadership. Cullors has received many awards, fellowships, and grants for making history, or for being named woman or person of the year, including from the NAACP, the National Center for Lesbian Rights, Essence, Glamour, Google, the LA Times, and the 2017 Sydney Peace Prize committee. The racial justice programs she has developed have been supported by organizations that range from liberal to radical; a sampling includes the Rosenberg Foundation, the ACLU, MomsRising, and Cullors's own initiative JusticeLA. As well, Cullors has been awarded honorary doctorates, has delivered keynote addresses at any number of universities, and since 2018 has held a faculty position at Arizona Prescott College, in an MA program in Social Justice and Community Organizing (Patrisse Cullors website).

The memoir's publication history itself registers Cullors's renown as a BLM leader. In 2017, St. Martin's outbid six other publishers at an auctioning of the book, paying "six figures" for what Cullors's agent Victoria Sanders described as the "first official Black Lives Matter book" (Deahl). The memoir's reception provides an indicator of the widespread interest in BLM and the substantial audience that exists for activist stories. *WTCYAT* made the *New York Times* Editor's Choice list and appeared on its Bestseller list its first week out. *Oprah Magazine* recommended it as a "Top 10" book and *Essence* featured the memoir on its cover. *Library Journal, Goodreads,* and *Time* all recommended the memoir or recognized it in their "Best of 2018" lists for memoir/autobiography and/or biography. *WTCYAT* has also been chosen as required reading for first-year college students, including for Northern Illinois University's Common Reading Experience. When it appeared in paperback in 2020, it became an instant *New York Times* Bestseller and Cullors began working to get copies to the California state prisons ("Two Years Ago Today"). That same year Cullors and bandele adapted the memoir for a Young Adult (YA) audience, one of the fastest-growing markets in book publishing.

In telling Cullors's story as "A Black Lives Matter Memoir," *WTCYAT* does not focus on Cullors's journey to reaching widespread acclaim. Its attention is not on her as an exceptional individual or a great writer, and Cullors does not direct her address to the white liberal audience that a St. Martin's publication makes possible. Instead, the memoir sends love out to Black readers and embraces the importance of community-based, nonhierarchical organizing. In the memoir's online Q&A, Cullors singles out Black Queer girls as her most desired audience and bandele describes the book as being "for anybody and everybody who cares about living in a world in which all of our children, all of our elders, all of humanity can survive" ("Q&A"). Cullors and bandele's use of the memoir genre to sidestep Cullors's celebrity standing, even while gaining a readership from it, is consonant with Cullors's approach in the many interviews she gives. While embracing the recognition she has received in cofounding BLM, in *WTCYAT* she simultaneously highlights BLM as a "leaderful" movement without clearly defined origins (Patrisse Cullors website), one in which people "stand beside each other, not in front of one another" (qtd. in Taylor, *From #BlackLivesMatter*). With a commitment to being a grassroots, horizontal movement, BLM by the time of the memoir's publication had come to include more than thirty regional chapters and had catalyzed or formed associations with any number of additional groups, some directly affiliated with BLM. These include Cullors's Reform LA Jails; Mothers of the Movement; #SayHerName; Campaign Zero (a pressure group that aims to end police violence through effecting legislative change); Black Youth Project 100 (BYP100); and the Movement for Black Lives (M4BL), under which fifty Black organizations—including thirty-six chapters of the BLMGN—have developed a "visionary agenda" that moves from local, to state, to federal, to global positions and policies aimed at implementing restorative justice for Black people. WTCYAT makes no attempt to tell Cullors's story as one that gives her ownership over or representative status in speaking on behalf of all these decentralized and wide-ranging but often interlinked initiatives. Instead, Cullors explains, she "shared deeply personal moments in my life to humanize #BlackLivesMatter" ("In July 2018 I published my first book").

The memoir tells a story of the BLM movement through attention to Cullors's life story as a daughter, sister, lover, mother, and community member. WTCYAT moves from Cullors's childhood up until 2016 and her marriage to Future and the birth of her child Shine. At its heart are her relationships to her birth father Gabriel and her brother Monte, and the state violence they experience that contributes to Gabriel's drug addiction and Monte's schizoaffective disorder. As readers learn of the individual and collective trauma that results from this violence, Cullors and bandele delve into the practices that provide a kind of blueprint for how to not only heal, but thrive: "My community of friends, this chosen family of mine, loves in a way that sets an example for love. Their love as a triumph, as a breathing and alive testimony to what we mean when we say another world is possible" (loc. 1188). In telling its love stories, WTCYAT serves simultaneously as a memoir of an individual and one that is of/for a movement committed to revolutionary change.

WTCYAT's collective aims in telling a deeply intimate story can be traced through attention to its coauthorship: bandele—a journalist, editor, and author, including of two memoirs, The Prisoner's Wife (1999) and Something Like Beautiful: One Single Mother's Story (2010)—is listed after Cullors as a full coauthor. In their appearances together, they highlight their shared politics and close collaboration. At the same time, bandele does not directly appear anywhere in the memoir's first-person account of Cullors's life, and bandele's marked/unmarked presence suggests the trust and intimacy between Cullors and bandele. (That said, in the YA edition, Cullors provides what is perhaps a corrective to bandele's absence in the body of the earlier edition, one that underlines the importance of acknowledging their relationship. There she adds, "when I set about this journey, and to this very day, I have been held by three veteran organizers and writers: asha, dream hampton and Rosa Clement. . . . And I name them here because just as I would not be erased on their watch, neither will they be erased on mine" [206].) Cullors and bandele's coauthorship also suggests that Cullors's story is not simply her own. This sense of a shared story is deepened by the memoir's frequent use of a first-person plural that at times expands to encompass all readers, and at other times is more particular to Cullors's loved ones, but always includes bandele.

Through a reading of bandele's other memoirs, one can trace her voice, and the profound affinities between bandele and Cullors. Like *WTCYAT*, they embody a poetics and a politics that value imagination and love as transformative forces. This is especially clear when reading *WTCYAT* alongside *The Prisoner's Wife*, a love story bandele writes about her relationship with her husband Rashid, whom she met at a poetry reading in a prison where he was serving time for a murder conviction. We witness how the strength of their relationship and their imaginations enable them to overcome the harsh institutional setting of the prison and "choose the rich, defiant tones and texture of our flesh, eyes, and humanity instead" (131). Like *WTCYAT*, *A Prisoner's Wife* denounces prison as a site of dehumanization. As well, both memoirs evidence faith in the power of love and care to enable (self) transformation (not redemption, because bandele and Cullors work from the premise that all humans matter). They also embrace a belief in the power of stories to heal trauma, overcome shame, and imagine better worlds into being. Reading *A Prisoner's Wife* alongside *WTCYAT* provides a window into how fully Cullors's and bandele's visions comingle.

In keeping with the lack of demarcations between Cullors's and bandele's lives or lines of authorship, the memoir does not distinguish between the individual and the collective when it comes to art or politics. As *WTCYAT* highlights the personal, political, spiritual, and emotional benefits of creative expression, it evidences no preoccupation with western understandings of authorship as an endeavor tied to singular intellectual accomplishment. Refusing a focus on literary greatness or memoir's privileging of individual consciousness, Cullors and bandele instead mobilize collective forms of narrated humanity that lift up community and that further BLM as a radical movement that reconceives the human through stories of (queer) Black kinship.

Sentencing Lives: The Fiction of "Self-Help" in a Racist Police State

In telling what is in large part a coming-of-age story, *WTCYAT* breaks from that genre by thoroughly critiquing narratives of self-making. Amplifying BLM's concerns with racist policing and the carceral state, *WTCYAT* demonstrates through Cullors's story how modes of narrative humanity repeatedly cast Black people as criminals, noncitizens, and terrorists. *WTCYAT* makes it possible for us to witness how narrative humanity can uphold white supremacist structures by unmaking Black humanity, that is, by representing Black people as criminals and terrorists against whom the citizen and the human are defined. The memoir thus exposes the ways that familiar antiblack narrative arcs, codes, conventions, and genres justify and sustain the school-to-prison pipeline that keeps white supremacist structures in place.

Readers repeatedly see how narrative formulas enable the criminal justice system to subject Cullors and her loved ones to the criminalization and incarceration that makes BLM necessary. Chapter 2 of WTCYAT begins with an account of Cullors being arrested at age twelve under false charges of marijuana possession—a formative and still-present trauma: "One sentence and I am back there, all that little girl fear and humiliation forever settled in me at the cellular level" (loc. 245). This reference to "one sentence" is not simply wordplay. The memoir shows how the sentencing of lives happens not only through police actions but also through language, through sedimented narratives that keep alive racist histories. WTCYAT powerfully demonstrates how dominant narratives dehumanize Black people, killing, incarcerating, or otherwise criminalizing them for merely existing. Though not focused on stories such as Tamir Rice's, Trayvon Martin's, and Aiyana Stanley-Jones's—police killings of children that BLM activists have brought to public attention—the memoir provides a firsthand account of how the police state terrorizes Black children and denies them their childhoods. For Cullors, this childhood trauma is constitutive of the criminalization and dehumanization that means that by age twelve, if Black children have not lost their lives, their "childhood [is] already gone," and confronted with the threat of imminent death, they find themselves "twelve, and out of time" (loc. 351).

WTCYAT shows how Black Americans who engage in political resistance, or who are unable to conform to societal norms owing to illness or addiction, are particularly targeted for criminalization, incarceration, and premature death by antiblack narratives that establish the humanity of others at their expense. In a vicious circular logic, these racist narratives often bring into being the very conditions they criminalize. The memoir shows how existing forms of narrative humanity, as well as the practices of white supremacy that they justify, both cause and compound mental illness and substance abuse. Throughout, even as Cullors and bandele marshal sociological data to establish how pervasively Black people are incarcerated, WTCYAT focuses on the lasting emotional and material harm of this criminalization, not least because of the assumptions and narratives that continue to imprison the previously incarcerated and deny them rights of citizenship. Through its focus on Cullors's family members, the memoir powerfully embodies the life stories that statistics cannot tell. As bandele puts this in a chapter title in *Something Like*

Beautiful, "statistics don't tell the story. the story tells the story." Cullors describes how her brother Monte, continuously arrested from early childhood, cannot find a job or achieve self-sufficiency owing to the stigma of having been incarcerated. She details how this "lifetime sentence" (loc. 1327) exacerbates a mental illness that cannot be separated from his subjection to white supremacist violence—and how this illness then codes him as a terrorist. Through her father Gabriel, Cullors tells the story of how "crack filled the empty spaces for a lot of people whose lives have been emptied out," and of how addiction without a safety net or the kind of assistance handed out to her father's "counterparts on Wall Street" (loc. 426) gets him "cages without compassion" (loc. 1284) and eventually kills him.

If racist criminalization and incarceration can cause as well as result from mental illness and substance abuse, Cullors and bandele reveal the hegemonic forms of healing and their accompanying forms of narrative humanity to be harmful because they hold only the suffering individual accountable. In particular, Cullors asserts the limits of 12-stepping, or self-help narratives. At the 12-step meetings Cullors attends to support her father as he strives to recover from drug addiction, and then later as an adult counselor, she finds the "honesty was life-giving." At the same time, as the men discuss joblessness, feeling hated, and being beaten up by the police, she asks, "Why are only individuals held accountable? Where were the supports these men needed?" (loc. 505). She wonders when thinking of her father who "is working hard, once again, to hold himself accountable. . . . Who has ever been accountable to Black people or to my father?" (loc. 1094). When she talks with her father about the determining force of societal structures (loc. 1110) and is unable to reach him with this analysis, or with her insights regarding the "coded language" that criminalizes Black people, she laments, "A decade of 12-stepping has ensured that he only really knows how to hold himself accountable" (loc. 1110). Through the telling of her father's story, she shows how 12-stepping foundationally sidesteps societal responsibility for the harms white supremacy inflicts, and instead disciplines individuals for the obstacles they face. (And here it is important to note that in her 2021 *An Abolitionist's Handbook: 12 Steps to Changing Yourself and the World,* Cullors appropriates the 12-step, self-help model not to align the individual within already-existing norms, but for world-changing purposes that will benefit, as they remake, individuals and communities.)

WTCYAT's critiques of 12-stepping and its attendant narratives as ultimately more harmful than helpful resonate with BLM's foregrounding of mental health as a crucial societal and political issue—and one connected to the sharing of stories, and the healing that love makes possible. As Kai M. Green, Je Naé Taylor, Pascale Ifé Williams, and Christopher Roberts put this in "#BlackHealingMatters,"

an account of internal work BLM organizers are doing in the name of healing and transformative justice, "The healing is in the telling. The story is in
the healing. The story is a healing. Because we said it. We told it. We will
continue to tell *it*, not always like *it* is now. Sometimes *it*, the story, is the ar-
ticulation of what we desire that has yet to come to pass" (940).[10] Cullors's
work in *WTCYAT* enacts this belief in the power of story as a form of healing
and transformative justice, and as integral to the work of BLM.[11] Whereas in
Fruitvale Station Oscar Grant's attempts to follow Oprah's self-help narrative
are interrupted by police violence, and whereas in *BTWAM* the indictment of
the self-made narrative is undone by Coates's investments in the Künstlerroman, *WTCYAT* shows the problems to reside in the very structures of self-
making and self-help narratives.

Ultimately, *WTCYAT* presents dominant narratives of self-making not only
as unavailable to Black people, who also often are poor, ill, gender queer, or
otherwise disenfranchised, but also as damaging fictions. In defining humans
in ways premised on the exclusions and cruelties that uphold racial capitalism
and colonialism, these narratives diminish life for all humans. In contrast to
Fruitvale Station, which presents as aspirational though it dashes the hopes of
an Oprah Winfrey–like ascent to self-transformation and success, Cullors and
bandele condemn such forms of narrative humanity as harmful. Their memoir shows how inserting Black people into established forms of narrative humanity intensifies rather than ameliorates racist injustice. Cullors asserts that
Black people are silenced "with false promises that if we just shut the fuck up
and did what we were told, maybe we'd be Oprah or Puffy or LeBron, or, dare
we say it, Barack Obama, when the truth was that the overwhelming majority
of us spent a good portion of our time battling white supremacy" (loc. 2468).
Rather than attempting to invest in hegemonic narratives of (Black) self-
making, *WTCYAT* dismisses them as being ways to *curtail* Black people's
agency. It is worth remembering that BLM began under the Obama presidency, and that Obama's endorsements of these individualist narratives kept
company with his acceleration of the militarization of the police, and often
led him to hold Black men responsible for antiblack violence, even as he also
expressed identification with African Americans killed by the police and those
grieving their loved ones' deaths.[12]

As *WTCYAT* shows the inhumanity of these existing narratives, it also creates forms of narrated humanity that are politically committed—that are inspired
by the BLM movement, and that draw as well on the Black radical tradition.
The phrase "I can't breathe," which runs throughout the memoir, does not only
register the often lethal violence Black people experience and its crushing
impact on Black health and well-being. The memoir's attention to breath also

reminds readers that WTCYAT is a BLM narrative that participates in collective grieving and resistance to this violence. The repetition of Eric Garner's—and what would also be George Floyd's—final words as a police officer choked him to death conveys what it means to live in a world in which Black lives don't matter as it also aligns the memoir with the BLM movement that has made these words into a rallying call, part of a collective assertion that Black lives do indeed matter. (And here it is interesting to note how Frantz Fanon's assertion of solidarity with Indo-Chinese anti-imperialists in *Black Skin, White Masks* has been taken up since 2014 and changed to a first-person plural expression of support for a Black uprising against suffocating conditions. In the wake of Garner's murder, Fanon's proclamation, "It is not because the Indo-Chinese has discovered a culture of his own that he is in revolt. It is because 'quite simply' it was, in more than one way, becoming impossible for him to breathe" (226), has been widely circulated as, "When we revolt it's not for a particular culture. We revolt because, for many reasons, we can no longer breathe."[13] Even as this is a misquotation, taking up Fanon in this way to accompany BLM's "I can't breathe" remains true to the spirit of Fanon's commitment to antiracist, anti-imperialist revolution.) When Cullors reads a report about the Los Angeles County jail's torture techniques, she explains how "I begin to hyperventilate and remember my brother on his knees drinking out of the toilet. My God. // I can't breathe. // We can't breathe" (loc. 1884). As Cullors moves from information she discovers in a news report to a first-person account of her brother's torture, to her own visceral reaction to this memory, and then finally to a collective Black "we," she shows how this suffocating violence impacts not only Eric Garner, and not only prisoners including her brother. She also conveys how it imperils her own ability to breathe, and that of Black people as a collectivity. When Cullors describes first seeing her brother Monte, released after he has been incarcerated for four years, hunched over, swollen from all the medication he is on, wearing "underwear, but no pants, their final fuck you, you ain't human to this man whom I have loved for all of my life," she is "left breathless" (loc. 773). So, too, the lack of help she finds in existing narratives leaves her unable to breathe—she explains that because there are no rulebooks or self-help books *"to guide you through losing a parent to incarceration"* (loc. 552) and because *"Angela Davis hasn't yet asked us Are Prisons Obsolete? and Ruthie Gilmore has not yet done breathtaking research on prisons in California, and beyond"* (loc. 568), *"This is why sometimes you think, I can't breathe. / I can't breathe. / I can't breathe"* (loc. 586).

As the memoir makes clear, the inability to breathe did not begin with Eric Garner, nor does this violence derive only from prisons and police. With their erasure of Black humanity, white supremacy's modes of narrative humanity

can suffocate Black people emotionally as well as physically. That Cullors focuses on breath not only on behalf of those the police state kills, but also in
support of the living, is clear in her explanation of the M4BL's 2020 proposed
Breathe Act: "Yes, we are honoring #EricGarner and #GeorgeFlloyd's [sic] last
words. But this is also for the millions of us who want to breathe freely" ("BLM
Co-founder Patrisse Cullors-Brignac"). To return to Billy-Ray Belcourt's
words at the outset of this chapter, "Freedom is a measure of breathability"
(127). WTCYAT's insistent refrains of "I can't breathe" and its accounts of
breath communicate how the state denies freedom, and life, to Black people.
Its recurring references to breath also convey the life-giving organized resistance in narratives by Angela Davis and Ruth Wilson Gilmore—and by Cullors
and bandele themselves—that, together with the BLM movement, inspire Black
people not only to grieve together, but also to rise up to revolt, in order to
breathe and heal together.

Terrorist v. Citizen

Just as attention to breathing operates in the memoir both to register antiblack
police violence and to participate in BLM's resistance to it, so too the figure
of the terrorist serves these dual purposes. The terrorist/Black subject appears
in narrative humanity as a figure against whom the citizen/human is defined.
Cullors and bandele do not flip but reconfigure this script and its conflations
of human and citizen, and Black and terrorist. In the stories WTCYAT tells, it
is state actors who are the terrorists, and we witness how, after labeling Black
citizens as terrorists, they then use this designation as grounds to dehumanize
and terrorize them. As Cullors and bandele expose this violence, rather than
insisting on Black people's status as citizens or their conformity to dominant
narratives of good citizenship, WTCYAT refuses altogether the human/citizen
conflation that is so central to forms of narrative humanity that dictate who is
deserving of human rights. The memoir instead narrates forms of human being that emerge out of a BLM framework. These acts of narrated humanity
show the policing of Black bodies within the United States to be mutually reinforcing with its acts of imperial violence, and the memoir relays stories of
human becoming and belonging that build global solidarity among those the
US government designates as terrorists, whether they be inside or outside its
borders.[14]

Throughout WTCYAT, Cullors and bandele reveal ways the narrative humanity that produces the Black person as terrorist aligns with narratives that
help promulgate state-sponsored terrorism in other parts of the world. Their
stories bring to life Christina Sharpe's contention that, in public discourses

about terror, Black people "become the *carriers* of terror, terror's embodiment, and not the primary object of terror's multiple enactments; the ground of terror's possibility globally" (*In the Wake*, 15). Cullors and bandele connect the current war on terror to the ongoing exclusion of Black people from the realm of the human/citizen. Even with the end of Jim Crow, they note that these exclusions have persisted, ensuring that "the terrorism that had always been the primary experience of Black people living in the United States continued" (loc. 2453). At the outset of the memoir, they describe how in a petition sent to the White House, those involved in BLM were depicted as terrorists: "We, who in response to the killing of that child [Trayvon Martin], said Black Lives Matter" (loc. 112). Following the memoir's publication, under the presidency of Donald Trump, such representations have only increased. In 2019, the FBI placed BLM activists, labeled as "identity extremists," as a top concern in its counterterrorism priorities (Fearnow). Particularly in the wake of the 2020 uprisings, Black people, men especially, already criminalized and cast as terrorists, have been unable to safely wear masks even when mandated to do so as part of COVID-19 safety protocols.[15] The strength of narratives in which Black activists are perceived as terroristic threats have also been on full display in the 2021 attacks on Cullors and BLM. When the right-wing publications Dirt .com and the *New York Post* covered Cullors's purchase of four houses for family members, not only did they insinuate that Cullors was a grifter engaged in a "real estate buying binge" (Vincent). This coverage also spawned commentary casting her as a terrorist on the basis of owning property—a foundational right of US citizenship—but not, apparently, a legitimate one for Black activists (or Black people more generally?) to exercise. Even as it was Cullors who was being subjected to death threats, readers' incendiary responses to her purchase of a Topanga Canyon home included the following: "Evidently it pays Big to burn, loot, kill in the name of Oppression, and Social Justice. People who live around them look out!"; "Use the BLM playbook. Burn it to the ground"; and "What if she bought it to burn it down and take out Topanga?" (Mark David). Since its publication, in other words, *WTCYAT* has only gained in relevance for its insights into how, in dominant modes of narrative humanity, protesting or refusing exclusion from the rights of US citizenship only confirms Black people's status as terrorists, thereby legitimating their subjection to terrorizing violence.

Through the global framework afforded by attention to the figure of the terrorist, *WTCYAT* shows how being labeled as a terrorist leads to being terrorized—and deprived of human rights and citizenship status—not only for Black activists, but also for Black people who are poor and/or sick. The memoir situates Cullors's own story in relation to this international context. In "Zero

Dark Thirty," a chapter titled after the movie by the same name, Cullors describes how the police perceive her brother Monte as a terrorist when he is suffering from mania. With this chapter title, Cullors and bandele liken the police's relentless pursuit of Cullors's brother to the US war on terror and to the hunt for Osama bin Laden. After the police tase Monte and charge him with terrorism for getting into a fender bender with a white woman, they put him in solitary confinement, starve him, and deny him his medication. Cullors says of her brother's treatment, "torture is terrorism" (loc. 1855). Abu Ghraib's human rights violations, she asserts, originated on US soil: "The skills to torture people were honed in this nation on people who were not terrorists. They were the victims of terrorism" (loc. 1869). Through connecting US human rights abuses in the war on terror to those leveled against Black Americans, Cullors and bandele show how discourses of terrorism serve as a deadly way to deny any recognition of citizenship or, by extension, humanity to Black people who either deliberately or not defy the societal norms on which white supremacist structures and capitalist and colonial agendas depend.

The memoir powerfully calls on readers to contend with how policing is not a system that offers Black people protection and safety, but one that subjects them to state terror with what Colin Dayan describes as "casual but calculated disregard" ("Can't Breathe"). During one of the memoir's central moments, when Cullors is living with her then-husband Mark Anthony in a cottage that is part of an artists' cooperative village, the police invade their home. Describing how he is "yanked out of bed by armed men dressed in riot gear, who possess no warrant," she asks readers, "How is this different from tactics used by the SS, the KGB, the Tonton Macoutes? And who is the real criminal, the real terrorist, and how will they be held accountable?" (loc. 2299). In posing such questions, Cullors draws Black readers into collective conversation as she also invites non-Black readers into her intimate domestic space and calls on us to contend with forms of state terror that have dehumanized Black people for centuries, and that require accountability and action. Rather than tell a story that inserts Black Americans into established pathways of good citizenship, WTCYAT characterizes the United States as a police state indistinguishable from the most brutal of regimes, in which the true terrorists are its rights-bearing and most powerful citizens. Cullors and bandele then enlist readers to align with those whom the state designates as terrorists.

The memoir's focus on what it means to be called a terrorist is not necessarily the most obvious way to address how systemically the United States casts Black people outside the status of human and citizen. More common racist appellations might be "criminal," "animal," "gangster," "mobster," "looter," or "thug." By choosing to foreground how the state defines Black people as terrorists, Cullors and bandele reinforce BLM's commitment to approaching US police violence within a global framework. From its inception, BLM organizers have acted in solidarity with international liberation struggles. And it is this commitment that ensures their designation as terrorists.

BLM's solidarity with Palestine has been especially noteworthy—and the memoir's focus on the figure of the terrorist bolsters this solidarity even as Palestine is largely absent from Cullors's story. Black-Palestinian solidarity dates at least back to the Third World Liberation movements of the late 1960s and the 1970s.[16] It derives from the understanding that Palestinians' resistance to Zionism and apartheid are similar or analogous to Black people's struggles against white supremacy and apartheid. So, too, this solidarity is based on articulated struggles against what Jewish Voice for Peace has described in their program "Deadly Exchange" as the direct interconnections that exist between the United States and Israel as sites of settler colonialism ("About Deadly Exchange"). The solidarity that has emerged between BLM and Palestine has gained momentum, in 2014 and then again in 2020, in response to what Grace Lee Boggs and James Lee Boggs call "the clock of the world." The summer of 2014 decisively marked BLM's shift from a hashtag to a movement as people converged in Ferguson to share grief and protest the police murder of Michael Brown. (Distinguishing between the two, Alicia Garza insists, "Hashtags do not start movements—people do" [*The Purpose of Power*, xi]). That same summer, Israel launched another offensive against Palestine in its ongoing settler colonial project, including laying siege to the Gaza strip with patterned but still shocking brutality. Israel bombed Gaza for 51 days, ravaging its infrastructure and killing an estimated 2,200 people, over 500 of them children. As BLM gathered strength and protesters in Ferguson came face to face with a militarized police force, Palestinians tweeted advice from the West Bank about how to recover from tear gas, and Black and Palestinian activists exchanged messages of support, joined BLM and BDS protests, and connected the militarization of US police forces in the United States (often trained in Israel and using Israeli weaponry) to the Israeli military's genocidal attack on Gaza, noting the US funding and munitions supply sustaining this siege and Israel's decades-long occupation of Palestine (Erakat, "Geographies of Intimacy").[17] Then, in May 2020, the US police murder of George Floyd that sparked uprisings over racist injustice coincided with events in Israel/Palestine: Prime Minister Benjamin Netanyahu's announced plans, in coordination with the Trump administration, to annex the West Bank; Israeli soldiers' gunning down of Eyad Hallaq, an autistic man on his way to his special-needs school in occupied East Jerusalem; and then the Israeli military's extrajudicial killing of Ahmad Erekat (cousin of Noura Erakat, a US-based scholar/activist known for her solidarity with BLM), as Erekat was crossing a West Bank checkpoint on his way to pick up his sister from a beauty salon on her wedding day. These conjunctures led to renewed and deeper forms of BLM-Palestine solidarity. These were evident in the spate of events that, shaped by the COVID-19 pandemic and the turn to online events, have taken the form of webinars attended by hundreds and sometimes thousands, plus actions on the streets of Palestine in support of BLM—and, at BLM protests, expressions of solidarity with Palestine. In the contexts of societies in which ordinary policing poses a greater risk to Palestinian and Black lives than does the Coronavirus (Wrigley-Field), people have risked viral infection to fight even deadlier interconnected and allied forms of oppression.

Cullors has played an important role in supporting BLM's solidarity with Palestine. In July 2014, she and other BLM organizers participated in a ten-day delegation to Palestine, co-organized by the Dream Defenders and the Black Youth Project (Khalek, "Watch"). During her time on the West Bank, Cullors coordinated a flash mob in Nazareth at which delegates danced dabke to Sweet Honey in the Rock's "Ella's Song" (fig. 3). While singing "We who believe in freedom cannot rest," participants issued a call to support the Palestinian-led Boycott, Divestment and Sanctions (BDS) campaign. The Dream Defenders then released a video of the flash mob, described by the filmmaker, Susanne Rostock, as "a breath of history." The M4BL also endorsed this campaign at no small cost, given how widely BDS is misperceived to be

Figure 3. Still from Nazareth flash mob video organized by Patrisse Cullors during the Dream Defenders' and Black Youth Project's delegation to Palestine. Cullors appears to the right of Cherrell Brown (*center*). (Photo credit: Thorsten Thielow / Susanne Rostock)

antisemitic. Like the 2014 "When I See Them, I See Us" (a video produced by Noura Erakat, which includes the Dream Defenders delegation among its sixty Palestinian and Black artists and activists), this flash mob video insists on the interrelatedness of Black and Palestinian struggles against US and Israeli state terror as it conjoins Black and Palestinian cultural expression.

Through its attention to the figure of the terrorist, Cullors's memoir continues to link antiblack and anti-Palestinian racism—and the BLM movement to the Palestinian and other global liberation struggles. Angela Davis's foreword to the memoir, in which she discusses the rhetoric of terrorism, immediately positions the life narratives of Cullors and of BLM in this international context that is simultaneously critical and revolutionary in intent. Davis's lifelong work for Black liberation and prison abolition, her autobiography that stands as a predecessor to Cullors's (along with the autobiographical writings of James Baldwin, Elaine Brown, Audre Lorde, Assata Shakur, and Malcolm X), as well as her commitment to connecting Black and Palestinian struggles, make her a fitting choice to introduce the memoir of a movement profoundly influenced by Davis's decades of writing and activism. So, too, does that fact that since 1970, because of her work for Black liberation, Davis has carried the designation, initiated by President Richard Nixon, of being a "dangerous terrorist." In her foreword and in her many public appearances with Cullors, Davis presents WTCYAT as a work of importance not only to prison abolitionism but also to coalitional and conjunctural freedom struggles, and to a genealogy of Black radicalism that the state perceives as terrorist. In her foreword, she notes that the memoir's title "asks the reader to engage critically with the rhetoric of terrorism—not only, for example, the way in which it has occasioned and justified a global surge in Islamophobia, and how it has impeded thoughtful reflection on the continued occupation of Palestine, but also how this rhetoric attempts to discredit antiracist movements in the United States" (loc. 53). This foreword establishes the memoir not as one directed to a white liberal readership, but rather as one that, like Davis's own autobiography, participates in a Black radical tradition with a long history of commitment to international solidarity.

In the memoir's body, Cullors and bandele tell stories that unite different freedom struggles. In Ferguson, when Cullors describes how she stands shoulder to shoulder with Black women as she faces tanks and machine guns, she states, "We have already learned from people in Palestine to douse our eyes with milk, not water, when attacked with tear gas" (loc. 2546). Here, the strength, fortitude, and intimacy Cullors experiences as she stands with Black women facing down state terror extends to include Palestinians from across the world, who are also, and in entangled ways, being subjected to state terror. The memoir demonstrates how if structures of imperialism connect settler states, so too, those who are called terrorists for opposing the terror of these structures establish ties, as they find their grounding in forms of love and care that are based on intimate relations and material practices. Cullors and bandele make this perspective even more explicit in the YA edition, which includes numerous annotations in the margins in a "handwritten" font, quoting Black revolutionary thinkers including Davis, June Jordan, Huey Newton, Assata Shakur, and Malcolm X. In this way, *WTCYAT* draws on and participates in the work of BLM and the movement's predecessors.

"Magnitude and Bond": Solidarity without Borders and Queer Kinship

Cullors and bandele have no interest in seeking recognition of (good) citizenship as a way for Black people to counter the terrorism they regularly experience. Their memoir disregards forms of narrative humanity that, as they naturalize the nation-state and conflate the human and citizen, subject Black people to persecution, torture, and ill health. Instead, *WTCYAT* activates forms of narrated humanity that emerge from a BLM framework, and that refuse the nationalist framework and the citizen/human versus Black/terrorist binary that narrative humanity naturalizes. Whereas Coates, even as he directly addresses his son, works within forms of narrative humanity that speak to a (white) mainstream liberal readership, Cullors and bandele constitute their readers by working within a framework that emerges from BLM and other collective, intersectional, and solidarity-based political movements. This framework, in which the nation-state becomes obsolete, extends from one's most intimate relations, to chosen community, to global solidarity formations, and then ultimately skyward to the stars from which all humans come. In this way, the memoir helps materialize alternative ways of being human founded on radical interrelationality, as it makes its Black readers its primary but not exclusive audience.

In other words, Cullors and bandele do not look to tell a story of model citizenry and social ascent, but rather of community building and societal *dissent*. Such a story requires deliberately political as well as deeply personal forms of narrated humanity that approach Black readers with abolitionist love rather than trying to persuade non-Black readers in need of such an education that Black lives matter. The pronouns in the memoir—often first-person plural or second-person—extend in concentric circles beginning with Cullors, to Cullors and bandele, to loved ones, to Black activists, to Black people more generally, to any readers willing to enter the world Cullors lives in and the movement she cocreates to survive and thrive. As when readers are invited into the intimacy of Cullors's and Mark Anthony's bedroom when it is stormed by the police in riot gear—"Close your eyes and come close. // Try to imagine this with me: // You are a graduate student whose work is in Chinese medicine . . ." (loc. 2299)—rather than persuade readers, "I am just like you," the memoir instead reverses that process. This intimate mode of address, which begins with those who are Black and most vulnerable, is at the heart of the BLM movement and its understanding that when Black lives matter, all lives will matter, and that this mattering cannot be individual but interrelational and practiced through collective Black-centering forms of care.

As the memoir focuses on Cullors's most intimate family relationships, *WTCYAT* tells a story that is at once recognizable, and one that defies the modes of narrative humanity that exclude Black people from good citizenship, and indeed the realm of the human. *WTCYAT* follows established pathways for a life story by giving a roughly chronological account of Cullors that moves from her childhood and attention to her birth family, to the relations she establishes as an adult, including getting married and having a child. However, the memoir breaks with forms of narrative humanity that, in upholding antiblack formulations of the human and the citizen, either insist that "model" Black families can look just like white ones, or else posit Black families as broken or pathological, as less than human and undeserving of love, owing to some combination of absent fathers, poverty, drug addiction, and crime. In the memoir, even when present, these conditions do not lessen the value of Cullors's family members or the bonds that connect them to one another. This radical revaluing necessitates new narratives. As Cullors states in relation to her birth father, Gabriel, a man she never lived with and did not even know of in early childhood, and who, until his premature death in a homeless shelter, battled addiction, "We are a father and daughter determined to write our own history" (loc. 1204). This history she/they write is not one of brokenness, of lack, or of Gabriel as a "deadbeat dad." It is a story of abundance, love, and Black men's tenderness, including from her two fathers, but not in a way that idealizes heartbreaking conditions. Cullors does not find her "hardworking parents" failing when she says her survival depended on the Black Panthers and their Breakfast for Children program (loc. 1469). Nor does she represent her father's cycling in and out of drug use, or Monte's illness, as diminishing their value. When Cullors finds her "precious father" relapsed, "high as fuck and drunk," she says, "I refuse to turn away. If he matters to me at all then he has to matter to me at every moment" (loc. 1173). The memoir's stories of Black lives that matter do not require recuperating Black lives into the familiar narrative arcs of redemption, conversion, progress, respectability, societal success, or good citizenship. Nor do they depend on dominant society and its narratives that determine which lives matter. And the survival of the family members is enabled not by the state, or the government-granted opportunities that depend on citizenship status. Survival depends on the care that comes from radical Black organizing—for Cullors, starting with the Black Panthers.

As with her father's drug addiction, Cullors approaches Monte's mental illness not as a personal deficit, but as an index of the cruelty that structures the United States and its narratives that make her brother's life without value. In participating in Kenneth Paul Rosenberg's 2019 documentary film *Bedlam*, as Cullors tells of Monte's own and her family's struggles with his mental illness, she shares a diary entry in which she states that Monte "really is perfect to me." She also describes how when he is diagnosed, she "refused to let it tell a different story than I already had about my brother" (Rosenberg). As in *Bedlam*, in *WTCYAT* her fight for her brother's survival involves creating alternatives to the narratives that render him not only imperfect, but undeserving of life. She states, "Our nation, one big damn *Survivor* reality nightmare. I am filled with a sense of rage and a call to action at the idea that my brother, my Monte, is considered someone disposable to these people" (loc. 1422). For her and her family members, Cullors explains, "Monte was never disposable. Not him nor the measure of his great heart or beautiful broken brain, which perhaps wrestles so mightily because my God, how the fuck does any of this make sense?" (loc. 1422). With this reference to *Survivor*, *WTCYAT* indicates how staying alive in the United States requires killing off or beating out those of greater physical or emotional vulnerability. Here it bears noting that despite their claims to being spontaneous and unscripted, reality shows follow conventions of narrative humanity, be they those of self-making or improvement (as in weight-loss shows), marriage plots (as in dating shows), or "survival of the fittest" (as in shows like *Survivor*). It is precisely the values of competitive individualism and domination encoded in scripts like *Survivor* that Cullors and bandele reject in favor of a different kind of survival story, a love story of family and community members who try their best to help each other stay alive in a white supremacist world.

Through her story, Cullors shows how those who do not survive matter to their loved ones, in ways that defy the usual metrics and the dominant expressions of kinship that determine human value and flourishing. In *WTCYAT*, a lack of food and of time with parents, a psychotic brother rolled out of the courthouse on a gurney yelling for his mother, a birth father with drug addiction who missed his daughter's childhood—none of these indicate a deficit of love. Instead, they evidence the debility—to draw on Jasbir Puar's use of this term to describe disabling conditions imposed on groups of oppressed people—that comes with being Black. And rather than brokenness or failure, Cullors asserts her family's strength and unity: "My mother wove us together, my brothers, sister and I, into a tight and strong complex quilt and she called it us and it was, and it is, us./Magnitude and Bond" (822). The quilt, with its Black womanist resonances, serves in *WTCYAT* as an apt metaphor for the cohesion and protective warmth achieved through her family members' combination of labor and love. So, too, by evoking Gwendolyn Brooks's 1970 ode to Paul Robeson here—

> we are each other's
> harvest:
> we are each other's
> business:
> we are each other's
> magnitude and bond. (Brooks)

—Cullors and bandele draw on a history of Black artistic expression and activism as they locate via forebearers including Brooks "what we now commonly call self-care" (Danticat) within the fabric of family, unconventionally formulated.

WTCYAT tells a story of creating a chosen family—one that defies heteronorms and extends outward into the creation of a beloved community that does not replace or compete with, but supports, her birth family. The vocabulary Cullors and bandele draw on in telling this story comes out of movement politics. Phrases such as "intentional family," "chosen community," "accountability," "holding space," and "uplift" figure prominently. So, too, Cullors's story articulates with even as it is not contained within the tropes and narratives that come out of contemporary queer cultural politics—including but not limited to BLM. From its origins story, in its organizational structures, and in the writings about BLM, the movement emerges in large part as a love story that puts at its center queer Black women and their circles of kinship and care. When, in July 2013, an all-white jury acquitted George Zimmerman for the 2012 killing of seventeen-year-old Trayvon Martin, #BLM began as Alicia Garza's Facebook post titled "A Love Note to Black People" in which she said: "black people. I love you. I love us. Our lives matter."[18] Patrisse Cullors replied: "#BlackLivesMatter." They then enlisted Tometi for her expertise in social media, to spread this message. In Garza's posting, and in the tellings of BLM's genesis and continued life, the focus on nurturing the love that Black people have for one another has persisted, in a way that explicitly attends to intersectional identities and makes room for the most vulnerable of Black people, emphasizing the need for Black people to create communities of care and accountability for one another and for themselves.

If BLM originates as a love note, as a BLM memoir *WTCYAT* tells many love stories that expand upon Garza's message. These include romances between

Cullors and partners who are men, women, and gender queer. In forging these relationships and in working through their difficulties, Cullors conforms neither strictly to queer nor to hegemonic heterosexual codes, formulas, or story lines. After coming out and claiming her love for women, she tells of unexpectedly falling in love with her friend Mark Anthony, and of coming to marry him as she finds with him a love "we could not have predicted but always imagined. A love that rocks us and a love that holds us" (loc. 1846). When their marriage ends, she describes their divorce not as a failure but as a transition that, although painful, allows them to grow while sustaining their connection "as family," explaining, "We know it just has to be family in a new way" (loc. 2658). Although she describes behaviors that show Mark Anthony's adherence to heteronorms, Cullors focuses instead on the "love not ordinary" (loc. 1846) that connects them and on the ways that they "still soar." When she meets and—at nine months pregnant—marries her gender queer partner Future (Janaya Khan), a BLM activist living in Toronto, they parent Shine. At their wedding, she writes, "Among those gathered in the crowd is Mark Anthony, my family forever, my cherished friend. He takes me in his arms" (loc. 2845). The love stories in the memoir are plural, many-gendered, and not premised on ownership or adherence to "happily-ever-after" scripts. Nor do they depend on refusing forms such as marriage that queer activists sometimes dismiss. Cullors not only enters into marriages; she also tells of becoming ordained so she can marry same-sex couples, as well as prisoners and any others without legal rights to marry (loc. 2121). Her description of fostering these forms of kinship echoes with those of the BLM group BYP100, and their mobilization of a Black queer feminist approach "to create space for compassion, patience, and gentleness," and their choice "to collectively center the least of these, people who are forgotten and discarded" (Green et al., 924). As Cullors overrides the state's limitations on who counts as legal or deserving of kinship, she acts in concert with BLM's abolitionist politics, envisioning ways to attend to the spiritual, emotional, and material well-being of those whose humanity the state denies.[19]

The memoir's expansive understandings of kinship and community, which are the heart of BLM's political vision and activism, involve creating forms of narrated humanity that draw on queer, abolitionist, and radical Black politics in forging a future in which Black people can live and love freely. As Mary Hooks, codirector of SONG and cofounder of Black Lives Matter Atlanta, puts this, "Black lives matter is an old prayer spoken in new tongues, articulated in a hashtag" (Wortham). Cullors shows her chosen relationships and communities of care as at once necessary to collective Black survival, and rooted in a

Black past. When her brother's PTSD takes the form of drinking from the toilet (loc. 1614), a loving and steady circle of Black men are there to catch him. Cullors presents this moment as "the image of Black men that lives in my head" (loc. 1646). She offers it to her readers as an example of community control, and a pathway to reviving a Black past to survive an antiblack present and create a Black future:

> . . . this is what community control looks like
> This is what the love of Black men looks like.
> This is what our Black yesterday once looked like.
> And I think: If we are to survive this is what our future must look like.
>   (loc. 1646)

By sharing this image that "lives in her head," she unites the personal and the political, and joins together past and present, to embody an abolitionist politics and to create forms of narrated humanity that will carry into a future in which Black lives matter.

As an adult, the various relationships Cullors chooses are with those who share her politics, and her romantic relationships further rather than strain against her activism, as does the work of bringing up a child. These relationships are integral to her commitment to a future in which all Black people thrive. She looks to Emma Goldman as she tries out experimental forms of love that put into practice the lesson "that relationships do not come before community liberation, that possessiveness and jealousy can undo the best of us" (loc. 1765). Thus, her aspirations and the love she seeks are often expressed in a collective first-person plural. She says of Black people, "We deserve love. Thick, full-bodied and healthy. Love" (loc. 2359). Her vision for BLM, of a global Black family that practices accountability, empathy, liberation, justice, and peace, is seamless with the love stories she tells that involve creating intergenerational community that is safe for women, queer and transgender people, and children.

The metaphor of building the BLM movement out from "our Black Lives Matter-Los Angeles DNA" (loc. 2326) is emblematic of the memoir's refusal of divisions between "genetic" families, intentional family, chosen community, and BLM as a political movement. In the introduction to Cullors's *An Abolitionist's Handbook*, Prentis Hemphill remarks how "the transformation of systems happens in our most intimate places as much as anywhere else" (Hemphill, xvi). BLM is indeed a movement that starts close to/at home, in one's families, neighborhoods, and communities, and it does not ever move beyond them in a vision that is also global. In keeping with this expansive understanding of

family that BLM inspires, *WTCYAT* concludes by Cullors refusing a distinction between her own child, Shine, and the children of other mothers:

> If ever someone calls my child a terrorist, if they call any of the
> children in my life terrorists, I will hold my child, any child, closer to
> me and I will explain that terrorism is being stalked and surveilled
> simply because you are alive. And terrorism is being put in solitary
> confinement and starved and beaten. And terrorism is not being able
> to feed your children despite working three jobs. And terrorism is not
> having a decent school or place to play. I will tell them that what
> freedom looks like, what democracy looks like, in the push for and
> realization of justice, dignity and peace.
>
> And I will say that to my precious Shine, or Malik, or Nisa, or Nina,
> or any of the children and young people we cherish and lift up, that
> you are brilliant beings of light. You have the power to shape-shift not
> only yourselves but the whole of the world. You, each one, are en-
> dowed with gifts you don't even yet know, and you, each one, are what
> love and the possibility of a world in which our lives truly matter looks
> like. (loc. 2989)

Kinship in *WTCYAT* involves Cullors caring not only for her own son and bandele's daughter Nisa and other beloveds. In the shift from first-person singular
to second-person and first-person plural, Cullors also conveys care for all the
children in her life, in a form of address that is at once intimate, often one-to-
one, and also far-reaching in its embrace of Black women's activist mothering
as part of "a praxis of politicized care" (Story, 892).[20]

WTCYAT further situates Cullors and her kin not only as human and rooted
in a Black past, but also with lives that matter in ways that exceed human-made
parameters of time and space—and structures of race and white supremacy.
In the above passage, Cullors and bandele, looking to the future, reference
children as "brilliant beings of light" with shape-shifting power. Starting with
the introduction, "We Are Stardust," this description is part of a constellation
of assembled images, in which Cullors and bandele represent Cullors and those
who come before and after her not as terrorists, and not only as human, but
also as made of stars, in ways that are at once scientifically grounded (Lotzof)
and visionary in approach to the past and future. Describing how she comes
from a line of "human beings legislated as not human beings," Cullors says
with respect to her ancestors: "What could they be but stardust, these people
who refused to die, who refused to accept the idea that their lives did not matter,
that their children's lives did not matter?" (loc. 3089). When she names her
and Future's son Shine, she situates him in this celestial framework in a joy-

ous and optimistic counterpart to Coates's also epic but resoundingly pessi-mistic vision of Black life. WTCYAT connects humans not to nation-states but to one another, and to a more cosmic sense of what it means to be alive and interrelated, to belong to an entire universe.[21]

As Cullors and bandele narrate Cullors's past through the prism of that which BLM makes possible, they situate the memoir at the intersections of a Black past, present, and future, in a way that makes clear their own—and BLM's—universality. The memoir's vision resonates with Je Naé Taylor's ac-count of the work done by BYP100 and BLM, in "holding the hands of the elders and the unborn. Standing in the middle of the clay and the sky" (Kai Green et al., 928). So, too, in WTCYAT Cullors and Future create a present and a future in which their child and all children can shine like the stars that, in another lifetime, they were/are. Cullors and bandele capture in memoir form the yearning for Black power that exists in Coogler's and Coates's turn to Black Panther as a superhero story, but theirs is not a longing rooted in fan-tasy, nor is it one that requires abjuring the Black Panther Party. WTCYAT's vision for the future, already taking shape in the present, does not require extra-human scientifically derived superpowers, or travel to another planet. Its forms of narrated humanity build on a radical Black past and historically rooted present-day solidarities that understand the power of love and connection to bring new futures into being, and to make a world in which Black people, and all humans, can flourish and experience joy.

Telling Memoirist from Memoir and Movement

During the spring 2022 academic year, I was teaching a graduate class on "Genres of Protest" when the *Washington Examiner* broke a story about BLMGNF's delayed 2020 tax filings, and the 2021 right-wing attacks on Cul-lors resumed. As we began our reading of the YA version of WTCYAT that February, students were following the smear campaigns against Cullors and the BLMGNF, as well as BLM responses to them. (There was particular hi-larity over Khan's response on Instagram to what they called the *New York Post's* "salacious" attacks on them for the BLMGNF-facilitated purchase of the Toronto "mansion" by Black Lives Matter Canada: as Khan leans into the camera, they explain in an ironic, drawn-out, drag-inflected tone, "It's an ART CENTER. For queer and trans people!" [Khan]). In our discussions of the attacks coming from far-right quarters—as well as the sometimes-angry critiques from within BLM about the BLMGNF's, Cullors's, and other high-profile BLM activists' priorities and decision-making—student activists brought up the complexities that inhere in movement organizing. We talked about the inevitable challenges of occupying leadership positions, and of the interpersonal and political tensions that exist within any political community. We discussed the difficulties of addressing these dynamics in ways that do not undermine a movement; the drawbacks and necessity of being paid for activist work; and the problems that can arise when radical organizations and activists experience mainstream success and receive large amounts of money. We also observed how the timing of the renewed racist attacks on Cullors corresponded with the publication of *An Abolitionist's Handbook* in an attempt to undermine the growing popularity of abolitionist demands, including calls to defund the police. However, we spent most of our time diving into *WTCYAT*, which we all found inspiring for the ways it supports the revolutionary internationalist vision and abolitionist dreams of the BLM movement. In other words, our analysis of Cullors and bandele's memoir was not derailed by the public debates surrounding Cullors and the BLMGNF.

Our continuing appreciation for *WTCYAT* markedly contrasts to the ways that, as discussed in chapter 2 of *Narrating Humanity*, the controversies surrounding Abdulrahman Zeitoun upended *Zeitoun*'s representation of him and undermined Eggers's efforts to combat Islamophobia and condemn the war on terror. In large part, of course, this difference derives from the fact that Zeitoun was not being targeted by white supremacists working to delegitimate a liberatory political movement. The scandal that attended *Zeitoun* postpublication resulted from his being convicted of acts of domestic violence. But also of significance are Eggers's investments in making his hero conform to textbook forms of narrative humanity that idealize heteropatriarchy, racial capitalism, and American exceptionalism. *Zeitoun* could not sustain its political objectives when its eponymous hero exited Eggers's text and exposed the ugly underbelly of what it means to be an ideal husband and American citizen.

The controversies surrounding Cullors and the BLMGNF, on the other hand, do not disrupt *WTCYAT*'s power as a BLM memoir. The right-wing trolls and media out to delegitimate BLM and dehumanize Cullors rely on racial capitalist and heteropatriarchal forms of narrative humanity (outrage over Black women and organizations owning property, the casting of Black activists as criminals and terrorists) that *WTCYAT* and the BLM movement resist and provide alternatives to. In addition, the memoir makes room for the messiness of movements and lives as it values abolitionist forms of love, accountability, and restorative justice. In its accounts of kinship and community, Cullors and bandele do not depend on Cullors's or her loved ones' perfect conformity to narrative formulas or movement ideals. The memoir's acts of narrated humanity leave room for making mistakes, for messing up and then mending relationships, for remaking the world alongside others who are rising up in ways that are not fixed or known, but yet-to-be-discovered or imagined. For this reason, as with the BLM movement, the memoir's life continues beyond the controversies and contestations that center on Cullors and the BLMGN.

In the next chapter, I turn to Steven Salaita's *Uncivil Rites*. Whereas Cullors and bandele's memoir precedes the public attacks that target Cullors, Salaita's memoir responds to charges that associate him with terrorism and incivility. In ways I will be exploring, *Uncivil Rites* tells a story that refutes and also refuses to be contained within formulas of narrative humanity that underwrite Zionist assaults on Salaita's character. Through acts of narrated humanity, Salaita instead forges inter/national solidarity and imagines ways of human being and belonging that are not circumscribed by nation-states and their violent exclusions.

As also chronicled in *WTCYAT*, and as evident in Black-Palestinian texts and events discussed in this chapter (e.g., "When I See Them," Cullors's and the Dream Defenders' dabke flash mob), what we see in *Uncivil Rites* are people engaged in liberation movements linking arms, conjoining their freedom struggles, and addressing one another while shrugging off narratives that have long represented those resisting state terror as terrorists. As we will see in chapter 4, what is perhaps the most threatening to those who weaponize narrative humanity is how powerfully the narratives emerging out of radical political movements show resistance to oppression to be fueled not by hatred or reactionary violence, but by commitments to freedom and justice, and bonds of love, kinship, and community. This is the story that *When They Call You a Terrorist: A Black Lives Memoir* tells, and this is the story in which Steven Salaita also participates.

4

"Nursing Visions of the Unimagined"

BDS and Steven Salaita's World-Making Narratives of Fatherhood, Affiliation, and Freedom

There is a huge gap between us and our enemies—not just in ability but in morality, culture, sanctity of life, and conscience. . . . [Palestinians] are people who don't belong to our continent, to our world, but actually belong to a different galaxy.

—ISRAELI PRESIDENT MOSHE KATSAV
(QTD. IN STEVEN SALAITA, *ANTI-ARAB RACISM*)

For in the end, revolution, like its counterpart, decolonization, isn't about reimagining the world as we currently know it, but about nursing visions of the unimagined, just out of view but always there, demanding penury, providing abundance, somewhere to the left.

—STEVEN SALAITA, "PALESTINE IN THE REVOLUTIONARY IMAGINATION"

On January 4, 2014, just before going abroad to participate in a conference on transnational American studies, Steven Salaita posted Jack Johnson's "Upside Down" video to his Facebook page. Salaita wrote, "Listening to this with my little boy before departure to Beirut. He adores the video. I do, too, and think it's a lovely song. Hate being away from him!" ("Listening to this"). In this music video, Johnson, at home in Hawai'i, walking along an oceanside ridge barefoot, slips on a banana peel planted by a mischievous monkey (Curious George), and tumbles into the ocean. Once underwater, Johnson is led through an animated ocean world by the little monkey. When they come upon a lush land filled with flowers and trees, animal friends greet him and dance with delight as Johnson sings to them. Strumming his guitar, Johnson lets them know he wants "to turn this whole world upside down" ("who's to say

144

what's impossible?"). The song is about imagination ("as my mind begins to spread its wings / There's no stopping curiosity") and love ("I'll share this love I find with everyone"). As night falls, Johnson and the little monkey gaze at the stars, which meld into ocean as Johnson surfaces up out of the water and back into "reality." In this video, Jack Johnson, a musician beloved for his up-beat music, his respect for Native Hawaiian culture, and his advocacy for children's well-being and environmental justice, frees Curious George from his colonial contexts, conjuring a world in which there is balance between humans and other animals, water, earth, and sky.

Salaita's post can be seen as a father sharing a video that borders on senti-mentality as it upholds uncontroversial values of curiosity, creativity, and kind-ness. Yet taken in context, it gestures toward Salaita's radical humanism. Zionist vilifications of Salaita as a terrorist propelled him into national attention dur-ing the summer of 2014 after he tweeted his outrage over the Israeli military's rampage through the West Bank and all-out assault on Gaza. But if Israel's defenders brought infamy to Salaita through distorted reporting of his angry tweets that would soon be weaponized to fire him from a tenured position, those of us who have worked with him and know the range of his work ap-preciate him for his generative humanism. As a prodigiously prolific scholar and a public intellectual, as a passionate teacher, as a regular contributor to social media, and as an organizer for the US Campaign for the Academic and Cultural Boycott of Israel (USACBI), Salaita gives expression to this human-ism through wonder-filled stories about and for his son; and also through his acerbic responses to Zionism, settlerism, racial capitalism, the corporate acad-emy, and the hypocrisies that attend liberal or "progressive" politics, particu-larly those that are, as he puts it in *Uncivil Rites*, "RbI," or "regressive because of Israel" (93). From this vantage point, I viewed Salaita's "Upside Down" post as resonant with his belief in a revolutionary politics premised on love and imagination. It also seemed a fitting companion for work he was on his way to do at the Center for American Studies and Research (CASAR) at the Ameri-can University of Beirut (AUB), participating with scholars working at the in-tersections of Native American and Indigenous studies, American studies, and Middle East studies in building what Salaita calls "inter/nationalism," or "mu-tually affirmational national struggles with interlocking destinies" ("Decolo-nization: Survival").

Given the savagery of the Zionist attacks that sabotaged Salaita's career just months after that CASAR conference, I find it bittersweet to think back to this shared father-son moment, but I also begin with it because it speaks to this chapter's concerns with the contextual nature of what counts as radi-cal, political, and revolutionary. Memoirs work within a tradition of liberal

humanism insofar as they represent their authors as complex individuals constituted in relation to their time and place. And yet, in the Palestinian context—if not, as previous chapters show, uniquely so—such uses of narrative
humanity are not merely liberal. Because they counter the dehumanization
on which the Israeli state depends, Palestinian memoirs do not merely open a
multicultural umbrella. Almost all of narrative humanity's pathways cast Palestinians as terrorists, as inhuman others, and as security threats.[1] In such a
world, for a Palestinian father to narrate his nurturing love for his son and for
other children, and to express the joy of imagining and then entering a world
animated by kindness, care, and harmony ("nursing visions of the unimagined,
just out of view but always there" [Salaita, "Palestine in the Revolutionary
Imagination"]), counts as a world-upending, decolonial practice.

In *Uncivil Rites: Palestine and the Limits of Academic Freedom* (2015), a
memoir catalyzed by his 2014 firing from a tenured position at the University
of Illinois Urbana-Champaign (UIUC), Salaita continues this love story to
and for his son—and for all children, including those under siege in Palestine.
He responds to interconnected issues surrounding his firing: the colonial and
racist violence inherent to institutional demands for "civility"; the dehumanization of Palestinians and the Palestinian exception to academic freedom
and free speech; the undue influence of Zionism in the United States and the
criminalization of the Boycott, Divestment and Sanctions (BDS) movement;
the white supremacy and militarism of US and Israeli settler colonial societies;
the corporatization of the university and its systematic undermining of Indigenous studies and solidarities. Through telling a family story, Salaita mobilizes
the liberal tenets of narrative humanity toward transformative ends and
advances the BDS movement and the Palestinian struggle for justice. Not
simply anticolonial but also decolonial, his memoir supersedes Zionist efforts
to circumscribe his and all Palestinians' life stories.

Accompanying its contextually radical elements of *narrative* humanity are
Salaita's acts of *narrated* humanity. Sometimes contributing to the memoir's
father-son narrative and at other times more explicitly political, these instances
of narrated humanity further Salaita's work to support a free Palestine as a parent, scholar, teacher, member of the USACBI Organizing Collective, and, in
the tradition of Edward Said, intellectual in exile. As his genre-bending
memoir combines autobiographical elements that are profoundly political with
political analysis that is deeply personal, Salaita does not merely expand understandings of the human and the civil. Instead, he reconfigures the human
as he exposes an articulated set of oppressive conditions in the United States
and Palestine/Israel. Through deployments of narrated humanity, Salaita re-

works and provides alternatives to forms of narrative humanity that, in the name of civility, support settler violence. In a post to his website written in response to the Israeli army's execution of beloved Palestinian American journalist Shireen Abu-Akleh on May 11, 2022, Salaita remarked of the endlessness of the settler's violence, "It is the only way he knows how to be a good citizen. And it is the only way, in the end, he can imagine a meaningful existence" ("Why Did Israel Execute Shireen Abu-Akleh?"). Salaita's memoir exposes and refuses such formulations of citizenship—ones that make settlers into what Ali Musleh calls "human-weapon ensembles"—while embracing both a way of being human that is instead based on inter/nationalism and radical forms of empathy and equality.

In the latter part of this chapter, as I explore Salaita's website entries, I look to how this decolonial way of being human comes more sharply into focus once Salaita leaves academe and moves more fully into modes of narrated humanity in which he asserts his newfound freedom. No longer willing to combat a four-continent blacklist, Salaita began work as a school bus driver. He also started a website which frees him to write what and when he wants and to reach out to his large social media following (over 55,000 on Twitter, almost 20,000 on Facebook). In postings to this site, as a father and caretaker of schoolchildren, he continues to extend his filial love to all children, and to tell family stories with elements that increasingly shift them from narrative to narrated humanity. These entries provide glimpses of what a decolonial mode of life writing can look like as they participate in and promulgate Angela Davis's insight that rather than an achieved or achievable destination or state of being, "freedom is a constant struggle."

Before turning to a section on BDS that prepares for my discussion of Salaita's life writing, I want to situate myself in relation to this chapter's concerns. Since participating in 2013 in a faculty development seminar in Palestine, my work has come to include a focus on Palestine. I grew up in a white Jewish home and in a white Christian neighborhood, both Zionist by default. In college, and then as an American Studies and life writing scholar located in Hawai'i, I developed an antipathy to settlerism and Zionism. I contribute what I can to Kanaka Maoli, or Native Hawaiian, decolonial movements, and advocate for the call from Palestinian civil society to boycott Israeli academic institutions. Acting in solidarity for a free Palestine has also involved using the privileges that come with being tenured, Jewish, and white in a university with only a small and ineffective (though vociferous and well-funded!) Zionist presence: to host and teach the work of Palestinian scholars, writers, and activists; to help organize events bringing Palestinians into conversation with Kanaka

Maoli student activists; and to work on academic boycott resolutions and divestment initiatives.

Through these efforts, I have come to know Steve (as I will refer to him in the more personal moments in this chapter) not only as a scholar and leading proponent for BDS, but also as a comrade and friend. The Zionist website *Canary Mission*'s description of me as Steve's "avid supporter" is an attempted aspersion in which I take pride ("Cynthia Franklin"). I began working with Steve when we were both organizing with the Academic and Community Activism Caucus of the American Studies Association (ASA), to pass a Resolution to Boycott Israeli Academic Institutions, which, after years of groundwork, was adopted with overwhelming support from the membership in 2013.[2] In 2013, I also joined the Organizing Collective of USACBI, which included Steve as a member (he has since moved to the USACBI Advisory Board). Based on this work, I was happy to be part of a group that David Lloyd brought together to nominate Steve for the 2016 ASA Angela Davis Award, which recognizes scholars who have made an outstanding contribution to the public good, and to celebrate with Steve and other comrades in Denver when he received this award. I also invited Steve to Hawai'i in 2017 for "Decolonial November" (more on this later), a visit that inspired students to join the University of Hawai'i's Students and Faculty for Justice in Palestine organization (SFJP@UH) and participate in ongoing inter/national exchanges. Steve stands as a beacon for me and students and faculty I work with. His politics are principled, uncompromising, and courageous. He also is kind, decent, and compassionate. Steve exemplifies how it is possible to uphold humanism and value the human in ways that work within, against, and beyond narrative humanity, in practices of decolonial love, and in collective pursuit of freedom and justice.

In attending to how Steve does this through genre-mixing engagements with both narrative and narrated humanity, and how his involvement in the BDS movement informs his writings, my commitments to him and to BDS are personal and political. They take this book into a more explicit crossing over from literary, cultural, and life writing studies into personal narrative, and engaged scholarship. In part, I attribute this move to what I have learned from Steve. In his attention to form as well as content, as his work advocates for better ways of being human, it not only reinvigorates the maxim that the personal is political—it also illuminates ways the political is personal. In this chapter, by blurring the lines between life writing studies and life writing, and between scholarship and activism, I explore possibilities that open for politically engaged cultural criticism when it includes attempted acts of narrated humanity.

In taking this approach, I flip Said's formulation, "never solidarity before criticism" (*Representations of the Intellectual*, 32), specifically conceiving of how to act in solidarity not only as a critic, but also as a comrade and as an ally. Putting solidarity before criticism does not mean that I am withholding criticisms that would challenge my arguments. It does, however, mean not attempting to do research or tell stories that cross lines I would not venture beyond as a movement participant. And it also means being willing to test my academic freedoms and cross lines of "professionalism" or "civility" in order to exist "in a contradictory relationship to the academy," as graduate student 'Ilima Long put it on an *Arab Studies Quarterly* conference panel we organized on solidarity. It means being willing to call out university administrators using a tactic my brilliant and badass student 'Ihilani Lasconia named, on that same *ASQ* panel, "shame, blame and follow the money" (Lasconia). It also means putting what close-reading skills and audiences I have access to as a literary critic into the service of supporting not only movements in which I believe, but also those I respect and am connected to through political solidarity, friendship, and love.

Zionist Narratives, "The 'Salaitification' of Higher Education," and BDS

Before turning to readings of Salaita's life writing texts, it is necessary to place them in context. Salaita's firing directly connects to events that took place during the summer of 2014 in Palestine/Israel and the United States. For 51 days of that long summer, over the course of "Operation Protective Edge," Israel's fourteenth military campaign since unilaterally disengaging from Gaza in 2005, Israel ravaged Gaza's infrastructure, bombing homes, refugee sites, hospitals, and schools. The Israeli army killed more than 2,200 Palestinians trapped inside Gaza's shrinking borders, 521 of them children ("50 days"). That July, Salaita issued furious tweets condemning Israel's assault against Palestine and the complicity of the United States and anyone supporting Israel's decades of occupation and settler violence. His tweets offered in compressed form critiques he makes of the Zionist state in his eight books, in his many scholarly essays, and in journalistic articles in venues ranging from Mondoweiss to Colorlines to *Salon*. This work includes his 2006 *Anti-Arab Racism in the USA*, recognized with an Outstanding Book Award by the Gustavus Myers Center for the Study of Bigotry and Human Rights. Salaita's most scathing commentary concerned Israel's unchecked murder of children. In one of his most controversy-arousing tweets, he asked, "At this point, if Netanyahu appeared on TV with a necklace made from the teeth of Palestinian children, would anybody be surprised? #Gaza." Zionist groups and individuals seized upon Salaita's tweets. Claiming that they proved his antisemitism, his incivility, his "professional unfitness," and the lack of safety his students would feel, they pressured UIUC to fire Salaita from a tenured position he had just been hired into in the American Indian Studies (AIS) Department. On August 1, 2014, Phyllis Wise, chancellor of UIUC, acting at what turned out to be the bidding of UI trustees and donors, revoked his contract. Salaita and the AIS Department received notice of his firing after Salaita, having given up a tenured position at Virginia Tech, had sold his house to move with his family to Champaign, and was preparing classes for which students were already enrolled. This all unfolded as Israel continued its onslaught against the 2.1 million Palestinians in Gaza.

The firing of Salaita for exercising his rights of free speech as a private citizen catapulted him into the public eye. As Salaita puts this in *Uncivil Rites*, "I had become a virus on Facebook" (14). Amid widespread media coverage, the American Association of University Professors (AAUP) condemned his firing; 17,000 people signed a petition protesting it; over 5,000 academics pledged to boycott UIUC; and some 400 academics wrote in support of Chancellor Wise's actions. Salaita's firing also resulted in the wholesale dismantling of the world-renowned AIS Department. Salaita fought back with a lawsuit against UIUC and, in a bold move, against its "John Doe" donors. By including donors, Salaita, together with Palestine Legal and the Center for Constitutional Rights, succeeded in exposing, through Freedom of Information Act (FOIA) requests, donors' influence on an increasingly corporatized university. Focused on UIUC's violation of Salaita's free speech and the breaking of his employment contract, the lawsuit revealed the malfeasance of the administration, trustees, and donors. Salaita was awarded $875,000, with over half going to legal fees ("Salaita v. Kennedy, et al.").

The settlement did not result in the restoration of Salaita's job or academic career. After moving to Beirut in 2015 to serve one year at AUB as the Edward Said Chair, Salaita was chosen by CASAR as the top candidate to occupy the position permanently. However, as Salaita explains in "AUB Limited," his initial hiring caused "consternation among board members, investors, administrators, and US politicians."[3] When selected for the permanent position, he discovered how fully Zionist pressure born of what he calls "corporate kinship" extends to the Arab world. As at UIUC, his hiring at AUB, "a site of soft power for the State department," was blocked, leading to the collapse of the CASAR program despite its $5 million endowment (Salaita, "An Honest Living"). The following year, on July 22, 2017, Salaita made a public statement via a Facebook posting, declaring his decision to leave academe owing to his refusal "to bear the indignities of a blacklist" ("A few thoughts"). He explained, "Despite applying to positions on four continents, I was unable to find an academic job, so I no longer count myself among the professoriate. A number of colleagues have attempted to recruit me, but their efforts always get shut down by management." In February 2019, Salaita inaugurated a website and, in his first entry, "An Honest Living," announced his transition from a tenured professorship to an hourly-wage position as a school bus driver.

Zionist responses to his tweets, which then broadened into the smear campaign that, through ad hominem attacks on his scholarship and teaching, destroyed his academic career, represent Salaita as not human. This dehumanization—representing him as uncivil, as a terrorist, as antisemitic—followed post-9/11 as well as deeply grooved forms of narrative humanity. Attacks from administrators relied on charges of antisemitism and drew from more recently fashioned discourses of "incivility" that Heike Schotten contends in "Against Academic Freedom" are the post-9/11 mode by which the academy carries out its settler colonial operations of dominance and dispossession. Christopher Kennedy, chair of the UI Board of Trustees, successfully led the charge to fire Salaita by labeling his tweets "blatantly anti-Semitic" (Wurth)—an action that earned Kennedy a "Spirit of Courage" award from the Simon Wiesenthal Center. UIUC senior Josh Cooper spearheaded a petition signed by 1,000 students that ascribed "hate speech" and a lack of civility to Salaita (Elizabeth Nolan Brown). The editorial board of the *Chicago Tribune* agreed. Finding Salaita guilty of "hate speech" in an op-ed released on September 11, they opined, "Some of his remarks come uncomfortably and irresponsibly close to endorsing violence against individuals or groups of people" ("U. of I. Right"). As a complement to these "civil" charges from management and mainstream media, trolls depicted Salaita as a terrorist and antisemite, in rhetoric that gave expression to the crudely racist, Islamophobic, and colonial views that have long constituted civility's underbelly. Death threats, diatribes, and gaslighting memes spread via social media and were sent directly to Salaita. One example—to which Salaita responded, "enjoy your new BFFs, upper administration"—consisted of a headshot of Salaita, with a swastika Photoshopped onto his forehead. The caption read: "Anti-freedom Moslem religious bigot Steve Salaita does not believe all humans are created equal" (Salaita, "Enjoy your new BFFs"). This meme is characteristic in its conflations of being Palestinian (or Arab), Muslim (as his name indicates, Salaita is Christian), antisemitic, fascist, and genocidal. Years later, these attacks persist. When Salaita posted his inaugural essay to his website about his new job driving a bus, one of the first remarks was "Steven Salaita should not be around buses. Curious—will he still defend blowing them up?" ("An Honest Living"). Whether packaged in or stripped of the language of civility, this commentary puts into sharp relief the reversals and hypocrisies at work in formulas of narrative humanity that characterize Palestinians as uncivil and inhuman. In addition to their ugliness, these formulaic character attacks have a material impact: they legitimate and displace the racist and colonial violence that underwrites the everyday workings of civil society.

In part, Salaita's firing has garnered so much attention because it reveals a creeping fascism on college campuses, or what Tithi Bhattacharya and Bill V. Mullen have called "the 'Salaitification' of higher education." In the first press conference following his firing, Salaita warned that UIUC's bowing to pressure from donors "risks creating a Palestinian exception to academic freedom and the First Amendment" (Salaita, "Salaita Speaks Publicly"). Although "the 'Salaitification' of higher education" affects academics engaged in other struggles, including against antiblack racism (e.g., Johnny Eric Williams, Keeanga-Yamahtta Taylor, George Ciccariello-Maher, Garrett Felber), attacks on those engaged in Palestine advocacy stand out in the broader crackdown on free speech and academic freedom. Along with Salaita, targets include both Palestinians (e.g., Rabab Abdulhadi, Sami Al-Arian, Nadia Abu El-Haj, Joseph Massad) and allies (e.g., Angela Davis, Bruce Duthu, Norman Finkelstein, Terri Ginsberg, Marc Lamont Hill, Jasbir Puar, and Cornel West). As Schotten observes, Palestinian liberation "simultaneously compresses and stands in for a host of struggles" on college campuses; thus, it is not "a lightning rod but rather a tuning fork" (298). Sunaina Maira similarly observes, "The boycott is at the center of battles over the neoliberal structuring of the university and academic labor, helping to advance a politics of decolonizing the academy" (118). *The Palestine Exception to Free Speech*, a report issued by Palestine Legal that substantiates Salaita's formulation, documents how "in the first six months of 2015 alone, Palestine Legal responded to 140 incidents and 33 requests for assistance," over 80 percent of them involving students and scholars targeted for being pro-Palestinian.

Salaita's firing and the other findings in *The Palestine Exception* demonstrate the centrality of the American university in supporting colonial projects materially and ideologically, and in contesting them. Ali Abunimah focuses on the role of the American university in his analysis of Israel's apartheid regime, and he remarks upon Zionist awareness of its importance in the struggle for justice in Palestine: "Israel's most aggressive proponents understand that the future of US support for the Zionist settler-colony—without which the apartheid regime cannot survive—will be won or lost at universities" (x). The battle over Palestine-Israel is particularly pitched when it comes to academic boycott and divestment initiatives. Omar Barghouti observes, "Few forms of pressure have triggered as much alarm in Israel's establishment as the growing divestment movement on college campuses and the mushrooming support for academic boycott of Israel among US academic associations" (Maira, 87). This alarm translates into well-funded and ruthless attacks on Palestine solidarity activists and organizations on college campuses.

The well-resourced entities and individuals exercising this repression often exceed, with impunity, the very parameters of free speech and the academic freedom they claim to be defending. Often based in or funded by the Israeli state, Zionist organizations play a key role in instigating lawfare and campaigns of harassment and intimidation as they posit not only Palestinian solidarity organizing but also any anti-Zionist or Palestine-based scholarship as antisemitic and a threat to academic freedom. Such groups include Canary Mission, the David Horowitz Freedom Center, AMCHA Initiative, Campus Watch, Stand With US, the Simon Wiesenthal Center, Middle East Forum, the Zionist Organization of America, and the Lawfare Project. In the name of protecting constitutional rights and democratic ideals, these groups operate "as kind of like a navigation system for trolls" ("A guide to surviving"), as Salaita notes of Canary Mission, an anonymous website that features hundreds of slanderous profiles of faculty and students that they tweet to students' prospective employers and admissions committees.[4]

These groups particularly target academic boycott, and in ways Salaita details in *Uncivil Rites*, his firing cannot be understood independently of his vocal support for USACBI (45). His activism on behalf of the ASA's 2013 boycott resolution, the passage of which made the front page of the *New York Times*, drew especially intense fire. Zionist groups and individuals leading the charge against Salaita have been at the forefront of working to defeat it and related boycott initiatives. One such person is Cary Nelson, former AAUP president and faculty member at UIUC, and collaborator with the Israeli security state. Nelson was instrumental in Salaita's firing in ways both public and, as revealed in documents obtained through FOIA, involving back-door dealings. His obsessive pursuit of Salaita predates the UIUC scandal and cannot be separated from his Israeli-backed agitating against academic boycott resolutions, including his authorship of an MLA antiboycott resolution (Hassan).[5] (I have witnessed Nelson's haunting firsthand: at conference panels featuring Salaita or focused on his firing, Nelson has sat in unwelcome attendance, his physical presence casting a noticeable pall over the proceedings.) Nelson's and other Zionist individuals' and organizations' attacks on Salaita have occurred in tandem with their involvement in these more broadly focused campaigns. Indeed, as Salaita notes in *Uncivil Rites*, a slew of other anti-BDS actions by groups including AMCHA, Canary Mission, and other "professional trolls" took place the same month he was fired (52). The persecution of Salaita, along with other proponents of academic boycott, particularly those who are queer and BIPOC, continues past Salaita's firing: Salaita is one of several USACBI Organizing Collective members targeted in ongoing nuisance lawsuits waged by the Louis D. Brandeis Center for Human Rights, contesting the ASA Boycott Resolution.[6] Founded by Kenneth Marcus, Trump appointee to head the Office for Civil Rights at the Department of Education, the Brandeis Center's objectives are, in Marcus's own words, "to send a signal" (Redden) to other associations thinking about boycott resolutions.

In fomenting criminalization, censure, and silencing, Zionist groups rely on formulas of narrative humanity that associate Palestinians and Palestine solidarity with antisemitism and terrorism. The David Horowitz Freedom Center, which supported Salaita's firing, collaborates with Canary Mission. Both encourage students to report on anti-Zionist faculty members and to orchestrate racist and Islamophobic smear campaigns designed to quell dissent. The Freedom Center systematically plasters college campuses with posters that name and provide caricatured images of faculty and students active in Students for Justice in Palestine (SJP) chapters or in other BDS-related organizing. These posters dehumanize and label their targets as "Jew Haters," "Terrorist," "Neo-Nazi," and "Hamas Terrorists," and level accusations at them for perpetrating "Neo-Nazi Incidents on Campus," spreading "Genocidal Hamas Propaganda," and supporting "a culture that teaches children to slaughter Jews" (Palestine Poster Project Archives). Their targets include not only well-known pro-BDS scholars such as Rabab Abdulhadi, Hatem Bazian, Judith Butler, Angela Davis, and WJT Mitchell, but also individual students and SJP chapters.[7]

University administrators' responses indicate that Salaita's firing is but an intensification of business as usual in what Piya Chatterjee and Sunaina Maira call "the Imperial University," as they also demonstrate how powerfully Zionist narratives have worked to define Jews' humanity over against Palestinians'. When right-wing Zionist individuals and organizations weaponize these forms of narrative humanity, administrators have responded either with silence or with active support. Not a single university president has condemned Canary Mission, upholding Salaita's contention that this anonymous site "exemplifies the problems of the corporate university more broadly: donor meddling, institutional racism, adamant Zionism, right-wing structures, top-down governance, arbitrary decision-making, shadowy influences and political suppression" ("A guide to surviving"). San Francisco State University met the June 2017 federal lawsuit filed against Professor Rabab Abdulhadi, the entire Ethnic Studies Department, and the SFSU General Union of Palestinian Students (GUPS) with silence. In this lawsuit, which conflates criticism of Israel and support for

Palestinian rights with antisemitism, the Lawfare Project charged SFSU with violating the constitutional and civil rights of Jewish students and community members ("SF State"). More recently, under its new president, Lynn Mahoney, SFSU also was complicit in the shutdown by Zoom, YouTube, and Facebook of Abdulhadi and Tomomi Kinukawa's Open Classroom featuring Leila Khaled. Administrators at other universities similarly fell into line when Zoom again canceled events protesting this censorship one month later in a Day of Action organized by USACBI (Barrows-Friedman; Zahzah). This included my own administration, which disavowed UH's connection to our event, "We Will Not Be Silenced: The Case of Khaled and Solidarity from Hawai'i to Palestine," and refused to help the sponsoring departments and SFJP@UH secure another platform.

Often, university support is more than tacit. At San Diego State University, the administration defended posters from the Horowitz Freedom Center on the grounds that the students deserved them. Hundreds of university presidents issued statements condemning the passage of the ASA boycott resolution. (At UH, in a closed meeting, an administrator threatened to withdraw contractually committed funding after UH won the bid to house the ASA's journal *American Quarterly* at UH from 2014 to 2024.) Numerous SJP chapters have been sanctioned or silenced by campus administrators for "incivility" or antisemitism on the basis of calling out Israel's human rights violations. Fordham University denied organizational status to Students for Justice in Palestine on the grounds that it "might stir controversy" (Garrison). Students at Butler University faced—although ultimately defeated, with the assistance of Palestine Legal—anti-BDS "emergency" resolutions after holding educational boycott events ("Butler Students").

This repression reveals the extent to which forms of narrative humanity that dehumanize Palestinians have been codified in punishing policies and laws at the state and federal levels. The Israel lobby, most notably AIPAC, not only has succeeded in seeing that Israel receives $3.8 billion of federal aid a year, but also has secured Israel's special status through anti-BDS legislation (MJ Rosenberg). Over 30 federal and state laws that aim to stigmatize or penalize participation in BDS or Palestine advocacy have been adopted; 218 have been proposed.[8] US and intergovernmental definitions of antisemitism have been especially consequential for educational institutions. The US State Department's definition of antisemitism features examples that place any criticism of Israel in violation of free speech and academic freedom. Such censorship intensified under the Trump presidency. A 2019 executive order instructs government agencies tasked with enforcing antidiscrimination laws to consider the 2016 definition for antisemitism provided by the International Holocaust

Remembrance Alliance (IHRA). Owing to seven of the IHRA's eleven examples, any criticism of Israel can be deemed hate speech.[9] The Biden administration, busy in its first weeks undoing Trump's executive orders, announced that it "embraces and champions" the IHRA definition (Arria). In addition to the passage of state laws directing adoption of the IHRA in Florida, Ohio, South Carolina, and Tennessee educational institutions, twenty-one college and university student governments reportedly have passed resolutions to adopt it (Khalili).

Despite being afforded the protections that come with being white, Jewish, tenured, and working at an institution with a relatively small Zionist footprint, I am intimately acquainted with legally abetted and administratively enabled Zionist campaigns of intimidation. I offer a few examples to illustrate just how commonly they occur, and also how often outlandish forms of harassment and threats rely on formulaic messaging that rarely deviates from the pathways carved by narrative humanity. Made in response to my participation in USACBI-related initiatives (especially the MLA and ASA boycott resolutions), and to having edited work and organized events featuring Palestinians, this sampling includes being featured in a fake press release, circulated widely enough to reach a family member at the University of Michigan, in which "I" with the support of "press secretary" J. Kēhaulani Kauanui supposedly led a rally attended by hundreds at the Honolulu Convention Center and called for elderly Jewish people to be refused medical treatment. At the height of the MLA campaign, my head was Photoshopped onto a porn video sent to a USACBI comrade by text from a cell phone number that spoofed my own. I have received emails with threats and death wishes—one, a gun pointing at me when I opened the email; another, forecasting that I would be the next Jew sent to the showers and turned into worm dust. I have lost many hours responding to FOIA requests based on charges that I had set up my website for a special *Biography* issue on "Life in Occupied Palestine" as a Hamas portal. This accusation involved a convoluted conspiracy theory about an ad for fixing a leaky toilet. (I cannot resist connecting this desperate and paranoid fantasy to Salaita's satirical list of names for the IDF's military campaigns, one of which is "Operation Blame Hamas for Everything from Hadassah to the Leaky Sink in That One Bathroom in the Knesset (because Hamas)" [*Uncivil Rites*, 85]). A series of articles claims that I am bringing terrorism to the University of Hawai'i. A Zionist colleague has sent me hundreds of harassing emails, often with university administrators copied, alleging my antisemitism and impropriety. (I take pride in having answered zero of them.) After I appeared on a television show in which a former student interviewed me about a trip to Palestine, the show's director censored the episode, then brought in a Zionist rabbi for a hastily arranged "response" in which they denounced me as a "monster" for having made antisemitic remarks that they themselves fabricated. Canary Mission has activated trolls on Twitter; my favorite from the stream of vitriol calls me a "wizened old bag" before instructing me to "read a fucking book!" As unpleasant as such incidents are, worse still is the climate that normalizes their underlying assumptions about what it means to support Palestine. Many of these incidents have resulted in my being summoned to meetings or receiving emails in which, addressing me in blandly "civil" language, administrators have dismissed, ignored, lightly chastised me for, and in some cases intensified instances of censorship and harassment.

If these examples suggest the multifaceted attacks that attend support for Palestine, they also provide an occasion to remark on their differential impact, as well as the pleasures and power of BDS. For me these incidents have been annoying, at times amusing, and occasionally infuriating. But for Palestinians, such targeting often carries serious material consequences: in addition to job loss and lawfare, the inability to travel home and see family. Another difference: when aimed at white Jewish allies, these attacks, however personal, constitute responses to our politics, not vilifications, denials of or efforts to eliminate our very existence. If Salaita is tasked with defending "the very humanity of the Palestinian people" (*Uncivil Rites*, 88), a Jew taking an anti-Zionist stand is cast as standing alone, as a betrayer of one's people. In ways the next section develops, Salaita uses personal narrative not only to expose the impact of Zionists' uncivil rites, but also to speak as part of a political community that includes but goes beyond Palestinians. As I weave my own experiences participating in that collectivity into my analysis of Salaita's life writing, I seek to puncture and provide an alternative to the Zionist narrative about anti-Zionist Jews. Far from an individual act of self-hatred or betrayal, for Jews to oppose Zionism and support Palestinian freedom is to keep the very best of company and to participate in a collective struggle for justice fueled by decolonial love. As attention to Salaita's writings will show, this struggle involves forms of filiation as well as (in the Saidian sense) often joyful affiliation. I believe these bonds will outlast and ultimately triumph over the ugliness and increasing desperation of Zionism; its ethnonationalist and settler colonial practices of racist apartheid, ethnic cleansing, and military occupation; and the forms of narrative humanity that underwrite civil society's uncivil rites.

It is because Palestine solidarity work proffers more ethical and loving ways to be human that BDS, as its most important expression, is under such concerted attack. Since its formation in 2005, this Palestinian-led international movement has called attention to Israel's human rights violations and put faces to Palestinians living under, refusing to be defined by, and nonviolently resisting this violence. BDS has been instrumental in changing the narrative that casts Palestinians as terrorists, as inhuman, as nonexistent, and as antisemites. As a result, the demands of BDS and their consonance with democratic ideals are becoming better known and gaining popular ground (if not to the point where, as with BLM, CEOs and university administrators are attempting to appropriate the movement!). Divestment initiatives have swept across US college campuses, largely powered by SJP chapters, and boycott resolutions have been adopted by academic associations. BDS is also being popularized by church groups, Jewish Voice for Peace, and trade unions. High-visibility artists, film directors, and writers including Elvis Costello, Brian Enos, Danny Glover, Naomi Klein, Ken Loach, and Roger Waters are supporting the cultural boycott, and athletes, too, are refusing trips to Israel. In addition, renewed forms of inter/national solidarity are conjoining Palestinian and other liberatory movements, including the Movement for Black Lives, whose platform includes an endorsement of BDS, and other Black abolitionist movements (*The Struggle for Abolition: From the US to Palestine*; Rosenthal); NoDAPL, the Indigenous-led opposition to the Dakota Access Pipeline; and (in ways the final chapter takes up) the movement to protect Mauna a Wākea.

BDS's appeal, which ranges from the popular to the politically radical, owes in large part to how it makes humanist appeals and works within a liberal framework toward radical ends. Its campaign is fueled by three demands: (1) to end the occupation of the Palestinian territories, dismantle the apartheid wall, and return to the 1967 borders; (2) to give equality to Arab Palestinian citizens inside Israel; and (3) to respect and promote the United Nations Right of Return (US Campaign). On the one hand, these planks, insofar as they are rights-based and demand "only" that Israel comply with international law, are solidly liberal. On the other, they are contextually radical. As a solidarity movement, BDS quite deliberately abstains from advancing a solution or specific vision for the future; it aims to establish a floor, not a ceiling. Nonetheless, meeting its three demands would put an end to a state defined by practices of occupation, ethnic cleansing, and apartheid. Conditions would exist for a true democracy in which everyone counts as human. Here it is important to note that Israel discriminates not only against Muslim Palestinians, but also against anyone who is not white and Jewish—this includes not only Muslims, but also Christian Palestinians, African immigrants and refugees, and Mizrahim (Arab Jews). Moreover, simply to organize on behalf of BDS's demands, however liberal in form, is to engage in a transformative process of education and a reconstituting of dominant narratives of the human.

"For He Who Ignites": *Uncivil Rites*, and the Potency of Salaita's Radical Humanism

I want to make a related argument about Palestinian memoirs—in particular, Salaita's. Written in the wake of his high-stakes firing, *Uncivil Rites*, as it rethinks the human, is shaped by and strengthens the BDS movement so centrally at issue in the attacks on Salaita. As mentioned in the introduction, Palestinian memoirs challenge liberal narratives of humanity. That is why, despite Palestinian auto/biographies being in no short supply,[10] they rarely appear on the lists of US mainstream publishers—Salaita's is published by Haymarket, an independent, nonprofit radical press dedicated to social change. Edward Said's 1999 *Out of Place*, published by Knopf, constitutes one of the rare exceptions. Although Salaita's style differs greatly, he follows in Said's legacy as a public intellectual dedicated to understanding the discourses that underwrite colonial displacement and dispossession: Orientalism and imperialism for Said; Zionism and settler colonialism for Salaita. Both men have been deemed threats for speaking truth to power. After serving for two years as the Edward W. Said Chair of American Studies at the American University of Beirut, Salaita was unceremoniously unseated from this position by the same US congressional body that in 2003 passed House Resolution 3077 targeting Said in an effort to regulate postcolonial studies, a field of study to which Said had an ambivalent relationship (Rowe). Both Said's and Salaita's memoirs demonstrate how the Western humanist tradition has at every turn denied human status to Palestinians along with permission to narrate, while their writings simultaneously advance a radical humanism. How Salaita relates as an intellectual and activist to BDS, humanism, inter/nationalism, and freedom can be productively positioned in relation to Said's investments in humanism, affiliation, worldliness, and exile (or being "out of place").

Even as it breaks with the belles lettres style of *Out of Place*, *Uncivil Rites* adheres to a Saidian model of humanism in the ways Salaita engages forms of narrative humanity, while also participating in acts of narrated humanity. With this combination, as Salaita co-constitutes the creation of self and political community, *Uncivil Rites* furthers his BDS activism and, along with other contemporary movement memoirs such as Cullors's *When They Call You a Terrorist*, anticipates new ways of human being and belonging. Writing in hotel rooms and airports while he traversed the United States, visiting more than fifty college campuses and giving public lectures in response to his firing, Salaita pronounces his memoir "a communal project" (4). In telling "an autobiographical story that is anything but personal" (4), Salaita narrates a larger history of settlerism and racial capitalism and shares his experience collectively organizing against these forces through participation in USACBI and other activist communities. In *Anti-Arab Racism in the USA*, Salaita asserts the decolonial power of collective acts of storytelling. Describing nights spent with friends during a summer in Palestine, when, robbed by the Israelis of water and electricity, they chatted by candlelight, he says, "Those nights proved to me yet again that no matter what sort of technology humans invent, stories will forever be our greatest resource" (182). *Uncivil Rites* can be seen as a fleshing out, a realization, of that conviction. It suggests how immersion in activism that is personal can generate new ways to narrate the human that, as they sustain political movements and community building, can rework, refuse, and provide alternatives to existing narrative codes, genres, and conventions that advance bourgeois individualist and settler ideologies.

Through its mix of narrative and narrated humanity, *Uncivil Rites* challenges the parameters of autobiographical narrative and, along with this, what counts as scholarly and political writing—and life writing and activism. In addition to including documents pertaining to his firing and their impact on him and his family, *Uncivil Rites* also provides analysis of broader issues and events that are intimately related to Salaita's case. Through its acts of narrated humanity, the memoir illuminates how the political and historical are deeply personal. The stories *Uncivil Rites* tells about Salaita and his family stand as, and are accompanied by, movement-building narratives. *Uncivil Rites* supports BDS and other, interconnected, decolonial movements; it offers solidarity and advice to those (perhaps especially students) who have been or might be targeted as Salaita has been; and it provides polemical and often satirical commentary on anti-Indigenous and Zionist ideologies, on the corporatization of the university, and on what passes in it for civility. Footnotes range from typical scholarly ones, to irreverent smackdowns of Zionists, to confessions about failing to comply with "bougie habits like taking regular showers and making mortgage payments" (3). As the memoir's different modes and forms of address play off one another and satirize the civil, they also suggest ways to (re)think the human that neither exceptionalize nor exclude but begin with Palestinians. Premised on values of compassion, solidarity, and decolonial love that Salaita shows to be in keeping with his collective work for USACBI, the human in *Uncivil Rites* is antithetical to understandings that emerge from settlerism and its attending narratives of civility.

Uncivil Rites is at once a memoir and an unruly, antidisciplinary, genre-defying, and deliberately nonchronological text. It comprises an introduction, twenty-three brief chapters, an addendum, an epilogue, and appendices consisting of AAUP Statements and Hiring/Termination documents. It also includes a 2013 *Salon* article Salaita wrote, along with Virginia Tech's response to it that, as it affirms the institution's support for the military, demonstrates the convergence of patriotism and ethnonationalism also at work at UIUC. Chapter titles suggest the range of subjects, rhetorical styles, and approaches: a sampling includes "Imaginary Students," "The Pro-Israel Activist Handbook, Unabridged," "On Being Palestinian and Other Things," "Shame on Me," and "The Evolution of 'Anti-Semitism.'"

Unifying these chapters is an exposé of civility as a disciplinary regime. Admonishments to be "civil" regularly operate as policing mechanisms that support the settler state. Charges of "incivility" rely on conflations of docile conformity with good citizenship, and displace the state's violence onto those it subjugates. As Salaita well understands regarding the chorus of administrators, media pundits, and donors charging him with incivility, "civility" is a stand-in for the settler state, and "incivility" is a code word for being Palestinian, Arab, Muslim, terrorist, Indigenous.[11] He notes, "Troublesome assumptions underlie questions about my fitness for the classroom. It is impossible to separate questions about my 'civility' from broader narratives of inherent Arab violence" (45). Through his accounts, readers learn of ways Palestinians and (other) Indigenous peoples have been killed, terrorized, and erased in the name of "civility," and of how BDS activists have been demonized, criminalized, and silenced. *Uncivil Rites* illuminates how narrative humanity, in dehumanizing Palestinians, Native Americans, and anyone who resists the settler state, legitimates colonial violence in all its guises in the name of the civil.

Salaita's indictment of civility builds not only on his own experiences but also on his work as a literary critic with a keen interest in the power of narrative. Much of his previous scholarship concentrates on how literary and cultural texts relentlessly represent Palestinians, and all Arabs, as terrorists and as uncivil in ways that sanitize the violence of conquest. In *The Holy Land in Transit* (2006), he demonstrates how both colonial and decolonial politics "are essentially inseparable from literature" (4). He extends that book's analysis of the dehumanizing narratives on which settler colonialism as a "terrorist enterprise" (50) depends in *Anti-Arab Racism in the USA*, including accounts of how this dehumanization affects him personally. He describes what movies and TV shows teach him: "My grandfather was a terrorist, a romance, an obedient servant. In fact, everybody in my family, I learned at a young age, was afflicted with innately violent tendencies" (11). In *Israel's Dead Soul* (2011), Salaita turns his attention to understanding "how scholars and artists have constantly reproduced the formulations that conflate Zionism with multicultural humanism" (9). He explicates how binaries between the Israeli as human/humanist and the Palestinian as inhuman/terrorist are produced and explains how similar formulations make possible the imperial and capitalist structures that result in global injustices.

In the face of such demonization, Salaita does not use his memoir to make appeals "proving" his or Palestinians' civility and humanity. Instead, he faces his opponents head-on. The book's cover image introduces his approach and establishes how, to draw on Angela Davis's words, Salaita "does not capitulate" (qtd. in Lloyd, "Toast for Steven"). In this headshot, Salaita meets his readers' eyes, unapologetic and resolute. His dedication of the book, "For he who ignites," embraces the explosive power of words (not bombs). Through this dedication, Salaita declines to assuage the anxieties of those who associate him and Palestinian/Arab men more generally with terrorism. (Because the gendering of this dedication is not in keeping with Salaita's usual more inclusive practices, as I discuss later, the "he" might well refer to his son or to someone else he chooses not to name.) Throughout *Uncivil Rites*, as he denounces the role civil discourse plays in sanitizing and sanctifying colonialism, he refuses the demand that "to be considered human" Palestinians must "grovel" or "genuflect in order to earn the trust of those by whom we are conquered and defined" (122). In contrast to Said, who conveys his scathing critiques of imperialism with the utmost elegance and urbanity, as a polemicist Salaita repudiates civility's codes and conventions.

Salaita's refusal of civility often takes the form of the bold sarcasm that Eman Ghanayem notes, via her reading of Ghassan Kanafani, is a quintessential feature of Palestinian resistance literature ("'Popular Intelligence'"). In "Tweet, Tweet," when Salaita states, "I cuss sometimes, because why the fuck not?" (6), this salvo is not merely defiant humor any more than is, for example, "Civilized Twitter." In that brief chapter, he gives Twitter handles to the likes of Andrew Jackson, Menachem Begin, Theodore Roosevelt, Golda Meir, and Ronald Reagan. He then issues as tweets their statements that demonstrate civility's racist and genocidal policies and practices. For example, Winston Churchill, dubbed "@EmpireFalls," tweets, "I am strongly in favour of using poisoned gas against uncivilized tribes." Or, from @ThePeacefulOne, "Break their bones"—a reference to Yitzhak Rabin's directive to the military to maim Palestinians participating in the First Intifada. Through these satirical tweets, Salaita provides a riposte to charges regarding the incivility of his own tweets while also proving how "civility" is the "lexicon of conquest" and "the discourse of educated racism" (105). In "The Chief Features of Civility," Salaita similarly denounces civility from a context that is at once personal and trans-Indigenous. He opens this chapter, "Here is what civility looks like at the University of Illinois:"; Salaita follows this announcement with a photo of the (now retired) UI mascot "Chief Illiniwek" in full "Indian" regalia. Salaita's punning on civility's "chief features" connects the story of his firing to the broader racist, eliminatory, and often genocidal logics of settlerism as they extend from UI, to the US, to Palestine.

By intermixing discussion of the role that discourses of civility play in enabling settler states to violently disappear Palestinians and Native Americans with an account of how he has experienced attacks made in the name of "civility," Salaita uses memoir to challenge forms of narrative humanity that, in aligning the civil and the human, perpetuate regimes of settlerism. A particularly powerful example of this occurs in "Entry Not Approved." This chapter takes its title from paperwork from the UI Board of Trustees overturning Salaita's appointment. In it, Salaita remarks on the inhumanity of bureaucratic conventions and civil discourse: "During the vote, the trustees referred to me as 'Item 14, page 23, number 4.' It's not exactly a prison tattoo, but it nevertheless does an excellent job illuminating the dehumanizing, technocratic conventions of the corporate boardroom" (33). He notes, "The university meant it as a public record, but I read it as a thoroughly personal episode" (33), and comments on how, through the symbolism of the document's 9/11 date, "Palestine is (falsely) implicated in the tragedy" (34). As well, he considers the layered meanings the language stamped on this public record hold, for him personally, and for others subjected to violent exclusions. He explains how, for Palestinians, "'entry not approved' pertains to their ancestral land. . . . 'Entry not approved' also pertained at one point to Jewish college and country club applications in the United States. The line is painfully reminiscent of 'whites only' signs in southern diners, the exclusivity of an aristocratic soiree, or an electrified fence encircling governmental secrets" (34). Moving through these different associations, Salaita conveys how larger historical traumas intensify his already-dehumanizing experience, and he relates it to the "many communities and individuals who experience disapproval through the locutions of an unexamined rectitude" (34). As chapters such as "Entry Not Approved" intermix with ones such as "Civilized Twitter," *Uncivil Rites* makes room for polemics and challenges memoir as a form of narrative humanity that consolidates the human and the civil.

Salaita rejects the civil, but not the human. Stories of being human that are antithetical to civility's dependence on perpetual war and dehumanization animate *Uncivil Rites*. Children, and especially Salaita's son, figure centrally in stories premised on values of empathy, kinship, community, safety, and kindness.[12] In "Uncivil Rites," the chapter that follows "Entry Not Approved," Salaita muses on the ethical need to occasionally lie to children. He then describes his son's birth, and, when his wife Diana returned to work, treasured time spent feeding his son, taking him for walks, shading him from the sun, and experiencing his own life "completely integrated into his" (36). As Salaita reflects on his son's developmental benchmarks, he discloses that it was empathy that mattered most to him. When at age two, his son begins asking

"'Okay?' . . . whenever something seemed amiss," Salaita states. "It was the biggest indication yet that he would grow into the type of person I so badly want him to become" (37). The chapter ends with his son's response when Salaita receives UIUC's letter of termination. Perceiving his father's anguish, he stops his play:

> Placing his hand on my thigh, his inky pupils wide with concern, he asked, "Okay, Papa?"
> "Yes my love," I replied, squeezing his hand. "Papa's okay." (39)

The tenderness at the heart of this encounter—his son's empathy, Salaita's protective lie (also the truth, given the primary importance he places on bringing his son up well)—starkly contrasts to the bureaucratic mendacity and colonial cruelty of both "Entry Not Approved" and the chapter that follows "Uncivil Rites." In "Survival of the Fitness," as Salaita reflects on being deemed "unfit" for the classroom on the basis of his tweets, he poses the rhetorical question, "You tell me which is worse: cussing in condemnation of the murder of children or using impeccable manners to justify their murder" (44). In "Uncivil Rites," we see how his loving family life is rudely disrupted by—and serves as a bastion against—"civil" missives and missions. This and other chapters focused on his wife and son are themselves interrupted by those that address the dehumanizing violence at the heart of civility and settler states. Through these dynamics within and between chapters, *Uncivil Rites* at once works within and upends a familiar form of narrative humanity in which family relations, as they establish human value, align the human and the civil.

Salaita's stories of fatherhood offer powerful counters to representations of Palestinian parents and children in Zionist narratives. They also reflect the protective love for children that is threaded throughout all of his writings: as Salaita tweeted in response to the May 2022 massacre of children in Uvalde, Texas, "Killing kids is a cruelty that my brain simply refuses to process. Nothing makes this world feel more desolate and beyond repair" ("Killing kids"). Throughout this study, we have looked at how contemporary forms of narrative humanity code those who are Arab, Muslim, or Middle Eastern as terrorists. Explicitly Zionist narratives amplify such representations, often through stories that cast Palestinians (or, when refusing to acknowledge Palestinian existence, "Arabs") as terrorists with no regard for children, including their own. An iconic quotation attributed to Israel's former prime minister Golda Meir encapsulates the logic such narratives deploy: "Peace will come when the Arabs will love their children more than they hate us."[13] As this statement tacitly acknowledges that the Israeli state kills Palestinian children, it displaces the blame for this onto Palestinians and converts parents' grief into anti-Jewish hatred. During the summer of 2014, as the Israeli army bombed schools and killed hundreds of children, Zionists updated and doubled down on this narrative. Nobel Peace Prize laureate and author Elie Wiesel turned to the biblical story of Abraham and Isaac to contend that as in Nazi Germany, we were witnessing "a battle of civilization versus barbarism" in which Islamist militants were sacrificing Palestinian children by using them as human shields. This essay appeared as a paid advertisement in major US newspapers under the headline, "Jews rejected child sacrifice 3,500 years ago. Now it's Hamas' turn" (Mackey). Other accounts charged Palestinians with sacrificing their children as a publicity ploy: Netanyahu asserted that Hamas was tricking Israel into killing civilians in order to use "telegenetically dead Palestinians" to tarnish Israel's reputation (Mackey). To account for photos circulating on social media of grieving parents holding their children's bodies, Alan Dershowitz deployed (and as Salaita notes, falsely took credit for inventing) the phrase "dead baby strategy," explaining of Hamas, "They want Palestinian babies to be killed precisely so that they can display the kind of photographs that were shown around the world" (*Uncivil Rites*, 65). Zionist narratives also demonize Palestinian children in a process Nadera Shalhoub-Kevorkian calls "unchilding." In *Incarcerated Childhood and the Politics of Unchilding*, Shalhoub-Kevorkian analyzes how, through their representation as dangerous, racialized others and as terrorists, Palestinian children are evicted from the realm of childhood. In defining Jews as humans who value family, nation, and civilization in contrast with depictions of Arabs or Palestinians as savages, terrorists, or uncivil antisemites who destroy families and nation, these Zionist narratives heighten the binary oppositions that attend liberal forms of narrative humanity. By representing his loving relationship to his son in stories that refuse these binaries, Salaita at once inhabits a familial form of narrative humanity and disrupts the racism and colonialism that inheres within it.

Uncivil Rites also advances a form of narrated humanity through its interplay of chapters that further decouple family and nation while broadening Salaita's care for his son to all children. The interrelations between the "personal" and more "political" chapters expand what it means to write a narrative about being a father as they evidence how Salaita cannot separate his response to Israel's siege on Gaza from his identity as a parent. A look at a cluster of chapters illustrates this. In "The Darling That Can No Longer Be Defended," he addresses Naftali Bennett's charge that "Hamas is butchering its own children," issued to attempt damage control after international journalists witnessed the Israeli army kill the Bakr boys, four young cousins playing soccer on a beach close to their hotel. He also analyzes Bennett's proclamation that Palestinians were "conducting massive self-genocide" because of their

insistence on placing their "missile launcher rooms" in their homes, thus requiring the Israeli army to bomb whole families. Salaita jokes, "I have to give
Bennett credit for his deep knowledge of the enemy. We don't like to admit it,
but the missile launcher room is the lifeblood of every Arab household" (172).
Even as he focuses on the absurdity of Bennett's commentary, his next chapter
shows how Israel's slaughter of children and global complicity in this horror is
for Salaita the stuff of nightmares. In "Consumption," he recounts a recurring
dream of being at the mall with Diana and his son, who tumbles from the
second floor as Salaita is trapped upstairs surrounded by oblivious shoppers.
He concludes this one-page chapter with Diana's response to his dream:
"'You have to quit reading about Gaza,' she finally tells me" (175). "A Politics
of the Child" comes a few pages later. Contending that he "cannot separate
parenthood from politics" (181), Salaita explains his vow to do well by his son
as "an aspiration toward a worldly ethics as much as it was a proclamation of
fatherly responsibility" (180). His explication of this ethics, which includes
empathizing with Israeli parents who have lost children (181), culminates at
the chapter's end, when he shares his memory of an "episode of unmitigated
Israeli brutality in Gaza: the ice cream freezers" (181). He explains, "Few things
better exemplify the gaiety and innocence of childhood than rummaging
through boxes of frozen confections. During Israel's recent bombing campaign in Gaza, however, the ice cream freezers weren't stacked with popsicles
and sorbet. Instead, they stored the bodies of dead children" (183–84). Salaita
concludes this chapter by standing by the tweets he wrote in response to this
horror: "I am a man who was fired because I condemned Israeli policy in
language appropriate to a horrible occasion rather than in the meek platitudes of civility. I prefer moral clarity. After all, there is nothing civil about
dead children in an ice cream freezer" (184). In Uncivil Rites, Salaita's stories
about fatherhood are integral to his refusal of civility, his activism against the
Israeli state, and his formulation of a radical humanism premised on love and
empathy for all humans.

   In its fierce opposition to the disregard, devaluation, or expendability of any
people, Uncivil Rites employs forms of narrative and narrated humanity that
bring to life the radical humanism of intellectuals including B. R. Ambedkar,
Arendt, Fanon, C. L. R. James, Marx, and perhaps especially Said. Salaita's
humanism strongly resonates with Said's belief in secular humanism as a form
of worldliness (by which Said means attention to how texts are deeply rooted
in their time and place) that enables resistance to the nationalism and imperialism that Western humanist texts sustain and naturalize.[14] For Said, "Humanism is the only—I would go so far as saying the final—resistance we have
against the inhuman practices and injustices that disfigure human history"

(*Humanism and Democratic Criticism*). This statement finds its counterpart in Salaita's assertion that his empathy for Israeli Jews is not merely "an instinctive act, a shared biological sensitivity, but . . . also a political choice" (*Uncivil Rites*, 181), and that "this basic statement of mutual humanity should be the groundwork for creating a society in which both communities live in love and safety" (181). Salaita's humanist vision upends Israel's claims to being a state that is at once Jewish and democratic. It also overturns the Zionist—and hegemonic Western—narrative that positions Israeli Zionists as Jewish victims rather than agents of violence in a "conflict" that is intractably ancient and religious. Noting that though it might sound impossible to realize this humanist proposition (one that resonates with Cullors's abolitionism), Salaita contends that "we have to be more creative than the state, able to imagine ways of being that expand the limited options afforded us by neoliberalism" (181). As its father-son narrative intermixes with and embodies the political and ethical convictions Salaita reflects on in other chapters, *Uncivil Rites* enacts a form of narrated humanity. While drawing on tenets of narrative humanity, this narrated humanity advances a humanism and a way of being human that challenges narrative humanity's grounding in colonialism. And through its plays with genre, Salaita's memoir realizes Said's belief that the humanities offer a way to "challenge and defeat both an imposed silence and the normalized quiet of unseen power wherever and whenever possible" (Said, "Public Role"). In keeping with Said's vision, Salaita's humanism exposes and resists the violence that civil discourse disguises, as his memoir advances a humanism premised on all people living together in safety and love.

Salaita is well aware of the power his humanism poses to a racist and colonial status quo that takes its cover in liberal humanism. Explaining why his opponents have culled and decontextualized his tweets, entirely ignoring those "condemning anti-Semitism or proclaiming that Arabs and Jews are brethren," he observes, "The tweets that critics ignore are more important to understanding my firing than the tweets they cite. My denunciations of Israel and Zionism aren't as threatening as my calm appeals to humanism" (118). In other words, Salaita's fireable offense is not only his "incivility," but perhaps even more, the way he puts within reach a humanism that does not define the human as a zero-sum game, one that establishes the settler's humanity over against the inhumanity or very existence of those who challenge the settler's claims to land and power.

As *Uncivil Rites* embodies a humanism that counters settlerism, it also finds its grounding in and lifts up BDS as an international movement that, like *Uncivil Rites*, is liberal in its demands but radical in its implications and intersectional commitments. When Salaita observes what administrators dislike about

BDS "beyond its Palestine advocacy," his list provides a concise summary of concerns his memoir supports: "grassroots organizing, faculty autonomy, anti-racism, decolonization, systemic critique, class consciousness, democratic co-operation" (56–57). So, too, he makes clear that his opposition to antisemitism, which he distinguishes from anti-Zionism, is part of a collective political vision "to eradicate the existence of anti-Semitism throughout the world" (130) that he shares with other Palestine activists. He notes that this includes the "mul-tiethnic and multidenominational" USACBI Organizing Collective (130). Salaita explicitly ties his memoir's humanist vision to the principles guiding USACBI. When he asserts that Palestinian liberation cannot entail Jewish displacement, he explains, "A free Palestine means that all its citizens enjoy freedom. I don't make up this stuff; these ethics are hallmarks of Palestine's national liberation movement. They guide USACBI and the many activists who daily risk their lives inside and beyond Palestine" (182–83). He further elab-orates that he and his comrades condemn Israel's deeds "because we think deeply and often about what it means to be kind and empathetic" (183). Such reflections infuse the memoir's more personal moments, providing them with a political context, while also illuminating the humanism of BDS.

As Salaita shows the consonance between the humanist values his memoir embodies and those that animate BDS, *Uncivil Rites* serves as an important complement to the more directly political forms the BDS campaign takes. These range from social media postings, to campus and other community panels and events, to divestment and boycott resolutions, all of which are susceptible to censorship and criminalization. As in Salaita's case, this includes tweets, which occupy an as-yet-unsettled status as public statements and private speech acts. Given the current clampdown on political speech, especially if it is pro-BDS, forms of narrative and narrated humanity can flesh out USACBI's hu-manist commitments—to kindness, empathy, equality, and freedom from oppres-sion—while exposing the violence and hypocrisies that define democracy in the United States. (This is less true for "the only democracy in the Middle East," in part because literature and especially poetry has such popularity with Palestin-ians as a political form of expression. Deemed therefore by Israel a dangerous activity, literary writing can lead, as it did for Dareen Tartour, to imprisonment.) In an interview with Oishik Sircar, Jasbir Puar, while agreeing with Sircar that human rights are "pharmakon-like (both medicine and poison)," distinguishes human rights from liberalism. She contends that because of "the exclusionary practices and politics of liberal inclusion . . . there is no liberal 'solution' to Pal-estine" (Sircar). As Salaita centers Palestinians whose humanity persists in the face of (un)civil rites, he disarticulates liberalism from humanism and a con-cern with human rights. In his memoir, seemingly liberal tenets of narrative humanity and rights-based claims are folded into forms of narrated humanity that support BDS and its demands that should—but cannot—be accommodated within the value system of liberalism.

Even as *Uncivil Rites* powerfully challenges liberal readers in a form resistant to being criminalized or censored, its primary address is to Salaita's comrades, including the USACBI Organizing Collective, as it advances a vision of what Salaita calls "inter/nationalism." As theorized in his *Inter/Nationalism: Decolonizing Native America and Palestine* (2016), the term bespeaks a "commitment to mutual liberation," and consists of "an amalgamation of what is sometimes called solidarity, transnationalism, intersectionality, kinship, or intercommunalism" (ix). Envisioning "a Palestine disaggregated from its own geography" (152), *Inter/Nationalism* develops Salaita's long-standing commitment to a deterritorialized imaginary based on forms of kinship and "the play of decolonial narratives across cultures and colonial borders" (xv). This striving to bring together those engaged in materially interconnected struggles for liberation dates back to Salaita's earliest scholarly work. *The Holy Land in Transit* (2006) grew out of his dissertation, written under the mentorship of Robert Warrior (Osage). As Salaita explores shared discourses in Native American and Palestinian history, he states, "I hope to help intellectually unite ethnic and national groups that on some level share common histories" (4). This commitment—so key to Salaita's hire by the American Indian Studies department of which Warrior was a member—is not only intellectual. It also characterizes Salaita's activism, which begins but does not end with Palestine and BDS. Noting that "Native and Indigenous support of, and participation in, the Boycott, Divestment, and Sanctions (BDS) movement constitutes a quintessential form of inter/nationalism" (*Inter/Nationalism*, xvii), Salaita advocates for BDS to "conjoin itself to a global politics of Indigenism rather than to a liberal notion of multicultural dialogue" (63).[15] He insists that opposition to Indigenous dispossession requires prioritizing "economic, racial, sexual and geographic issues in addition to its traditional uses of rights-based discourse" (69). Without, in other words, forgoing the demand for rights from national and international bodies, inter/nationalism involves forms of liberation that come from recognition of how different struggles articulate, and from relationships oppressed people form with one another.

Published the same year as *Inter/Nationalism*, in many ways *Uncivil Rites* can be seen as its companion piece, one that helps build the kinship Salaita envisions as a crucial component of inter/nationalism. In *Inter/Nationalism*, Salaita postulates that "Kinship is more than an emotion. . . . It entails the intellectual rigors of theorization and political labor" (58). If *Inter/Nationalism* theorizes kinship, *Uncivil Rites* puts it into practice by engaging in a form of political labor. As the memoir enacts Salaita's vision of inter/nationalism, it not only describes but also participates in formulating, through acts of narrated humanity, relationships of decolonial love and chosen kinship on which BDS and other solidarity movements depend. As summed up in the chapter "Incivility Manifesto" but evident throughout his memoir, Salaita insists on linking Palestine solidarity work to struggles by those fighting corporations, contingent labor, homophobia, transphobia, ableism, classism, racism, anti-indigeneity, sexism, and militarization. In addressing academic communities, this manifesto is explicitly pro-student, decolonial, pro–faculty governance, pro-BDS, and pro-Indigenous in a global context (177–78). Such chapters position his memoir as an endeavor that is not only personal but also collective, political, and community-building.

The heart of this memoir beats for "the uncivilized" who are Salaita's chosen kin. Complementing its stories of family are those of solidarity premised not on political pragmatism but on decolonial love. As acts of narrated humanity, these stories embody "inter/nationalism" and lovingly represent and build on the comradery that gives life to the BDS movement and that in the wake of Salaita's firing offered him "salvation" and "a lifeline" (115). *Uncivil Rites* is full of stories of solidarity that are not abstract but material: they include offers of "money, homes, encouragement, acupuncture, yoga via skype, dental care" (63) that are expressions of "unfiltered, undiluted love" (63). Salaita also voices appreciation for friends like Lisa Kahaleole Hall and J. Kēhaulani Kauanui who schooled him "on the abusive dynamics of colonial induction" (113). This love and inter/national kinship—not anger or a desire for vengeance—are what inspire him to sue UIUC and its John Doe donors. Salaita explains that the support he received from principled lawyers and from "the folks at UIUC who had become like family to me" (115) took away any doubts that "I would fight. And, just like the Palestinians on whose behalf so many of us work, I have no intention of stopping" (116). In its model of kinship, *Uncivil Rites* brings together the values of filiation in the Saidian sense (the organic connection to inherited location) and affiliation, which Said defines as allegiances chosen out of "social and political conviction, economic and historical circumstances, voluntary effort and willed deliberation" (*The World*, 24–25). Salaita's dedication—to "he who ignites"—might well apply both to his son as his inspiration, and to the inter/national collectivity with whom he has chosen to affiliate.

Salaita ends on a collective note at once personal and political, individual and collective, as he makes memoir a vehicle for organizing and for "igniting" Palestinian students and scholars, along with other student activists and faculty (contingent, tenure-track, and tenured) who oppose the workings of unjust power. In the final chapter, he inspires us in direct addresses that accord with our different degrees of vulnerability to participate in principled actions against interconnected forms of oppression (188). His memoir ends not with "I," but with a collective and rousing "we":

> . . . as long as all people who suffer continue to endure, despite the dangers of endurance,
> So, too, must we. (192)

An epilogue follows, in which he reports on the findings of the UI lawsuit: although they confirmed the violation of his rights, they did not result in the restoration of his job. Rather than reflecting on what this means for him personally, once again, he breaks with memoir's mode of individualism and ends on a kinship-forging note. In his role of provocateur to power, pedagogue, and friend, he imparts his last words to those who share his political vision and to those dispossessed by colonialism and racial capitalism: "it's often worthwhile to push back. . . . Be steadfast and persistent. Behave ethically. Invoke the dignity of children and ancestors. Accept the love and support of friends" (195). He promises that, in persisting in this work, "you're left with something amusingly simple: sub-mediocre sycophants and inheritors of privilege who display all the psychological complexity of a mosquito buzzing around your ankles" (195). With these final words, although he withers his opponents with ridicule, more important than his righteous anger and resistance is how, in this address to his comrades, his memoir participates in political activism that he shows to be founded on relations of kinship and community.

Like *When They Call You a Terrorist*, *Uncivil Rites* is a memoir ignited by a movement that seeks to remake the world in accordance with principles arrived at collectively of justice, equality, and love. Both memoirs posit revolutionary change not in the future tense, and not as necessitating a violent overthrowing of implacable power (think here of the mosquitos!). Instead, like Cullors, Salaita advocates for daily practices of love and kinship that look back (to the ancestors) and forward (to the children). The resulting forms of narrated humanity show memoir's capacity to help carry the work of inter/national movements in conceiving radical forms of humanism that remake understandings of human being and belonging.

Creating Lifelines to a Decolonial Present and Future in SteveSalaita.com

Catalyzed as it is by his firing, *Uncivil Rites* is written in a reactive mode. Its forms of narrative and narrated humanity refute Zionist narratives and expose civility as a regime of dehumanization, while also championing BDS and other inter/national political movements. This section focuses on the website Salaita started in 2019, when having cut free of academe and the soul-sapping fight against Zionist blacklisting and lawfare, he became a school bus driver. In postings that accompany shorter polemics about politics, Salaita writes about the freedom that has come with time spent with his son and in his new job. Requiring no adherence to academic standards and publishing norms (though some will be featured as part of his memoir *An Honest Living*, forthcoming with Fordham University Press), these long-form, often associative essays take Salaita deeper into forms of narrated humanity. In them, as he works from the foundations of his life outside academe—as a Palestinian, as a father, as a writer, as an educator, as a longtime BDS activist, and as a school bus driver—he experiments with a decolonial mode of life writing.

Salaita's website opens to his name and, under it, the words, "No Flags, No Slogans," then under that, a photograph of a drawing made by Salaita's son that encapsulates his stance (fig. 4). Off to one side of a piece of slightly crumpled paper, his son has crayoned a tall blue podium and behind it, a small stick figure. On close inspection, this bald man with brown skin appears to be smiling. His feet, big blue blobs pointing downward, do not touch ground. By featuring this artwork, Salaita establishes his disinterest in a "professional" website and his freedom from the need to be marketable or accountable to administrators. This portrait also captures how fundamentally Salaita is both an educator and a doting father. At the same time, the figure at the podium appears dislocated, floating alone and perhaps a little lonely against an expanse of whiteness. Poignantly present in this picture are themes of fatherhood and of the freedom as well as aloneness that come with being an intellectual in exile.

Salaita develops these themes in his website, in essays that emerge from and continue his work as a public intellectual, educator, and activist committed to BDS and other inter/national movements for liberation. In his essay "The Big Picture," Salaita explains his decision not to participate in "an economy of self-absorption" or to capitalize on "sites of conflict," but instead to "derive material from necessary motion, a new and novel livelihood nearly absent as a setting in both fiction and nonfiction." Making clear the liberation that his website and his new job afford him, he states, "I post essays to a basic WordPress design, without worrying over deadlines and editorial politics. I barely know how to operate the site: I can upload and edit entries and create a thumbnail picture; everything else is a mystery. I dislike paywalls and don't really care about page clicks. My goal is to create a decent body of writing in a space conducive to experimentation" ("The Big Picture"). *Uncivil Rites*, through its mix of narrative and narrated humanity, refuses the inhumanity of civility and all it stands for.

Figure 4. Screenshot of Steven Salaita's website, featuring a drawing made by his son. (Permission granted by Steven Salaita)

In the experimental essays that accompany Salaita's exit from academe, as he writes about the "necessary motion" of driving a school bus, he imagines, and at moments realizes, kinder and freer ways of being human. In this life writing, he builds upon even as he does not consistently reference his engagement with decolonial and abolitionist theories and movements, or the political positions, often Palestine-related, that he takes up in the website's other essays.

Salaita's experiments with genre are as deliberate as his decision to pursue a "novel livelihood." Both constitute breaks with established forms of narrative humanity that equate moral rectitude with capitalist obedience, that promote spirit-killing and colonial conceptualizations of progress, and that posit education as the conduit to achieving these ill-begotten goals. As he puts this in "The Influence of Anxiety," when recalling the Victorian prison-like school building where he was to be civilized and "shaped into a good boy," "Even at the age of five, I understood that death feels like the hypostasis of progress." Charting a life narrative that overturns conventions of progress is not easy. As he wryly remarks, "It's hard to imagine coming of age in reverse. Hollywood doesn't make inspirational movies about struggling to overcome material comfort. . . . But forward progress as material comfort is cultivated through the ubiquitous lie that upward mobility equals righteousness" ("An Honest Living"). Despite these difficulties, in the story he tells, his career move, which defies capitalist understandings of success, appears neither as regression nor as failure.

In Salaita's acts of narrated humanity, his stories of education and coming of age do not serve as they regularly do in forms of narrative humanity to establish good citizenship, academic achievements, and money in the bank as markers of the human. In his website's inaugural essay, "An Honest Living," as he writes about his career move, the school bus emerges both as metaphor and as, quite literally, a vehicle for achieving an honest living. Salaita's new job allows him to leave behind the hypocrisies and cruelties of the corporatized academy and reconnect to the parts of a life in school that he values. After Salaita describes how his earliest memories are of going to work with his father, a physics professor who dubbed his curious young son "Prof.," he explains that he "went to college at seventeen knowing I would never leave." Thus, when he is expelled from academe, "Becoming a school bus driver wasn't random." He is attracted to the school bus for its role as equalizer ("Nearly everybody who grew up in the United States rode the bus as a child, even private school kids") and also for how it "induces primal expressions of love. School buses supersede their physical structure; they anchor a huge apparatus designed to guard the vulnerable. . . . The school bus is one of the few institutions in the United States that protects the powerless from the depredations of commerce." Explaining his lifelong search for "a space where I could conform to my surroundings without feeling unmoored from an inner sense of decency," he discovers, "That space, it turns out, is equivalent to the volume of a school bus." At the end of this beautiful and moving essay, he tells of how his son, with a child's "boundless ambition," learns from him how to operate a bus and run its routes. As his own father did, he begins referring to his son "as my little professor." This ending is tinged with wistfulness and a sense of loss. But it also captures a way of being in the world—

as a father, and as an educator/school bus driver—committed to imparting values of curiosity, equality, care, and decency that capitalist and colonial forms of success cannot accommodate.

Salaita goes on to develop this vision in subsequent essays. In "Left-Rights," when a little girl is being bullied, he tells of springing from his seat and grabbing the intercom mic to announce, "Nobody on this bus is ugly. Nobody." As the children stare at him, his voice breaking, he lets them know, "You're all beautiful. Every single one of you." These "coming of age in reverse" stories about time spent with his son and other school-aged children enact his conviction, as he reflects on the ordinary exchanges that contribute to both his job and his parenting, that "a decent life needn't follow conventional notions of excitement and success (fame, wealth, gratification, power), but is available in millions of transactions that cultures of profit and accumulation dismiss as insignificant" ("I miss igniting my bus"). In these stories, as teaching and parenting converge, Salaita insists on the interrelatedness of all humans; on the right of all humans to feel protected and loved; and on the honorableness of doing work that in the most everyday ways creates a world that accords with these convictions.

As in *Uncivil Rites*, this is not a liberal but an inter/national and radical humanism. In his narratives about children—his son, and those he transports on the school bus—Salaita advances an understanding of security not as money, and not as police presence or military might, but as community practices of humanity and decolonial care.

For this reason, Steve's stories return me to Palestine, to the spring of 2018 when I spent time at Al Quds University (AQU) as a visiting scholar, and to a bus ride I took back to Abu Dis from Occupied Jerusalem.[16] Let me preface this story by saying that during my four trips to Palestine, I have come to understand the daily heroism of Palestinian bus and cab drivers. Given how dangerous and complex Israelis have made it to drive West Bank roads, with their elaborately inhumane systems of checkpoints and their eruptions of militarized as well as vigilante settler violence, these jobs require courage, composure, quick thinking, and resourcefulness. On this particular bus ride, we were taking a route that had become familiar to me. So too had the generosity of this driver, Magid, who insisted on maneuvering the bus down a steep road to the AQU guesthouse, rather than dropping me at the final stop. I liked to sit up front—to chat with him, and also because I enjoyed witnessing his exchanges with friends who ran up to the bus midroute to hand him a sandwich or a coffee. On this evening, a man wandered into the middle of the street. When Magid ground the bus to a halt, the man pressed his face up against the wide expanse of glass at the front of the bus. He looked angry, disoriented, and disheveled. As the man's agitation increased, Magid stepped down from the bus, and another man watching from a produce shop came and joined him. They each put an arm around this young man, cradling him in the midst of all the stopped traffic until he became calm. Still holding him, they walked him gently to the sidewalk. Magid returned to the bus, and we continued on our way. To this day, I am struck by the kindness, the compassion, and the humanity of that act, especially when imagining his (and the driver's) fate at the hands of Israeli soldiers—or how in the United States, that man could well have ended up shot by police. When Steve announced he was leaving academe to drive a bus, that experience was still fresh in my mind. And although Steve and this bus driver live across the world from one another, when I read "An Honest Living," what came to mind were not only the lies of the Zionist playbook that demonize men like Steve and Magid to legitimate their own acts of terror. Steve's essay also brought home how bus drivers, through small acts of kindness, create conditions for genuine security, and touch the lives of those with whom they have the briefest and most regular of encounters.

This story of my time in Abu Dis speaks to me not only because of the connection I see between Steve and this bus driver, but also because of their separation. If I have the freedom to enter Palestine (however tenuously, given Israel's anti-BDS laws) or even claim it as my "birthright," Steve, as a perceived "security threat," is unable to exercise his right of return. And it is this state of exile along with Zionist violence that haunts his essays.

Even when his narratives about bus driving include no mention of Palestine, the way he "derive[s] material from necessary motion" and inhabits his exile from academe as a mixed state of freedom, alienation, recalcitrance, uncertainty, and nostalgia makes Palestine a palpable presence, one that can be placed in fruitful relationship to Said's theorizations of dispossession and intellectual exile. For both Salaita and Said, the condition of exile—of "a solitude experienced outside the group: the deprivations felt at not being with others in communal habitation" (Said, "Reflections on Exile," 2000)—is integral to being Palestinian, and also to being an intellectual whose allegiances are not to the academy or to preserving the status quo. In *The Politics of Dispossession*, Said notes, "The Palestinians are a people who move a lot, who are always carrying bags from one place to another." He explains that in the face of Zionist dispossession, this constant movement and the strident assertion of a continuing Palestinian presence "[give] us a further sense of identity as a people" (115). Said's contrapuntal understanding of Palestinian identity predates Zionism. As well, it is one that is both imposed by and also a "pessoptimistic" political response to Zionist dispossession. Being Palestinian therefore intersects with his identification as a secular critic, or intellectual exile who "exists in a median state, neither completely at one with the new setting nor fully disencumbered of the old, beset with half-involvements and half-detachments, nostalgic and sentimental on one level, an adept mimic or a secret outcast on another" ("Intellectual Exile," 49). Both as a Palestinian and as an intellectual, for Said, exile entails existing within and resisting a situation defined by imperialism (*Culture and Imperialism*, 79).

Salaita's explorations of his exilic state resonate with Said's. In "The Big Picture," Salaita reflects on his visit to South Africa to deliver a lecture at the University of Cape Town. He considers the "aftereffects" that come with being an "ex-academic," and his realization that "no amount of bitterness or cynicism will untether me from my original avocation. It's a strange sort of liminality, exile combined with disgust, which distorts my sense of belonging. The school bus or the campus? I can function in both spaces, but neither feels comprehensive, permanent; contradiction is the only steady variable." In this essay, and in "An Honest Living," he details pre-daylight hours spent pondering this mixed state and experiencing "pronounced moments of loneliness" ("An Honest Living"). In "The Big Picture," as he struggles during another such moment to make sense of his past and former jobs, he concludes, "It's not really a job, I realized. . . . It's more of a spiritual occupation." In these essays, as Salaita shuttles between the school bus and the college campus—connecting Israeli brutality in Palestine to Zionist repression in the US academy—the constant motion that comes with exile and dispossession is not only a source of loneliness, sadness, anger, and uncertainty. It is also a necessary existential condition for Salaita as a Palestinian and as an intellectual who refuses the status quo—a spiritual vocation that is not to be overcome as much as inhabited in an ongoing struggle for freedom and justice.

Writing during the era of BDS, and of Standing Rock and BLM, Salaita draws on an understanding of freedom in his acts of narrated humanity that emerges out of and contributes to contemporary Palestinian and other intersectional struggles for justice. These struggles are expressly abolitionist and/or Indigenous. In them, activists assert independence from the nation-state and its logics. Salaita's self-published stories about parenting and bus driving not only enact his freedom from publishing conventions and academic systems of evaluation but also declare his freedom from university administrators and their disciplinary actions, corporate donors and their undue influences, and Zionist lawfare. In his Cape Town lecture, "The Inhumanity of Academic Freedom," posted to his website, as he makes clear the limits of freedom that can be granted by the academy, he puts forth an alternative and urges his audience to help him collectively realize it: "Let us not wait for institutions to authorize our imagination. Let us create unsanctioned solidarities. Let us redefine disrepute. Let us harbor intellectual fugitives." The freedom he envisions, and brings into being through his acts of imagination, runs counter to contemporary forms of narrative humanity that advance freedom as a fixed state that is determined by and upheld in the form of nations and institutions; protected via policing, war, and other imperialist and militarized ventures; guaranteed in the form of individual rights and national belonging; and manifested as material wealth and ownership of property.

In contrast to such formulations, which further an exclusionary understanding of who counts as human, Salaita imagines freedom, to draw on Angela Davis's words, as "a constant struggle." He envisions it not as future goal or already-achieved state, but as a process directed toward creating a world in which all people live together in conditions of equality, safety, and care. Although such a world does not yet exist for humans who are confined within the domain of the civil, to spend time with children, and also to participate in the work to create such a world, constitute ways to realize freedom as a practice. Salaita explores this approach in "The Inhumanity of Academic Freedom." In that essay, he reflects on contexts that led to his firing: the criminalization of BDS and of any revolutionary political speech in a corporatized, militarized, imperial academy. He interweaves this analysis with considerations regarding the ascendancy of fascism; South African–Palestinian solidarity; and the joys of spending time with his young son, which he explains is "the only time I know freedom. . . . He hasn't yet discovered the enervating logic of civility." Toward this essay's end, he brings its different threads together by way of a story about parenting. He describes the pleasure he has taken in attending his son's baseball practices: "There I sat on a grassy hillside and watched my boy run and smile and I'd remember the meaning of freedom—not as a term, but a feeling, its most essential incarnation." After Salaita, having urged his son to practice hitting because "it will pay off," faces his son's disappointment when he strikes out, he connects this experience back to his own "unwillingness to grovel my way back into academe's good graces." He concludes, "But it's been almost impossible to understand the stakes because the story is ongoing, its plot out of my control." Despite the uncertainties that accompany this unscripted story line, he states his determination "to keep alive the idea of freedom. If I back down from a dangerously simple vision of Palestinian liberation, one intolerant of anything less than equality, then I will have betrayed the people with whom my destiny is aligned. . . . I endure the punishment not because I'm a sucker or a martyr . . . but because I want the vision of freedom ubiquitous among the dispossessed to survive." Stating his refusal to "abdicate my commitment to human beings dismissed as surplus, devoid of influence, unloved by power," he states of his "unapologetic defiance": "That's how we win. That's how the downtrodden have always won. . . . That's why they hate me. . . . Because I'll never compromise the humanity of the Palestinian people in order to assuage a colonizer."[17] Despite all the efforts to destroy him—to take his health insurance, drag him repeatedly into court, force him to hourly labor—he says that what he has left is "the one thing they can't extinguish: a fixation on equality, recorded in steady rhythms with an uncapped pen. In other words: freedom." In concluding this essay, he brings his child back into the picture:

> Institutions wring humanity out of social relations and so the indescribable closeness of filial love, in whispered exchanges of hope and anxiety, becomes a lifeline to meaningful futures. I don't want to conceptualize justice as an attempt to curtail our worst tendencies, but as a disposition that reproduces the imperatives of filial love in spaces of mercy and compassion.
>
> . . .
>
> I want to take up residence with you in a world of impossible ideas.
>
> And the main idea we must nurture isn't academic freedom; it's simply freedom, unadorned, unmediated, unmodified.

Through this essay's associative moves, Salaita brings together writing freely, the disciplined practice (or "steady rhythms") of his filial love, and building freedom and community with his readers through shared commitments to intersectional movements for justice.

Taking as his starting point those who are most vulnerable and dispossessed, in this essay and its companion pieces, Salaita counters the inhumanity of racial capitalism, civility, and the settler state as he participates in the making of a world premised on care for and commitment to the liberation of all humans. The vision Salaita enacts through his website demonstrates how, as with participating in movements for freedom and justice, engaging in acts of narrated humanity provides both a way to get free that need not wait for the demise of racial capitalism and settlerism and also a way to imagine better ways of human being and belonging.

"Milk, Stones and Water": From the Inter/National to the Inter/Species, a Love Story

By way of concluding this chapter, and transitioning to the final chapter's consideration of the need to stay with but move beyond the human as an elemental concern, a story:

In 2016, I organized a visit for Steve as part of a running series, "Decolonial November." Each November since 2013, as a founder and then faculty
adviser for SFJP@UH, I have committed to bringing out a Palestinian visi-
tor to build solidarity between Hawaiʻi and Palestine as interconnected sites
of settlerism. Since meeting Steve during the sustained campaign to pass
the ASA boycott resolution and working with him on the USACBI Organizing Collective, I had wanted to bring him to Hawaiʻi. Other UH faculty
and students were equally enthusiastic. Members of SFJP@UH had spent
the summer and the first part of the semester reading and discussing his recently published *Inter/Nationalism*. We were primed to continue conversations started in previous Decolonial Novembers with Noura Erakat, Remi
Kanazi, Nadera Shalhoub, and also Noor Daglhas and Mai Hasan, under-
graduates from Birzeit University (BZU) who had come in spring 2016 as
part of a "Right to Education" (R2E) tour organized by the National SJP and
BZU's R2E.

Steve's visit was packed. He delivered lectures at a church ("Why Palestine
Is Everyone's Moral Issue") and at the university ("Freedom to Boycott: BDS
and the Modern University"); led a seminar on *Inter/Nationalism*; and participated in a roundtable discussion at the Kamakakūokalani Center for Hawaiian Studies titled "Inter/Nationalism: From Palestine to Hawaiʻi" with UH
students and faculty Joy Enomoto, Noelani Goodyear-Kaʻōpua, Kahala Johnson, ʻIlima Long, and Ali Musleh (fig. 5). In addition, Steve went on a DeTour
with demilitarization activists Kyle Kajihiro and Aunty Terri Kekoʻolani; and
attended meals and beach gatherings with students, faculty, and community
organizers.

Steve's time in Honolulu coincided with other significant events: the 100-
year anniversary of the Balfour Declaration, in which the British government
promised Jewish people a "national home" in Palestine; a visit by Donald
Trump to Honolulu; and the founding of a UH chapter of the Campus Anti-
fascism Network (CAN) in response to the Trump presidency and the Proud
Boys' presence on the UH campus. His visit also followed Rocky the monk
seal giving birth to her pup Kaimana on Kamaina Beach, a favorite spot for
locals adjacent to the small Waikīkī hotel where Steve was staying. So, too,
the movement to protect Mauna Kea, the world's tallest mountain and an ancestor to Native Hawaiians, from construction of a Thirty Meter Telescope
(TMT) was well under way. We discussed all of this, including on Steve's final
day in Honolulu, when we gathered at Kaimana for an SFJP@UH potluck. Talking as we shared food and took ocean dips, we punctuated our conversation
with visits to the edge of the cordoned-off part of the beach. There, without
words, we watched Rocky lounging with her pup.

Figure 5. Roundtable discussion titled "Inter/Nationalism: From Palestine to Hawai'i" at the Kamakakūokalani Center for Hawaiian Studies Hālau o Haumea with (*left to right*) Joy Enomoto, Noelani Goodyear-Ka'ōpua, Steven Salaita, Ali Musleh, 'Ilima Long, and Kahala Johnson. (Photo taken by author. Permissions granted by Salaita, Enomoto, Goodyear-Ka'ōpua, Musleh, Long, and Johnson)

In his Mondoweiss article "Washing Ashore in Hawaii," Steve reflects on several of these conjunctures (fig. 6). In the interest of building "communal activism," he situates Trump and the ills of military occupation, land theft, foreign settlement, and structural racism in the US/Hawai'i in relation to "the same colonial apparatus" in Israel/Palestine. Characteristically, what concerns Salaita is how "the colonial imagination" perpetuates this violence, and how Kanaka Maoli and Palestinians engage in decolonial refusal. After outlining manifestations of settlerism in both places, he urges his readers to "Listen to Hawaiians and Palestinians. They constantly attempt to conceptualize a world unbound by commonsensical notions of the possible." From there he turns his attention from Trump's visit to Mauna Kea, repudiating the binary understanding that the struggle over the TMT pits science against superstition and savagery. He concludes the article with a description of Kaimana:

Little Kaimana had skin like jet black patent leather, dusted with grains of sand and adorned by pliant whiskers. She sometimes smiled

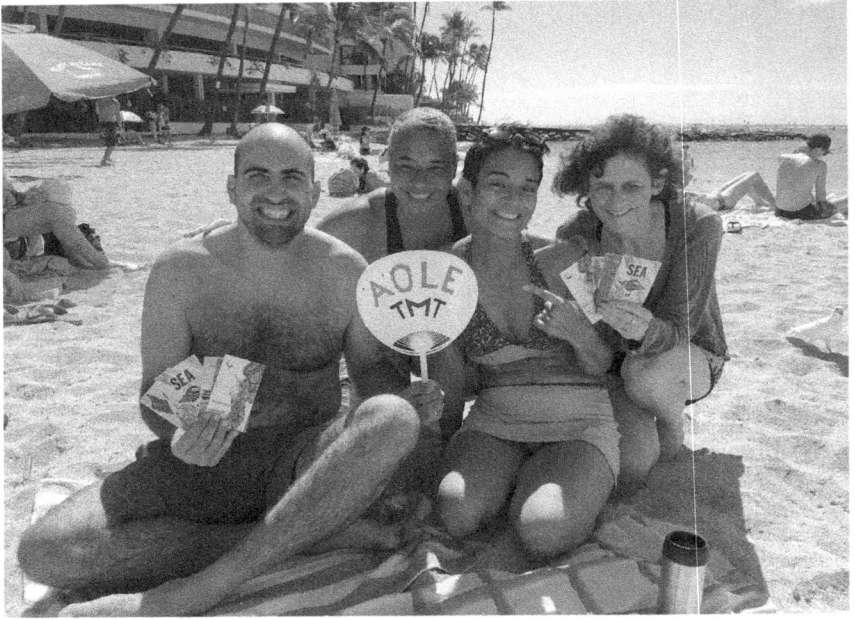

Figure 6. Trip to Kaimana Beach during Steven Salaita's visit. *Left to right:* Steven Salaita, Joy Enomoto, Kim Compoc, Cynthia Franklin holding "sea of islands" artwork by Enomoto and "'A'OLE TMT" fan. (Photo taken by author. Permission granted by Salaita, Enomoto, and Compoc)

for photographers and liked to show affection, nestling with Rocky and occasionally kissing her mouth. People spoke of the seals in a reverent tone, as if cognizant of the world's fragility. It was a moment of agreement, an existential reckoning around dark flesh on tan sand, a reemergence of wilderness in the suburbs, the contrasts offering an incisive answer to the world's most complicated questions.

Steve notes, "In the presence of Rocky and Kaimana, people felt secure. That sense of security didn't arise from an abundance of bases and armaments, but from the simplicity of milk, stones, and water."

In the stead of military proliferation, and what Sherene Seikaly notes are mottos of safety and security that function "to dispossess the Palestinian" who "stands as a threat to security, not a subject who may desire security" (Hanhardt et al.), Steve embraces a radically different sense of security. His is a security premised on care—of a mother for her pup; of humans making space to protect that mother-child dyad and a fragile and interconnected ecosystem. He also captures the collective human wonder over that monk seal birthing, on a beach crowded with humans on the outskirts of Waikīkī. And he dwells on ways answers to large questions lie not in high-tech outer space exploration, but through close and respectful attention to the elemental care encapsulated in that birthing, and in the responses to it that honor intimate, everyday, and extraordinary relations between humans and nonhumans. When Steve advocates for decolonial imagination, for conceptualizing "a world unbound by commonsensical notions of the possible," this does not require space travel or the tools of western astronomy. Nor is it bound only to inter/national forms of human solidarity. The making of a new world also demands attention to time immemorial if often forgotten human-more-than-human relations,[18] to monk seals, and to the elemental simplicity and sanctuary to be found in milk, stones, and water.

In this way, Salaita's "Washing Ashore" takes us back to this chapter's beginning, and to the pleasure he and his son take in "Upside Down," a video that, as Jack Johnson plunges from land into water, values imagination, care, and connection among humans, animals, the ocean, land, and stars. As "Washing Ashore" and a return to "Upside Down" take us onto Kanaka Maoli land, these texts transition us to this book's concluding chapter, which concerns the movement to protect Mauna Kea and the need to think beyond without skipping over the human. And here it is fitting that Johnson played "Upside Down" at a rally at the Hawai'i State Capitol in support of Mauna Kea, and went to the Mauna to play music, lending his voice to Kanaka Maoli kia'i (protectors) standing for aloha 'āina. When it comes to acts of narrated humanity and what they make possible, context, as I have been arguing, is crucial. Whether it be thousands of kia'i and allies, gathered not only on the Mauna but also at the center of State power, singing a joy-filled song about turning things upside down, or Salaita, sharing visions of cross-species care with his son and readers in ways that resonate with his expressions of inter/national kinship and filial love, we can glimpse the power of decolonial imaginings. We also can envision in such movement-building acts of narrated humanity not only freedom as a constant struggle, but also the true security that comes with decolonial formulations of the human that depend on practices—simultaneously forward-facing and time immemorial—of care and respect for human and more-than-human beings and for the elements that sustain us all.

PART III

*Narrated Humanity and
Grounded Narrative Humanity*

5

"E Hū ē" (Rising Like a Mighty Wave)

Mauna Kea and the Movement beyond the Human

E nā hoaʻāina e
E nā hoawelo like e
E nā hoapili e
E nā hoaaloha e
ALOHA ʻĀINA!
Kūkulu e, nā kūkulu ʻehā e
KŪKULU!
He mau maka koa e nā maka kaʻeo
EŌ!
E hū e
HŪ!
He kū kiaʻi Mauna
KŪ!
He pōhaku kū
KŪʻ&!
He ʻili ʻili kapu
ALOHA!
He koa wai e ola
OLA!
E hū e
HŪ!

Natives, the backbone of Hawaiʻi,
Relatives of the big ocean of Kiwa
Relations of the first nation of Turtle Island,
Friends, supports from around the world,

Pillars, the four cardinal points,
We are beloved warriors,
We are strong (wearing our topknots on our heads)
Rise . . . A mountain guardian,
A standing rock,
A sacred stone,
A water protector
Rise . . .

—PUA CASE, "NA KŪKULU OLI"

In every Indigenous story tradition I know . . . we learned to be human
in large part from the land and our other-than-human relatives.
—DANIEL HEATH JUSTICE, *WHY INDIGENOUS LITERATURES MATTER*

In this concluding chapter, through attention to the movement to protect
Mauna Kea from construction of the Thirty Meter Telescope (TMT), I continue my inquiry into narrative and narrated humanity by exploring the importance of the human in relation to other-than-human lives and elemental
forces. To engage the movement for Mauna Kea is to confront the limits of
focusing on the human, and of working within this book's referenced framework of narrative humanity. The stories emerging from and as part of the movement for Mauna Kea (also known as Mauna a Wākea and Maunakea) not
only counter the dehumanization that inheres in hegemonic narrative humanity but also evidence an Indigenous system of narrative humanity, one I will
be calling "grounded narrative humanity." In coming up with this name, I am
indebted to Yellowknives Dene scholar Glen Sean Coulthard's theorization
of "grounded normativity." By this he means "the modalities of Indigenous
land-connected practices and longstanding experiential knowledge that inform
and structure our ethical engagements with the world and our relationships
with human and nonhuman others over time" (13).[1] In naming this way of being "grounded normativity," Coulthard unsettles settler norms and lays collective claim to a world that is decolonial rather than anticolonial—one with
norms that predate, and do not derive from or talk back to, the settler state.
Following his lead, I make what I hope is a complementary move in proposing
the term "grounded narrative humanity," to reference a framework for narrating and understanding the human that is normative within Indigenous worldviews. Stories based in grounded narrative humanity sustain modalities of
Coulthard's grounded normativity as they posit humans in profound, long-
standing relationships to land and other-than-humans. Grounded narrative
humanity posits as normative a distinctly anticapitalist and decolonial under-

standing of the human as part of a story still in the making, one in which humans exist in reciprocal, caring, and nonhierarchical kinship with one another and a living, breathing world. Stories of grounded narrative humanity also often simultaneously constitute acts of narrated humanity. Not clearly demarcated from grounded *narrative* humanity, these instances of *narrated* humanity work in concert with other interconnected, inter/national liberation movements. In so doing, they sometimes work beyond but not against grounded narrative humanity's understandings of the human to realize a decolonial future. Taken together, as they help materialize as-yet-unconceived ways of being human, these modes of grounded narrative humanity and narrated humanity shape, energize, and form dynamic relationships among movements in the making, including the movements for Mauna Kea and those considered in previous chapters (BLM and BDS).

In this last chapter, as I dwell on—and seek to participate in—acts of grounded narrative and narrated humanity that animate the movement for Mauna Kea, in a departure from the previous chapters, my focus is not on stories that have occasioned or intervened in controversies in the public sphere concerning who counts as human. Instead, some of the stories I tell are small ones that take place in the spaces between public ceremonies or events. Others unfold off the pages or outside the frames—but as part of the process—of the many vibrant texts and protocols produced as part of the movement to protect Mauna Kea. Because many of the stories and insights I share, the questions I raise, and the approaches I consider come from my experiences and personal relationships, I often move into an autobiographical mode. When I use first names, it is to mark stories or experiences that have come out of these more intimate contexts.

I also share movement- and public-facing narratives, sometimes by the same people who are part of the more personal stories I tell.[2] These narratives bring together Kanaka Maoli and all their relations, including the land and elements, other peoples engaged in articulated struggles, and an international audience. We see an example of this in kumu hula (master hulu teacher) and Mauna leader Pua Case's 2017 composition, "Na Kūkulu Oli." This call-and-response oli that unites Kanaka, Maori, and Turtle Islander protectors and their friends concludes protocols held on and far beyond the reaches of Mauna a Wākea. At the center of such chants and stories is aloha ʻāina—a concept that translates (roughly, insufficiently) to a dedication to Hawaiian independence, and to love and care for the land that gives life to all its relations. As I take up acts of narrated humanity that emerge out of a grounded narrative humanity and that participate in inter/national movement making, my interest is also in the radical and necessary challenges they pose to assumptions that the human, however defined, is a distinct category. This last chapter, then, serves both as a conclusion and as an opening, an aperture that builds upon as it also departs from the previous chapters.

As Indigenous movements, including the one to protect Mauna Kea, make clear, to consider forms of kinship and relationality that include but go beyond human beings is necessary for planetary as well as human survival. A foundational assumption of grounded narrative humanity, this relationality extends from humans to standing rocks and sacred stones, from mountains to monk seals and the elements Steven Salaita evokes when he reflects on his visit to Hawaiʻi (see chapter 4). So too, these movements evidence why situating humans in intimate relation to more-than-human life-forms cannot mean homogenizing or jumping over the human. Kaleikoa Kaʻeo makes this clear in an April 2015 speech opposing the TMT: "How can you dehumanize us, and call yourselves scientists? . . . Either we're human beings, or we're not; either we have a place to decide what is sacred, or we don't!" ("Speech").

Located on the island of Hawaiʻi, and the world's highest mountain at 32,000 feet when measured from its underwater base, Mauna Kea is both ancestor and sacred site to Kanaka Maoli. The Mauna is the piko, the summit and the umbilical connection or point of origin, that connects Kanaka Maoli to those who have come before them and to those yet to come, and it is a source of life-giving waters.[3] As Pua Case explains, "Mauna Kea is known as our *kupuna*, our ancestor, our teacher, our protector, our corrector and our guide" (Democracy Now!, "'If Not Now'"). The movement to protect Mauna Kea is not only an act of decolonial love, an assertion of aloha ʻāina that situates the human in loving and respectful kinship and interdependency with the more-than-human. It is simultaneously a specifically human struggle. It involves acts of resistance and nonconsent—or what Michi Saagiig Nishnaabeg writer Leanne Betasamosake Simpson calls "generative refusal" (*As We Have Always Done*, 9)—not only to the TMT, but to man-made structures of settlerism, racial capitalism, and heteropatriarchy that are dehumanizing as well as destructive of all life-forms. To stand for Mauna Kea is also to rise up with people engaged in related, inter/national movements. Both anticolonial resistance and a decolonial embrace of Indigenous cultural and political practices, the movement for Mauna Kea is one of world making. As aloha ʻāina follow the call of Pua Case and other leaders to "E hū ē"—to envision and activate themselves as elemental forces in order to rise like a wave to protect the Mauna,[4] through acts of grounded narrative and narrated humanity that include but do not give primacy to the human, they contribute to what Simpson calls "radical resurgence" (*As We Have Always Done*; see esp. 34–37).

As aloha ʻāina rise up and bring to life ways of human being at once old and new, stories and storytelling play a central role. Drawn as they are from

Indigenous epistemologies and told as part of a resurgent movement that creates a decolonial future, these stories operate outside the logics of hegemonic narrative humanity. Instead, as they indicate the presence of another (grounded) narrative humanity, they also partake in movement making, or narrated humanity. Their substance and the movement contexts in which kiaʻi (protectors) and allies share and reshare Mauna Kea stories make possible alternatives to the capitalist, colonial, racist, and heteropatriarchal structures that underwrite narrative humanity's hegemonic formulations of the human. In the acts of grounded narrative and narrated humanity that feed and are fed by the movement for the Mauna, sovereignty, life, and independence (known in Hawaiian as "ea," a word that also means breath, and rising) are not individualist, premised on dominance, contractual, or extractive. They are not measured by possession of money or land, nor are they achieved through claiming mastery over other humans, more-than-human beings, or elemental forces. Instead, sovereignty, freedom, and other qualities so central to understandings of human flourishing are premised on deep bonds and interdependence (pilina); being part of a collective, self-governing people (lāhui); place- and land-based responsibilities, authority and rights (kuleana); practices of aloha ʻāina; and compassion and adherence to prohibitions against violence and harm, even to one's opponents (kapu aloha); all of which come into being through the communal telling and sharing of stories.[5] Kawena Kapahua, the youngest member of the kiaʻi-led media team Nā Leo Kākoʻo, speaks to the power of stories in the movement for the Mauna: "For a young Hawaiian like me, the breath and stories of the kūpuna [ancestors] fill my lungs, allowing me to breathe and pass on breath to the next generation, so that one day soon we'll no longer be gasping for air, no longer breathless. What there will be is ea—life/breath/sovereignty/rising" (581). Kapahua's reflections on the importance of being able to breathe are particularly resonant because he writes during the time of COVID-19, BLM, and climate crisis fires. The ea, the ways of being human, this storytelling breathes into life centers Kanaka ʻŌiwi,[6] their lāhui, and the sacred Mauna they rise up, in struggle, to protect.

Kū Kiaʻi Mauna!: The Movement for Mauna Kea

Kanaka-led organizing to protect Mauna Kea dates back decades before the movement to stop construction of the TMT.[7] For over fifty years, kiaʻi have opposed the desecration of Mauna Kea—and also, on Maui, Haleakalā—as the state, the University of Hawaiʻi (UH), and their governmental, corporate, and university partners have erected thirteen observatories housing twenty-two telescopes on Mauna Kea, and thirteen observatories on Haleakalā. Planned to be the most massive observatory yet, budgeted at 1.4 billion dollars, and already outdated in its technology, the TMT would stand eighteen stories high, with a footprint of over five acres. The TMT Corporation, UH, and the settler state are joined in this project by partners in Canada, China, India, Japan, and the United States, with the largest single donor being the Gordon and Betty Moore Foundation in Palo Alto, California. Although these corporate and colonial entities represent the TMT project as a pure and noble enterprise that supports science while casting kia'i as antiscience and atavistic, even UH-Hilo's *Final Environmental Impact Statement* acknowledges that the TMT would contribute to the already "substantial, significant, and adverse" harm caused by telescopes on Mauna Kea (University of Hawai'i). As J. Kēhaulani Kauanui observes, "In addition to desecrating the sacred site, which would also cause gross ecological damage, particularly to the Mauna Kea aquifer, the TMT project is a violation of the state of Hawai'i's responsibility to manage the 'public lands' constituted in part by Mauna Kea and to fulfill constitutional and statutory obligations to Kanaka Maoli" ("Introduction"). Stands for Mauna Kea and Haleakalā have taken place over the past decades in the courts as well as through direct action, "EAducation" (education related to ea), and cultural practices and events that constitute articulated and often overlapping expressions of aloha 'āina.

The rallying calls throughout Hawai'i and worldwide to stand in protection of Mauna Kea ("Kū Kia'i Mauna") and to shut down the TMT ("'Aole TMT") build on years of organizing against the TMT—and over one hundred years of Kanaka Maoli coming together as a lāhui to assert never-relinquished sovereignty over the illegally expropriated Crown and Government Lands of the Hawaiian Kingdom. Since 2011, Kanaka Maoli have opposed the TMT by engaging in legal challenges, ceremony, cultural practices, EAducation, social media campaigns, protests, and civil disobedience, all in keeping with the practice and philosophy of kapu aloha. With legal cases based on settler state and Hawaiian Kingdom laws still pending, the TMT Corporation moved anyway in April 2015 to begin moving equipment up Mauna Kea Access Road. Protectors formed a blockade to stop the crews. Police arrested thirty-one kia'i during this action that staved off construction. Then, in June 2015, when the TMT and its partners again acted to move trucks up the Mauna, protectors sent out a kāhea (summons, call). Over eight hundred Kānaka Maoli and allies came to the Mauna in response. Under the leadership of Kaho'okahi Kanuha, starting at what became known as the "Aloha 'Āina Checkpoint" or the "Legendary Crosswalk," and stretching up to the summit, protectors formed sixteen lines. Blocking the Access Road with the strength and life-force of pōhaku (rocks), these protectors enacted the living structure of the Kumulipo, the cosmogonic genealogical chant whose sixteen sections establish humans' kinship with more-than-human creatures, land, ocean, and skies.[8] At the Aloha 'Āina Checkpoint, described by Noelani Goodyear-Ka'ōpua as "a space of engagement" ("Protectors," 190), kia'i invited police, construction crews, and tourists to join protectors and act in kapu aloha. As they chanted in ceremony, children and other kia'i greeted law enforcement officials with lei under the protective watch of legal observers. Without further arrests, this action, in coordination with others across the archipelago, effectively stopped construction. It also enacted and extended as an invitation a decolonial way to be human.

Kia'i again came together to protect Mauna Kea in the summer of 2019, in an all-out mobilization made possible by years of concerted organizing, testifying, and building pilina with one another and those engaged in related struggles, especially Indigenous-led ones. After the Hawaii Supreme Court ruled in 2018 in support of the TMT and the Board of Land and Natural Resources' decision to issue a building permit, Governor David Ige announced in June 2019 that construction would begin on July 15, 2019. On July 10, in conjunction with other state and UH officials, Ige announced a partial closure of the Mauna Kea Access Road. Kanaka 'Ōiwi across the political spectrum unified in response, and on July 13, together with the activist group HULI (the Hawai'i Unity and Liberation Institute), the Royal Order of Kamehameha established Pu'uhonua o Pu'uhuluhulu as a place of refuge at the base of the Mauna Kea Access Road, where it met with the Daniel K. Inouye Highway. Before dawn on July 15, eight kia'i (Adam Mahi'ai Dochin, Malia Hulleman, Kaleikoa Ka'eo, Noelani Goodyear-Ka'ōpua, Jamaica Heolimeleikalani Osorio, Kamuela Park, Walter Ritte, and 'Imaikalani Winchester) chained themselves to the cattle guard on the Access Road, remaining for twelve hours until the state promised not to move equipment up the road that day. At the start of what became an eight-month blockade stopped only by COVID-19, kūpuna and other kia'i came together on the Access Road (since renamed by kia'i as the Ala Hulu Kūpuna, or the Road of Our Cherished Elders) and, as the state again geared up to violently remove kia'i, HULI issued a kāhea for people to gather at the Pu'uhonua. HULI members Camille Kalama, 'Ilima Long, and Andre Perez orchestrated trainings in direct non-violent action. Within days, the forty people on the Mauna grew to hundreds, and then thousands. On July 17, Governor Ige declared a state of emergency and called in the National Guard and police forces. They arrived in riot gear, armed with chemical dispersants, sonic weaponry, semiautomatic guns, and batons.[9] That day, a line of kūpuna met a militarized police force with linked arms and kapu aloha. After police arrested thirty-eight kūpuna and their assistants, some of the kūpuna in wheelchairs, some lifted prostrate to the waiting paddy wagons, a line of "mana wāhine" formed: some seventy-five powerful women, arm-in-arm, chanting, put their bodies on the line for the Mauna.

Coordinated actions took place throughout the islands. At UH-Mānoa, in response to the arrests, protectors held a press conference on the steps of the central administration's building, Bachman Hall, calling out UH president and CEO David Lassner. Afterward, a kiaʻi, beckoning us to "come close," invited participation in an airport convoy. Our line of cars and trucks, bedecked with red ribbons, Hawaiian flags, and ʻAole TMT signs, stopped traffic as we drove on the H-1 freeway at 10 mph to the airport. Not only did the Convoy send a message to arriving tourists, but, along with protectors acting across the islands and in other parts of the US, we sent solidarity to the kiaʻi on the Mauna, and a clear signal to UH and the settler state that what happened on the Mauna would not stay on the Mauna. As Uahikea Maile noted, "the convoy caused such a fright for the state's central hub of economic activity that State of Hawaii leaders called off the police operation at the base of Maunakea" ("Ka Lei o ka Lanakila"). Radiating out from Mauna Kea as piko, a massive Hawaiʻi-wide *and* international mobilization was under way, with the numbers of protectors traveling to the Mauna that summer reaching 5,000–7,000 on any given day. These included NoDAPL (No Dakota Access Pipeline) Water Protectors that Mauna leaders Pua Case, Hāwane Rios, Andre Perez, Camille Kalama, Gwen Kim, Malia Hulleman, and other kiaʻi had built relations with during their time at Standing Rock and Sacred Stone Camp.

In the coming months, as the state poured more than eleven million dollars into "security" to stop them, protectors established a whole world in the parking-lot-turned-puʻuhonua. They did so in the face of constant threats of militarized state violence and a panoply of state and university administrative rules and regulations, all designed to foment fear, criminalize free speech, quell dissent, and break protectors' bank accounts. So too those occupying the Mauna endured blistering heat, formidable cold, and restricted oxygen from the 6,000-foot elevation. As the movement to protect the Mauna swelled, kiaʻi organized Puʻuhonua o Puʻuhuluhulu in accordance with principles of true security, care, consent, kapu aloha, and aloha ʻāina. Māhealani Ahia, a Mauna leader who spent months living at Puʻuhonua o Puʻuhuluhulu, notes that this space of refuge evolved organically as "an autonomous zone, a social justice experiment in community empowerment, a kauhale [group of houses] village, an ʻohana [family]. What I witnessed was the continual spontaneous eruption of need and fulfillment. Grounded in ancestral understandings of puʻuhonua as places of refuge, protection from punishment by governing authorities, and spaces of healing and restitution, the puʻuhonua established in 2019 has evolved uniquely." This evolution, she goes on to explain, was the result of kiaʻi enacting their kuleana through their *"ability to respond"* ("Mālama Mauna," 609). Exercising this kuleana with discipline and imagination, as the movement grew exponentially, kiaʻi camped out in cars and tents worked to ensure safe crossing of the highway, made supply runs, and maintained the cleanest port-a-potties I have ever stepped foot in. They established a check-in tent to orient visitors and accept donations; set up a kitchen that fed as many as a few thousand people three meals a day; started a supply tent, Hale Hoʻolako, to which people donated blankets, warm clothing, and sleeping bags; created a childcare tent; formed an art center, run, in part, by Standing Rock artist/organizers; and established media quarters. They also staffed a Mauna Medics Hale with a hui (group) of healers skilled in traditional Hawaiian healing, homeopathy, acupuncture, and allopathic medicine; and founded Hale Mauna Māhū and Hale Mauna Wāhine as what Ahia described as "brave space-making" places for women, māhū, and queer folx (607). As well, kiaʻi created Puʻuhuluhulu University. Initiated and run by Presley Keʻalaanuhea Ah Mook Sang (affectionately dubbed as Chancellor), ʻIlima Long, Kahala Johnson, and Ahia, the university offered twenty classes a day (approximately one thousand altogether) taught by hundreds of educators, in classrooms set up on the lava fields at the base of Puʻuhuluhulu. In front of the tent for kūpuna and their caretakers, kiaʻi and visitors gathered three times a day along the Ala Hulu Kūpuna for ceremony, for concerts, and to learn hula and other protocols. This paved access road to the Mauna was transformed into a ceremonial space, one lined with flags from those who came from all over the world to be in solidarity with the aloha ʻāina occupying the Mauna. As described by Marie Alohalani Brown, one of the thirty-eight arrested and creator of Hale Hoʻolako, "The Puʻuhonua o Puʻuhuluhulu remains an incredible example of lāhui, in both the sense of nation and people, as a sovereign space/place run organically by intelligent, hardworking, dedicated, selfless aloha ʻāina who embody the best of our culture and what it means to be Kanaka ʻŌiwi. I have never experienced such sustained unconditional love as I did at the puʻuhonua" ("Aloha Wale," 584).[10] During my three 2019 trips to Mauna Kea, I experienced how kiaʻi created this decolonial space of love and connectivity, and through ceremony along with everyday practices of reproductive labor, brought into being at this crossroads a world of abundance, mutual aid, and care, welcoming all who came to support their vision.

The world making on the Mauna ignited an inter/national movement as it also helped spark uprisings across Hawaiʻi—the Hanapēpē salt ponds,

Hūnānāniho, Kalaeloa, Kahuku, Kaua'ula, and Nā Wai 'Ehā. In the words of Maile, kia'i set in motion a "cultural resurgence" through which protectors "are crafting alternatives to the death-dealing of corporate development linked to global capital and settler colonialism" ("For Mauna Kea"). Mauna protocols, including traditional as well as contemporary hula, chants and songs that have served as the movement's anthems have spread throughout and beyond Hawai'i. At UH-Mānoa, Professors Davianna Pōmaika'i McGregor, Ty P. Kāwika Tengan, and Kahikina de Silva—along with students with Kia'i Ke Kahaukani (Kaipulaumakaniolono Baker, Tiele-Lauren Doudt, Jonathan Fiske, Keahinuinakeakua Johnson, Kawaipuna Kalipi, Beau Shishido, Bruce Ka'imi Watson), many of whom were occupying Bachman Hall in protest of the TMT—also held protocol three times daily, and after, people shared action items and updates from the Mauna. Different groups came together and organized a unity march on October 5, 2019, through Waikīkī attended by some fifteen thousand people, almost all of us in red Mauna wear. Massive rallies took place at the State Capitol, with hundreds dancing, singing, and chanting together. Trucks and cars flew Kū Kia'i Mauna and Hawaiian hae (flags), even after the state responded by outlawing them when appended to vehicles. Members of paddling clubs, baseball teams, hula hālau, and K-12 schools chanted and participated in Mauna Kea actions. Under the leadership of Healani Sonoda-Pale, Ka Lāhui Political Action Committee (part of the sovereignty group Ka Lāhui) initiated a range of political actions ranging from the legislative to the grassroots. Kumu hula taught oli and hula workshops on university and school campuses, and in parks and parking lots. At UH, professors held open-access Hawaiian language classes on Wednesday afternoons attended by hundreds. Students, faculty, and staff held art days and teach-ins; acted in Hawaiian language plays; and testified and protested at UH Board of Regents meetings. Musicians jammed for and at the Mauna, and people across the world testified, danced, sang, and sent videos and photos expressing solidarity.[11] Celebrities and politicians caught the Mauna wave—Jason Momoa made a Mauna Kea video, and in Honolulu, Janet Jackson invited kia'i to lead an audience of thousands in Mauna mele and oli (and it was especially moving to see Mauna Kea leaders 'Ilima Long, and Andre Perez and Camille Kalama on stage with their young daughters, becoming part of this history in the making). Bernie Sanders, Elizabeth Warren, and Alexandria Ocasio-Cortez took positions opposing the TMT. More important than any big-name endorsements, however, the movement for the Mauna was and remains a vibrant movement for anyone to enter, and an invitation for anyone willing to rethink how to be human and live in better balance with other humans and the world and all its forms of life.

Baby Steps: Growing Kuleana through Story

As I go on in this chapter to tell stories that emerge out of my experiences participating in the movement for Mauna Kea, I keep my evolving understanding of (my) kuleana front and center. Moving to a more autobiographical mode, and engaging with the concept of kuleana, I continue part 2's efforts to reconfigure the role of the scholar as an individual who theorizes movements and abstracts meanings from the stories of activists. I instead seek to work within a mode that is more dynamic and reciprocal, including through attempts at my own acts of narrated humanity. In doing so, I strive to foreground and, in however modest a way, emulate as well as honor all I have learned from aloha ʻāina, many of them UH students, whose work in the world refuses boundaries between storytelling, theorizing, pedagogy, and activism. In telling stories that emerge from my own experiences, in other words, my aim is not to center myself. Instead, I mean for this chapter to be an offering, a hoʻokupu, that attempts to fulfill my kuleana as a scholar and to extend my participation as a settler ally in the movement for Mauna Kea.

Perhaps, then, it is fitting to enter this attempt at narrated humanity with a story about kuleana. On March 13, 2019, I attended a Kuleana Circle, during a teach-in at UH-Mānoa. The event was part of a National Mauna Kea Awareness Day I had helped to organize with a Kanaka Maoli-led group of UH students, faculty, and staff. Faculty and staff later coalesced into Mauna Kea Protectors at the University of Hawaiʻi; students, into Kiaʻi Ke Kahaukani. Approximately forty to fifty of us gathered at Wise Field, the grassy area designated as "Bachman Lawn" by the upper administrators housed in the adjacent edifice, Bachman Hall. Kanaka ʻŌiwi at UH had reclaimed this area and its former name, given in 1937 to commemorate Native Hawaiian educator and politician John Henry Wise, a UH football player and one of the first Hawaiian language faculty members. We stood barefoot in a circle under some trees, near an ahu (altar made of stones). With attention to the life-force of pōhaku as kūpuna who feed their descendants, aloha ʻāina had erected the ahu in 2015 as an assertion of ea and in opposition to the University's move to construct the TMT. By late July 2019, this ahu would be the site for daily ceremonies (ʻaha), and ringed by thirty-eight bamboo structures, one for each of the kūpuna and their assistants arrested for blocking the access road to Mauna Kea.

The Kuleana Circle was an exercise designed by members of MANA (the Movement for Aloha no ka ʻĀina) to teach the "responsibilities, authority and rights that are tied to one's relationship to place, genealogy, and commitment and effort put forth toward a community and landbase" (MANA, 74). Noelani Goodyear-Kaʻōpua, MANA member, UH-Mānoa political science professor, and a beloved EAducator, mother, and community organizer, led us in locating ourselves in relation to the circle's center, or its piko, as a way to help us understand our kuleana, or our different places in the movement for Mauna Kea. Noe asked us about our genealogy; how long we have lived in Hawai'i; our familiarity with the stories and rhythms of the land; and about whether community members had affirmed our kuleana to care for the 'āina. Depending on our responses, we moved closer to or remained at a distance from the piko. I found myself standing in one of the outer rings of the concentric circles we formed—without genealogical ties; with very limited knowledge of the 'āina, 'ōlelo (language), and cultural practices; but with relations and awareness that had come from living since 1994 on O'ahu, and contributing what I can as a faculty and community member to Kanaka-led movements. This circle manifested Simpson's understanding of the "radiating responsibilities" (*As We Have Always Done*, 8) that make up a nation as it made clear that no one was without kuleana, even as our responsibilities and privileges differed.

This circle showed kuleana to be not about individual and exclusive ownership of land or rights, but about the invitations that come from learning one's place, growing connections by stepping forward or standing back, with respectful awareness of one's relations to other people and 'āina. As MANA members explain in their activist handbook, "The term 'kuleana' allows us to see how different people can maintain different kinds of connections to lands. These different interests are layered in the 'āina, like a layer cake. This way of relating to land and to others provides an alternative to private property frameworks. The capitalist principle of private property is individualistic and ultimately based on exclusion. Everyone is out to get their own piece of the pie" (MANA, 75). Along with rainbows and mosaics, food metaphors (hot pots, soups, salads) often serve to obscure or make digestible oppressive capitalist and colonial power relations. MANA members here do the reverse. Not only do they expose the problems with capitalism's relations of scarcity, competition, and individual ownership. Through their praxis that "grow[s] the abundance that capital fears" (Fujikane, 216), they also counter these logics with kuleana, a concept that invites multilayered, pleasurable, and collective participation (as they go on to note, layer cake is tasty, or 'ono).

Throughout this chapter, the Kuleana Circle has served as a touchstone as I have grappled with deciding which stories I feel it pono (right, just, ethical) to share; as I have shared drafts with those it includes; and as I strive to acknowledge and leave room for rather than erase or attempt to represent experiences, worldways, and stories I do not know or should not write about. I work on this chapter with the commitment to make my efforts contributory, not extractive, and with gratitude to the many aloha ʻāina and settler allies who, as students, teachers, activists, theorists, critics, and guides, illuminate alternatives to producing scholarship that, however anticapitalist in content, remains mired in the competitive individualism, privileging of "originality," and ownership of ideas that regularly count as hallmarks of the human.[12] Embracing the concept of kuleana enables another way of being human, and of conducting scholarship. Premised on multilayered sharing, and nourishing interdependency with other humans and with ʻāina, valuing kuleana presents possibilities for breaking with dominant modes of narrative humanity and for participating in acts of narrated humanity that take as their basis grounded narrative humanity.

That acts of narrated humanity can be at once small, to keep with one's kuleana, *and* significant is itself an understanding I have learned from the stories, theorizing, and activism of those engaged in the movement for the Mauna—and in related movements, including BLM and the movement for a free Palestine. To put this as Carol Lighor Carl did in a July 26, 2021, panel, "Together We Rise: Kanaka Maoli and Micronesian Solidarity," when addressing how to support Hawaiian-Micronesian solidarity, "small streams fill big rivers, and create a resilient watershed." adrienne maree brown's work on fractals and her insight that "what we practice at a small scale sets the patterns for the whole system" also inspire my approach. Perhaps most of all, my understanding of the value of small stories has been shaped by reading Aiko Yamashiro's blog posting, "Some Baby Steps toward a Decolonial Love Story," and also by learning from the stories it has moved my students to share. In this piece, Yamashiro writes,

> I know I am not changing the world by telling you this small story, but I also know that my world has already changed. And I will tend that ground of possibility quietly and tenderly, in case you need some land to grow your own love story. Baby steps. When people say 'baby steps,' they often mean an action that is slow, contained, tentative. . . . But when I watch our dear friends' baby Kaikainaliʻi take her first steps, I feel the fences in my mind fall away. Her body plummets across the room, laughing, falling. She teaches me that baby steps are the bravest steps I know: fierce and impossible, rushing headlong into imagination.

For me, this story and those it has inspired embody how, as with baby steps or other small movements that are at once ordinary and remarkable, small stories can be liberating, investigatory, joyful, generative, and transformative. Yamashiro's love story appears in a blog, *Ke Kaʻupu Hehi ʻAle*, started by eleven friends with decolonial commitments who share a belief in the "power in being part of stories, in sharing stories, in telling them, in listening to them, in putting them out into the world." As they explain, "this is how we show our love, how we reach out to others in the struggle." A product and practice of community and kuleana, as their blog circulates—on social media, among their friends and friends of friends—they "seed the world with our stories" ("About"). Animated by this understanding of stories as seeds, this concluding chapter is born out of a belief in the power that stories hold for anyone willing to tell, listen to, and share them, as a means of participating in Indigenous-led, old and new, anticolonial and decolonial ways of human being.

From "Mākou" to "Kākou": Grounding and Expanding Narrative Humanity

Just as Black intellectuals and organizers have been at the forefront of exposing racist violence and challenging hegemonic understandings of the human (see chapters 2 and 3), Indigenous writers, activists, and scholars lead the way in realizing the possibilities of working outside the logics of the narrative humanity engaged in this book. In hegemonic forms of narrative humanity, the human is a fixed and known entity, positioned at the top of a chain of being or evolutionary process of linear development. By contrast, one of the hallmarks of grounded narrative humanity is an insistence on how human being is a verb, not a noun, and constitutes a form of emergence premised on profound interdependence with rather than dominion over or possession of all deemed non- or less-than-human. As Kaleikoa Kaʻeo observes, in Kanaka Maoli cosmogony, "Creation is not an event that occurred. Creation is an event that is ongoing" ("Walter H. Capps"). His account of human becoming in the Kumulipo resonates with the account given by Daniel Heath Justice in *Why Indigenous Literatures Matter*: "In thinking about how we learn to be human, we also have to keep firmly in mind that Indigenous traditions generally don't limit the category of person solely to the human. As humans, we're simply one of many peoples, and depending on the tradition, there are also animal people, bird people, rock people, fish people, and so on" (37). In the words excerpted to serve as this chapter's epigraph, Justice notes that it is through relations to these peoples, passed on in and through stories, that humans come into being: "While the details differ across geographies and cultures, stories like this are common in every Indigenous story tradition I know: we learned to be human in large part from the land and our other-than-human relatives" (76). A poem by Jamaica Heolimeleikalani Osorio addressing Mauna Kea as a beloved protector and ancestor beautifully captures this process that is so central to grounded narrative humanity:

As constant as the summit
With all your magic
Rising beside me
Holding out your hands to catch everything I am
And am not quite yet.

(Lacy)

Through this insistence on profound and reverent relationality, grounded narrative humanity counters hegemonic narrative humanity's reliance on forms of belonging—national, heteropatriarchal—that, as they perpetuate the legal and other structures that uphold racial capitalism and colonialism, divide humans from one another and from other life-forms and elements in ways that imperil the planet. Nick Estes (Kul Wicasa) makes this point when telling the story of the NoDAPL movement. He describes how Indigenous forms of kinship "exist in opposition to capitalism's twin, settler colonialism, which calls for the annihilation of Indigenous peoples and their other-than-human kin," and explains: "While corporations take on legal personhood under current US law, Water Protectors personify water and enact kinship to the water, the river, enforcing a legal order of their own. If the water, a relative, is not protected, then the river is not free, and neither are its people" (*Our History*). Kaʻeo similarly contrasts the "prevailing worldview" that is wreaking such havoc, in which the earth is there to be dominated and exploited, to a Hawaiian cosmogony passed down through the Kumulipo and other stories, in which "everything around us is familial . . . everything is ancestral" ("Walter H. Capps"). When protectors initiated legal action to stop construction of the TMT in 2011, they drew on this cosmogony to insist on a consensual relationship to the ʻāina and all its inhabitants. This includes, for example, E. Kalani Flores's May 13 petition on behalf of Moʻoinanea, a reptilian water guardian. Flores's legal challenge is premised on the storied understanding that elemental forms have a consciousness and communicate back and forth with humans, and that the water guardian had not consented to the TMT.[13] As they break with the extractive, alienating, killing, and commodifying logics of capitalism and colonialism that underwrite hegemonic formulations of the human, protectors enlist forms of grounded narrative humanity to tell stories that instead create and re-create a practice of being human premised on the values of grounded normativity, of loving and consensual connection to ʻāina.

In their acts of decolonial world making, Indigenous activists also draw on forms of grounded narrative humanity that defy the linear notions of time and progress that characterize dominant modes of narrative humanity. To counter the devastation that comes with capitalist and colonial worldviews, Kaʻeo looks to the Kumulipo as "not so much a story of the past," but rather one "that provides us guidance and nutrients, . . . to push us where we need to go in the future" ("Walter H. Capps").[14] Similarly, drawing on stories of the past, Kauwila Mahi looks to how, in response to the settler state's authoritarian emergency orders, kiaʻi once more are rising, connecting with their "elemental ancestors" by activating themselves as "Pōhaku (Stones), Hau (Ice), Kēhau (Dew), ʻUhiwai (Mists), Hū (Surges), Kūkulu (Pillars), Ua (Rains), ʻAwa (Bitter-Cold Mountain Rains), Wai (Waters), Pele (Lava), Ehu (Dust), and as Hunalepo (Dust/Dirt Motes)." In this way, as part of an "emergent-sea," "Kiaʻi are ancestral animators of past and future memories" (Mahi, "Emergent-Seas"). In "We Live in the Future. Come Join Us," Bryan Kamaoli Kuwada also reflects on the power of stories to connect Kanaka Maoli "to the very inception of these islands" and, thus, to a decolonial future: "Standing on our mountain of connections, our foundation of history and stories and love, we can see both where the path behind us has come from and where the path ahead leads. . . . The future is a realm we have inhabited for thousands of years." As he situates protectors "operating on geological and genealogical time," he posits this vantage point as one that values land, people, and the sacred over the faulty and limited sightlines afforded by construction companies that work within capitalism's and colonialism's linear narratives of progress.[15]

Because from an Indigenous perspective what it means to be human is a story still in the making—and one that, in facing future, looks back—there is no clear demarcation between grounded narrative humanity and narrated humanity. As I have been discussing, grounded narrative humanity's hallmarks include an understanding that the human is continuously being made, through stories that tell of a foundational kinship and interdependency with other-than-human creatures and land, waters, and sky. In other words, in grounded narrative humanity, it is normative to assume that because the human is not a fixed and finished entity, the human emerges through the acts of narrated humanity that accompany movements. For this reason, the line between grounded narrative humanity and narrated humanity is a blurred one. Nonetheless, I find it worth preserving a distinction between the two and considering how they work together. In the movement for Mauna Kea and related Indigenous-led movements, we can trace ways grounded narrative humanity, as it also includes narrated humanity, comes to include non-Indigenous allies, moving as Kuwada and Noʻu Revilla do from a restricted "we" (or mākou) to an expansive "we" (or kākou) when they assert "we are Maunakea" ("Introduction," 518). We also can look to how the movement for the Mauna—and the stories that make up this movement—take shape in dynamic relationality with movements and acts of narrated humanity that at times exist outside of or extend beyond grounded narrative humanity, and that foreground issues and identities that are not (only) Indigenous, but that are (also) queer, trans, Black, Palestinian, migrant, abolitionist, feminist, environmental, labor-based, antiracist, antiableist, and so on.

The Mauna Kea Syllabus Project, which "traces its genealogy to Puʻuhuluhulu University" ("About the Mauna Kea Syllabus Project"), provides one way to map how the movement for the Mauna draws on and is fed by grounded narrative humanity, as well as acts of narrated humanity that put other traditions, movements, identities, and ways of knowing into the mix.[16] Inspired by other syllabi, including the BLM and Immigration Syllabi, and created in dialogue with makers of the NoDAPL Syllabus,[17] stories (including visual texts) that the Mauna Kea Syllabus Project includes move between grounded narrative humanity and narrated humanity. Several of these stories shift the lāhui to what QTPI (Queer/Trans Pacific Islander)/Kanaka māhū including Ākea Kahikina, Kahala Johnson, and T. Kalaniʻōpua Young call the māhūi, or the hui (collective) of māhū. These stories make central formulations of gender and sexuality that emerge out of both traditional Kanaka Maoli stories (or grounded narrative humanity), and also queer-of-color, feminist, trans, and abolitionist accounts of kinship, being, and belonging.[18] As these stories move into unknown terrain, they constitute acts of narrated humanity.[19] In "notes towards a huli: gender, sexuality, & pilina," for example, Revilla playfully draws on akua in conjuring a decolonial present that is anchored in the past *and* animated by contemporary queer theory and activism:

> Like Haumea, in ultimate femme fashion, readying herself to rescue Wākea by adorning her kino in forest finery, we are preparing our bodies for a huli. . . . Like Haumea, we ready our bodies in and with the ʻāina. Like Haumea, we queer ʻŌiwi are rigorous, pāhaʻohaʻo & unfuckwithable. Cue the kukui nuts. The huli is here.

This vision of a "huli," or an overturning, is one made possible both by traditional moʻolelo and by lesbian and queer-of-color writer/activists including Gloria Anzaldúa, Audre Lorde, Cherríe Moraga, and Jose Muñoz, all of whom Revilla references following this contemporary moʻolelo. As with the Syllabus Project's artwork by Joy Lehuanani Enomoto, which includes stunning representations of akua as badass, sexy, imperfect, gender-bending, larger-than-life beings who allow "for us to dream impossible things" (Kuwada and Revilla,

"'We're Asking,'" 596), Revilla's story of (herself as) Haumea, an akua nui (major god) of childbirth, war and politics—and a manifestation of Papahānaumoku, or Earth Mother—is an act of radical resurgence, an act of queer reproduction at once grounded and uncharted. So, too, we see this radical resurgence at work in Goodyear-Kaʻōpua's "On the Cattle Guard," a story/poem included as part of the Syllabus Project. When she writes in second person of her experience of being chained to the cattle guard, "your back is a bridge you offer to kiaʻi of generations past, present, and future, crossing to meet one another, to touch noses and share ea," she evokes *This Bridge Called My Back*. As she brings Moraga and Anzaldúa's vision into a genealogy that is at once distinctly Kanaka Maoli, she also narrates into being a Mauna movement that is expansively queer and feminist.[20]

In their acts of narrated humanity, Enomoto, Goodyear-Kaʻōpua, and Revilla point to a "beyond" to the grounded narrative humanity in which it is simultaneously situated. In "What's Normative Got to Do with It? Towards Indigenous Queer Relationality," Jodi Byrd (Chickasaw) speculates about limitations to grounded normativity as they instead consider the possibilities of a framework of "grounded relationality" that attends to how, like the land and water that are their relations, all Indigenous bodies "are fluid, capacious; they transform over time; and they exist outside settler gender binaries, normativities, and even nonnormativities. . . . Though Indigenous and queer studies may not yet know exactly what the other means to their respective fields, what is left for both is to find the ground between the nowhere and nothing of the vacated Indigenous queer and imagine an everywhere and everything that the two fields might instantiate at the site of decolonization when they finally meet" (120). This meeting place is one that Goodyear-Kaʻōpua, along with Enomoto, Revilla, and other queer-identified kiaʻi including Māhealani Ahia, Ruth Aloua, Lanakila Mangauil, Greg Pōmaikaʻi Gushiken, Kahala Johnson, Ākea Kahikina, ʻIhilani Lasconia, Adam Keawe Manalo-Camp, Heoli Osorio, Malia Hulleman Osorio, Leilani Portillo, Hāwane Rios, Kānealiʻi Williams, Hinaleimoana Wong-Kalu, and Kalaniʻōpua Young explore through acts of narrated humanity that, as they look back and forward, daringly transform the lāhui into a māhūi that makes room for new and freer ways of being human (or what Johnson calls "pre/posthumanity" ["Anti-humanism"]) as they rise up to protect their ancestor, Mauna a Wākea.

"Life Narrative versus Life Narrative"

Kiaʻi narratives about the Mauna, and those that the state promotes, are at the heart of the struggle over Mauna Kea: in their push to construct the TMT, the state as well as the university and its corporate partners crucially rely on hegemonic modes of narrative humanity. As they do so, they participate in an ongoing history of dehumanizing Indigenous peoples in order to maintain structures of settlerism and racial capitalism. Estes comments on this history when he connects state violence and surveillance against Water Protectors at Standing Rock to the Indian Wars of the nineteenth century: "To justify conquest, enslavement, and genocide under European law, Indigenous peoples, and the darker nations, have been categorically excluded from the realm of humanity."

In ways this book has been analyzing, and as is clear in the efforts to curtail the movement for Mauna Kea, this categorical exclusion crucially relies on narrative humanity. The familiar narratives the state, corporate interests, and UH promote represent those supporting the TMT as being on the side of science, progress, knowledge, development, and modernity. Meanwhile, they cast kiaʻi as terrorists, savages, premodern or atavistic, antiscience, and ignorant.[21] During a July 19, 2019, press conference, Governor David Ige relied on these racist stereotypes when he described the puʻuhonua as unsafe, lawless, full of "drug and alcohol use," badly maintained, lacking in organization and purpose, and overrun by disobedient protesters in need of "crowd control" by law enforcement. He charged Mauna leadership with spreading rumors and fear instead of participating in "real world conversations" ("Governor Ige").[22] In these representations, which recycle those employed to represent NoDAPL water protectors, Ige and other university and state actors also contribute to a long history in Hawaiʻi of dehumanizing Kanaka Maoli. In ways critics including Cristina Bacchilega, Vernadette Gonzalez, kuʻualoha hoʻomanawanui, Paul Lyons, Brandy Nālani McDougall, Ty Kāwika Tengan, and Haunani-Kay Trask have powerfully analyzed, the dehumanization that accompanies what McDougall calls "colonial entitlement" ("Moʻokūʻauhau") and that exists within what Patrick Wolfe calls settler colonialism's "logics of elimination" ("Settler Colonialism") takes contradictory but complementary forms. In dominant forms of narrative humanity, Kanaka Maoli are erased; cast as welcoming and childlike Natives happy to serve tourists and settlers who now occupy their lands; and appear as lesser humans who are lazy and shiftless, or primitive and criminal and in "need" of colonization and assimilation into the settler state.[23]

Kiaʻi well recognize the power of life narratives in contestations over the Mauna, and have deployed them with strategic brilliance to protect their sacred ancestor and, as Kaʻeo succinctly states, to "demand our humanity" (Inouye, *Like a Mighty Wave*). Working with forms of grounded narrative humanity and narrated humanity, they have countered hegemonic modes of narrative humanity pro-TMT forces rely upon in what Kuwada and Revilla describe as a battle of "life narrative versus life narrative" ("Introduction," 518), and through what Goodyear-Kaʻōpua notes was a "story-based" media strategy ("Protecting Maunakea"). The Mauna Kea Media team and protectors worldwide have held press conferences; testified at public hearings and in courts of law; organized rallies, concerts, demonstrations, teach-ins, and other events; issued petitions; produced documentaries; created websites; participated in interviews and podcasts; written op-eds, poems, songs, personal narratives, essays, and articles; edited special issues of journals; and performed chants and hula. They have gained international support by sharing all these storied events and texts via social media. Reflecting in an interview on her decision to chain herself to the cattle grate, Goodyear-Kaʻōpua discloses that she did so at the invitation of Kaʻeo, who "asked the seven of us because he thought we [alongside himself] were people who could speak to the media and also could tell the story later" (Kuwada and Revilla, "'It Could've Been You,'" 536). In their special *Biography* issue in which this interview appears—itself part of the powerful body of life writing texts that contributes to the movement for Mauna Kea, and one viewed over six thousand times in the first two months after appearing as Open Access on Project Muse—Revilla and Kuwada, himself a member of the Kanaeokana media team, explain,

> The kiaʻi knew the importance of optics, of how their lives were going to be narrated, and they knew that traditional media was not their friend in this regard, so they seized control of the news cycle, creating and utilizing their own social media channels, holding press conferences of their own, and creating high-quality video content that ran the gamut from historical overviews to interviews to music videos to poetry to travelogues and more. Across social media platforms such as Facebook and Instagram, the main channels through which the kiaʻi communicated—Puʻuhonua o Puʻuhuluhulu, Kākoʻo Haleakalā, Protect Maunakea, and Kanaeokana—had around 800,000 followers. Via Kanaeokana's Facebook page alone, the general public viewed 6.5 million minutes of video that kiaʻi produced during the Mauna standoff. ("Introduction," 520)

In the life stories kiaʻi circulated, as they counter stereotypes of Native Hawaiians as antiscience, atavistic, and ignorant, they insist on the connections—and deep and often scientific ways of knowing—among humans and land, skies, and waters.[24] In addition, pro-TMT representations of Hawaiians as angry, unruly, violent protesters are overturned by kiaʻi's signs and banners, and through protocols and disciplined practices of kapu aloha in meeting militarized po-

lice forces and mainstream media with nonviolence and compassion. As embodied acts of grounded narrative and narrated humanity, such messaging
and performance of ceremony that assert Kanaka ʻŌiwi kinship with and
guardianship over their revered Mauna counter hegemonic narrative humanity's anti-Indigenous formulations of the human.

Stories as "Constellations of Coresistance"

These Mauna Kea texts and actions are not only or even primarily for the media: first and foremost, they matter for those who participate in them, and the
stories participants tell about them not only come out of but also become part
of the movement for Mauna Kea. Jamaica Heolimeleikalani Osorio calls attention to this powerful role story plays. Noting that Kanaka Maoli are engaged
in "the greatest creative outpouring of our collective lifetime," she describes
how in creating moʻolelo about Mauna Kea, Kanaka Maoli "are writing the
histories of our time in our own voices, with our own melodies and dancing
them with our own bodies, just as our kūpuna did for us. . . . Our creativity
both describes and expands our current movement" ("On the Frontlines"). As
these stories beget more stories, they strengthen pilina, among generations of
Kanaka, land, and the gods or elements.

We can see a clear example of the powerful role these acts of narrated and
grounded narrative humanity play in perpetuating the movement for the
Mauna and in reproducing decolonial ways of being human if we look to the
poem and other stories Goodyear-Kaʻōpua tells of the cattle guard. Her poem
"On the Cattle Guard" has circulated on social media, on the show run by
DJPhD Anjoli Roy "It's Lit," and in the special *Biography* issue. She has also
shared it at gatherings, and she discusses its meaning in an interview in *Biography* as a companion piece to the poem. There, she states her intention for
the poem to be "one more moʻolelo of the many that are to be told about Maunakea. That it would be for our keiki and the next generation who wonders
what it was like to be there" (Kuwada and Revilla, "It Could've Been You,"
535). She explains the poem's second-person address as an invitation to the
"group of people I was trying to remember for" (539) to share in her experience—
to participate in moʻolelo as a verb. So, too, even as they are open access, what
makes "It Could've Been You" and the other interviews in the special issue
remarkable is the intimacy between participants who laugh and cry together
and share stories only partially accessible to a wide readership. As opposed to
stories of nation building that are part of hegemonic narrative humanity, the
sharing of these stories becomes part of the movement for the Mauna, as
they also model ways of being human. Goodyear-Kaʻōpua tells the story of

the cattle guard as one of building a lāhui that is based not on individual acts of heroic conquest, or one-off events of revolution, but rather on practices, at once everyday and extraordinary, of love, mutual aid, true security, and aloha ʻāina:

> From the very beginning, with Kahala [Johnson] and Māhea [Ahia] being there with lights, making sure that when the first officers were coming, they saw us and they stopped before they ran us over. Then the Mauna Medics started to come and they brought blankets. . . . Throughout the day, there was always somebody with us. . . . I never ever felt alone. I never felt endangered because nobody ever let us feel alone. [pauses] So yeah, when I think about what was so overwhelming about it . . . people just started coming up. Kumu Jon Osorio came and sang . . . seeing him sing to Heoli [his daughter, Jamaica Heolimelei-kalani Osorio] and to all of us. Kaʻikena Scanlan came up singing, all kinds of people. Uncle Liko Martin came up. People were just coming to the cattle guard and giving whatever they could so that we didn't feel alone. [pauses again] I don't think I've ever felt so cared for in my life. (537)

When we discussed Goodyear-Kaʻōpua's poem in a graduate class I taught in Spring 2022, Kauwila Mahi aptly described it as a "PDA" or public display of affection that, in a world "plagued by colonialist trauma and pain," works to "bind ourselves and future generations to that moment on a cattle guard where kiaʻi had so much love for the land that they made a commitment that they were willing to be at the very least arrested for it."

Other kiaʻi also tell related stories of the cattleguard that, as they proliferate and as one gives rise to another, capture the dual meanings of moʻolelo as tradition and as "a succession of talk."[25] For Heoli Osorio, for example, it is a legendary story about her love for ʻāina and the kiaʻi who surrounded her with care (*Remembering*, 143–45). It is also a story of the place where she meets the wahine who becomes her life partner—a moʻolelo that turns into another moʻolelo as she returns with Malia Hulleman (now Osorio) to this place as they prepare for the birth of their child Kaleiwohi ʻAʻahulīhauikalaʻikūokekuamauna Osorio whose name carries this story ("When I arrived"; "Kaleiwohi"). The telling of these moʻolelo enact a genealogy of resistance to settlerism as these PDAs also strengthen and participate in the creation of kiaʻi's ties to their ancestors, to their descendants, to their lāhui, and to ʻāina.

Accompanying stories of the stories behind media events are those shared primarily among the participants in the daily protocols that served as grounding anchor—and form of rising—in the movement for the Mauna. Important as the protocols were for taking control of the narrative about the Mauna and overturning the state's representation of protectors as unruly protesters, the practice of daily ceremony, open to anyone standing for Mauna Kea, served as an embodied praxis of human being and becoming. Made up of stories that unfolded through ritualized movement and chant—through hula, mele, and oli—these ceremonies invited participants into a spiritual practice, one that offered a way to be human rooted in ʻāina.

As they involved participants in enacting forms of grounded narrative humanity and narrated humanity, these daily ceremonies served as a pillar in the movement for Mauna Kea. I have never considered myself a spiritual person. Nor have I been particularly adept at integrating my mind with my body, emotions, and the land on which I stand (indeed, this formulation is itself symptomatic of habitual practices of compartmentalization and separation). So for me, attending daily protocols was not normative, but transformative. As we danced to Pua Case's "He Kūkulu," a composition which poses the question, "What is a pillar?," the answers we chanted along with the accompanying actions brought together standing as kūkulu (pillar), Mauna (mountain), ahu (altar), pōhaku (stone), and kanaka (human):

He aha la he kūkulu? (What Is a Pillar?)
He Mauna! (a mountain)
He aha la he kūkulu?
He ahu! (an altar)
He aha la he kūkulu?
He pōhaku! (a stone)
He aha la he kūkulu?
He kanaka! (we the people) (x3) ("He Kūkulu")

Participating in this and other chants and hula connected my feet to the ground under me and gave me an experience of expansiveness, of being part of something beyond myself and the more-than-human. Legendary kumu hulu such as Pualani Kanakaʻole Kanahele, and also Pua Case, Lanakila Mangauil, Vicky Holt Takamine, and Hinaleimoana Wong-Kalu, led sometimes a few and sometimes hundreds or thousands of us through some of these protocols, while others were reserved for those with genealogical connections and cultural training. Under blazing sun and on hot pavement or cooling grass, in lashing rains, or shrouded in mist, we formed lines across Ala Hulu Kūpuna, and crowded together for rallies at the State Capitol rotunda, and spread out across Kapiʻolani Park. At Wise Field, small groups of us learned from Snowbird Puananiopaoakalani Bento (who taught hula there on Sundays) or from Kahikina de Silva, Kaipulaumakaniolono Baker, Ty Kāwika Tengan, and the students occupying Bachman Hall who led the protocols three times daily. Participating in this ritualized practice connected me in a new way to land on which I have lived for decades, and introduced an understanding, however rudimentary, of what it means to feel a relation to stones, and to the mountains, pillars, and altars that they form. Emalani Case, reflecting on the protocols held on Mauna Kea, said this:

> Every day, three times a day, we stood at the pu'uhonua and chanted and danced for us: for our continuance as people tied to the land, to the mountain, and to our inherited right to be Indigenous in our place. Each chant was a practice in breath, in how to exhale meaning wrapped in vowel sounds, carried by vibrato coming from the gut, and maintained by ancient vocabularies constantly made new. Each dance was a practice in using my breath intentionally, holding it where necessary, releasing it where it could help my body reach down to the land or to the sky above, shaping stories with my hands. Using breath in this way is a sovereign act. It is a reassertion of who we are and an enactment of our commitment to each other, to the land, and to our futures. (570)

As a settler ally, what I experienced was not the assertion of sovereignty Case speaks of, but a way to exhale, to release toxic ways of being in the world. This (for me) profoundly unsettling and grounded practice offered an antidote to spirit-sapping capitalist and colonial ways of being. Participation in protocols suggested more balanced, reciprocal, and caring ways to exist as a human and in relation to other humans and more-than-humans, while also growing my kuleana, to Mauna Kea and to the Kū Kia'i Mauna movement.

In addition to mo'olelo that are the stuff of legends, as with the Cattle Guard 8, and that make up ceremonial practices are the smaller, more everyday stories behind the making of media events, ones that involve putting into practice ways of being human that these storied events themselves tell of. One such story involves the making of the banners and signs kia'i held and posted on Mauna Kea. Part of virtually every media capture of the stand-off, they represented the kia'i not as protesters, but as peaceful protectors and guardians of their sacred Mauna. Photos of kūpuna blocking the Access Road that have become iconic feature them in the predawn hours on July 17, sitting in a line with linked arms, bundled up under blankets. Their caretakers stand behind them, holding signs that say, "We are here to Protect Mauna Kea" and "Crown Lands, Kū Kia'i Mauna." In the months that followed, these signs have appeared in hundreds of photos and stories, held by kia'i, and also lining Ala Hulu Kūpuna, looking weatherworn and tattered as the Makahiki season advanced, but still beautiful.

Each time I have seen the signs and banners—while on the Mauna, but also on social media, on the news, in the messages Mauna Kea Protectors at UH sent back and forth—I think not only of the kiaʻi who stood holding them while facing a militarized police force and countering narratives criminalizing their stand for Mauna Kea. I also think about the stories that attend their making—stories I share here for what they taught me about decolonial and anticapitalist practices of community, solidarity, movement building, and human becoming and belonging.

On July 4, 2019, I attended a HULI Art Build that Andre Perez and Camille Kalama held at their Hanakēhau Learning Farm, located on the shores of Puʻuloa, in cooptation of a holiday Andre calls "4th of you lie, end dependence day."[26] As he shared the story of the Art Build with me, Andre told me of how the Action Art Tent at Standing Rock served as a model.[27] In October 2016, Andre and Camille spent eight days at Red Warrior Camp, supporting the NoDAPL movement. After they returned, the Indigenous Peoples Power Project (IP3) called Andre back, to run daily nonviolent direct action training sessions from November to December (Andre provided related trainings in Spring 2019, to ready protectors to occupy Mauna Kea; and Camille, legal observer trainings). Andre gave up a job in Honolulu and stayed for a month at the IP3 Camp, serving as the nonviolent direct action trainer for the entire encampment in what were mandatory two-hour orientation sessions. He explained that the IP3 Camp also included a huge event tent where Indigenous and non-Indigenous artists worked together making signs, banners, and back patches. There, he learned just how crucial action art is for messaging, for narrative, and for controlling the narrative. As Andre put this in a November 29, 2016, Facebook update about his five weeks at Standing Rock, "Art is critical to messaging, consciousness raising and political expression," remarking, "Take notes for Mauna Kea" ("Art"). Back on Oʻahu in 2016, with Mauna Kea in mind, he fundraised to bring out four Standing Rock artists, and organized a weeklong action art camp at Hanakēhau. Those who attended learned from Standing Rock Protectors how to make low-tech, low-budget art (stenciling, silk screening, hand painting) that was highly visible and clear in its messaging. So, when the state and the TMT moved to begin construction in 2019, Andre was ready to work with other members of HULI to organize an Art Build implementing these skills passed on from Standing Rock Protectors, and with the understanding that in nonviolent direct action, "messaging comes first, then visuals, and only then, logistics and an action plan" (Perez, phone interview).

On June 30, 2019, Andre initiated the Maunakea Movement Art Hui Facebook page and put out a call: "If you can draw, trace, paint with a brush, glue, staple, sew, measure, cut fabric etc. you can be of important value." People organized through that page to rideshare and bring materials. Responding to his kāhea—and inspired by the photo catalog he shared on June 26 of NoDAPL artwork by Christi Belcourt (Métis), Isaac Murdoch (Ojibwe), and others—local artists designed signs and banners, weaving in local cultural and political contexts.

The stories behind the designing of these signs, including how they relate to those from Standing Rock, themselves constitute instances of grounded narrative and narrated humanity. Andre explained how, working from Canada, Isaac Murdoch (aka Bomgiizhik) adapted his fierce, joyful NoDAPL artwork featuring Thunderbird Woman. Murdoch's artwork asserts Water Protectors' kinship with Thunderbird—for Sioux, a sacred shapeshifting being who protects humans from the Unktehila, dangerous reptilian monsters. Endowing protectors with this spiritual power and in sacred connection to land and water, Murdoch's artwork positions the pipeline and those supporting it as modern-day monsters. In conversation with Andre, Murdoch made a related sign for Mauna Kea, featuring, at Andre's suggestion, the ʻIwa. Underlining the importance of symbolism in action art, Andre explained this choice. ʻIwa birds are known as thieves. One of the highest-flying birds, when they circle, they also are known as foreboding indicators of a coming storm. For the artwork, then, the ʻIwa is a symbol of warning, of the approach of a thief (the TMT), and also of protectors' awareness, wisdom, and ability to see the lay of the land with clarity. In conversation with each other, the two signs also tell a story—an act of narrated humanity—a story about the friendship and solidarity between NoDAPL and Mauna Kea protectors, and one that emerges out of a shared way of being human, a form of grounded narrative humanity, premised on a oneness with and guardianship over the land, and kinship with more-than-human creatures. (This solidarity continued on the Mauna, when Standing Rock artists came for a month at a time to run the Art Tent Andre set up with the recognition that as a movement evolves, so too must the messaging, and also because of awareness of the important role art plays in creating pleasure and community for those engaged in a sustained blockade.)

The story of the July 4th art build suggests how different struggles feed one another as they participate in building the movement for the Mauna. Telling this story from my own experience of it also, I hope, serves to illustrate the small but significant ways participation in this movement for aloha ʻāina invites allies, too, into a freer, decolonial way of being human that, as it comes out of grounded narrative humanity, leaves behind fireworks and celebrations of individualist and national freedom and independence that cover over—and perpetuate—racial capitalism, militarism, and settlerism.

On the day of the art build, along with dozens of others, I headed over to Hanakēhau with art supplies, food to share, and a T-shirt to silkscreen. When I arrived that morning, it was to a gathering of people of all ages, all hard at work. (As a result of the art build, Andre went to the Mauna with eight 12′ × 8′ banners and 160 fabric signs.) Working with other kiaʻi, Andre and Camille had set up big work tables under tents, equipped with bolts of muslin fabric, rulers, stencil material, acrylics and spray paints, markers, pencils, irons, glue guns, a sewing machine, silkscreen ink, cutting mats, silk screens, and squeegees. In addition to seeing old friends there—including artist Joy Enomoto, a taskmaster who made sure hems for the giant banner that Candace Fujikane, Cristina Bacchilega, Monisha Das Gupta, Kim Compoc, and I were working on were tight and professional—I worked alongside and talked story with people from all over Oʻahu as we colored in "Protect Maunakea" signs and painted the lettering of banners stating "We Are This Land / Maunakea Is Our Origin," and "Road Closed to Desecration." I met women including Rhonda Vincent, who I later learned made up the behind-the-scenes backbone of this and other movements for ea, young activists, UH students, children, and artists. (After meeting Nicole Naone that day, I was able to ask her to design fliers and a logo for Mauna Kea Protectors at UH; she later also contributed her skills as an artist to an SFJP@UH project.) Participating in this event awakened a deep pleasure in making art that I had not experienced for decades, as I followed the lead of the artists around me who were bringing the black-and-white signs to life with colorful beams, spirals, and Mauna triangles, and mixing alaeʻa, or red clay, into paint for signs that were, as Sierra Dew explained of her "Protect Maunakea" artwork, "a form of prayer" and "a gift to send [to the Mauna] of protection and connection." As we worked together creating art—some, including Sierra, stayed until past 2 A.M. painting banners with ʻIlima Long's and Andre's daughters—we also built pilina with one another, and through the sharing of practices in these articulated struggles, between Mauna Kea and Standing Rock (fig. 7).

As I hope this small story suggests, the movement for Mauna Kea—as manifested in the accumulation of actions that include the Art Build—realizes a vision that corresponds to Simpson's "radical resurgence." In her manifesto on radical resurgence, Simpson calls for people "to join together in a rebellion of love, persistence, commitment, and profound caring and create constellations of coresistance, working together toward a radical alternative present based on deep reciprocity and the gorgeous generative refusal of colonial recognition" (*As We Have Always Done*, 9). After reading Simpson and Coulthard in an undergraduate course on decolonial love, a brilliant student, Gabriel Verduzco,

Figure 7. July 4, 2019, Art Build at Andre Perez and Camille Kalama's Hanakēhau Learning Farm. *Left to right:* Andre Perez, Imani Altemus-Williams, Hoʻoleia Kaʻeo, Sierra Dew. (Photo credit: Andre Perez. Permission granted by Perez, Altemus-Williams, Kaʻeo, and Dew)

wrote this meditation on constellations that illuminates their power as decolonial guides and maps:

> Being literate in star reading allows for a connection to past, to ancestors, to the unborn, and to the future. . . . Constellations are also conceptual doorways that return us to the core of Indigenous thought. Constellations are constantly in motion, shifting with the seasons, serving as signposts indicating when it is time to tell winter stories, when the ice is no longer safe, or when it is time to move to the sugar bush. Some constellations are ceremonies, like the sweat lodge or shaking tent formations, while others are animals of the clan system. The constellations are maps, read by animals who use the stars as

guides in migration; they can also be used by us, using the skyworld knowledge to guide us out of settler colonialism. A map that colonizers can't read because they aren't rooted in grounded normativity.

The stories behind the posters and banners on Mauna Kea—themselves not only signposts but also past and future portals to the stars and maps rooted in grounded normativity—materialize a vision of grounded narrative humanity. They show how this vision can be realized not only through ceremony but also through the most everyday of practices. And, in creating new forms of connectivity and solidarity, they partake in acts of narrated humanity that emerge out of constellations of coresistance.

Autobiography as Activism

In addition to the texts that participate in the movement for Mauna Kea, and the stories behind those stories, are others based on more intimate exchanges that, as they constitute forms of grounded narrative and narrated humanity, also open up decolonial ways of being human that enable survival and flourishing. In thinking about the NoDAPL movement and its connection to a long history of revolutionary activism, Estes remarks on the significance of everyday life in seeding extraordinary change: "Hidden from view to outsiders, this constant tunneling, plotting, planning, harvesting, remembering, and conspiring for freedom—the collective faith that another world is possible—is the most important aspect of revolutionary work. It is from everyday life that the collective confidence to change reality grows, giving rise to extraordinary events." Stories made and shared among friends and comrades constitute an important part of this revolutionary process. These stories not only serve to create collective forms of remembering that lay the groundwork for a revolutionary future; they also can themselves serve to grow kuleana, and create collective faith and confidence, human community, and connectedness to the more-than-human world. They are part of practicing hope not as a feeling but as what Mariame Kaba contends is "a discipline" we must practice "every single day" (Kaba). To return to brown's thinking about fractals, Yamashiro's baby steps, and Carl's small streams, the telling, tending, and sharing of little stories of decolonial love have a part to play in creating large-scale change that can "huli the system" and upend the networked forms of state violence this book has been addressing.

Here, then, are a few of my own small acts of narrated humanity.

I did not initially intend to go to Mauna Kea: I felt it more in keeping with my kuleana to support the movement from my location at UH. My work with the Mauna Kea Protectors at UH shifted this, as I built relations with Kanaka ʻŌiwi faculty members, staff, and students through participation in ceremony, writing statements and testimony, planning teach-ins, and other actions at UH. In July 2019, we organized a trip to the Mauna with the intention of holding a UH Protectors press conference, one we ended up canceling when conditions shifted. I again felt called to the Mauna when Rana Barakat and Yousef Aljamal, Palestinians I was hosting as part of Decolonial November, visited. We took this trip with J. Kēhaulani Kauanui, a longtime USACBI organizer as well as scholar and activist for Hawaiian independence, so that Rana and Yousef could experience the world-making on the Mauna, and offer hoʻokupu and teach at Puʻuhuluhulu University. Then later that month, Candace Fujikane, Vernadette Gonzalez, and I went on behalf of the 2019 American Studies Association Site Committee, to present in person money to the Mauna leadership that the committee had raised by selling tote bags Joy Enomoto had designed, of the line of mana wāhine on the Mauna.

What I took most from these trips was an understanding of the significance of ceremony, but also of the importance more intimate moments and everyday acts of reproductive labor hold for movement making—and insights into ways acts of narrated humanity can help materialize the "re-education, re-culturation, and re-humanization" that Kaʻeo contends is necessary to achieve Hawaiian independence ("Hawaiian independence"). My times on the Mauna were made up of storied moments, or what Kuwada and Revilla call "living maps of aloha ʻāina" ("Introduction," 523), that emerged out of and participated in Simpson's "ecology of intimacy"—respectful and freeing interspecies relations of kinship, kuleana, and community that unfold "in the absence of coercion, hierarchy, or authoritarian power" (As We Have Always Done, 8). These moments included talking story with Noenoe Silva and Marie Alohalani Brown in Hale Hoʻolako, and, as Alohalani stacked beanies and sweatshirts on shelves, hearing about the evolution of that tent that was not, as some joked, a Kanaka Costco, but part of an economy that defied the logics of capitalism. They included skipping out on Jason Momoa's noontime presentation of hoʻokupu to work in the kitchen, where as I scooped rice and chicken onto people's plates, I learned how kiaʻi were managing without running water, working to reduce plastic and waste, and providing healthy and delicious food to anyone gathered on the Mauna. They included hearing about the work of Mauna Medics while waiting in line for Haley Kailiehu to silkscreen a T-shirt with one of her stunning designs of Haumea, lying on her side, water or a shoot of green life streaming from her piko, her hair melding into the earth. They included talking with Punahele, Rana, and Yousef about Punahele's recent trip to Palestine with the Palestinian Youth Movement, while taking photos under the Palestinian flag, one of the many lining Ala Hulu Kūpuna, and hearing Rana and Yousef talk about the gift of feeling so legible and welcomed as Palestinians on the Mauna (fig. 8).[28] They included

Figure 8. Mauna Kea, along the Ala Hulu Kūpuna (Road of Our Cherished Elders). *Left to right:* Yousef Aljamal, Rana Barakat, Punahele. (Photo taken by author. Permission granted by Aljamal, Barakat, and Punahele)

sitting in a circle in the evening hours with ʻIlima, Māhea, Kahala, Rana, Yousef, and Kēhaulani, plotting future exchanges between Hawaiʻi and Palestine, and learning from Māhea and Kahala about the work of creating true security on the Mauna for trans, māhū, and queer kiaʻi. They included heading from the airport to Costco and then, with a carload of food, to Mauna Kea, and hearing from Candace about Uncle Ku Chingʻs stories of the Mauna waterways. They included talking story at the Mauna Medics Hale with Noe Ahia as she shared herbs and homeopathic remedies. The acts of narrated humanity that accompanied the daily operations at Puʻuhonua—each one unfolding amid the fierce and changing elements and the massive, gorgeous omnipresence of the Mauna—gave me glimpses into the future coming into being in the movement for Mauna Kea. These stories about the world being created in that crossroads-turned-space-of-refuge carry teachings for ways of human becoming and belonging premised on everyday acts of reproductive labor and mutual aid, and based on love, care, compassion, and respect for the sacred interrelatedness of people, land, and elements.

Perhaps my most moving lessons from the storied world making on the Mauna came when teaching courses on "(Auto)biography as Activism" at Puʻuhuluhulu University. My first time doing so, across the lava field, a group of men gathered, engrossed in Ty Tengan and Keawe Kaholokuaʻs workshop, "Aia i hea ka wai a kāne? What Makes a Healthy Kāne?" The intensity and power of that class, the movement of the November sun as it lowered and came in and out of the clouds, the presence of the Mauna—I felt all of this as those who showed up for "(Auto)biography as Activism" formed a circle on folding metal and camping chairs. UH brands itself as a "Native Hawaiian place of learning" and an "aloha ʻāina" university, a move that Kekailoa Perry contends attempts to turn "aloha ʻāina" into "a slogan for settler colonial imagination and native erasure" (Kaʻeo and Perry).[29] At the base of Mauna Kea, those who created Puʻuhuluhulu University as a freedom school took back these appropriated terms. As explained by Presley Keʻalaanuhea Ah Mook Sang, "Unlike the current actions of the University of Hawaiʻi administration, Puʻuhuluhulu University therefore intentionally allowed and encouraged individuals of our kaiāulu (community) to take ownership of the ʻike (knowledge) they possess, and transfer those knowledge systems to the lāhui" (Sang, 266). What she and other aloha ʻaina brought into being was a vision of life outside the circuits of the corporate and colonial university, and a space to unlearn violence-inducing sexual and gender roles so foundational to hegemonic formulations of the human.

Those who showed up for "(Auto)biography as Activism" included graduate students who had taken classes from me at UH, and people of all ages and from

different walks of life. Most were from Hawaiʻi, but some were from the conti-
nental US, Aotearoa, Taiwan, and Tonga. I started class by asking them, as they
introduced themselves, to answer the following questions: What is your connection to Mauna Kea? What has brought you here? What role, if any, have stories
played and have they been from those you know personally? From there, we
discussed what stories they might tell of their time on the Mauna, and to whom
and why. We thought about the meaning of "the personal is political" in relation
to what they might say about their experience on Mauna Kea—to their children,
to their ancestors, to the legislature, to scientists. I asked those at UH to think
about how they might narrate their time on the Mauna to the UH Board of
Regents and UH president/CEO David Lassner. We talked about what an account
of their personal experiences might accomplish in each of these instances,
and if or how they might share them and why. I also asked them about the photos they were taking—and deliberately not taking. Then we read a brief excerpt
of autobiographical writing by Malia Hulleman, one of the Cattle Guard 8 (from
"An Ode to My Sanity"), and passages from James Baldwin, June Jordan, and
Patrisse Cullors that brought together considerations of personal and political
transformation in relation to the stars, in ways I hoped would be generative. I
then invited them to take some time to write about their experience on the Mauna,
whether it be as BOR testimony, an op-ed, a diary entry, or a letter to a family
member. I passed around paper and pens for those not writing on phones,
laptops, or notebooks. As we wrote, we could hear chanting from men in the kāne
workshop. With the sun angling down and a chilly wind blowing across the lava
field, we drew closer. About fifteen minutes later, we formed small groups so
people could read or reflect on what they had written. We then came back together to share our experiences and, for those who wished to do so, their writing.

   Although this class was similar in structure to any number I have taught
at UH, this experience was a world apart. I have often been moved by the
trust, honesty, generosity, and vulnerability of students in my Autobiographical
Writing classes, but with this one, there was a new and exhilarating experience of working within rather than against the grain of the university, and of
being part of something bigger than ourselves. The students I knew from UH
shared ways they felt transformed and healed by their time on Mauna Kea.
They talked about how they felt connected in new ways to the land and to one
another. Many of us cried as one young protector shared a story about the difficulty of coming out as queer and having their heart broken, and of how coming to stand for the Mauna proved unexpectedly healing. They and others
talked about coming in solidarity, and about the surprise of the Mauna giving
them what they had needed without knowing they needed it.

This sharing of our stories—these acts of narrated humanity—became part of the movement we were making together. I had entered the class intending for us to think about life narratives in relation to activism. How are they part of the struggle for human rights? Who gets to tell stories and who doesn't? What are the political and ethical effects of "personal" stories? How might we share our experiences to support the movement for Mauna Kea and what venues were open to us? By the end of class, these questions seemed less important than what was transpiring among us, the pilina we were creating with each other through sharing stories that needed no analytical framework nor any life beyond that class to matter. So, too, the transformation many of us were experiencing had everything to do with the lava that felt at once so solid but alive under our feet, with the immensity of the Mauna, with our elevation and closeness to the clouds, the sun, and the emerging stars. All of this created an experience of aloha ʻāina that came alive in and through story.

Solidarity Stories: Thickening the "Rope of Resistance"

Through the movement for Mauna Kea, I have come to discover how the values and practices of aloha ʻāina inspire solidarity. Threaded through this chapter have been instances of solidarity, and examples of how the Mauna Kea movement exists in a constellation with other movements. In tracing the history of Standing Rock, and its "brief vision of what a future premised on Indigenous justice would look like," how it guaranteed to all "free food, free education, free health care, free legal aid, a strong sense of community, safety, and security," Estes links this vision to organizing by AIM (American Indian Movement) and the Black Panthers, and to an "infrastructure of Indigenous resistance, its ideas and practices of solidarity" that counter "settler colonialism's own physical infrastructure—trade routes, railroads, dams, and oil pipelines." With its clear and highly conscious connections to past and contemporary struggles, the movement for Mauna Kea emerges out of and partakes in this history that Estes maps—and that kiaʻi make legible, whether it be through the keffiyah that Perez, Kaʻeo, Hulleman, and Punahele wear; or the signs protectors hold that speak in concert with those at Standing Rock; or the flags that line Ala Hulu Kūpuna, gifted by people who came from all over the world to stand in solidarity with Mauna Kea.

This story of solidarity is part of a living moʻolelo that, even during a global pandemic that brought kiaʻi down from the Mauna, has continued to grow as kiaʻi participate in storytelling events that celebrate and insist on making space for queer and māhū aloha ʻāina; participate in unprecedented numbers in the BLM movement; organize against anti-Micronesian racism; support Maori protectors fighting for landback at Ihumātao; strike for hotel workers' rights; stand for a free Palestine; and more. When the police killed 16-year-old Iremamber Sykap on April 5, 2021, kiaʻi not only organized and showed up at protests. They also extended support to his family through offerings of stories—as at the 2021 Na Hua Ea, the art, poetry and music event held each year as part of the celebration of Lā Hoʻi Hoʻi Ea (Hawaiian independence). So too, they have stood for Palestine: when in May 2021, Israel moved again to dispossess Palestinians of their land and homes in Occupied Jerusalem's Sheikh Jarrah, ʻIhilani Lasconia, an aloha ʻāina, student, organizer, and artist, initiated an SJFP@UH protest that brought together Kanaka Maoli organizers, longtime Palestine activists, and young women with the Muslim Association of Hawaii. The following week, more than sixty people came together for a Solidarity Gathering, and we broke into study groups to explore connections between Hawaiʻi and Palestine, and to plan film nights, panels, and a march cosponsored by SFJP@UH, Sabeel Hawaiʻi, JVP-Hawaiʻi, Kiaʻi Ke Kahaukani, the anti-imperialist fourth-wave feminist organization AF3IRM Hawaiʻi, Anakbayan, Hawaiʻi for Black Lives, Refuse Fascism, Hawaiʻi Peace and Justice, Decolonial Pin@ys, and Coronacare.

The power of solidarity, and the mobilizing power of the movement for Mauna Kea, were on full display at the historic June 6, 2020, BLM march, organized by teens with Hawaiʻi for Black Lives. Following the police murders of George Floyd and Breonna Taylor, in an unprecedented stand for BLM, ten to fifteen thousand people marched during the COVID-19 lockdown from Ala Moana Beach Park to the State Capitol (see chapter 3). In contrast to the police presence, along with the mutual aid organization Coronacare, the Mauna Medics supported the march by ensuring our safety. Speaking as a Black Kanaka kiaʻi, Joy Enomoto rocked the Capitol that day as she highlighted the global nature of the struggle against anti-Blackness and the interconnections of BLM, abolitionist movements, and the stand for Mauna Kea; and as she enjoined those of us gathered at the Capitol "to imagine what genuine security feels like." Insisting on the inseparability of peace and freedom, she called on us to "make puʻuhonua within each other" and to "imagine alternatives to capitalism," and for Kanaka Maoli to reclaim their ʻaina ("Joy Enomoto's Speech"). As she took those of us at the Capitol that day back to Puʻuhonua o Puʻuhuluhulu, she dared us to begin realizing a future that refuses anything less than freedom and safety for us all.

Sharing stories has everything to do with forging this solidarity, and with how involvement in different movements can help narrate into existence ways of being human that create freedom and true security on a more-than-human, planetary scale. My own understanding of the power that comes from

Figure 9. Nā Hua EA gathering at Papahana Kuaola, 2018. Dancing to 47Soul's "Dabeekeh." (Photo taken by author)

the cross-pollination of different struggles and movements, and story's role in this process, has come largely through participating in Palestine solidarity work in Hawai'i (fig. 9).[30] One of the many things I have learned through supporting anticolonial and decolonial movements from Hawai'i to Palestine is how seemingly different movements can strengthen and energize one another, and how stories connect humans and movements that exist oceans and lands apart—and enable the creation of decolonial futures that, circling back to this book's introduction, leave behind Sylvia Wynter's Man.

By way of illustrating this contention, here is one telling of the meeting of the movements for Palestine and Mauna Kea.

When Rana Barakat, Yousef Aljamal, and Noura Erakat came to Honolulu in November 2019 for a visit sponsored by SFJP@UH and Sabeel Hawai'i, and also with the support of the ASA, their visits built on previous ones, especially those taking place for "Decolonial November" (see chapter 4).[31] Timed to coincide with the Honolulu American Studies Association Conference, the 2019 Decolonial November included more than formal talks and the trip to Mauna Kea: Rana, Noura, and Yousef also participated on a solidarity panel at the ASA; attended noontime 'aha at Wise Field; and after that, participated in a rally alongside some twenty kiaʻi and ASA participants. At this rally, we presented testimony opposing the UH administration's authoritarian rules for Mauna Kea. Although our plan had been to present this testimony to the UH Board of Regents, they moved their meeting at the last moment from the Mānoa to the Hilo campus, presumably to avoid precisely this inter/national show of solidarity.

Perhaps most productive of all in building pilina from Hawaiʻi to Palestine have been the stories shared during and in between organized actions and events. That November, Noura, Rana, and Yousef spent time with Kanaka Maoli and other Palestinian and Hawaiʻi activists talking story—at restaurants; during potlucks on my lānai or hookah sessions at the home of Political Science PhD candidate Ali Musleh; in the early morning hours at the Honolulu airport; at the home that former UH-M student and UH Hilo professor Mark Panek and his mother Jane Panek shared with Kēhaulani, Rana, Yousef, and me; at a karaoke night to celebrate Hōkūlani K. Aikau and Vernadette Vicuña Gonzalez's coedited collection, *Detours: A Decolonial Guide to Hawaiʻi*; at the beach; and on hikes. The exchanging of stories created a solidarity that was nontransactional, a solidarity that goes beyond shared political beliefs and objectives (though surely those are important)—a solidarity premised on its close cousin kuleana, and on decolonial love.

In the interviews for the "Cultivating Allies" unit of the Mauna Kea Syllabus—themselves acts of solidarity—Rana, Noura, and Yousef all stress the significance of stories in creating solidarity, a sense of belonging to the Mauna Kea movement, and a glimpse into emergent ways of being human. Reflecting on the importance of sharing stories with kiaʻi Mauna, Rana observed to me that settler colonialism is "about preventing shared collective stories and the sharing of personal stories" (Barakat, *Interview with Rana*). During her time in Hawaiʻi, she says that she learned how "incredibly powerful stories and storytelling" are as "a core part of an arsenal of resistance against settler colonialism." Through story, she goes on to describe how she became part of the Mauna Kea movement. Along with being in a space she describes as sacred and ceremonial, she says, it was "also very human to sit with people and talk story and be part of something bigger than ourselves." Through the relationships that unfolded on the Mauna, she says, "I was not only legible and recognizable [as a Palestinian], I was part of what was happening."

The movement Rana describes becoming part of through the sharing of stories was about a deepening relationship, decolonial and spiritual in nature, not only to people, but also to Kanaka and Palestinian land. As she tells her story of the Mauna, beginning with the drive from the airport, the drop in temperature, and the rise in altitude, she says, "I knew where I was headed but there was a feeling throughout my body . . . it was a spiritual experience"—and one that, as she came to understand aloha ʻāina, gave her a new understanding of her relationship to Palestine as "a place you long for and belong to." Noura's story about her experience of Hawaiʻi in many ways echoed Rana's. Explaining she came expecting a cerebral connection, she says, "I was not prepared at all for the feeling I would have, coming to a place where the relationship to the land was so fundamental. . . . You cannot be prepared for the energy of the earth itself, of the land itself, of the people themselves and how they frame it, and what was going on in terms of indigenous resurgence" (Erakat, interview). Yousef, too, expressed the at-homeness he felt in Hawaiʻi coming out of a shared sense of the understanding, passed on through story from one generation to the next, that "To the land we belong and to the land we shall return" (Aljamal).

As they narrate their time in Hawaiʻi, both Rana and Noura describe coming to the limits of language as they consider the meaning of aloha ʻāina and what it means to be part of a movement in the making. Noura tells of how through participating in noontime protocol and learning of the concept of aloha ʻāina, she experienced "an overwhelming feeling that left me shaken . . . filled with metaphysical commitment to something that our writing and our reading could not possibly say." She also looks back on a dinnertime conversation with Jon Osorio and the power of discovering from him that the ceremony she attended that day was not one fixed in the past, but a process still in the making. She describes her understanding that "on the Mauna itself what was being created was the alternative future, it was a space of mutual aid, of mutual existence, an alternative economy, an alternative government, an alternative decision-making structure," and a glimpse into "what it would mean to overcome capitalism and settler colonialism. . . . If not what it is, what it could be, what it might be." When I asked Rana about this future she saw unfolding at Mauna Kea, she replied that as she engages in decolonization as "our practice and our praxis," "we are constantly trying to free ourselves and I don't know what that will look like, but we're doing it together."

As kiaʻi create this undetermined future in conversation with other Indigenous peoples and allies engaged in articulated struggles, through the sharing of stories, what is taking shape is the making of movements that offer new forms of kinship, and still inchoate ways of being human that nonetheless allow for legibility and feelings of belonging. And just as Palestinians and other allies are showing up for Kanaka ʻŌiwi as they rise up, so too are Kanaka ʻŌiwi and other allies showing up for Palestinians. This rising continues—during COVID-19, in the form of masked protests and panels and webinars and publications that bring together the movements for Mauna Kea, BLM, and Palestine.[32] In October 2020, when USACBI organized a Day of Action in response to Zoom, Facebook, and YouTube having censored Rabab Abdulhadi and Tomomi Kinukawa's open classroom featuring Leila Khaled and other freedom fighters, SFJP@UH and the Hawaiʻi Peace and Justice base-building demilitarization initiative Koa Futures organized a Zoom event, "We Will Not Be Silenced: The Case of Khaled and Solidarity from Hawaiʻi to Palestine." Co-sponsored by Ethnic Studies and Political Science, this webinar was to feature Enomoto, Kaʻeo, and Maʻan Odeh. Zoom shut that down too, with complicity from UH administrators who declined to provide us with another site, and who ignored a letter from Palestine Legal challenging the constitutionality of the censorship ("Unconstitutional Censorship"). At the brilliant suggestion of Kaleikoa, students and faculty then organized a reading, on Zoom, of Khaled's words, read by tenured faculty, many of them kiaʻi who are part of the story this chapter has been telling.[33] This willingness to act in the face of administrative chill and Zionist harassment, including in the form of FOIAs, came not only out of political conviction, but friendships, and ongoing conversations with Palestinian comrades that have taken place in classrooms and lecture halls, but also at dinner tables, and on sand, on lava fields, and in water. As we show up for each other, we share stories that thicken what Haunani-Kay Trask calls the "rope of resistance" ("Sons") as, together, we narrate into being a freer, more expansive and caring approach to being human.

"End Dependence Day": An Ending, and a Projection into a Freer Future Perfect

By way of concluding this chapter, I want to take July 4 as an occasion to consider how the grounded narrative and narrated humanity that feed and are fed by the movement for Mauna Kea continue to foster freeing ways of being human, premised on ʻāina-based forms of solidarity, kuleana, and kinship that break the circuits of heteropatriarchy, racial capitalism, and settlerism.

On July 3, 2021, I learned of the passing of Haunani-Kay Trask. My Facebook, Instagram, and Twitter feeds were flooded with memories and tributes from Hawaiʻi to Turtle Island to Aotearoa to Palestine, as friends grieved the loss of this internationally renowned public intellectual, poet, critic of settler colonialism, leader of the sovereignty group Ka Lāhui Hawaiʻi, founder and longtime director of the UH-M Kamakakūokalani Center for Hawaiian Studies, and teacher who mentored generations of Kanaka Maoli activist/scholars. When I opened my Facebook, it was to send a reminder post about that day's "From Hawaiʻi to Palestine" march. My first thought was, How could we possibly go forward with the event in the face of this devastating loss? My second was, How could we not? So much solidarity for Palestine in Hawaiʻi traces back to Haunani, who was passionate about Palestinian liberation and its connections to

Hawaiian independence, and staunchly internationalist in her fight for Indigenous rights (activists and scholars she brought to UH included Angela Davis, Winona LaDuke, Rigoberta Menchú, Ngugi wa Thiong'o, Albert Wendt, and Patrick Wolfe). When we gathered in a circle before the march at Ala Moana Beach Park that afternoon, after we held a moment of silence for Haunani, 'Ihilani Lasconia dedicated our march to her, and spoke of how Haunani was her kumu, although she had been too young to have taken classes with her.

As 'Ihilani spoke, I thought of all the postings I had read, particularly by Kanaka Maoli women Haunani had mentored, who, like 'Ihilani, identified as her "slyly reproductive daughters"—a reference to Trask's poem "Sons," in which she proclaims, "I am slyly/reproductive: ideas/books, history/politics, reproducing/the rope of resistance/for unborn generations" (Trask, *Light in the Crevice*, 55–56). Revilla provides a gorgeous meditation on this, in words she addresses to Haunani, proclaiming herself and other "aloha 'āina who are also intersectional feminists as well as queer, lesbian, trans, māhū, and nonbinary kanaka" as Haunani's "slyly reproductive daughters" (qtd. in ho'omanawanui, "He Hali'a"). Haunani continues to be a felt presence in all contemporary organizing for ea, including the movement for Mauna Kea. ku'ualoha ho'omanawanui's story of going to the Mauna beautifully exemplifies this. She describes how it was "an honor to carry her [Trask] with me to Mauna Kea in the summer and fall of 2019, as her life partner David Stannard gifted me with one of her iconic pareu. . . . Because my aloha 'āina activism began on the Mānoa campus under her mentorship in 1985, gathering on the Mauna seemed incomplete without her. What a privilege to teach a class in the Mana Wahine tent one rainy morning under her photo the kia'i of that space had hung" (ho'omanawanui, "He Hali'a"). Haunani-Kay Trask is indeed "slyly reproductive," as a mana wahine who taught her students, her nieces and nephews, her lāhui, and allies how to analyze, resist, and organize against the theft of land to which she belongs and fiercely loved.

Just as kia'i brought Haunani to the Mauna, so too her spirit of kū'ē, or resistance, animates their tributes to her that also continue her legacy. Haunani's passing on July 3 seemed a fitting refusal of another "4th of you lie" that Mauna Kea leadership brilliantly foregrounded at the State Capitol on the evening of her death, as they slyly reproduced a way of being human that refuses the imperialist and militarized freedom and belonging blasted into the skies each Fourth of July.

On January 17, 1993, in an electrifying speech marking the one hundredth anniversary of the illegal overthrow of the Hawaiian Kingdom, Trask stood in front of 'Iolani Palace and proclaimed, "We are not American! Say it in your heart! Say it when you sleep! We are not American! We will die as Hawaiians!" (Lander and Puhipau). On the eve of July 4, 2021, aloha 'āina gathered and, using a giant projector, lit up the State Capitol with the words "We Are Not American," along with "LANDBACK" and, in response to a bill seeking to extend state control over stolen Hawaiian lands, "HB499 LANDTHEFT." The distinctive "LANDBACK" font aligned their action with the Indigenous-led NDN Collective and their Landback movement (and here it is worth noting that Andre Perez is one of the twenty-one people from Turtle Island and surrounding island nations named as a 2021 NDN Changemaker Fellow [NDN Collective, "Meet the 2021 Cohort"]). In their LANDBACK Manifesto, the NDN Collective proclaims the interconnection of all struggles against oppression; their belonging to the land "because—we are the land"; and the understanding that if the earth is not well, they as her children cannot be well. In their antiracist, anticapitalist, decolonial vision, they espouse principles of staying in community; moving from abundance; refusing to "let our oppressors' inhumanity take away from ours"; and engaging in honest and unapologetic organizing to dismantle white supremacy. They demand the defunding of the police, the military industrial complex, Border Patrol, and ICE; the return of "all public lands back into Indigenous hands"; and the establishment of an era of consent ("LANDBACK Manifesto"). Each of these principles and demands is embodied in the making and messaging of the art action at the Capitol. So, too, as a kind of sequel to the July 4, 2019, Mauna Kea Art Build, this art action two years later traces back to and builds on the movement for the Mauna, and before that, Standing Rock, and before that, to Indigenous visionaries like Trask and their movements for aloha ʻāina. And, like the movement for Mauna Kea, as a mobilization against HB 499, this landback action is at once time and place specific, and global. It is part of a moʻolelo that, based in grounded normativity, projects a decolonial future and helps bring into focus an ongoing story of human freedom and becoming that will continue, through acts of narrated humanity, to create alternatives to the dehumanization that hegemonic narrative humanity perpetuates, in the name of freedom and humanity.

One of the kiaʻi from whom I learned about this art action was the not-quite-teenaged daughter of one of the Mauna Kea leaders, ʻIlima Long. On Instagram, Kahele posted the iconic photo of Haunani-Kay Trask with her fist raised as she delivered her 1993 speech. As part of the same story, she followed this image with photos of the messages projected onto the State Capitol (@sistakahele). Over the years, this young kiaʻi has sat quietly through any number of meetings, workshops, and events her mother has been at the forefront of—for Mauna Kea, for labor, for the rights of undocumented students, for Palestine solidarity, for uniting student activists from different organizations. I have seen her together with other children of kiaʻi on the Mauna, at direct action nonviolent training sessions, at BLM marches, at anti-Asian hate protests, at reproductive

Figure 10. Mauna Kea, July 2019. *Left to right*: Konakaimehela'i Kealoha, Ka'uiki Kalama, Kahelekaiaulu Seto-Long, La'ila'ikūhonua Ka'ōpua-Winchester. (Photo credit: Noelani Goodyear-Ka'ōpua. Permissions granted by all in the photo and their parents)

rights rallies, and at potlucks and sign wavings for Palestine (fig. 10). Through these children and their parents, we can see what Nadine Naber calls "The Radical Potential of Mothering." In her article by that name, Naber contends that the women she spoke with about their involvement with the Egyptian revolution "reframe[d] mothering from biological responsibility to collective radical pedagogy. . . . As children and revolutionary mothers envision a new future together, they participate in building a new kind of society *and* forging new forms of being, both of which are essential to bringing about a revolutionary future" (31). Naber's insights into mothering as a collective radical pedagogy, and as a revolutionary practice of reproductive labor, resonate with Goodyear-Ka'ōpua's understanding in *The Seeds We Planted* of how students at the Native Hawaiian Charter school Hālau Kū Mana "come to see themselves as important actors within a genealogically situated movement for self-determination and sovereignty" (13). The words of both mother/teacher/activist/scholars speak to the significance of the reproductive labor that is part of the movement for Mauna Kea's history and future—work that Noe, like 'Ilima, has undertaken in visionary ways. To see on Instagram 'Ilima's daughter Kahele emerging as a storyteller in her own right, and claiming this connection to Trask, is to witness the power of living forms of kinship, kuleana, and solidarity that start but do not end with grounded normativity, and that bring into being old as well as slyly reproductive new alternatives to narrative humanity's dominant—and killing—forms of kinship, self-making, and discovery.

One of the stories this book has been telling concerns the critical role kinship plays in narrative and narrated humanity. Its narrative trajectory starts with chapter 1's consideration of *Zeitoun*, a story of marriage and family that, with its reliance on heteronorms, perpetuates violent exclusions, forms of (domestic) violence, racial capitalism, and imperialism. Via *Fruitvale Station* and *Between the World and Me*, chapter 2 delves into searing accounts of police murders that expose and challenge ways narrative humanity's antiblack norms support the state in robbing mothers and fathers of their children, and children of their parents. Part 2 departs from stories of family that are constituted within and against narrative humanity's norms. Instead, we see how acts of narrated humanity that partake in political movements can bring into being forms of kinship that overturn and offer alternatives to the violence encoded in narrative humanity. In chapter 3's reading of *When They Call You a Terrorist*, we see how through her queer and abolitionist BLM-inspired vision for the future, Patrice Cullors connects her and Future's child, Shine, to the stars, and to children everywhere, whom she addresses as "brilliant beings of light [who] have the power to shape-shift not only yourselves but the whole of the world." Through Steven Salaita's acts of narrated humanity, we consider in chapter 4 how he extends the love and security he provides for his son to all children—those he transports to school each day, and those in Gaza. Through these stories, he insists on a way of human being premised on elemental forms of love and belonging that emerge out of his BDS activism, and that go beyond biological ties and national borders. Through attention to the movement for Mauna Kea, this fifth and final chapter brings more-than-human relations—sky, land, ocean, elements, all living creatures— into this book's story of human being and becoming, considering how crucial these and other more expansive forms of kinship are for human as well as planetary survival and thriving. As they become part of one story, my hope is that the stories, movements, and relations chronicled in this book help engender other stories—and that these stories will continue to create ways of being human that will enable all of us, together, to rise like a mighty wave, buoyed up by radical and resurgent relations of care, connection, and love.

Postscript

Hope, Joy, and "The Struggle for Ea"

Joy is an art is an ethics of resistance.

—BILLY-RAY BELCOURT, *A HISTORY OF MY BRIEF BODY*

It's work to be hopeful. It's not like a fuzzy feeling. Like, you have to actually put in energy, time, and you have to be clear-eyed, and you have to hold fast to having a vision. It's a hard thing to maintain. But it matters to have it, to believe that it's possible, to change the world. . . .

People are doing work all the time and consistently and constantly. And I don't know where that's going to go. I don't know what the end result is going to look like. But it's part of a long legacy, what we call *la longue durée*. This is a long term arc of work and I'm not a progress-narrative person, so I think everything happens at the same time. So we're resisting and we're being crushed at the same time always, like they're parallel tracks happening.

—MARIAME KABA, "HOPE IS A DISCIPLINE"

. . . I like you because you hold this all together with the parts I can't see
I breathe it in
You breathe it out

—LEANNE BETASAMOSAKE SIMPSON, "THE OLDEST TREE"

On Friday, March 5, 2022, Sumaya Awad gave a talk at the University of Hawai'i as part of a SFJP@UH (Students and Faculty for Justice in Palestine) "Decolonial November" visit that had been postponed until spring because of the pandemic. Our title for Sumaya's visit, "Inter/nationalism, from Hawaiʻi to Palestine," came from Steven Salaita's time here and also from our collective study of his book *Inter/Nationalism*, which we read together when preparing for his visit. The week of Sumaya's visit, Kauwila Mahi, an ʻŌiwi Hawaiʻi artist, rapper, sound designer, and a student in my graduate course, "Genres of Protest," posted a letter to the class website. Salaita was on our syllabus, and Kauwila wrote that Salaita's theorization of "intersectionality as a mutual liberation . . . helped me prepare some new lyrics for this Friday!" (Mahi, "Class Letter"). After Sumaya's inspiring talk and Q&A, Kauwila and ʻIhilani Lasconia, an aloha ʻāina, graduate student, organizer, and artist, closed out the event with the song they cowrote for the occasion. As the audience cheered them on, they invited us to join them as they rapped,

> From olive tree to olive tree, from Niʻihau to Hawaiʻi
> We see you in your struggle and we won't stop til we all are free
> Kū ana ka paia
> Intifada Intifada Intifada! . . .
> Free ya people, free ya mind
> Deoccupy Hawaiʻi *and Palestine!*
> (Lasconia and Mahi)

It was thrilling, especially after the isolation and fragmentation of the pandemic, to see everyone in the Kamakakūokalani Center for Hawaiian Studies Hālau o Haumea on their feet (except, that is, for the one lurking Zionist), unified, fists raised, joyful and joining together in song (fig. 11). Past Decolonial Novembers were a felt presence in the Hālau that day, as Sumaya, Kauwila, ʻIhi, and audience members experienced a deepening inter/national relationality and sense of past and present collective power.[1]

In its mix of hip-hop rhythms and ancestral chants, and as performed with the audience in that Hālau, ʻIhi and Kauwila's song was an act of what I have called throughout this book narrated humanity, one based in grounded narrative humanity. Inspired by the ties fostered through inter/national solidarity and a commitment to creating decolonial futures, as they performed their song, they embodied how acts of narrated humanity can breathe life into resistance against state violence while lifting up decolonial ways of human being and belonging. Their proclamation, "Kū ana ka paia," comes from an oli said to be a prophecy from Kapihe, who lived during the time of Kamehameha I. Kapihe forecasted an overturning that, as Noelle Kahanu explains, "came to pass with the overthrow of the Hawaiian religious system in 1819 and the coming of American Protestant missionaries just a year later." The oli predicts that the high will be brought low, and the low lifted up, as the islands unite and

Figure 11. Kauwila Mahi and 'Ihilani Lasconia, performing at the Kamakakūokalani Center for Hawaiian Studies Hālau o Haumea, during Sumaya Awad's visit to Hawai'i. (Photo taken by author. Permissions granted by Mahi and Lasconia)

the people stand firm.[2] Kahanu finds that this chant "acknowledges difficulty and sorrow, heartache and turmoil, warfare and destruction. It acknowledges that despite these profound changes, we are still here. We have survived and we will continue to come together as a people—a hui ana nā moku." Kanaka Maoli have returned to this oli, including in the movement for Mauna Kea, in their struggle for ea. 'Ihi and Kauwila evoke this oli, while also declaring "liberation's the cause for those near and those far/We choose to join hands when they only bear arms/So hands off Mākua and hands off Sheikh Jarrah." In their rendering, the choice to unify not only draws on the past but also exists in the present and future. As they put this ancestral oli into the present tense (changing "E kū ana ka paia" to "Kū ana ka paia"), they extend its call to include everyone gathered in Hālau o Haumea, and they urge us to continue to kū'ē, to resist, in friendship and solidarity, ongoing settler violence and the dispossession of land, from Hawai'i to Palestine.

I thought of 'Ihi and Kauwila's song, and this moment of joyous rising together in struggle from Mākua to Sheikh Jarrah, and "from olive tree to olive tree," when I first saw the image Joy Lehuanani Enomoto designed for *Narrating Humanity*. When I commissioned Joy to come up with a cover image, she searched for the book's through-line and found in it "the struggle to breathe and for self-determination, for ea. But there is always an attending violence." Joy's image, "The Struggle for Ea," captures this dynamic, or what in this postscript's epigraph Mariame Kaba describes as "parallel tracks" where "we're resisting and we're being crushed at the same time always." Indeed, this same dynamic emerges throughout this book in the ways friendship and community are co-constituted with decolonial and abolitionist struggles. On the one hand, there is the racist, heteropatriarchal, colonial, capitalist state violence (what 'Ihi and Kauwila call "the same colonial apparatus round the atlas") that fills the air that we and our other-than-human relations—including trees— breathe in with smoke and toxins. There is the state violence that drowns the most vulnerable in floods of petroleum-filled waters; that puts the police's knees to the necks of Black boys and men, also leaving their loved ones breathless; that teargasses and chokes the speech of those standing up to or taking cover from university upper administrators, soldiers, and police; that crushes the living, breathing bodies of Palestinians through bombs and bureaucratic maneuvers. On the other hand, there are human and more-than-human assertions of life, and sovereignty; there are stories that breathe life into struggles for human being and belonging to one another, to more-than-humans, and to water, stars, sky, 'āina.

Even as Joy's "Struggle for Ea" features a trachea that is damaged, this passageway into the lung is still intact and, also treelike, it branches into rhizomatic roots that hold together all the parts we can't see, bringing the human and the land into one interdependent organism—to return to the lines quoted in the introduction from Leanne Betasamosake Simpson's poem "The Oldest Tree" and then again in this postscript's epigraph, "I breathe it in /You breathe it out." Indeed, Joy's image captures this book's attention to interdependent and intersectional forms of rising and resistance through the sharing of stories even when—especially when—state violence makes it hard to breathe. Joy's gorgeous, fleshy, all-at-the-same-time image of the struggle for ea also struck me as a visual accompaniment to 'Ihi and Kauwila's song. Both evoke the power and urgency of individual and collective breath, life, human and other-than-human interconnection, and inter/national and rhizomatic risings. With all these valences that acknowledge colonial violence, but that also assert what this book has been suggesting—the strength and joy of political movements and human and more-than-human in(ter)dependence—"The Struggle for Ea" and "Free Ya People" provide an image and a soundtrack for the story of human making and unmaking that *Narrating Humanity* strives to tell.

Joy's art and 'Ihi and Kauwila's song also put into play just how much this book has emerged out of friendships made through teaching, through study and learning, through organizing, and through showing up in spaces where people are standing up for mutual liberation, for the right not only to breathe, but also to shout and sing together and to create and share stories about human being and becoming, in ways that feed and are fed by theories and movements and dreams of liberation. The activists and storytellers whose work animates this book have guided both its theories of the human and my methodology. Being in community with them has moved me to produce scholarship that, through my own acts of narrated humanity, participates in political movements. During Sumaya's visit to Hawaiʻi, as we thought about all the time spent between public events sharing food and stories and thinking about water and ways to create true safety and inter/national, abolitionist communities of mutual aid and care, graduate student Ali Musleh and I cast back to Remi Kanazi's 2015 visit, and to a day we spent at Kailua Beach, talking about academic boycott, but also about parenting, food, and family. As we walked along the sand, the ocean lapping at our feet, I remember saying to Remi how much it meant to meet him outside of online organizing for the USACBI Organizing Collective. Remi responded that it was forging friendships in these small gatherings and during these quiet moments ("before the next bomb drops," to quote the title of Remi's book of poetry) that the real work gets done. As with organizing, so too with this book: the seeds for it were planted and watered during such moments on beaches, in cafes, over potluck dinners on the lānai, with the companions to whom I dedicate this book. It is my sincerest hope that in the long arc of the struggle for ea, through daily practices of organizing, dreaming, and sharing our stories, we narrate into being more stories that will continue to create as-yet-undetermined ways of human being and joyful belonging that will be breath-giving, and, like "The Struggle for Ea," rooted in land and life, and breathtakingly beautiful.

Notes

Introduction: The Human in Crisis

Portions of this introduction appeared previously in "Eichmann and His Ghosts: Affective States and the Unstable Status of the Human," *Cultural Critique* 88 (Fall 2014): 79–124.

1. Here, I particularly want to note the special *Biography* issues on topics that include BLM, Mauna Kea, Palestine, testimony and witnessing, caste, #MeToo, "baleful postcoloniality," and Indigeneity that, as they contribute to a variety of other fields, also make interventions into the field of life writing studies.

2. The way I am using "abolition" corresponds to the "Manifesto for Abolition" written by the Abolition Collective for *Abolition: A Journal of Insurgent Politics*: "'Abolition' refers partly to the historical and contemporary movements that have identified themselves as 'abolitionist': those against slavery, prisons, the wage system, animal and earth exploitation, human trafficking, and the death penalty, among others. But we also refer to all revolutionary movements, insofar as they have abolitionist elements—whether the abolition of patriarchy, capitalism, heteronormativity, ableism, colonialism, the state, or white supremacy. Rather than just seeking to abolish a list of oppressive institutions, we aim to support studies of the entanglement of different systems of oppression, not to erase the tensions between different movements, but to create spaces for collective experimentation with those tensions."

By "decolonial," I mean ways of knowing, relating, and being that are based on Indigenous values and epistemologies. For a useful delimiting of this term, see Cana Uluak Itchuaqiyaq and Breeanne Matheson.

3. Wilderson elaborates on this position in "'We're Trying to Destroy the World,'" the interview, taped during the 2014 antipolice protests in Ferguson, Missouri, in which he makes this statement: "As I told a friend of mine, 'Yeah we're going to help you get rid of Israel, but the moment that you set up your shit we're going to be right

there to jack you up, because anti-Blackness is as important and necessary to the formation of Arab psychic life as it is to the formation of Jewish psychic life. . . . We know, once they get over [their own hurdles], the anti-Blackness that sustains them will rear its ugly head again against us. So that we don't fall into a sort of genuine bonding with people who are really, primarily, using Black energy to catalyse and energize their struggle'" (13). Critics echoing this skepticism about engaging in coalitional politics from an Afro-pessimist perspective include Jared Sexton and Nicolas Brady.

4. Spillers unequivocally states she is not an Afro-pessimist in "Afropessimism and Its Others: A Discussion between Hortense J. Spillers and Lewis R. Gordon," explaining that she concludes her work by looking to the future, in distinction to Afro-pessimism.

5. In their assessments, they attend to its boycotting of Wynter (Thomas, 300) and misreadings and mistranslations of Fanon to arrive at a fixed and despairing understanding of the human (Gordon has a particularly sharp take on this); its Eurocentric distortions of African history, culture, and politics (Okoth, Gordon, Thomas); its dismissal of Marxism (Reed); and its erasures and put-downs of revolutionary anticolonial politics (as Spillers puts this, Afro-pessimists' reified understanding of Blackness acts as a "stop sign" that precludes movement). They also point to Afro-pessimists' obfuscation of their privileged location in the US academy (Mitchell, Thomas), and connect this to how Afro-pessimism facilitates the neoliberal university's and corporate America's cooptation of Blackness (Okoth) and quelling of political activism, including the movement to defund the police (Mitchell). Wilderson's 2021 article in *The Nation*, "An Afropessimist on the Year since George Floyd Was Murdered," provides a particularly good example of this as he uses this platform and occasion to liken an investment in political change to youthful naivete, and to equate the call to defund the police with liberal antiblackness (https://www.thenation.com/article/society/george-floyd-afropessimism/).

6. As I discuss in chapter 5, Coulthard defines grounded normativity as "the modalities of Indigenous land-connected practices and longstanding experiential knowledge that inform and structure our ethical engagements with the world and our relationships with human and nonhuman others over time" (13).

1. Love and Terror: Formulas of Citizenship in *Zeitoun* and *Trouble the Water*

Portions of this chapter appeared previously in "Narrative Humanity and Post-9/11 Dehumanization: *Zeitoun* as Case Study," *American Quarterly* 69, no. 4 (December 2017): 857–81.

1. As critics including Ed Morales have pointed out, Hurricane María exposed how the island serves the US as "a colonial satellite, a dumping ground for U.S. manufactured goods, and a tax shelter/investment casino in a land of temptation for tourists" (2–3).

2. The Jones Act, which had a stranglehold on Puerto Rico's economy even before María, "requires that goods shipped from one American port to another be transported on a ship that is American-built, American-owned, and crewed by US citizens or permanent residents. . . . That makes everything Puerto Ricans buy unnecessarily expensive relative to goods purchased on either the US mainland or other Caribbean islands, and drives up the cost of living on the island overall" (Yglesias).

3. In addition, a substantial body of Katrina scholarship exists, including special journal issues (e.g., the September 2010 issue of *American Quarterly*, "In the Wake of Katrina: New Paradigms and Social Movements," ed. Clyde Woods) and monographs (see, e.g., Douglas Brinkley, *The Great Deluge*).

4. Eggers continues his reliance on this pattern in *The Monk of Mokha* (2018). He describes this idealized narrative nonfiction about the entrepreneurial and hard-working young Yemeni American Mokhtar Alkhanshali as being "chiefly about the American Dream, which is very much alive and very much under threat" (qtd. in Seghal).

5. The film version was quietly canceled. Stories have appeared questioning the Zeitoun Foundation's finances and Eggers's ethical integrity and silence about the charges against Zeitoun (Champion).

6. This article includes a chart that documents the dramatic rise in pre- and post-2004 media mentions of "radicalization" from approximately 10 per year to around 120 by 2009.

7. For analysis of this dynamic, see Elia.

8. See, e.g., True.

9. Marullo also discounted testimony from the family friend who introduced the couple (Martin).

10. The same is not true for women. Law professor Tania Tetlow found that nationwide, while men who kill their female partners average two to six years in prison, women who kill male partners average fifteen years. In DeBerry, "Trayvon Martin."

11. Thanks here go to Lauren Barbour, who pointed out *Zeitoun's* biologically based understanding of family in a graduate seminar.

12. For a brief account of the Indigenous presence in New Orleans and Louisiana, see "Indigenous Tributes of New Orleans & Louisiana."

13. For example, Robert Holden, from the National Congress of American Indians (NCAI), reported that a tribal representative from an area near Chalmette, Louisiana, nine miles from New Orleans, told him of a total lack of government outreach, and of having to use Chalmette High School as a morgue (C. Stone Brown).

14. For an account of the longer history of anti-Arab racism and Islamophobia, see Maira and Shihade, "Meeting Asian/Arab American Studies"; Jamal and Naber's *Race and Arab Americans*; and Salaita's *Anti-Arab Racism*.

15. For one of the most definitive analyses of the model minority myth, see Lisa Lowe's *Immigrant Acts*.

16. As critics including Steven Salaita have noted, *Fahrenheit 9/11* is problematic. To put it in Salaita's words in *Anti-Arab Racism*, "Moore either whitewashed the anti-Arab racism of the Patriot Act unintentionally, in which case he failed to produce

an analysis worthy of the applause he received from liberals and progressives; or he whitewashed that racism intentionally, for the sake of rhetorical persuasiveness, in which case he pandered to an assumed ethos of White supremacy on the part of his imagined audience; an assumption, it turns out, that was totally correct" (31). *Trouble the Water*, which attends to issues of class and race, nonetheless adheres to a Black and white vision of racism that, in later chapters, Salaita and others productively challenge.

17. In *Lose Your Mother*, Hartman writes, "If slavery persists as an issue in the political life of black America, it is not because of an antiquarian obsession with bygone days or the burden of a too-long memory, but because black lives are still imperiled and devalued by a racial calculus and a political arithmetic that were entrenched centuries ago. This is the afterlife of slavery—skewed life chances, limited access to health and education, premature death, incarceration, and impoverishment. I, too, am the afterlife of slavery" (6). For discussions of contemporary uses of the slave narrative, see Sharpe's *Monstrous Intimacies*, especially her chapter on *Corregidora*.

18. For a discussion of the slave narrative as a Christian abolitionist genre, see Hopkins and Cummings; Hopkins; and Carter.

19. Exceptions to this constitute some of the best-known slave narratives, such as those by Mary Prince and Harriet Jacobs; thus, as Hannah Manshel pointed out to me, Roberts can be seen to be drawing on a legacy of working within forms that have white editorial oversight, while nonetheless finding ways to put forth *Black form* that is not wholly overdetermined by the white-directed vehicle.

20. The label's website, Bornhustler Records, promises "stone cold protest" as it embraces Black pride and profit—it includes a graphic of a small Black girl whose braids are clipped with money bills, adorned in rapper's bling that includes a large "born hustler" pendant, sitting in front of a pile of money.

21. Even as the film can be seen to allude to the scene in Zora Neale Hurston's *Their Eyes Were Watching God* where Janie and the folks on the muck await the arrival of the 1928 Okeechobee hurricane, in contrast to this scene, the Robertses' relationship to Christianity does not leave room for irony.

22. This happens within some slave narratives, as well. For example, Harriet Jacobs troubles this arc, and with it the genre of the sentimental novel / marriage plot, in her conclusion to *Incidents in the Life of a Slave Girl*. See Manshel's "'Never Allowed for Property.'"

2. Criminals and Kinship: *Fruitvale Station, Between the World and Me, and Black Selfhood in the Age of BLM*

1. For other commentaries on its influence, see Mizoeff (6), or, for a mainstream venue, *Fortune* magazine's "The Black Lives Matter Founders Are among the World's Great Leaders" (Griffith). After its first five years, some scholar-activists questioned the status of BLM even as they also underlined its ongoing relevance

and impact. See for example Taylor's "Five Years Later." The prescience of Taylor's analysis became evident in 2020 when BLM returned in full force, in ways I address in chapter 3.

2. I am drawing here on Mbembe's "Necropolitics." In defining this term, he explains that "to kill or to allow to live constitute the limits of sovereignty, its fundamental attributes" (11). In a necropolitical order, to assert sovereignty "is to exercise control over mortality and to define life as the deployment and manifestation of power" (12).

3. My usage varies in this chapter between "antiblack racism" (or antiblackness) and "anti-Black racism" (or anti-Blackness). As also noted in the book's introduction, I use the former except when working within a specifically Afro-pessimist frame, or one that describes a form of racism posited as ontological rather than historically variable, and changeable.

4. A number of the films or series that are arguably catalyzed by and carry forward the BLM movement remind us of this long historical arc; to name but a few, *Get Out!*; *Selma*; *I Am Not Your Negro*; *The Underground Railroad*; and *When They See Us*.

5. An antecedent to BLM, the Katrina Complex (see chapter 1) showed the US's continuing refusal to recognize Black Americans as US citizens. At the close of 2017, Eric Garner's twenty-seven-year-old daughter, Erica Garner, died from asthma and heart failure. These are conditions linked not only to poverty and environmental racism, but also to heartbreak and stress, conditions that numerous studies confirm lead to premature death for Black people. An important body of literature exists on racism as a source of illness. See, for example, Threadcraft's "North American Necropolitics," 555.

6. Less publicized, Garner also proclaimed, "This stops today"—a proclamation that, when police killed him moments later and medical staff failed to attend to him, proved with chilling precision what it means for a Black man to issue such a claim.

7. Cooper made this statement in a workshop discussion for the special *Biography* issue, "M4BL and the Critical Matter of Black Lives," that she coedited with Treva Lindsey. This chapter is informed not only by that special issue, but also by what I learned about BLM from its scholar/activist contributors during that three-day workshop held in Honolulu.

8. The affinities between Coogler and Coates are further suggested by the fact that, in addition to their Black Panther connection, they are currently working together on a film dramatizing the 2006 Atlanta public school cheating scandal (Rao).

9. Responding to negative attention given to property destruction in the contexts of the Floyd uprisings, both Garza (Remnick) and Tometi (Ellen Jones) call for the focus to remain on the valuing of people over property.

10. As protesters, chained together, blocked the passage of consumers rather than goods through key nodes of transport, they offered an innovative alternative for disrupting what Stefano Harney and Fred Moten refer to as logistical capitalism's "choke points" ("Leave Our Mikes Alone"). By chaining themselves together, protesters

also evoke as they resist the past enslavement of African Americans and slavery's aftermath. For an account of the protest, see Heather Smith.

11. Smith's logic, which depends upon focusing on the humanity of the shooter/police officer and the dehumanization of the Black person shot, is key to acquitting cops who kill. In his analysis of the transcripts of Darren Wilson's trial, Mirzoeff finds that as the trial becomes "all about Darren Wilson" (82), his exoneration hinges on establishing that Wilson's fear of Brown is "reasonable" given racist stereotypes that render Black men powerful and scary.

12. Coogler's political orientation becomes increasingly clear over the course of his career to date. His blockbuster hit *Black Panther* earns its popularity and claims to radicality by featuring a strong Black cast. And it has been critiqued for staying away from, when it does not condemn, protest or resistance. However, whereas *Fruitvale Station*'s inattention to politics arguably aligns the film with BLM, *Black Panther*'s representation of political activism, including its dismissal of the work of the revolutionary Black Panther Party, disparages and approaches criminalizing political organizing, especially in US contexts. See LeBron.

13. The family narrative that appears in the "Love Not Blood" campaign, cofounded by Grant's Uncle Bobby, who also served as a consultant for *Fruitvale Station*, resembles but broadens and more directly politicizes the story the movie tells. On the website, after a video containing documentary footage of Grant's death come videos from different family members (his mother, grandmother, daughter, sister, Sophina Mesa, and two uncles) who tell stories that commemorate Grant as a family member and honor his personal growth. Those videos are followed by others documenting organizing against police violence, created in Grant's name. The website's tabs link to "know your rights" resources. The soundtrack, as in the movie, begins with a moving BART train, but then, in a look toward a more just future, the conductor announces the train's approach to Grant Station. (Despite mobilization from Grant's mother, Wanda Johnson, to rename the station after her son, the BART board has yet to rename Fruitvale Station.) The soundtrack moves from there to songs in Oscar Grant's honor.

14. See Yingling and Parry.

15. Coates's 2019 novel *The Water Dancer* continues to manifest this belief in the power of story (and the importance of family), albeit in a more optimistic vein. Its release was timed to mark what is commonly if problematically (see Carby) perceived to be the 400-year anniversary of the institution of slavery in what is now the United States. In this work of speculative fiction, the enslaved protagonist Hiram finds his supernatural power to transport himself and others across impossible distances by learning from Moses (Harriet Tubman) that "the jump" from slavery to freedom happens through "the power of story" (*Water Dancer*, 278).

16. A different version of this chapter might productively position Coogler and Coates in relation to the Black Panther story and consider the relationship between Afro-pessimism and Afrofuturism.

17. The interrelations between BLM and Afro-pessimism—an analytic that has taken hold in the academy at the same time as BLM, and one often linked to

BTWAM—merit more exploration than I provide in this chapter. Like BLM, Afro-pessimism exposes the exclusionary and violently antiblack underpinnings of "the human." However, whereas BLM is a political movement that insists on working intersectionally and coalitionally, Afro-pessimism, as discussed in this book's introduction, is a singularly focused analytic that sees anti-Blackness as omnipresent and ontological. *BTWAM* draws in significant if inconsistent ways on both BLM and Afro-pessimism. *BTWAM* shares BLM's insistence that Black lives matter, and dovetails with Afro-pessimism in its understanding that the world is foundationally anti-Black. However, in a departure from Afro-pessimism, as critics have noted, Coates's anti-Blackness is more cosmological than ontological, and at times is subsumed into a liberal humanism, and his ideas of freedom are neoliberal and individualistic. As well, *BTWAM* departs from BLM's commitment to collective organizing, and from the desire for revolution that fuels Afro-pessimism's categorical refusal of "the human" as Afro-pessimists call for the end of the world. My contention is that Afro-pessimism, in refusing any and all conceptions of the human as foundationally anti-Black, and so, by extension, any and all forms of narrative humanity, can—if not complemented by a commitment to political organizing—stabilize the anti-Black status quo. I believe that *BTWAM*'s impact as a BLM memoir is lessened by its oscillating and competing investments in a distinctly literary humanism on the one hand and in Afro-pessimist thought on the other that, when taken together, paradoxically combine to foreclose the collective organizing that defines BLM.

18. These criticisms have been made most harshly against Coates by Cornel West, who has lambasted Coates for being a neoliberal sellout. For a critical assessment of West's position, see Muhammad.

19. So, too, Coates's references to the weather reverberate with representations of rain in Rankine's *Citizen*, and with meditations by theorists including Christina Sharpe; see esp. 106 and 110.

20. In *Israel's Dead Soul*, Steven Salaita takes note of Coates's complicity in anti-Arab racism and of his investments in a hegemonic and exclusionary American multiculturalism in his recounting of a story told to him by NAACP president Benjamin Jealous (92).

21. During the pandemic, the café transitioned to become a commissary kitchen furthering Reem Assil's commitments to social justice and community building, while Assil also opened a Reem's restaurant in the Mission District of San Francisco.

22. Israelis sexually tortured Odeh until she was coerced into confessing in 1970 to participating in a 1969 Jerusalem supermarket bombing. After moving to the US following her 1980 release from prison in a prisoner exchange, she became a beloved Chicago community organizer. In 2014, Zionist forces conspired to charge Odeh with immigration fraud and, after a rigged high-profile trail, she was deported to Jordan in 2015. The Reem's mural of Odeh sparked protests that Reem's was supporting terrorism, and led to Reem Assil being terrorized and targeted with death threats. However, Assil's dedication in making her café a gathering space for political

education and community organizing and transformation—"a place of life, a place of nourishment and sustenance"—also resulted in an outpouring of love and solidarity, including from Black and Palestinian community members (Carroll).

23. Uncle Bobby notes that one of BLM's cofounders (Alicia Garza) was among those who came together on the Fruitvale Station platform on the night his nephew was murdered, and that she continued to work for justice for Oscar Grant (29:40–32:00); he also connects Oscar's murder—including Oscar's cries of "I can't breathe, I can't breathe"—to Garner's and, in 2020, George Floyd's.

3. From Movement to Memoir: *When They Call You a Terrorist* and the Power of Queer Black Kinship

1. As discussed in the introduction and chapter 2, I distinguish the Afro-pessimist use of this term through capitalization (anti-Blackness) from a more general description of antiblack racism (antiblackness).

2. For an in-depth exploration of how the policing of Black bodies at home cannot be understood apart from the workings of US Empire, or the long war on terror, including in Palestine, and of solidarities that have long been part of intertwined struggle against state violence, see Edwards. See also Andrea Ritchie, who insists that we not understand human rights violations against women "as 'horribles' that happen elsewhere, fueling anti-Muslim/anti-Black/Orientalist logics justifying a never-ending machinery of war, but as tools of subjugation used against communities of color within the United States and around the world."

3. BLM and attention to its cofounders headlined newspapers and magazines through the month of June. Cullors, for example, was featured on June covers and/or in interviews with *British Vogue, Rolling Stone, LA Times, Newsweek, Hollywood Reporter,* and the *Daily Show.*

4. The BLMGF is distinct from other BLM groups and organizations. Difficulties in tracking and distinguishing among different BLM organizations has been a source of confusion and messiness; for a partial account of this, see Campbell, who explains, "The BLM Global Network Foundation is distinct from the dissolved BLM Global Network, which is distinct from the BLM Action Fund, BLM Grassroots, and the BLM Political Action Committee."

5. In "LA Riots 2020," Ryan Lee provides a detailed account and class analysis of this history.

6. The BLMGN Foundation also categorically denied insinuations that Cullors used Foundation money to buy personal property and released documents verifying that Cullors received a total of $120,000 between 2013 and 2018 for work she undertook for the BLMGN, and confirming that she was not paid a salary between 2019 and 2021 when she served as the Foundation's executive director (Campbell). For Cullors's responses to charges of financial malfeasance, see her interviews with Marc Lamont Hill ("Activist Patrisse Cullors Talks") and Nesrine Malik.

7. Here it is important to note that the BLM movement builds on a long legacy of civil and human rights struggles. As Rinaldo Walcott observes, BLM "sits in a genealogy of Black activists' eruptions meant to transform the state as we presently know it" (Simpson, Walcott, and Coulthard). For textured histories that trace this genealogy, see, for example, Garza's *The Purpose of Power*, Ransby's *Making All Black Lives Matter*, or Taylor's *From #BlackLivesMatter*.

8. As part of her artivism, Cullors not only creates but also has prioritized building infrastructure for art and culture. After resigning as BLMGN executive director in 2021, Cullors cofounded the Crenshaw Dairy Mart, which she describes as "a reimagined art gallery and studio dedicated to shifting the trauma-induced conditions of poverty and economic injustice through the lens of Inglewood and its community" ("Mission"). This vision is consonant with BLM's commitments to creating spaces to nurture Black creativity, community, and possibilities for radical transformation. So, too, was BLMGN's transfer of funds to Black Lives Matter–Canada (M4BJ) to buy and turn the former Toronto-based headquarters of the Communist Party into the Wildseed Centre for Art and Activism. Although right-wing attacks on Cullors and BLM cast this purchase of a "mansion" as a misuse of funds and as an act of hypocrisy coming from self-proclaimed Marxists (and here the historical significance of the Toronto building was apparently lost on these critics), this investment in building infrastructure for the arts is consistent with BLM organizers' insistence on the need to establish spaces for Black people to create, to heal, to dream, and to thrive.

9. Whereas Robinson looks to the surrealists to find the embrace of "the unconscious, the spirit, desire, magic, and love" (xxi) that he claims are all suppressed key elements of Black culture, Cullors and other queer folx at the forefront of BLM look to the women who have come before them as they value these qualities.

10. See also Jameta Nicole's "Restoring Optimal Black Mental Health and Reversing Intergenerational Trauma in an Era of Black Lives Matter."

11. Cullors does similar work through her participation in Kenneth Paul Rosenberg's 2019 documentary *Bedlam*. Cullors, Monte, and their other family members make up one of its story lines that evidence the hardship and heartbreak that "treatments" for mental illness carry for patients and their loved ones. At once a wrenching expose of the failures of the US mental health system, especially but not only for those who are Black, poor, or otherwise marginalized, the documentary is also a loving tribute to many of the health care workers and family members (Cullors included) who do their best within its profoundly dehumanizing structures that only intensify racial capitalism and other root causes of mental illness. Thanks go to Ebony Coletu for suggesting I situate Cullors's memoir in relation to this documentary.

12. Under the Obama presidency, only one police officer was prosecuted for murder, while the DOD 1033 program expanded by 2,400 percent the transfer of

military equipment to the police. For a searing critique of Obama's failures in relation to BLM, see Taylor's *From #BlackLivesMatter.*

13. One index of the hold this misquotation has taken is that Googling it brings up over 1.5 million hits, most of them post-2014.

14. For analysis of these dynamics, see Andrea Ritchie.

15. Trump's July 4, 2020, Mount Rushmore speech makes this dynamic clear as it casts BLM participants as a "they" out to destroy America ("Remarks by President Trump").

16. See Erakat and Lamont Hill's curated special issue of the *Journal of Palestine Studies* on Black-Palestinian Transnational Solidarity; Erakat; Feldman; Fischbach; and Lubin.

17. In a public June 26, 2020, Facebook posting where she analyzes the bonds between Black and Palestinian communities that result from interconnections between "various systems and actors of oppression," Loubna Qutami notes:

> The importance of the 9/11 moment was that it facilitated a very material convergence of domestic racialized repression tactics [used against BIPOC and immigrants] with militarized logics and technologies used abroad. Proclaiming itself as the forerunner of this so called War on Terror immediately following 911, the Israeli state has indeed played a critical role in developing the racially manufactured hysteria that legitimized unabated expansions of borders and policing, militarized tactics of repression, extra-judicial killings, crowd-control and surveillance. Indeed Israel learned these logics and techniques from its intimate friendship with racist and colonial states throughout its history. But after 9/11 Israel secured itself in history as a leader of the war industry and US police forces certainly looked to it for new lessons and technologies. Those techniques and logics were extended to the US where so called Black/Brown "criminality" was met with the same weapons and police techniques that so called Arab/Palestinian/Muslim "terrorism" was facing by Western wars in Iraq, Afghanistan, and the ongoing colonial occupation of Palestine. The expansion of policing and surveillance systems also was accompanied by the militarization of borders driving forced displacement across the world. (Loubie Qutami)

18. For a beautiful meditation on the importance of letter writing to Black liberation, see Chester.

19. As Alicia Garza puts this when addressing the grief, despair, and trauma that attend being Black, "I am not, and we are not, defined by what we lack—we are defined by how we come together when we fall apart" (*The Purpose of Power,* 289).

20. This moment in the memoir echoes one in *Something Like Beautiful* where bandele lists the names of children, "the ones I made, the ones in my universe."

21. This future that *WTCYAT* works to bring into being—one rooted in a past that predates humans and human-made constructs such as race—articulates with tenets of Afrofuturism as it also disrupts linear notions of time (a disruption further explored in

chapter 5). A body of thinking concurrent in the academy with Afro-pessimism, Afrofuturist writings counter Afro-pessimism's ahistorical understanding of anti-Blackness as a totalizing narrative that defines the past, present, and future. Instead, Afro-futurist thought often takes the form of Black speculative fiction and fantasy and explores Black American themes in relation to contemporary and future technologies to imagine queer new futures free from capitalism, racism, colonialism, and heteropatriarchy. See, for example, Kara Keeling's *Queer Times, Black Futures*, which explores how Afrofuturism "combats miserablism by calling attention to the systematic rationalization of the unlivable, often imagining scenarios and sometimes movements that (re)turn to the cosmic, where 'life' perhaps can be perceived, even (re) conceived, as existence beyond measure." See also Rifkin's *Fictions of Land and Flesh* for an investigation of Black-Indigenous political solidarities and imaginaries.

4. "Nursing Visions of the Unimagined": BDS and Steven Salaita's World-Making Narratives of Fatherhood, Affiliation, and Freedom

1. See, for example, Naber's "'Look, Mohammed the Terrorist Is Coming!'" or Ghanayem's "Colonial Loops."

2. For accounts of this lawsuit and contexts for it, in addition to *Uncivil Rites*, see "American Studies Association Sued"; Dawson and Mullen's *Against Apartheid*; and Maira's *Boycott!*

3. See also Jaschik.

4. The Greyzone has identified Howard David Sterling as a key figure behind the site (Raza and Blumenthal).

5. During the 2016–17 MLA campaign to pass a boycott resolution, Nelson's collaborations with US and Israeli Zionist organizations resulted in the production of professionally made but highly misleading anti-BDS literature and videos and the data-scraping of MLA members' email addresses, as he and a few other MLA members zealously campaigned against a boycott resolution. As well, they proposed the passage of an unprecedented resolution for the MLA to "refrain" from supporting the PACBI boycott. This resolution passed, enabled by tactics that required not only significant funding but also the overriding of basic ethics and MLA rules. This resolution now positions the MLA as an organization that will further erode rather lift up the academic freedom of scholars being blacklisted or penalized for their BDS-related activism. See Hassan.

6. The original individuals named as defendants when *Bronner v. Duggan, et al.* was first filed in April 2016 were Lisa Duggan, Curtis Marez, Avery Gordon, Sunaina Maira, Chandan Reddy, and Neferti Tadiar. Later, in March 2018, Salaita, J. Kēhaulani Kauanui, Jasbir Puar, and John Stephens were added to the case. (Gordon was released by the plaintiffs in January 2018.)

7. For a partial account of Horowitz's hate speech, see "David Horowitz."

8. See Palestine Legal's resource on where and when legislative attacks have been issued against advocacy for Palestine ("Legislation"). As part of a more general

criminalization of BDS, in summer 2017, the federal Israel Anti-Boycott Act was proposed under bipartisan sponsorship, by over 250 representatives of the House. The bill aims to make it a felony for companies and also individuals to participate in an international commercial boycott of Israel. Those found guilty would potentially face anywhere from $250,000 up to $1 million in fines plus up to twenty years in prison. This criminalization of BDS in the US cannot be understood as separate from Israel's war on BDS—a movement that Prime Minister Benjamin Netanyahu has declared Israel's greatest strategic threat. Inside Israel, support for BDS is outlawed, and in 2017, the Knesset passed legislation banning boycott supporters from entering Israel. Israeli college students are paid for spreading hasbara (state propaganda) via social media. Israel also aggressively reaches out to Jewish students for Birthright trips and engages in faith-washing, and in pink-, green-, black-, yellow-, and red-washing. In other words, in addition to building its arsenal of weaponry used to ethnically cleanse and subjugate Palestinians, the state of Israel invests tens of millions of dollars into "Brand Israel" campaigns—hasbara that, often by way of cultural ambassadors, sustains the Zionist narrative. See the four-part Al Jazeera investigative TV report, *The Lobby—USA*.

9. This intergovernmental organization made up of thirty-four countries adopted Kenneth Stern's definition of antisemitism—a move even Stern opposes as a way to determine campus hate speech. See the USACBI Webinar, "Weaponizing Anti-Semitism." See also Palestine Legal's "Backgrounder" and their timeline "Distorted Definition."

10. Examples include memoirs and autobiographies by Izzeldin Abuelaish, Suad Amiry, Mourid Barghouti, Yousef Bashir, Issa J. Boullata, Mahmoud Darwish, Jabra Ibrahim Jabra, Wasif Jawhariyyeh, Hatim Kanaaneh, Jamal Krayem Kanj, Ghada Karmi, Sari Nusseibeh, Jean Said, Najla Said, Raja Shehadeh, Salman Abu Sitta, and Atef Abu Saif.

11. See Daulatzai and Rana's *With Stones in Our Hands*; Schotten's "Against Academic Freedom"; Naber's "Look, Mohammed"; Volpe's "The Citizen and the Terrorist."

12. I take the fact that Salaita never names his son to be an act of protectiveness. Paradoxically, this anonymity makes his son more "real," and less a literary device, than happens in Coates's *Between the World and Me*.

13. There is uncertainty as to whether Meir actually said this, but not in question is the reverence and stock Zionists put in this oft-quoted formulation. See Rachlin.

14. For a discussion of Said's worldliness, see Matthew Abraham.

15. How Palestinians fit into comparative frameworks of Indigeneity and settler colonialism is a matter of extensive discussion. In addition to *Inter/Nationalism*, see Barakat's "Writing/Righting"; Bhandar and Ziadah's "Acts of Omission"; Desai's "Disrupting Settler-Colonial Capitalism"; Erakat's *Justice for Some*; Salamanca, Qato, et al.'s "Past Is Present" and their special issue of *Settler Colonial Studies*; Sayegh's *Zionist Colonialism*; and Wolfe's *Traces of History*.

16. Also very memorably, this trip coincided with the great March of Return. In solidarity with those in Gaza asserting their right to return, and in protest of the

Israeli army's violent response to this nonviolent collective action, Al Quds students and faculty organized a strike and a rally. In response, Israeli soldiers invaded the campus, dropping tear gas and opening fire with live ammunition and rubber bullets. Dramatic as this invasion was, what I best remember is the reluctance of the students and faculty to leave a test midstream—all too accustomed to this colonial violence, what stood out was their refusal to have it disrupt their education. See my "A Firsthand Account."

17. The essay "Sirhan Sirhan the Palestinian" provides another beautiful illustration of this. As Salaita considers the man imprisoned for killing Robert Kennedy "through the prism of fatherhood," this entails thinking of Kennedy's children, and also of how for Salaita, Sirhan evokes memories of conversing with his own father. In this exploration of "the daily intimacies of conflict and affection," he explores how the relentless need to describe Sirhan as Palestinian has shifted due to decades of activism, with the result that "what is supposed to be an incriminating descriptor acts more and more like an invitation to contemplate a deeper story"—one that refuses the inhumanity of the Palestinian people.

18. My reference to "time immemorial" draws on its usages by Indigenous writers including Leslie Marmon Silko (Laguna Pueblo) and Daniel Heath Justice (Cherokee).

5. "E Hū ē" (Rising Like a Mighty Wave): Mauna Kea and the Movement beyond the Human

1. See also Coulthard and Simpson's "Grounded Normativity/Place-Based Solidarity."

2. In other words, I move between first and last names in a way that is context specific, rather than determining usage based on whether I know the person. It also bears acknowledging that with my often personal approach, I do not even begin to do justice to the many kia'i, or protectors, who make up the multifaceted, "leaderfull" movement for Mauna Kea.

3. See chapter 3 of Fujikane, *Mapping Abundance*, esp. 86–88, for a careful delineation of the genealogies of the Mauna.

4. This rousing call is a regular feature of Mauna Kea rallies and protocols; in titling his short film *Like a Mighty Wave*, Mikey Inouye provides one register of this metaphor's importance to the movement.

5. For discussions of these key terms, see Noelani Goodyear-Ka'ōpua's "Reproducing the Ropes."

6. I follow Noelani Goodyear-Ka'ōpua in my usage of Kanaka/Kānaka. As she explains, "In my usage of Kanaka/Kānaka, 'Kānaka' is a countable plural form. It is not used for an indefinite plural, but only when the actual number can be estimated. 'Kanaka,' the singular-generic form, refers to an individual person or to the whole class of people. It is also the form that is used when the word is used as an adjective" ("Reproducing the Ropes," 19). Throughout this chapter, I use Kanaka Maoli, Kanaka 'Ōiwi, and Native Hawaiian interchangeably.

7. See chapter 6 of Osorio's *Remembering Our Intimacies*, and chapter 4 of Fujikane's *Mapping Abundance*.

8. See Fujikane for a reading of this action, and for a textured mapping of the movement for Mauna Kea in relation to other contemporary land struggles in Hawai'i.

9. For discussion of the "state of emergency" in relation to 'Ōiwi emergence, see the forum "States of Emergency/Emergence," edited by Uahikea Maile.

10. For discussion of the role that women in particular played, see Goodyear-Ka'ōpua's "Protecting Maunakea."

11. See, for example, Pu'uhonua o Pu'uhuluhulu Maunakea and Mana Maoli's *Worldwide #Jam4Maunakea*. This video brings together professional musicians, keiki, families, choirs, schools, and solidarity organizations worldwide who recorded performances of Mauna Kea anthems "Kū Ha'aheo E Ku'u Hawai'i" and "Hawai'i Loa" on August 11, 2019, at 11:11 A.M. for this eleven-minute video, participating in what its creators call a "prophecy unfolding." See also "We Stand with Mauna Kea," a petition issued by Mauna Kea Education and Awareness signed by over 450,000 people.

12. And here it bears remarking that when I asked her during a visit to my class in Spring 2022 about the common archive in the many Mauna videos, filmmaker Ciara Lacy explained that, in distinction to usual practices among documentary filmmakers, those filming for Mauna Kea worked from a different ethos, one made possible by the Mauna, as they shared their photos and footage with one another.

13. See an account of this in *Mapping Abundance* (90; and 102–3). Jamaica Heolimeleikalani Osorio also explores the importance of consent in *Remembering Our Intimacies: Mo'olelo, Aloha 'Āina, and Ea*. In that book she delves into how time on the Mauna taught her that consent from 'āina is integral to humans' ability to sustain healthy and loving relations with each other as well as the earth.

14. See Kame'eleihiwa's illumination of the Hawaiian proverb "I ka wā mua, ka wā ma hope," or "In what is in front of you is found what is behind you." As she explains, "The Hawaiian stands firmly in the present, with his back to the future, and his eyes fixed upon the past, seeking historical answers for present-day dilemmas."

15. See also Goodyear-Ka'ōpua, who contends, "While settler state officials cast the kia'i as impediments on the road to 'progress' (aka settler futurity) and passed regulations that would be used to specifically target and remove protectors from the Mauna, kia'i stewarded places and practices that invited their antagonists to join them in reaching toward more expansive and sustainable futures" ("Protectors," 191).

16. The practice I am describing here resonates in some ways with Fanon's third stage of the struggle for liberation, even as Fanon does not place value in conceptualizing the past as future. Following the first two stages, of assimilation and then an idealizing of the precolonial past, Fanon's third stage involves a revolutionary praxis that draws on the present-day struggle for liberation that "sets culture moving and opens to it the doors of creation" (243) in the formation of a "new humanity [that] cannot do otherwise than define a new humanism both for

itself and for others" (245). See chapter 4 of *Wretched of the Earth*, "On National Culture."

17. See the "Mauna Kea Syllabus Project" panel.

18. For a discussion of relationship between the traditional Kanaka Maoli understanding of māhū (or third sex) and queerness, see the chapter "Savage Sexualities" in Kauanui's *Paradoxes of Hawaiian Sovereignty*.

19. Māhealani Ahia and Kahala Johnson discussed this at the 2021 American Studies Association Conference, during the Q&A for the panel "Mana Māhū, Rebel Elements and Queer Indigeneity at Mauna a Wākea," and in their coauthored presentation for that panel, "Aha Kiaialoha Consent and Kuleana." See also "Kikī a Kūkā: Queer Kanaka Roundtable."

20. Similarly, Goodyear-Kaʻōpua describes the world being made at the Mauna as "filled with profound expressions of *mana wahine* and *mana māhū*: the power of womxn and nonbinary folx" ("Protecting Maunakea").

21. Representations of protectors borrow from and reinforce those the state uses to justify the War on Terror and US support for Israel: in his analysis of attacks on Water Protectors at Standing Rock, Estes looks to how security personnel frequently referred to Water Protectors as "terrorists," cast prayer actions as "attacks," and represented the camps as a "battlefield." He also notes that they tracked the presence of Middle Eastern and especially Palestinian Water Protectors, with TigerSwan calling the Indigenous uprising a "jihadist insurgency."

22. Kiaʻi held their own press conference to refute the governor's allegations. See "Kiai Reacts."

23. Small everyday acts of storytelling reproduce and perpetuate these dominant formulas of narrative humanity. At a meeting in January 2019, an Institute for Astronomy (IFA) faculty member remarked on how he had just arrived that morning on a flight he shared with directors of all the Mauna Kea telescopes. If someone were to have set off a bomb, he said, it would have taken out "the entire leadership of Mauna Kea." Registering my shock, he mumbled, "I guess I shouldn't have said that." I still do not know whether he regretted (publicly) implying that kiaʻi are terrorists, or disclosing that all the telescope top guns were on-island. What he did make clear, however, was his conviction that TMT cronies constitute "the leadership of Mauna Kea," and his view of kiaʻi as criminal and violent.

24. In 2015, in testimony opposing the TMT, Kaʻeo turns on its head equations of science with human development and progress as he tells a story about meeting with the head of the solar observatory: "I asked this person—his name is Craig Foltz, of the National Science Foundation—and I asked him directly: 'What is the humanity of this project? You tell me, as a Hawaiian—I can take the pain, I can bleed, if it's going to save some lives—tell me what it is.' And he looked me directly in my eyes and said: 'It's just pure selfish research'" (Hawaii Independent Staff).

25. See J. Uluwehi Hopkins's "Moʻolelo as Resistance." Scholarship on moʻolelo is vast and deep, and I do not pretend to address its complexities in this chapter. For scholars who do so, see Bacchilega's *Legendary Hawaiʻi*, Marie Alohalani Brown's

Ka Poʻe Moʻo Akua, McDougall's *Finding Meaning*, hoʻomanawanui's *Voices of Fire*, and Osorio's *Remembering Our Intimacies*. See also Noʻu Revilla's *Ask the Brindled*.

26. For more on this remarkable farm, see the Hanakēhau website (Koʻihonua).

27. The account that follows comes from phone interview with Perez, 30 Aug. 2021.

28. Both discuss this in their Mauna Kea Ally interviews. See Mauna Kea Syllabus Project website, Allies section.

29. In their jointly delivered keynote address for the "Mapping Aloha Aina" conference organized by Native Hawaiian Student Services, Kaʻeo elaborated on this appropriation, explaining how the UH administration, by defining "aloha ʻāina" as separate terms in its strategic plan (as "aloha" and "ʻāina"), is able to purposefully transform and reduce the term to corporatized and European ideas of "sustainability," or the recycling of cans and newspapers (Kaʻeo and Perry).

30. I have also been inspired by Monisha Das Gupta's engaged scholarship in her forthcoming *All of Us or None: Migrant Organizing in an Era of Deportation and Dispossession*; see in particular the chapter "Not DREAMING: Youth Organizing across LA and Hawaiʻi," which powerfully conjoins migrant and Indigenous struggles.

31. Following Steven Salaita, these visits have featured Ramzy Baroud, Tariq Luthun, Sumaya Awad, and Sarah Ihmoud. In addition to church and university talks focused on building support for BDS, events have included roundtables and poetry readings at the Kamakakūokalani Center for Hawaiian Studies to explore Hawaiʻi and Palestine as intersecting and distinct sites of occupation and settler colonialism. These have featured J. Kēhaulani Kauanui and, from UH, Māhealani Ahia, Joy Lehuanani Enomoto, Kaleikoa Kaʻeo, Noelani Goodyear-Kaʻōpua, Kahala Johnson, ʻIlima Long, Kauwila Mahi, Ali Musleh, Jonathan Kamakawiwoʻole Osorio, Andre Perez, and Punahele. These visits also have included DeTours with Kyle Kajihiro and Aunty Terri Kekoʻolani, with ʻIlima Long and Joy Enomoto, with Kekai Perry, and with Candace Fujikane and the Concerned Elders of Waianae. As well, the Reppuns, a family at the forefront of struggles for water rights and anticapitalist sustainability, have regularly hosted those visiting at their farm in Waiahole.

32. These events have included a September 9, 2020, USACBI Climate Crisis webinar featuring Kalaniʻōpua Young, BLM-Mauna Kea-Palestine webinars featuring Heoli Osorio and Joy Enomoto, and a November 15, 2020, panel titled "Global Uprising: Indigeneity, Land Heritage: Hawaiʻi and Palestine!"

33. See Sperri and Biddle's "Zoom Censorship" and Barrows-Friedman's "Zoom Censors," both of which include a link to the video.

Postscript: Hope, Joy, and "The Struggle for Ea"

1. In November 2021, when we had to postpone Sumaya's visit, we held a Zoom discussion instead. As she also did on March 5, Māhea Ahia opened this online event with an oli, and we closed it with a song by Punahele, a rapper recently back from a Palestinian Youth Movement (PYM) delegation to Palestine. Māhea's oli,

and Punahele's performance of his song "From the River to the Sea," also contributed
to the inter/nationalism that brought us all to our feet when we were finally able to
come together in person.

2. Kahanu translates the full oli:

E iho ana o luna
E pi'i ana o lalo
E hui ana nā moku
E kū ana ka paia

to

that which was above
would come down
that which was below
would rise up
the islands shall unite
the walls shall stand firm
(Kahanu)

Works Cited

Abolition Collective. "Manifesto for Abolition." *Abolition: A Journal of Insurgent Politics* (2018). Accessed 13 Sept. 2021. abolitionjournal.org/frontpage/.

"About." *Ke Kaʻupu Hehi ʻAle* (blog). Accessed 2 Oct. 2021. hehiale.com/about/.

"About Deadly Exchange." *Jewish Voice for Peace.* deadlyexchange.org/about-deadly -exchange/.

"About the Mauna Kea Syllabus Project." The Mauna Kea Syllabus Project. Accessed 2 June 2022. www.maunakeasyllabus.com/about/the-project/the -mauna-kea-syllabus.

Abraham, Matthew. "Introduction: Edward Said and After: Toward a New Humanism." *Cultural Critique* 67, no. 1 (Autumn 2007): 1–12.

Abunimah, Ali. Foreword to *Against Apartheid: The Case for Boycotting Israeli Universities,* edited by Ashley Dawson and Bill V. Mullen, ix–xi. Chicago: Haymarket Books, 2015.

"Activist Patrisse Cullors Talks Criticisms Surrounding Black Lives Matter Network Foundation: Pt. 1." YouTube, uploaded by *Black News Tonight,* 15 April 2021. www .youtube.com/watch?v=2z-rxVKcDSc.

Agrawal, Nina. "Black Lives Matter, Other Activists Protest to Stop Jail Expansion." *Los Angeles Times,* 26 Sept. 2017. www.latimes.com/local/lanow/la-me-ln-black -lives-matter-protests-jail-expansion-20170926-story.html.

Ahia, Māhealani. "Mālama Mauna: An Ethics of Care Culture and Kuleana." *Biography* 43, no. 3 (2020): 607–12.

Ahia, Māhealani, and Kahala Johnson. "Aha Kiaialoha Consent and Kuleana." Panel on "Mana Māhū, Rebel Elements and Queer Indigeneity at Mauna a Wākea," Virtual 2021 American Studies Association Conference, 12 Oct. 2021.

Alexander, Michelle. *The New Jim Crow: Mass Incarceration in the Age of Colorblindness.* Rev. ed. New York: New Press, 2012.

———. "Ta-Nehisi Coates's 'Between the World and Me.'" *New York Times*, 17
   Aug. 2015. www.nytimes.com/2015/08/17/books/review/ta-nehisi-coates-between
   -the-world and-me.html.
Aljamal, Yousef. Interview with Yousef Aljamal by Cynthia Franklin. "Cultivating
   Allyship." The Mauna Kea Syllabus Project, Sept. 2020. Accessed 18 Oct. 2021.
   www.maunakeasyllabus.com/units/cultivating-solidarities/allyship.
"American Studies Association Sued for Academic Boycott." Palestine Legal
   (website), 18 July 2018. palestinelegal.org/case-studies/2018/3/8/american-studies
   -association-sued-for-boycott.
Arendt, Hannah. *Eichmann in Jerusalem: A Report on the Banality of Evil.* London:
   Penguin, 2006.
———. *The Origins of Totalitarianism.* New York: Meridian Books, 1958.
Arria, Michael. "Biden Administration Embraces Antisemitism Definition That
   Includes Some Criticisms of Israel." Mondoweiss, 3 Feb. 2021. mondoweiss.net
   /2021/02/biden-administration-embraces-antisemitism-definition-that-includes
   -some-criticisms-of-israel/?fbclid=IwAR3xu09N5G8qCJEYy
   _mfguFEmYaVfTtk2YFphJHFaYix996_W9ab5wC3ioM.
"Artist." Patrisse Cullors (website). Accessed 25 Sept. 2021. patrissecullors.com/artist/.
Bacchilega, Cristina. *Legendary Hawai'i and the Politics of Place: Tradition,
   Translation, and Tourism.* Philadelphia: University of Pennsylvania Press, 2011.
"Backgrounder on Efforts to Redefine Antisemitism as a Means of Censoring
   Criticism of Israel." Palestine Legal (website), updated Jan. 2020. Accessed 1
   Oct. 2021. palestinelegal.org/redefinition-efforts.
Bailey, Julius, and David Leonard. "Black Lives Matter: Post-nihilistic Freedom
   Dreams." *Journal of Contemporary Rhetoric* 5, no. 3/4 (2015): 67–77.
bandele, asha. *The Prisoner's Wife: A Memoir.* 1999. New York: Washington Square, 2000.
———. *Something Like Beautiful: One Single Mother's Story.* 2009. New York:
   Harper Perennial, 2010. Kindle.
Barakat, Rana. Interview with Rana Barakat by Cynthia Franklin. "Cultivating
   Allyship." The Mauna Kea Syllabus Project, Aug. 2020. Accessed 18 Oct. 2020.
   www.maunakeasyllabus.com/units/cultivating-solidarities/allyship.
———. "Writing/Righting Palestine Studies: Settler Colonialism, Indigenous
   Sovereignty and Resisting the Ghost(s) of History." *Settler Colonial Studies* 8,
   no. 3 (2017): 349–63. DOI: 10.1080/2201473X.2017.1300048.
"Barbara Bush Calls Evacuees Better Off." *New York Times*, 7 Sept. 2005. www
   .nytimes.com/2005/09/07/us/nationalspecial/barbara-bush-calls-evacuees-better
   -off.html?_r=0.
Barlow, Jameta Nicole. "Restoring Optimal Black Mental Health and Reversing
   Intergenerational Trauma in an Era of Black Lives Matter." *Biography* 41, no. 4
   (2018): 895–908.
Barrows-Friedman, Nora. "Zoom Censors Events about Zoom Censorship."
   Electronic Intifada, 13 Nov. 2020. electronicintifada.net/content/zoom-censors
   -events-about-zoom-censorship/31696.

Begley, Sarah. "These Are the 30 People under 30 Changing the World." *Time*, 5 Dec. 2013. ideas.time.com/2013/12/06/these-are-the-30-people-under-30-changing -the-world/slide/michael-b-jordan/.

Belcourt, Billy-Ray. *A History of My Brief Body*. Columbus, OH: Two Dollar Radio, 2020. Kindle.

Bench, Ansfield. "Still Submerged: The Uninhabitability of Urban Redevelopment." In *Sylvia Wynter: On Being Human as Praxis*, edited by Katherine McKittrick, 124–41. Durham, NC: Duke University Press, 2015.

Benjamin, Ruha. "Black AfterLives Matter." *Boston Review*, 16 July 2018. www .bostonreview.net/race/ruha-benjamin-black-afterlives-matter.

Bennett, Brit. "Ta-Nehisi Coates and a Generation Waking Up." *New Yorker*, 15 July 2015. www.newyorker.com/culture/cultural-comment/ta-nehisi-coates-and-a -generation-waking-up.

Ben-Porath, E. N., and L. Shaker. "News Images, Race, and Attribution in the Wake of Hurricane Katrina." *Journal of Communication* 60, no. 3 (2010): 466–90. doi .org/10.1111/j.1460-2466.2010.01493.x.

Berkshire, Geoff. "Fruitvale." *Variety*, 20 Jan. 2013. variety.com/2013/film /marketsfestivals/fruitvale-1117949029/.

Berlant, Lauren. *Cruel Optimism*. Durham, NC: Duke University Press, 2011.

"'Between the World and Me': Ta-Nehisi Coates Extended Interview on Being Black in America." *Democracy Now!*, 22 July 2015. www.democracynow.org/2015/7/22 /between_the_world_and_me_ta.

Bhandar, Brenna, and Rafeef Ziadah. "Acts of Omission: Framing Settler Colonialism in Palestine Studies." *Jadaliyya*, 14 January 2016. www.jadaliyya.com/Details/32857.

Bhattacharya, Tithi and Bill V. Mullen. "Where Zionism and the 'Alt-Right' Meet." Mondoweiss, 28 July 2017. mondoweiss.net/2017/07/where-zionism-right/.

"#BlackLivesMatter Activists Disrupt Sanders and O'Malley Speeches." *Democracy Now!*, 20 July 2015. www.democracynow.org/2015/7/20/headlines/blacklivesmatter _activists_disrupt_sanders_and_o_malley_speeches.

Black Lives Matter. "About." Black Lives Matter (BLM website). Accessed 22 Sept. 2021. blacklivesmatter.com/about/.

"BLM Co-founder Patrisse Cullors-Brignac Explains Why You Should Support the Breathe Act." *Glitter*, 16 July 2020. glittermagrocks.com/connect/2020/07/16/blm -co-founder-patrisse-cullors-brignac-explains-why-you-should-support-the -breathe-act/.

Bloom, Harold. *Shakespeare: The Invention of the Human*. New York: Riverhead Books, 1999.

Bloomenthal, Andrew. "Ryan Coogler's *Fruitvale Station*." *CreativeScreenwriting*, 3 Aug. 2013. www.creativescreenwriting.com/ryan-cooglers-fruitvale-station/.

Boggs, James Lee, and Grace Lee Boggs. *Revolution and Evolution in the Twentieth Century*. New York: Monthly Review Press, 1974.

Bonilla, Yarimar, and Marisol LeBron, eds. *Aftershocks of Disaster: Puerto Rico before and after the Storm*. Chicago: Haymarket Books, 2019.

Boone, Stephen. "Fruitvale Station." RogerEbert.com, 15 July 2013. www.rogerebert
.com/reviews/fruitvale-station-2013.

Bornhustler Records. Accessed 18 Sept. 2021. www.bornhustlerrecords.com/.

Bouie, Jamelle. "Michael Brown Wasn't a Superhuman Demon." *Slate*, 26
Nov. 2014. slate.com/news-and-politics/2014/11/darren-wilsons-racial-portrayal-of
-michael-brown-as-a-superhuman-demon-the-ferguson-police-officers-account-is
-a-common-projection-of-racial-fears.html.

———. "Where Black Lives Matter Began." *Slate*, 23 Aug. 2015. www.slate.com
/articles/news_and_politics/politics/2015/08/hurricane_katrina_10th_anniversary
_how_the_black_lives_matter_movement_was.html.

Bradshaw, Peter. "Fruitvale Station Review—A Tough and Moving Drama."
Guardian Weekly, 5 June 2014. www.theguardian.com/film/2014/jun/05/fruitvale
-station-review-oscar-grant.

Brinkley, Douglas. *The Great Deluge: Hurricane Katrina, New Orleans, and the
Mississippi Gulf Coast.* New York: Harper Perennial, 2006.

Brooks, Gwendolyn. "Paul Robeson." In *The Essential Gwendolyn Brooks.* Library of
America, 2005. Reprinted at poets.org. Accessed 23 Sept. 2021. poets.org/poem
/paul-robeson.

Brooks, Xan. "Oscar Predictions 2014: *Fruitvale Station*." *The Guardian*, 20
Aug. 2013.

brown, adrienne maree. *Emergent Strategy: Shaping Change, Changing Worlds.*
Chico, CA: AK, 2017. Kindle.

Brown, C. Stone. "Katrina's Forgotten Victims: Native American Tribes." Freedom
Archives, 13 Sept. 2005. freedomarchives.org/pipermail/news_freedomarchives
.org/2005-September/001394.html.

Brown, Elizabeth Nolan. "Steven Salaita and the Tyranny of 'Hate Speech.'" *Reason*,
16 Sept. 2014. reason.com/2014/09/16/hate-speech-steve-salaita-and-civility/.

Brown, Marie Alohalani. "Aloha Wale Mauna Kea, Aloha Wale Kuʻu Poʻe Hoapili
Kiaʻi ma ke Anuanu." *Biography* 43, no. 3 (2020): 582–87. Project MUSE. doi.org
/10.1353/bio.2020.0063.

———. *Ka Poʻe Moʻo Akua: Hawaiian Reptilian Water Deities.* Honolulu: University
of Hawaiʻi Press, 2022.

Brown, Robbie. "Katrina Hero Facing Charges in New Orleans." *New York Times*, 9
Aug. 2012. www.nytimes.com/2012/08/10/us/celebrated-hero-in-zeitoun-book-faces
-murder-charges-in-new-orleans.html.

Buchanan, Larry, Quoctrung Bui, and Jugal K. Patel. "Black Lives Matter May Be
the Largest Movement in U.S. History." *New York Times*, 3 July 2020. www
.nytimes.com/interactive/2020/07/03/us/george-floyd-protests-crowd-size.html.

"Butler Students Defeat Measures to Censor Palestine." Palestine Legal (website), 23
Oct. 2020. palestinelegal.org/news/2020/10/23/butler-students-defeat-measures-to
-censor-palestine.

Byrd, Jodi A. "What's Normative Got to Do with It? Toward Indigenous Queer
Relationality." *Social Text* 45 (Dec. 2020): 105–23.

Campbell, Sean. "The BLM Mystery: Where Did the Money Go?" *New York Magazine*, 31 Jan. 2022. nymag.com/intelligencer/2022/01/black-lives-matter -finances.html.

Carby, Hazel V. "We Must Burn Them." *London Review of Books* 44, no. 10, 26 May 2022. www.lrb.co.uk/the-paper/v44/n10/hazel-v.-carby/we-must-burn-them ?fbclid=IwAR2-IzZyVGtdhhk9FMVTjWrdHxmyu.

Carroll, A. K. "Reem's: A New Arab Bakery Where Food, Activism and Culture Come Together." *Berkeleyside.com*, 17 May 2017. www.berkeleyside.com/2017/05 /17/reems-arab-bakery-oakland.

Carruthers, Charlene A. *Unapologetic: A Black, Feminist, Queer Mandate for Radical Movements*. Boston: Beacon, 2018. Kindle.

Carter, J. Kameron. *Race: A Theological Account*. Oxford: Oxford University Press, 2008.

Case, Emalani. "Ea: Lessons in Breath, Life, and Sovereignty from Mauna Kea." *Biography* 43, no. 3 (2020): 568–74.

Case, Pua. "He Kūkulu." *'O HĀNAU KA MAUNA KEA*. Lālākea. lalakea.org/wp -content/uploads/2019/07/'O-HĀNAU-KA-MAUNA-CHANT-PACKET-v.2-JULY -14-2019.pdf.

———. "Na Kūkulu Oli." *'O HĀNAU KA MAUNA KEA*. Lālākea. lalakea.org/wp -content/uploads/2019/07/'O-HĀNAU-KA-MAUNA-CHANT-PACKET-v.2-JULY -14-2019.pdf.

Champion, Edward. "Dave Eggers, National Book Award Finalist, Refuses to Answer about Abdulrahman's Violent Assaults." Reluctant Habits, 4 Nov. 2012. www.edrants.com/dave-eggers-national-book-award-finalist-refuses-to-answer -about-abdulrahman-zeitouns-violent-assaults/.

Chan, Melissa. "2013: Patrisse Cullors, Alicia Garza and Opal Tometi." *Time*, 5 March 2020. time.com/5793789/black-lives-matter-founders-100-women-of-the-year/.

Chatterjee, Piya, and Sunaina Maira. *The Imperial University: Academic Repression and Scholarly Dissent*. Minneapolis: University of Minnesota Press, 2014.

Cherry, Richard. "Making Freshmen Read 'Between the World and Me' Is a Mistake." *New York Post*, 22 Aug. 2016. nypost.com/2016/08/22/making-freshmen -read-between-the-world-and-me-is-a-mistake/.

Chester, Tabitha Jamie Mary. "Movement for Black Love: The Building of Critical Communities through the Relational Geography of Movement Spaces." *Biography* 41, no. 4 (2018), 741–59.

Clemmons, Zinzi. "Ta-Nehisi Coates Has Given #Black Lives Matter Its Foundational Text." *Literary Hub*, 8 Oct. 2015. lithub.com/ta-nehisi-coates-has-given -black-lives-matter-its-foundational-text/.

Coates, Ta-Nehisi. *Between the World and Me*. New York: Spiegel and Grau, 2015.

———. "The Case for Reparations." *The Atlantic*, June 2014. Accessed 30 Sept. 2021. www.theatlantic.com/magazine/archive/2014/06/the-case-for-reparations/361631/.

———. "Ta-Nehisi Coates on *Vanity Fair*'s September Issue The Great Fire." *Vanity Fair*, 24 Aug. 2020. www.vanityfair.com/culture/2020/08/ta-nehisi-coates-editor -letter.

————. *The Water Dancer*. New York: One World, 2019.

"Coates Leaves *The Atlantic*, Where He Rose to Prominence." *AP News*, 20 July 2018. apnews.com/1ad4c462a5d5411dbbed52d8e23dea3d.

Coogler, Ryan, dir. *Fruitvale Station*. The Weinstein Company, 2013.

Cooke, Rachel. "Dave Eggers: From 'Staggering Genius' to America's Conscience." *The Observer*, 6 March 2010. www.theguardian.com/books/2010/mar/07/dave -eggers-zeitoun-hurricane-katrina.

Cooper, Brittney, and Treva B. Lindsey. "Introduction: M4BL and the Critical Matter of Black Lives." *Biography* 41, no. 4 (2018): 731–40.

Coulthard, Glen Sean. *Red Skin, White Masks: Rejecting the Colonial Politics of Recognition*. Minneapolis: University of Minnesota Press, 2014.

Coulthard, Glen, and Leanne Betasamosake Simpson. "Grounded Normativ- ity/Place-Based Solidarity." *American Quarterly* 68, no. 2 (2016): 249–55.

Craven, Julia. "Black Lives Matter Co-founder Reflects on the Origins of the Movement." *HuffPost US*, 30 Sept. 2015. www.huffingtonpost.in/entry/black-lives -matter-opal-tometi_us_560c1c59e4b0768127003227.

Cullors, Patrisse [@Osopepatrisse]. "For hundreds of years." Instagram, 29 May 2020. www.instagram.com/p/CAxsxR_jXYN/?utm_source=ig_web_copy _link.

————. "In July 2018 I published my first book." Instagram, 27 July 2020. www .instagram.com/p/CDJjbGIDrah/?utm_source=ig_web_copy_link.

————. "Performance Piece." Instagram, 28 Feb. 2020. www.instagram.com/p /B9IkcNmHQ3P/?utm_source=ig_web_copy_link.

————. "Tonight I received the Durfee Stanton Fellowship." Instagram, 2 Dec. 2019. www.instagram.com/p/B5mDG4TnWC4/?utm_source=ig_web_copy_link.

————. "Two Years Ago Today." Instagram, 11 Jan. 2020. www.instagram.com/p /B7MN7soH7Ty/?utm_source=ig_web_copy_link.

Cullors, Patrisse, and asha bandele. *When They Call You a Terrorist: A Black Lives Matter Memoir*. New York: St. Martin's, 2018. Kindle.

Cunningham, Vinson. "The Argument of 'Afropessimism.'" *New Yorker*, 13 July 2020. www.newyorker.com/magazine/2020/07/20/the-argument-of -afropessimism.

"Cynthia Franklin." *Canary Mission*, 17 Aug. 2021. canarymission.org/professor /Cynthia_Franklin.

Daley, Ken. "Judge Frank Marullo's Son Pleads Not Guilty to Domestic Abuse Charge." *NOLA.com/Times-Picayune*, 1 Nov. 2015. www.nola.com/news/crime _police/article_46addb00-4314-59df-b90a-ed07b17edac3.html.

————. "Zeitoun Arrested Again as Ex-wife Pleads, 'We Don't Feel Like Enough Is Being Done.'" *NOLA/Times-Picayune*, 29 Oct. 2014. www.nola.com/crime/index .ssf/2014/10/zeitoun_arrested_again_as_ex-w.html.

Danielle, Brittni. "In Ta-Nehisi Coates' New Book, It's Clear All the Blacks Are Still Men." *The Root*, 16 July 2015. www.theroot.com/in-ta-nehisi-coates-new-book-it-s -clear-all-the-black-1790860550.

Danticat, Edwidge. "Poetry in a Time of Protest." *New Yorker*, 31 Jan. 2017. www
   .newyorker.com/culture/cultural-comment/poetry-in-a-time-of-protest.
Das Gupta, Monisha. *All of Us or None: Migrant Organizing in an Era of Deportation and Dispossession*, forthcoming with Duke University Press.
da Silva, Denise F. "No-bodies: Law, Raciality and Violence." *Griffith Law Review*
   18, no. 2 (2009): 212–36.
Daulatzai, Sohail, and Junaid Rana, eds. *With Stones in Our Hands: Writings on
   Muslims, Race, and Empire*. Minneapolis: University of Minnesota Press,
   2018.
David, Mark. "Black Lives Matter Co-founder Patrisse Khan-Cullors Lands
   Topanga Canyon Compound." *Dirt*, 7 April 2021. www.dirt.com/gallery/more
   -dirt/politicians/black-lives-matter-co-founder-patrisse-khan-cullors-lands
   -topanga-canyon-compound-1203374803/.
"David Horowitz." *Southern Poverty Law Center*. Accessed 29 Sept. 2021. www
   .splcenter.org/fighting-hate/extremist-files/individual/david-horowitz.
Davis, Angela Y. *Freedom Is a Constant Struggle: Ferguson, Palestine, and the
   Foundations of a Movement*. Chicago: Haymarket, 2015.
———. *Women, Race and Class*. New York: Vintage Books, 1983.
Dawson, Ashley, and Bill V. Mullen. *Against Apartheid: The Case for Boycotting
   Israeli Universities*. Chicago: Haymarket, 2015.
Dayan, Colin. "Police Power & Can't Breathe." *boundary 2*, 31 July 2020. www
   .boundary2.org/2020/07/colin-dayan-police-power-cant-breathe/?fbclid=IwAR26b
   Ng3icz-CU7moO91UqSpOfeY5zsABDFP5Qaxmo7Z2GeqPptB8JV2mj4.
Deahl, Rachel. "Book Deals." *Publishers Weekly*, 31 March 2017. www
   .publishersweekly.com/pw/by-topic/industry-news/book-deals/article/73239-book
   -deals-week-of-april-3-2017.html.
Deal, Carl, and Tia Lessin, directors. *Trouble the Water*. Zeitgeist Films, 2008.
DeBerry, Jarvis. "Trayvon Martin Travesty Has a New Orleans Parallel, but Not the
   One You Think." *NOLA*, 2 Aug. 2013. www.nola.com/opinions/index.ssf/2013/08
   /trayvon_martin_travesty_has_a.html.
———. "Zeitoun's Latest Arrest Made Possible by Judge Frank Marullo." *NOLA*, 20
   May 2014. www.nola.com/opinions/index.ssf/2014/05/zeitouns_latest_arrest
   _made_po.html.
Democracy Now! "'If Not Now, When Will We Stand?': Native Hawaiians Fight
   Construction of Telescope on Mauna Kea." *Democracy Now!*, 22 July 2019.
   democracynow.org/2019/7/22/mauna_kea_thirty_meter_telescope_resistance.
Desai, Chandni. "Disrupting Settler-Colonial Capitalism: Indigenous Intifadas and
   Resurgent Solidarities from Turtle Island to Palestine." *Journal of Palestine
   Studies* 50, no. 2 (2021): 43–66.
Desvarieux, Jessica. "Greg Palast: New Orleans Lost Half Its Black Population since
   Hurricane Katrina." *The Real News Network*, 27 Aug. 2013. therealnews.com
   /gpalastkatrinaanniversary0827.
Dew, Sierra. Personal interview. 25 Aug. 2021.

Ebert, Roger. "Keeping Your Head above Water." RogerEbert.com, 18 Sept. 2008. www.rogerebert.com/reviews/trouble-the-water-2008.

Edwards, Erica. *The Other Side of Terror: Black Women and the Culture of US Empire*. New York: New York University Press, 2021.

Eggers, David. *Zeitoun*. New York: Vintage, 2009.

Elia, Nada. "Islamophobia and the 'Privileging' of Arab American Women." *NWSA Journal* 18, no. 3 (Fall 2006): 155–61.

Erakat, Noura. "Geographies of Intimacy: Contemporary Renewals of Black–Palestinian Solidarity." *American Quarterly* 72, no. 2 (2020): 471–96.

———. Interview with Noura Erakat by Cynthia Franklin. In "Cultivating Allyship." The Mauna Kea Syllabus Project, Oct. 2020. www.maunakeasyllabus.com/units /cultivating-solidarities/allyship.

———. *Justice for Some: Law and the Question of Palestine*. Stanford, CA: Stanford University Press, 2019.

———, producer. "When I See Them I See Us." YouTube, uploaded by theprairie.fr, 22 Oct. 2015. www.youtube.com/watch?v=tFVijtMN4dU.

Erakat, Noura, and Marc Lamont Hill, curators. "Black-Palestinian Transnational Solidarity." Special issue, *Journal of Palestine Studies* 48, no. 4 (Summer 2019).

Esmeir, Samera. *Juridical Humanity: A Colonial History*. Stanford, CA: Stanford University Press, 2012. Kindle.

Estes, Nick. *Our History Is the Future: Standing Rock versus the Dakota Access Pipeline, and the Long Tradition of Indigenous Resistance*. London: Verso, 2019. Kindle.

Fanon, Frantz. *Black Skin, White Masks*. Translated by Charles Lam Markmann, 1967. London: Pluto, 1986.

———. "On National Culture." In *Wretched of the Earth*, 206–48. Translated by Constance Farrington, 1963. New York: Atlantic Monthly Press, 1965.

Fearnow, Benjamin. "FBI Ranks 'Black Identity Extremists' Bigger Threat Than Al Qaeda, White Supremacists: Leaked Documents." *Newsweek*, 8 Aug. 2019. www .newsweek.com/fbi-leak-black-identity-extremist-threat-1453362?fbclid=IwAR1wG AautEAowAmCFeAKMgSFrkhiBsYg5pBEHNLWd6DCS-kquLJT9ocdjo8.

Felber, Garrett. "Black Zionism, Reparations, and the 'Palestine Problem.'" *Black Perspectives*, 28 Aug. 2016. www.aaihs.org/black-zionism-reparations-and-the -palestine-problem/.

Feldman, Keith. *A Shadow over Palestine: The Imperial Life of Race in America*. Minneapolis: University of Minnesota Press, 2017.

Felman, Shoshana. "Theaters of Justice: Arendt in Jerusalem, the Eichmann Trial, and the Redefinition of Legal Meaning in the Wake of the Holocaust." *Critical Inquiry* 27, no. 2 (2001): 201–38.

"50 Days of Death & Destruction: Israel's 'Operation Protective Edge.'" Institute for Middle East Understanding, 10 Sept. 2014. imeu.org/article/50-days-of-death -destruction-israels operation-protective-edge.

Filosa, Gwen. "Domestic Violence Defendant Acquitted Despite Video Evidence." *NOLA.com/Times Picayune*, 14 April 2010. www.newsjs.com/url.php?p

=http://www.nola.com/crime/index.ssf/2010/04/domestic_violence_defendant_ac
.html.

———. "Recent Domestic Violence Tragedies Couldn't Be Prevented by Moving
Cases to State Court." *NOLA.com/Times-Picayune*, 15 May 2010. www.newsjs
.com/url.php?p=http://www.nola.com/crime/index.ssf/2010/05/domestic_violence
_tragedies.html.

Finn, Natalie. "Oprah Winfrey's 40-Year Weight Loss Struggle: Inside the Billion-
aire Star's Ongoing Quest for Self-Acceptance." E! News, 3 Aug. 2017. www
.eonline.com/news/871198/oprah-winfrey-s-40-year-weight-loss-struggle-inside-the
-billionaire-star-s-ongoing-quest-for-self-acceptance.

Fischbach, Michael. *Black Power and Palestine: Transnational Countries of Color*,
Stanford, CA: Stanford University Press, 2019.

Fleetwood, Nicole. "Failing Narratives, Initiating Technologies: Hurricane Katrina
and the Production of a Weather Media Event." *American Quarterly* 58, no. 3
(2006): 767–89.

———. *On Racial Icons: Blackness and the Public Imagination*. New Brunswick, NJ:
Rutgers University Press, 2015.

Franklin, Cynthia G. "Eichmann and His Ghosts: Affective States and the Unstable
Status of the Human." *Cultural Critique* 88 (Fall 2014): 79–124.

———. "A Firsthand Account of Israel's Siege on a Palestinian University." Truthout,
28 April 2018. truthout.org/articles/a-firsthand-account-of-israels-siege-on-a
-palestinian-university/.

Franklin, Cynthia G., and Laura E. Lyons. "'I Have a Family': Relational Witnessing and the Evidentiary Power of Grief in the Gwen Araujo Case." *GLQ* 22, no. 3
(2016): 437–66.

"Fruitvale Station Soundtrack with Composer Ludwig Goransson." SoundWorks
Collection, 10 Sept. 2013. soundworkscollection.com/post/fruitvale-station
-soundtrack-with-composer-ludwig-goransson.

Fujikane, Candace. *Mapping Abundance for a Planetary Future: Kanaka Maoli and
Critical Settler Cartographies in Hawai'i*. Durham, NC: Duke University Press, 2021.

Fussell, Elizabeth. "Constructing New Orleans, Constructing Race: A Population
History of New Orleans." *Journal of American History* 94 (Dec. 2007): 846–55.
archive.oah.org/special-issues/katrina/Fussellefd6.html?link_id=sco_earlyimmig.

Garrison, Ann. "Fordham University: One of Many Canaries in the Zionist Coal
Mine." LA Progressive, 19 April 2021. www.laprogressive.com/zionist-coal-mine/.

Garza, Alicia. *The Purpose of Power: How We Come Together When We Fall Apart*.
New York: One World, 2020.

Ghanayem, Eman. "Colonial Loops of Displacement in the United States and
Israel: The Case of Rasmea Odeh." *WSQ: Women's Studies Quarterly* 47, nos. 3
& 4 (Fall/Winter 2019): 71–91.

———. "'Popular' Intelligence: Indigenous Literary Resistance and the Diasporic
Question of Home." University of Illinois Urbana-Champaign lecture, delivered
31 March 2021 via Zoom.

Goodyear-Kaʻōpua, Noelani. "On the Cattle Grate." *Itʻs Lit with PhDJ*, uploaded to SoundCloud, 2019. Accessed 9 Oct. 2021. soundcloud.com/user-973486614 /noelani-goodyear-kaopua.

——. "Protecting Maunakea Is a Mission Grounded in Tradition." *Medium*, 5 Sept. 2019. zora.medium.com/protecting-maunakea-is-a-mission-grounded-in-tradition -38a62df57086.

——. "Protectors of the Future, Not Protestors of the Past: Indigenous Pacific Activism and Mauna a Wākea." *South Atlantic Quarterly* 116, no. 1 (Jan. 2017): 184–94.

——. "Reproducing the Ropes of Resistance: Hawaiian Studies Methodologies." In *Kanaka ʻŌiwi Methodologies: Moʻolelo and Metaphor*, edited by Katrina-Ann R. Kapaʻanaokalaokeola Nakoa Oliveira and Erin Kahunawaikaʻala Wright, 1–29. Honolulu: University of Hawaiʻi Press, 2015. doi.org/10.1515/9780824857516-004.

——. *The Seeds We Planted: Portraits of a Native Hawaiian Charter School.* Minneapolis: University of Minnesota Press, 2013.

Gorman, Ryan. "Katrina Hero, Celebrated in 'Zeitoun,' by Dave Eggers, in Jail for Beating Ex-wife, Now Accused of Trying to Have Her Killed." *New York Daily News*, 12 Oct. 2012. www.nydailynews.com/news/national/katrina-hero-beats-ex -wife-accused-killed-article-1.1134094.

"Governor Ige News Conference about Mauna Kea (July 19, 2019)." YouTube, uploaded by Big Island Video News. Accessed 3 Oct. 2021. www.youtube.com /watch?v=fkWaVFsos6k.

Grady, Constance. "Ta-Nehisi Coates Is a Great Writer. His New Book The Water Dancer Is Not a Great Novel." *The Atlantic*, 24 Sept. 2019. www.vox.com/culture /2019/9/24/20879736/water-dancer-review-ta-nehisi-coates.

Green, Kai M., Je Naé Taylor, Pascale Ifé Williams, and Christopher Roberts. "#BlackHealingMatters in the Time of #BlackLivesMatter." *Biography* 41, no. 4 (2018): 909–41.

Griffith, Erin. "The Black Lives Matter Founders Are among the World's Great Leaders." *Fortune*, 24 March 2016. fortune.com/2016/03/24/black-lives-matter -great-leaders/?fbclid=IwAR1UHcH9cM1rDc2sTRIyBue3mdEHiZBCi _UFdIOefLvsjtFHqk19u-bowS8.

Gualtieri, Sarah. "Strange Fruit? Syrian Immigrants, Extralegal Violence, and Racial Formation in the Jim Crow South." *Arab Studies Quarterly* 26, no. 3 (Summer 2004): 63–85.

Hamilton, Carolyn. *One Man Zeitgeist: Dave Eggers, Publishing and Publicity.* New York: Bloomsbury Academic, 2012.

Hanhardt, Christina B., Jasbir K. Puar, Neel Ahuja, Paul Amar, Aniruddha Dutta, Fatima El-Tayeb, Kwame Holmes, and Sherene Seikaly. "Beyond Trigger Warnings: Safety, Securitization, and Queer Left Critique." *Social Text* 38, no. 4 (Dec. 2020): 49–76. doi-org.eres.library.manoa.hawaii.edu/10.1215/01642472 -8680438.

Hankins, Leslie K. "The Thwarting of the Artist as a Young Working Class Woman: Gender and Class Acts in Eudora Welty's *The Golden Apples.*" In *Politics,*

Gender, and the Arts: Women, the Arts, and Society, edited by Ronald L. Dotterer and Susan Bowers, 158–65. Selinsgrove, PA: Susquehanna University Press, 1992.

Harlow, Barbara. *Resistance Literature.* New York: Methuen, 1987.

Harney, Stefano, and Fred Moten. "Leave Our Mikes Alone." Squarespace. Accessed 20 Sept. 2021. static1.squarespace.com/static/53a0503be4b0a429a2614e8b /t/59d81c2eedaed84653048f0d/1507335215476/Harney-Moten.pdf.

Hartman, Saidiya. *Lose Your Mother: A Journey along the Atlantic Slave Route.* New York: Farrar, Straus and Giroux, 2008.

Hassan, Salah. "The Modern Language Association and the 2017 Vote on the Academic Boycott of Israel." *Jadaliyya,* 18 Jan. 2017. www.jadaliyya.com/Details /33943.

Hawaii Independent Staff. "Speech: Kaleikoa Kaʻeo on the TMT." *Hawaii Independent,* transcript, 24 April 2015. thehawaiiindependent.com/story/speech-kaleikoa -kaeo-on-the-tmt.

Hemphill, Prentis. Introduction to *An Abolitionist's Handbook: 12 Steps to Changing Yourself and the World,* by Patrisse Khan Cullors. New York: St. Martin's, 2021.

Hermez, Sami. "Dehumanization in War and Peace: Encounters with Lebanon's Ex-Militia Fighters." *American Anthropologist* 121, no. 3 (2019): 583–94.

hoʻomanawanui, kuʻualoha. "He Haliʻa Aloha no Haunani Kay Trask." University of Hawaiʻi English Department, 2021. Accessed 3 Oct. 2021. english.hawaii.edu/wp -content/uploads/2021/08/HKT-aloha-edited-with-photos-1.pdf.

———. *Voices of Fire: Reweaving the Literary Lei of Pele and Hiʻiaka.* Minneapolis: University of Minnesota Press, 2014.

"Hope Is a Discipline: Mariame Kaba on Dismantling the Carceral State." "Intercepted" with Jeremy Scahill. *The Intercept,* 17 March 2021. theintercept.com/2021 /03/17/intercepted-mariame-kaba-abolitionist-organizing/.

Hopkins, Dwight N. *Down, Up, and Over: Slave Religion and Black Theology.* Minneapolis, MN: Fortress, 1999.

Hopkins, Dwight N., and George C. L. Cummings. *Cut Loose Your Stammering Tongue: Black Theology in the Slave Narratives.* 2nd ed. Louisville, KY: Westminster John Knox, 2003.

Hopkins, J. Uluwehi. "Moʻolelo as Resistance: The Kaona of ʻKahalaopunaʼ in a Colonized Environment." *Narrative Culture* 6, no. 2 (2019). digitalcommons .wayne.edu/narrative/vol6/iss2/8.

Huehls, Mitchum. "Referring to the Human in Contemporary Human Rights Literature." *Modern Fiction Studies* 58, no. 1 (Spring 2012): 1–21.

"Human." *Online Etymology Dictionary,* 2021. Accessed 13 Sept. 2021. www .etymonline.com/search?q=human.

Hwang, Jung-Suk. "Post-9/11-Disaster Katrina: Reenacting American Innocence in Dave Eggers's *Zeitoun.*" *Texas Studies in Literature and Language* 63, no. 1 (2021): 28–52.

"Indian Tribes and Hurricane Katrina: Overlooked by the Federal Government, Relief Organizations and the Corporate Media." *Democracy Now!,* 10 Oct. 2005.

www.democracynow.org/2005/10/10/indian_tribes_and_hurricane_katrina
_overlooked.

"Indigenous Tributes of New Orleans & Louisiana." American Library Association,
13 April 2018. www.ala.org/aboutala/offices/nola-tribes. Document ID:
d7e52bf6-0acc-4316-9729-153b015059c7.

Inouye, Mikey, dir. *Like a Mighty Wave*. Short film. Pacific Islanders in Communications, 2020.

Itchuaqiyaq, Cana Uluak, and Breeanne Matheson. "Decolonizing Decoloniality:
Considering the (Mis)use of Decolonial Frameworks in TPC Scholarship."
Association for Computing Machinery (ACM) Special Interest Group on Design
of Communication (SIGDOC), 17 Feb. 2021. sigdoc.acm.org/cdq/decolonizing
-decoloniality-considering-the-misuse-of-decolonial-frameworks-in-tpc
-scholarship/?fbclid=IwAR3leT2srNHcJYplUr7y1KOoHeBMqXRfQnV6cilat3b05
CmowBDz409BgZY.

Jackson, Zakiyyah Iman. *Becoming Human: Matter and Meaning in an Antiblack
World*. New York: New York University Press, 2020.

Jamal, Amaney, and Nadine Naber, eds. *Race and Arab Americans before and after
9/11: From Invisible Citizens to Visible Subjects*. Syracuse, NY: Syracuse University Press, 2008.

Jaschik, Scott. "Another Lost Job for Salaita." *Inside Higher Ed*, 14 April 2016. www
.insidehighered.com/news/2016/04/14/reports-circulate-american-beirut-has
-blocked-permanent-appointment.

Johnson, Cedric. "An Open Letter to Ta-Nehisi Coates and the Liberals Who Love
Him." *Jacobin*, 3 Feb. 2016. www.jacobinmag.com/2016/02/ta-nehisi-coates-case
-for-reparations-bernie-sanders-racism/.

Johnson, Jack. "Jack Johnson - Upside Down (Official Video)." YouTube, uploaded
by Brushfire Records Inc, 16 June 2009. www.youtube.com/watch?v
=dqUdI4AIDFo.

Johnson, Kahala [@Kahala Johnson]. "Anti-humanism." Facebook, 12 Jan. 2020.
www.facebook.com/permalink.php?story_fbid=871253133294875&id
=100012305895692.

Jones, Bomani. "The Playboy Interview with Ta-Nehisi Coates." *Playboy*, 1 July 2016.
www.playboy.com/read/the-playboy-interview-with-ta-nehisi-coates.

Jones, Ellen E. "Opal Tometi, Cofounder of Black Lives Matter: 'I Do This Because
We Deserve to Live.'" *The Guardian*, 24 Sept. 2020. www.theguardian.com
/society/2020/sep/24/opal-tometi-co-founder-of-black-lives-matter-i-do-this
-because-we-deserve-to-live.

"Joy Enomoto's Speech." Uploaded to Facebook by @Kerry Kamakaokaʻilima, 7
June 2020. www.facebook.com/ItsIlima/videos/10223239014950431.

Justice, Daniel Heath. *Why Indigenous Literatures Matter*. Minneapolis: University
of Minnesota Press, 2018.

Kaba, Mariame. *We Do This 'Til We Free Us: Abolitionist Organizing and Transforming Justice*. Chicago: Haymarket, 2021.

Kaʻeo, Kaleikoa. "Walter H. Capps Center welcomes Professor Kaleikoa Kaʻeo." Lecture. Facebook video, uploaded by UCSB Religious Studies, 14 Oct. 2020. www.facebook.com/watch/?v=1039293826491941. http://voiceofwitness.org/about/

Kaʻeo, Kaleikoa [@ihikapalaumaewa]. "Hawaiian independence." Twitter, 19 Aug. 2021, 9:41 A.M. twitter.com/ihikapalaumaewa/status/1428442023376293888?s=20.

Kaʻeo, Kaleikoa, and Kekailoa Perry. "Hawaiian Place of Yearning: Settlerism in Higher Education." Opening keynote, Native Hawaiian Student Services Fifth Annual Lāhui Hawaiʻi Research Center Student Conference, "Mapping Aloha Aina," 2 April 2022, online via Zoom.

Kahanu, Noelle. "E Kū Ana Ka Paia: Finding Contemporary Relevance in an Ancient Prophecy." In *Restoring Bishop Museum's Hawaiian Hall: Hoʻi Hou Ka Wena i Kaiwiʻula*. Honolulu: Bishop Museum Press, 2009.

Kameʻeleihiwa, Lilikalā. *Native Lands and Foreign Desires: Pahea LA E Pono Ai? How Shall We Live in Harmony?* Honolulu: Bishop Museum Press, 1992. Kindle.

Kamugisha, Aaron, guest ed. "Sylvia Wynter's Black Metamorphosis: A Discussion." *Small Axe*, no. 49 (2016): 37–144.

Kanafani, Ghassan. *Resistance Literature in Occupied Palestine: 1948–1966*. Arabic edition. Cyprus: Rimal, 1966.

Kapahua, Kawena. "Stories from the Mauna, Kuʻu One Hānau." *Biography* 43, no. 3 (2020): 575–81.

Karoliszyn, Henrick. "'Trouble the Water' Star 10 Years Later: 'People Should Never Think Katrina Is Over.'" *Splinter*, 24 Aug. 2015. splinternews.com/trouble-the -water-star-10-years-later-people-should-ne-1793850182.

Kauanui, J. Kēhaulani. "Introduction." In *Forum 2 // Enduring Hawaiian Sovereignty: Protecting the Sacred at Mauna Kea. Radical History Review*, 14 Aug. 2019. www.radicalhistoryreview.org/abusablepast/forum-2-enduring-hawaiian -sovereignty-protecting-the-sacred-at-mauna-kea/.

——. *Paradoxes of Hawaiian Sovereignty: Land, Sex, and the Colonial Politics of State Nationalism*. Durham, NC: Duke University Press, 2018.

Keeling, Kara. *Queer Times, Black Futures*. New York: New York University Press, 2019.

Kelley, Robin D. G. *Freedom Dreams: The Black Radical Imagination*. Boston: Beacon, 2003.

——. "Thug Nation: On State Violence and Disposability." In *Policing the Planet: Why the Policing Crisis Led to Black Lives Matter*, edited by Jordan T. Camp and Christina Heatherton. London: Verso, 2016. E-book.

Khalek, Rania. "Ta-Nehisi Coates Sings of Zionism." Electronic Intifada, 23 Feb. 2016. electronicintifada.net/content/ta-nehisi-coates-sings-zionism/15776.

——. "Watch: Ferguson Activists Bring Message of 'Love and Struggle' to Palestine." Electronic Intifada, 16 Jan. 2015. electronicintifada.net/blogs/rania-khalek /watch-ferguson-activists-bring-message-love-and-struggle-palestine.

Khalili, Zoha. "Query about the IHRA." Email to Cynthia Franklin, 27 Dec. 2022.

Khan, Janaya Future [@janayathefuture]. "LOL." Instagram, 31 Jan. 2022. www .instagram.com/reel/CZaGToghUfz/?utm_source=ig_web_copy_link.

Khan-Cullors, Patrisse. *An Abolitionist's Handbook: 12 Steps to Changing Yourself and the World*. New York: St. Martin's, 2021.

Khan-Cullors, Patrisse, and asha bandele. *When They Call You a Terrorist: A Story of Black Lives Matter and the Power to Change the World*. Young Adult edition. New York: St. Martin's, 2020.

"Kiai Reacts to Ige's Press Conference in Hilo." Uploaded to YouTube by KHON2 News, 19 July 2021. www.youtube.com/watch?v=LWIXANbwdFc.

"Kikī a Kūkā: Queer Kanaka Roundtable." Livestreamed on Facebook by Native Hawaiian Student Services, 16 March 2021. www.facebook.com/groups/OPPOSE .Nai.Aupuni/posts/3000119066968964.

King, Tiffany Lethabo. *The Black Shoals: Offshore Formations of Black and Native Studies*. Durham, NC: Duke University Press, 2019.

———. "Humans Involved: Lurking in the Lines of Posthumanist Flight." *Critical Ethnic Studies* 3, no. 1 (Spring 2017): 162–85.

Klein, Naomi. *The Battle for Paradise: Puerto Rico Takes on the Disaster Capitalists*. Chicago: Haymarket Books, 2018.

Klein, Naomi, and Opal Tometi. "Forget Coates vs. West—We All Have a Duty to Confront the Full Reach of U.S. Empire." *The Intercept*, 21 Dec. 2017. theintercept.com/2017/12/21/cornel-west-ta-nehisi-coates-feud/.

Koʻihonua. "Hanakēhau Learning Farm." Accessed 16 Oct. 2021. hanakehau .wordpress.com/.

"Kold." *Urban Dictionary*. Accessed 18 Sept. 2021. www.urbandictionary.com/define .php?term=kold.

Krotov, Mark. "Spiegel & Grau Moves Up Publication Date of New Ta-Nehisi Coates Book." Melville House (website), 26 June 2015. www.mhpbooks.com /spiegel-grau-moves-up-publication-date-of-new-ta-nehisi-coates-book/.

Kundnani, Arun. "Radicalisation: The Journey of a Concept." *Race and Class* 54, no. 2 (2012): 3–25.

Kuwada, Bryan Kamaoli. "We Live in the Future. Come Join Us." *Ke Kaʻupu Hehi Ale*, 7 July 2015. hehiale.com/2015/04/03/we-live-in-the-future-come-join-us.

Kuwada, Bryan Kamaoli, and Noʻu Revilla. "Introduction: Mana from the Mauna." *Biography* 43, no. 3 (2020): 515–26.

———. "'It Could've Been You, It Could've Been You, It Could've Been So Many of Us': Interview with Noelani Goodyear-Kaʻōpua." *Biography* 43, no. 3 (2020): 530–40.

———. "'We're Asking You to Remember Why We're Here': Interview with Joy Enomoto. *Biography* 43, no. 3 (2020): 596–606.

Kwate, Naa Oyo A., and Shatema Threadcraft. "Dying Fast and Dying Slow in Black Space." *Du Bois Review* 14, no. 2 (2017): 535–56.

Lacy, Ciara, director. *Jamaica Heolimeleikalani Osorio: This Is the Way We Rise*. PBS, 14 Oct. 2020. www.pbs.org/video/jamaica-heolimeleikalani-osorio-this-is -the-way-we-rise-ndwixe/.

Lander, Joan, and Puhipau, directors. *Act of War: The Overthrow of the Hawaiian Kingdom*. 1993. Documentary uploaded on Vimeo by Joan Lander on 9 Aug. 2020. vimeo.com/ondemand/actofwar.

Lasconia, ʻIhilani, participant. "Deciphering and Defeating the Censorship of 'Whose Narrative? Gender, Justice, and Resistance: A Conversation with Leila Khaled.'" *Arab Studies Quarterly* Conference, University of Hawaiʻi, Honolulu, 26 March 2022.

Lasconia, ʻIhilani, and Kauwila Mahi. "Free Ya People." Performed at the University of Hawaiʻi Kamakakūokalani Center for Hawaiian Studies Hālau o Haumea, 5 March 2022.

LeBron, Christopher. "'Black Panther' Is Not the Movie We Deserve." *Boston Review*, 17 Feb. 2018. bostonreview.net/race/christopher-lebron-black-panther.

Lee, Ryan. "LA Riots." *End Notes*. Accessed 29 June 2022. endnotes.org.uk/posts /ryan-lee-la-riots-2020.

Lee, Suevon. "How 12 Teens Who'd Never Met before Organized Honolulu's Black Lives Matter Protest." Honolulu Civil Beat, 22 June 2020. www.civilbeat.org/2020 /06/how-12-teens-whod-never-met-before-organized-honolulus-black-lives-matter -protest/.

Leeb, Susanne, and Kerstin Stakemeier. "An End to 'This' World: Denise Ferreira da Silva Interviewed by Susanne Leeb and Kerstin Stakemeier." *Texte zur Kunst*. Accessed 13 Sept. 2021. www.textezurkunst.de/articles/interview-ferreira-da-silva/.

"Legislation." Palestine Legal (website). Accessed 1 Oct. 2021. legislation .palestinelegal.org/.

Levitz, Eric. "Ta-Nehisi Coates Is an Optimist Now: A Conversation about Race and 2020." *New York Magazine*, 17 March 2019. nymag.com/intelligencer/2019/03 /ta-nehisi-coates-race-politics-2020-elections.html.

Lipsitz, George. "From *Plessy* to Ferguson." *Cultural Critique* 90 (Spring 2015): 119–39. manifold.umn.edu/read/from-plessy-to-ferguson/section/d9524d57-5a48 -478e-8ede-49cf29e22571.

Lloyd, David. "Toast for Steven from Angela Davis." Email to Cynthia Franklin, 20 Nov. 2016, 10:11 A.M.

———. *Under Representation: The Racial Regime of Aesthetics*. New York: Fordham University Press, 2019.

The Lobby—USA. 4-part TV series. Al Jazeera, 2017.

Long, ʻIlima, participant. "Deciphering and Defeating the Censorship of 'Whose Narrative? Gender, Justice, and Resistance: A Conversation with Leila Khaled.'" *Arab Studies Quarterly* Conference, University of Hawaiʻi, Honolulu, 26 March 2022.

Lorde, Audre. "The Master's Tools Will Never Dismantle the Master's House." In *Sister Outsider: Essays and Speeches*, 110–14. Trumansburg, NY: Crossing, 1984.

Lotzof, Kerry. "Are We Really Made of Stardust?" Natural History Museum, 4 June 2018. www.nhm.ac.uk/discover/are-we-really-made-of-stardust.html.

Love Not Blood Campaign. Accessed 20 Sept. 2021. www.lovenotbloodcampaign.com.

Lowe, Lisa. *Immigrant Acts: On Asian American Cultural Politics.* Durham, NC: Duke University Press, 1996.

Lubin, Alex. *Geographies of Liberation: The Making of an Afro-Arab Political Imaginary.* Chapel Hill: University of North Carolina Press, 2014.

Luft, Rachel E. "Racialized Disaster Patriarchy: An Intersectional Model for Understanding Disaster Ten Years after Hurricane Katrina." *Feminist Formations* 28, no. 2 (2016): 1–26.

Mackey, Robert. "Israel's Supporters Try to Come to Terms with the Killing of Children in Gaza." *New York Times,* 7 Aug. 2014. www.nytimes.com/2014/08/08/world/middleeast/israel-supporters-try-to-come-to-terms-with-killing-of-children-in-gaza-strip.html.

Maggi, Laura. "Police Report Provides Details of Case against Abdulrahman Zeitoun, Subject of Best-Seller." *Nola.com,* 12 Aug. 2021. www.nola.com/news/crime_police/article_dd68bbe2-fe7b-56b4-9d6b-43440dc980aa.html.

Mahi, Kauwila. "Class Letter." English 775, "Class Letters." *Laulima,* 2 March 2022.

———. "Emergent-Seas: Ea mai ke kai mai." "States of Emergency/Emergence: Learning from Maunakea" (blog series). *Abolition Journal,* 11 July 2020. abolition-journal.org/emergent-seas/#more-3873.

Maile, David Uahikeaikalei'ohu. "For Mauna Kea to Live, TMT Must Leave." *Radical History,* Forum 2.1, 14 Aug. 2019. www.radicalhistoryreview.org/abusablepast/forum-2-1-for-mauna-kea-to-live-tmt-must-leave/.

Maile, Uahikea. "Ka Lei o ka Lanakila: Grasping Victory at Maunakea." States of Emergency/Emergence: Learning from Maunakea" (blog series). *Abolition Journal,* 17 July 2020. abolitionjournal.org/ka-lei-o-ka-lanakila/#more-3902.

Maira, Sunaina. *Boycott! The Academy and Justice for Palestine.* Berkeley: University of California Press, 2018.

Maira, Sunaina, and Magid Shihade. "Meeting Asian/Arab American Studies: Thinking Race, Empire, and Zionism in the U.S." *Journal of Asian American Studies* 9, no. 2 (June 2006): 117–40.

Malik, Nesrine. "'I Have a Lot of Resentment': Patrisse Cullors on Co-founding Black Lives Matter, the Backlash—and Why the Police Must Go." *The Guardian,* 28 Feb. 2022. www.theguardian.com/world/2022/feb/28/i-have-a-lot-of-resentment-patrisse-cullors-on-co-founding-black-lives-matter-the-backlash-and-why-the-police-must-go.

MANA. *Movement Building for Ea: A Workbook.* Movement for Aloha no ka 'Āina. Accessed 8 Oct. 2021. www.noegoodyearkaopua.com/_files/ugd/db9390_da542c230965466ea9f7c4fe873b0568.pdf.

Manshel, Hannah. "'Never Allowed for Property': Harriet Jacobs and Layli Long Soldier before the Law." *American Literature* 94, no. 2 (June 2022): 331–55.

Martin, Naomi. "Kathy Zeitoun Decries Ex-Husband's Acquittal on Charges He Tried to Kill Her." *NOLA.com/Times Picayune,* 31 July 2013. www.nola.com/crime/index.ssf/2013/07/kathy_zeitoun_interview.html.

"Matter of Culture Honors Women's History—March 2021." *Matter of Culture*, 1 March 2021. matterofculture.medium.com/matterofculturehonors-womens -history-month-2021-c9cb7447daa7.

Mauna Kea Education and Awareness. "We Stand with Mauna Kea." Petition. Accessed 8 Oct. 2021. www.change.org/p/gordon-and-betty-moore-foundation-the -immediate-halt-to-the-construction-of-the-tmt-on-mauna-kea?use_react =false&fbclid=IwAR38AOyVz220H7zoQJHwgxJHoy4hawI4TFAnLECe2C9OYL R4FWO-xFo-ZO8.

Maunakea Movement Art Hui (MMA Hui). Private Facebook page, 30 June 2019.

Mauna Kea Syllabus Project (website). Accessed 12 Oct. 2021. www .maunakeasyllabus.com/home.

"Mauna Kea Syllabus Project: From Standing Rock to Maunakea." Mauna Kea Syllabus Project, livestreamed to Facebook, 24 June, 2020. www.facebook.com /watch/live/?v=280859979783903&ref=search.

Mbembé, J.-A., and Libby Meintjes. "Necropolitics." *Public Culture* 15, no. 1 (2003): 11–40.

McDougall, Brandy Nālani. *Finding Meaning: Kaona and Contemporary Hawaiian Literature*. Tucson: University of Arizona Press, 2016.

———. "Moʻokūʻauhau versus Colonial Entitlement in English Translations of the Kumulipo." *American Quarterly* 67, no. 3 (2015): 749–79. Project MUSE. doi:10.1353/aq.2015.0054.

McKittrick, Katherine. "Yours in Intellectual Struggle: Sylvia Wynter and the Realization of the Living." In *Sylvia Wynter: On Being Human as Praxis*, edited by Katherine McKittrick, 1–8. Durham, NC: Duke University Press, 2015.

Mendoza, Jim. "Day 12: Shane Medeiros Testifies in Deedy Murder Trial." *Hawaii News Now*, 25 July 2013. www.hawaiinewsnow.com/story/22933849/day-12 -mcdonalds-workers-memory-questioned-in-deedy-murder-trial/.

Mignolo, Walter D. "Sylvia Wynter: What Does It Mean to Be Human." In *Sylvia Wynter: On Being Human as Praxis*, edited by Katherine McKittrick, 106–23. Durham, NC: Duke University Press, 2015.

Mignolo, Walter D., and Catherine E. Walsh. *On Decoloniality: Concepts, Analytics, Praxis*. Durham, NC: Duke University Press, 2018.

Mirzoeff, Nicholas. *The Appearance of Black Lives Matter*. Miami: [NAME], 2017. E-book.

Mishra, Pankaj. "'Why Do White People Like What I Write?' Review of *We Were Eight Years in Power: An American Tragedy* (2017)." *London Review of Books* 40, no. 4, 22 Feb. 2018. www.lrb.co.uk/the-paper/v40/n04/pankaj-mishra/why-do -white-people-like-what-i-write.

"Mission." Crenshaw Dairy Mart (website). Accessed 30 June 2022. www .crenshawdairymart.com/about-us.

Mitchell, Nick. "The View from Nowhere: On Frank Wilderson's Afropessimism." *Spectre* (Fall 2020): 110–22.

Morales, Ed. *Fantasy Island: Colonialism, Exploitation and Betrayal of Puerto Rico.* New York: Bold Type Books, 2019.

Moten, Fred. "Blackness and Nothingness (Mysticism in the Flesh)." *South Atlantic Quarterly* 112, no. 4 (2013): 737–80.

Moten, Fred, and Stefano Harney. "The University and the Undercommons: Seven Theses." *Social Text* 22, no. 2 (Summer 2004): 101–15.

Movement for Black Lives (M4BL) (website). Accessed 22 Sept. 2021. m4bl.org/.

Mowatt, Rasul A. "Black Lives as Snuff: The Silent Complicity in Viewing Black Death." *Biography* 41, no. 7 (Fall 2018): 777–806.

Muhammad, Ismail. "Cornel West's Reckless Criticism of Ta-Nehisi Coates." *Slate*, 20 Dec. 2017. slate.com/culture/2017/12/on-cornel-wests-reckless-disappointing -broadside-against-ta-nehisi-coates.html.

Murray, Charles. "Coming White Underclass." *Wall Street Journal*, 29 Oct. 1993. Repub. in contemporarythinkers.org. Accessed 19 Sept. 2021. contemporarythink-ers.org/charles-murray/essay/coming-white-underclass/.

Musleh, Ali H. "To What Abyss Does This Robot Take the Earth: On the Automa-tion of Settler Colonialism in Palestine." PhD diss., University of Hawai'i, 2022.

Naber, Nadine. "'Look, Mohammed the Terrorist Is Coming!' Cultural Racism, Nation-Based Racism, and the Intersectionality of Oppressions after 9/11." In *Race and Arab Americans before and after 9/11: From Invisible Citizens to Visible Subjects*, edited by Amaney Jamal and Nadine Naber, 276–304. Syracuse, NY: Syracuse University Press, 2008.

———. "The Radical Potential of Mothering during the Egyptian Revolution." *Feminist Studies* 47, no. 1 (2021): 1–31.

NDN Collective. "Meet the 2021 Cohort of NDN Changemaker Fellows." NDN Collective (website), 28 June 2021. ndncollective.org/meet-the-2021-cohort-of-ndn -changemaker-fellows/.

Ngowi, Kibo. "Ta-Nehisi Coates Is Not the Voice of Black People: Kibo Ngowi Considers the Cult of Intersectionality." *Johannesburg Review of Books*, 5 Feb. 2018.

Obama, Barack. "Transcript of Barack Obama's Victory Speech." NPR (website), 5 Nov. 2008. www.npr.org/2008/11/05/96624326/transcript-of-barack-obamas -victory-speech.

Okoth, Kevin Ochieng. "The Flatness of Blackness: Afro-Pessimism and the Erasure of Anti-colonial Thought." *Salvage*, 16 Jan. 2020. salvage.zone/issue-seven/ the-flatness-of-blackness-afro-pessimism-and-the-erasure-of-anti-colonial-thought/.

Osorio, Jamaica Heolimeleikalani. "On the Frontlines of Mauna Kea." Flux, April 2020. fluxhawaii.com/maunakea-movement/.

———. *Remembering Our Intimacies: Moʻolelo, Aloha ʻĀina, and Ea.* Minneapolis: University of Minnesota Press, 2021.

Osorio, Jamaica Heolimeleikalani [@Jamaica Heolimeleikalani Osorio]. "Kalei-wohi." Facebook, 28 Oct. 2021, 5:01 P.M. www.facebook.com/jamaicaosorio/posts /10219923558815893.

———. "When I arrived." Facebook, 18 July 2021. www.facebook.com/jamaicaosorio /posts/10219405229257978.

"Our Fight for Liberation: A Conversation with the Families of Eyad Hallaq and Oscar Grant." YouTube, uploaded by Palestinian Youth Movement, 11 July 2020. www.youtube.com/watch?v=qehpLsQ25qs.

Palestine Legal. "Distorted Definition: Redefining Antisemitism to Silence Advocacy for Palestinian Rights." Palestine Legal (website). Accessed 1 Oct. 2021. palestinelegal.org/distorted-definition.

———. "Unconstitutional Censorship." Letter sent via email to President Lassner, 22 Oct. 2020. static1.squarespace.com/static/548748b1e4b083fc03ebf70e/t/5f93228 dff537d4371b43a28/1603478158415/Civil+Rights+Orgs+Letter+to+UHM-post +final.pdf.

Palestine Legal and The Center for Constitutional Rights. *The Palestine Exception to Free Speech: A Movement under Attack in the US.* Sept. 2015. Accessed 29 Sept. 2021. ccrjustice.org/sites/default/files/attach/2015/09/ Palestine%20Exception%20 Report%20Final.pdf.

The Palestine Poster Project Archives. Liberation Graphics Collection of Palestine Posters. www.palestineposterproject.org/publishers/6333/poster-imaged-full. Accessed 29 Sept. 2021.

Palumbo-Liu, David. *Speaking Out of Place: Getting Our Political Voices Back.* Chicago: Haymarket Books, 2021.

Patrisse Cullors (website). patrissecullors.com/about/.

Patterson, Victoria. "Did Dave Eggers Get 'Zeitoun' Wrong?" *Salon,* 9 Dec. 2012. www.salon.com/2012/12/09/did_dave_eggers_get_zeitoun_wrong/.

Perez, Andre. Personal interview, 30 Aug. 2021.

Perez, Andre [@Andre Perez]. "Art." Facebook, 29 Nov. 2016. www.facebook.com /andre.perez.96/posts/10154714376258618.

Petski, Denise. "'Good Trouble': Patrisse Cullors Moves to Writers Room for Season 2 of Freeform Series." *Deadline,* 22 May 2019. deadline.com/2019/05/good-trouble -patrisse-cullors-writers-room-season-2-1202620887/.

Pilkington, Ed. "Black Americans Dying of Covid-19 at Three Times the Rate of White People." *Guardian Weekly,* 20 May 2020. www.theguardian.com/world /2020/may/20/black-americans-death-rate-covid-19-coronavirus.

Puar, Jasbir. *The Right to Maim: Debility, Capacity, Disability.* Durham, NC: Duke University Press, 2017.

Puʻuhonua o Puʻuhuluhulu Maunakea, and Mana Maoli. *Worldwide #Jam4Mauna.* Uploaded to YouTube by Mana Maoli, 13 Jan. 2020. www.youtube.com/watch?v =k1Ul5xp4PTg.

"Q&A—Patrisse Khan-Cullors and asha bandele." Macmillan.com. Accessed 28 June 2022. static.macmillan.com/static/smp/when-they-call-you/interview .html.

Rabinbach, Anson. "Eichmann in New York: The New York Intellectuals and the Hannah Arendt Controversy." *October* 108 (Spring 2004): 97–111.

Rachlin, Harvey. "Misquoting Golda Meir: Did She or Didn't She?" *Haaretz*, 10 April 2018. www.haaretz.com/golda-meir-s-gems-did-she-really-say-that-1.5371930.

Rankine, Claudia. *Citizen: An American Lyric*. Minneapolis, MN: Graywolf, 2014.

———. "The Condition of Black Life Is One of Mourning." *New York Times*, 22 June 2015. www.nytimes.com/2015/06/22/magazine/the-condition-of-black-life-is -one-of-mourning.html.

Ransby, Barbara. *Making All Black Lives Matter: Re-imagining Freedom in the Twenty-First Century*. Berkeley: University of California Press, 2018.

Rao, Sameer. "Ryan Coogler and Michael B. Jordan Reunite for Ta-Nehesi Coates- Penned 'Wrong Answer." *Colorlines*, 8 June 2017. www.colorlines.com/articles /ryan-coogler-and-michael-b-jordan-reunite-ta-nehisi-coates-penned-wrong -answer.

Raza, Hamzah, and Max Blumenthal. "Meet the Owner of Canary Mission's Anonymous Anti-Palestinian Blacklisting Website." Holylandjustice.org, 27 Aug. 2018. holylandjustice.org/2018/08/27/meet-the-owner-of-canary-missions -anonymous-anti-palestinian-blacklisting-website/.

Redden, Elizabeth. "Israel Boycott Battle Heads to Court." *Inside Higher Ed*, 21 April 2016. www.insidehighered.com/news/2016/04/21/lawsuit-targets-american -studies-associations-stance-israel-academic-boycott.

Red Nation. *The Red Deal: Indigenous Action to Save Our Earth. resilience*, 2021. Accessed 1 Oct. 2021. www.resilience.org/stories/2021-04-27/the-red-deal -indigenous-action-to-save-our-earth/.

Reed, Adolph. "Beyond the Great Awokening: Reassessing the Legacies of Past Blackorganizing." *New Republic*, 8 Dec. 2020. newrepublic.com/article/160305 /beyond-great-awokening.

"Remarks by President Trump at South Dakota's 2020 Mt. Rushmore Fireworks Celebration." 4 July 2020. trumpwhitehouse.archives.gov/briefings-statements /remarks-president-trump-south-dakotas-2020-mount-rushmore-fireworks -celebration-keystone-south-dakota/.

Remnick, David. "An American Uprising." *New Yorker*, 31 May 2020. www.thenation .com/article/activism/blm-looting-protest-vandalism/.

Revilla, No'u. *Ask the Brindled*. Minneapolis, MN: Milkweed Editions, 2022.

———. "notes towards a huli: gender, sexuality, & pilina." The Mauna Kea Syllabus Project. Accessed 13 Oct. 2021. www.maunakeasyllabus.com/units/gender -sexuality-pilina/notes-toward-a-huli-gender-sexuality-pilina.

Rhodes, Joe. "A Bay Area Killing Inspires Fruitvale Station." *New York Times*, 28 June 2013. www.nytimes.com/2013/06/30/movies/a-bay-area-killing-inspires -fruitvale-station.html.

Riesman, Abraham. "*Black Panther* Director Ryan Coogler: Ta-Nehisi Coates Has 'Absolutely' Influenced the Movie." *Vulture*, 24 July 2016. www.vulture.com/2016 /07/ryan-coogler-ta-nehisi-coates-panther.html.

Rifkin, Mark. *Fictions of Land and Flesh: Blackness, Indigeneity, Speculation*. Durham, NC: Duke University Press, 2019.

Ritchie, Andrea. *Invisible No More: Police Violence against Black Women and Women of Color.* Boston: Beacon, 2017. Kindle.

RITZ Crackers [@Ritzcrackers]. "We've come together." Twitter, 4 June 2020, 3:46 P.M. twitter.com/Ritzcrackers/status/1268720699302125571?s=20&t=qJVRTLE4Zn -Q_pAs6r_aOA.

Rivers-Roberts, Kimberly, dir. *Fear No Gumbo (Stop stealing our sh*t!).* IMDbPro, 2016.

———. "TEDxNOLA - Kimberly Rivers Roberts - Triumph + Adversity." YouTube, uploaded by TEDxNOLA, 15 Nov. 2010, www.youtube.com/watch?v =CV42VE9VgBg.

———. "Triumph over Tragedy—What Do You Win?" YouTube, uploaded by TEDxNewOrleans, 16 July 2015. www.youtube.com/watch?v=I1wwieZcSqA.

Robinson, Cedric. *Black Marxism: The Making of the Black Radical Tradition.* Chapel Hill: University of North Carolina Press, 2000.

Rosenberg, Kenneth Paul, dir. *Bedlam.* PBS, 2020.

Rosenberg, MJ. "Democrats Join Republicans in Bill Criminalizing Speech Critical of Israel." *Huffpost,* 27 July 2017. www.huffpost.com/entry/democrats-join -republicans-in-bill-criminalizing-speech_b_5978bc17e4b0c6616f7ce6d9.

Rosenthal, Keith. "BDS the Police," *Rampant,* 14 July 2021. rampantmag.com/2021 /07/bds-the-police/.

Rostock, Susanne. Phone conversation, 20 July 2022.

Rowe, John Carlos. "Edward Said and American Studies." In *The Cultural Politics of the New American Studies.* Ann Arbor: University of Michigan Press, 2012. quod .lib.umich.edu/o/ohp/10945585.0001.001/1:4.1/—cultural-politics-of-the-new -american-studies?rgn=div2;view=fulltext.

Rushin, Kate. "The Bridge Poem." In *This Bridge Called My Back: Writings by Radical Women of Color,* edited by Cherríe Moraga and Gloria Anzaldúa, 4th ed., xxxiii–xxxiv. Albany, NY: SUNY Press, 2015.

Saad, Nardine. "HBO, Ta-Nehisi Coates Team Up for Book Adaptation Special on Race in America." *LA Times,* 23 June 2020. www.latimes.com/entertainment-arts /tv/story/2020-07-23/hbo-ta-nehisi-coates-between-the-world-and-me-special ?fbclid=IwAR31yFSfNNjp4TmKYgNStRH19IN4OwB06 -vJvi2sKEr9cjHbgtjppi4tZhg.

Said, Edward W. *Culture and Imperialism.* New York: Vintage Books, 1994.

———. *Humanism and Democratic Criticism.* New York: Columbia University Press, 2004.

———. "Intellectual Exile: Expatriates and Marginals." In *Representations of the Intellectual.* New York: Pantheon Books, 1994.

———. *Out of Place: A Memoir.* New York: Knopf, 1999.

———. "Permission to Narrate." *Journal of Palestine Studies* 13, no. 3 (Spring 1984): 27–48.

———. *The Politics of Dispossession: The Struggle for Palestinian Self-Determination, 1969–1994.* London: Chatto and Windus, 1994.

——. "The Public Role of Writers and Intellectuals." *The Nation*, 17 Sept. 2001, reprinted in Tamilnation.org, tamilnation.org/ideology/said.htm.

——. *Representations of the Intellectual*. New York: Pantheon Books, 1994.

——. *The World, the Text, and the Critic*. Cambridge, MA: Harvard University Press, 1984.

Salaita, Steven. *Anti-Arab Racism in the USA: Where It Comes From and What It Means for Politics Today*. London: Pluto, 2006.

——. "AUB Limited." Mondoweiss, 21 Aug. 2017. mondoweiss.net/2017/08/aub -limited/.

——. "The Big Picture." Steve Salaita (website), 24 Oct. 2019. stevesalaita.com/the -big-picture/.

——. "Decolonization: Survival:: Water: Life." Steve Salaita (website), 19 April 2019. stevesalaita.com/?s=Decolonization+%3A+Survival+.

——. "A Guide to Surviving Canary Mission." *The Electronic Intifada*, 20 Dec. 2016. electronicintifada.net/blogs/steven-salaita/guide-surviving-canary -mission/.

——. *The Holy Land in Transit: Colonialism and the Quest for Canaan*. Syracuse, NY: Syracuse University Press, 2006.

——. "An Honest Living." Steve Salaita (website), 17 Feb. 2019. stevesalaita.com/an -honest-living/# more49.

——. "The Inhumanity of Academic Freedom." Steve Salaita (website), 7 Aug. 2019. stevesalaita.com/the-inhumanity-of-academic-freedom/.

——. *Inter/Nationalism: Decolonizing Native America and Palestine*. Minneapolis: University of Minnesota Press, 2016.

——. *Israel's Dead Soul*. Philadelphia: Temple University Press, 2011.

——. "Palestine in the Revolutionary Imagination." Steve Salaita (website), 3 April 2019. stevesalaita.com/palestine-in-the-revolutionary-imagination/.

——. "Salaita Speaks Publicly for the First Time since His Firing: 'I Am Here to Reaffirm My Commitment to Teaching and to a Position with the American Indian Studies Program at UIUC.'" Mondoweiss, 9 Sept. 2014. mondoweiss.net /2014/09/commitment-teaching-american/.

——. "Sirhan Sirhan the Palestinian." Steve Salaita (website), 16 Sept. 2021. stevesalaita.com/sirhan-sirhan-the-palestinian/?utm_source=rss&utm_medium =rss&utm_campaign=sirhan-sirhan-the-palestinian.

——. *Uncivil Rites: Palestine and the Limits of Academic Freedom*. Chicago: Haymarket Books, 2015.

——. "Washing Ashore in Hawaii." Mondoweiss, 15 Nov. 2017. mondoweiss.net/2017 /11/washing-ashore-hawaii/.

——. "Why Did Israel Execute Shireen Abu-Akleh?" Steve Salaita (website), 13 May 2022. stevesalaita.com/why-did-israel-execute-shireen-abu-akleh/.

Salaita, Steven [@stevesalaita]. "At this point." Twitter, 19 July 2014, 4:24 P.M. twitter .com/stevesalaita/status/490683700116738048?s=20.

———. "Enjoy your new BFFs, upper administration." Facebook, 31 Jan. 2015. www .facebook.com/photo/?fbid=10206017186497224&set=a.1319181068097.

———. "A few thoughts." Facebook, 22 July 2017. www.facebook.com/steven.salaita /posts/10213755322585790.

———. "I miss igniting my bus." Facebook, 14 May 2020. www.facebook.com/profile /1487894562/search/?q=a%20decent%20life%20needn%E2%80%99t%20follow%20 conventional%20notions%20of%20excitement%20.

———. "Killing kids." Twitter, 24 May 2022, 1:29 P.M. twitter.com/stevesalaita/status /1529243122810728449?s=20&t=fJPB3XS1DRObWbHyyWbfJQ.

———. "Listening to this." Facebook, 4 Jan. 2014. www.facebook.com/steven.salaita /posts/10202909889296736.

"Salaita v. Kennedy, et al." Center for Constitutional Rights, 15 Sept. 2016. ccrjustice .org/home/what-we-do/our-cases/salaita-v-kennedy-et-al.

Salamanca, Omar Jabary, Mezna Qato, Kareem Rabie, and Sobhi Samour. "Past Is Present." In "Settler Colonialism in Palestine." Special issue, *Settler Colonial Studies* 2, no. 1 (2012): 1–8. doi.org/10.1080/2201473X.2012.10648823.

———, eds. "Settler Colonialism in Palestine." Special issue, *Settler Colonial Studies* 2, no. 1 (2012).

Sang, Presley Keʻalaanuhea Ah Mook. "Puʻuhonua o Puʻuhuluhulu University: He Kīpuka Aloha ʻĀina no ka ʻImi Naʻauao." In *The Value of Hawaiʻi 3: Hulihia, the Turning*, edited by Noelani Goodyear-Kaʻōpua, Craig Howes, Jonathan Kay Kamakawiwoʻole Osorio, and Aiko Yamashiro. Honolulu: University of Hawaiʻi Press, 2020.

Saunders, Patricia J. "Fugitive Dreams of Diaspora: Conversations with Saidiya Hartman." *Anthurium: A Caribbean Studies Journal* 6, no. 1, Article 7 (June 2008): 1–16.

Sayegh, Fayez A. *Zionist Colonialism in Palestine.* Beirut: Palestine Liberation Organization Research Center, 1965.

Schotten, Heike C. "Against Academic Freedom: 'Terrorism,' Settler Colonialism, and Palestinian Liberation." In *Enforcing Silence: Academic Freedom, Palestine and the Criticism of Israel*, edited by David Landy, Ronit Lentin, and Conor McCarthy, 297–98. London: Zed Books, 2020.

Seghal, Parul. "Eggers's Latest PG-13 Story about the American Dream." *New York Times*, 23 Jan. 2018. www.nytimes.com/2018/01/23/books/review-dave-eggers-monk -of-mokha.html.

"SF State: Lawsuits Tried to Silence Research Advocacy on Palestine." Palestine Legal (website), 12 March 2018. palestinelegal.org/case-studies/2017/11/3/years-long -suppression-campaign-sfsu.

Shalhoub-Kevorkian, Nadera. *Incarcerated Childhood and the Politics of Unchilding.* Cambridge: Cambridge University Press, 2019.

Sharpe, Christina. *In the Wake: On Blackness and Being.* Durham, NC: Duke University Press, 2016.

——. *Monstrous Intimacies: Making Post-slavery Subjects*. Durham, NC: Duke University Press, 2010.

Simerman, John. "Katrina Literary Hero Abdulrahman Zeitoun Indicted on Stalking Charge." *The Advocate*, 23 June 2014. www.theadvocate.com/new _orleans/news/article_f33cbf03-3ab3-569d-9a08-6835ab34e460.html.

——. "Literary Hero Abdulrahman Zeitoun Convicted of Felony Stalking." *The Advocate*, 6 June 2016. theadvocate.com/news/neworleans/neworleansnews /16025090-123/katrina-literary-hero-abdulrahman-zeitoun-convicted-of-felony -stalking.

Simpson, Leanne Betasamosake. *As We Have Always Done: Indigenous Freedom through Radical Resistance*. Minneapolis: University of Minnesota Press, 2021.

——. "The Oldest Tree in the World." Track 3 on *F(l)ight*, produced by Jonas Bonnetta, 2016.

Simpson, Leanne Betasamosake, Rinaldo Walcott, and Glen Coulthard. "Panel Discussion: Idle No More and Black Lives Matter: An Exchange." *Studies in Social Justice* 12, no. 1 (2018): 75–89.

Sircar, Oishik. "'A Deep and Ongoing Dive into the Brutal Humanism That Undergirds Liberalism': An Interview with Jasbir K. Puar." *Humanity Journal* 11, no. 3, 17 Jan. 2021. humanityjournal.org/issue11-3/a-deep-and-ongoing-dive-into -the-brutal-humanism-that-undergirds-liberalism-an-interview-with-jasbir-k-puar/.

@sistakahele. "We are not American!" Instagram, 5 July 2021. www.instagram.com/p /CQHRwYj6CV/?utm_source=ig_web_copy_link.

Smith, Heather. "Meet the BART-Stopping Woman behind Black Lives Matter." *Grist*, 4 Dec. 2014. grist.org/politics/stopping-a-bart-train-in-michael-browns-name/.

Smith, Kyle. "'Fruitvale Station' Is Loose with the Facts about Oscar Grant." *Forbes*, 25 July 2013. www.forbes.com/sites/kylesmith/2013/07/25/fruitvale-station-is-loose -with-the-facts-in-an-effort-to-elicit-sympathy-for-oscar-grant/#7859ec7d693c.

——. "'Fruitvale Station' Tells Some, Omits Some." *NY Post*, 12 July 2013. nypost .com/2013/07/12/fruitvale-station-tells-some-omits-some/.

Sommers, Samuel R., Evan P. Apfelbaum, Kristin N. Dukes, Negin Toosi, and Elsie J. Wang. "Race and Media Coverage of Hurricane Katrina: Analysis, Implications, and Future Research Questions." *Analyses of Social Issues and Public Policy* 6, no. 1 (2006): 1–17.

"Speech: Kaleikoa Ka'eo on the TMT." *Hawaii Independent*, 24 April 2015. theha- waiiindependent.com/story/speech-kaleikoa-kaeo-on-the-tmt.

Sperri, Alice, and Sam Biddle. "Zoom Censorship of Palestine Seminars Sparks Fight Over Academic Freedom." *The Intercept*, 14 Nov. 2020. theintercept.com /2020/11/14/zoom-censorship-leila-khaled-palestine/?utm_source=twitter&utm _medium=social&utm_campaign=theintercept.

Spillers, Hortense J., and Lewis R. Gordon. "Afropessimism and Its Others: A Discussion between Hortense J. Spillers and Lewis R. Gordon." YouTube, uploaded by Soka University of America, 24 May 2021. www.youtube.com/watch ?v=Z-s-Ltu06NI&t=1s.

Stephens, R. L. "Between the Black Body and Me." *Jacobin*, 31 May 2017. www
.jacobinmag.com/2017/05/ta-nehisi-coates-racism-afro-pessimism-reparations
-class-struggle.

Story, Kaila Adia. "Mama's Gon' Buy You a Mocking Bird: Why #BlackMoth-
ersStillMatter: A Short Genealogy of Black Mothers' Maternal Activism and
Politicized Care." *Biograph* 41, no. 4 (2018): 876–94.

"Street Artists Clash with Weinstein Company over 'Fruitvale' Murals." False Art
(website), 14 July 2013. www.falseart.com/street-artists-clash-with-weinstein
-company-over-fruitvale-murals/.

The Struggle for Abolition: From the US to Palestine. Haymarket Books Teach-In,
YouTube, 20 Aug. 2020. www.youtube.com/watch?v=dND8keciMFo.

Tadiar, Neferti X. M. "Life-Times of Becoming Human." *Occasion: Interdisciplinary
Studies in the Humanities* 3 (2012): 1–17.

TallBear, Kim. "Making Love and Relations beyond Settler Sex and Family." In
Making Kin Not Population: Reconceiving Generations, edited by Adele E.
Clarke and Donna Haraway, 145–64. Chicago: Prickly Paradigm, 2018.

"Ta-Nehisi Coates & Cornel West: Black Academics and Activists Give Their
Verdict." Portside (website), 27 Dec. 2017. portside.org/2017-12-27/ta-nehisi-coates
-cornel-west-black-academics-and-activists-give-their-verdict.

Taylor, Keeanga-Yamahtta. "Five Years Later, Do Black Lives Matter?" *Jacobin*,
30 Sept. 2019. www.jacobinmag.com/2019/09/black-lives-matter-laquan-mcdonald
-mike-brown-eric-garner.

———. *From #BlackLivesMatter to Black Liberation*. Chicago: Haymarket Books,
2016. E-book.

———. "How Do We Change America? The Quest to Transform This Country
Cannot Be Limited to Challenging Its Brutal Police." *New Yorker*, 8
June 2020.

Thomas, Greg. "Afro-Blue Notes: The Death of Afro-pessimism (2.0)?" *Theory &
Event* 21, no. 1 (2018): 282–317.

Threadcraft, Shatema. "North American Necropolitics and Gender: On #Black-
LivesMatter and Black Femicide." *South Atlantic Quarterly* 116, no. 3 (July 2017):
553–79.

"Together We Rise: Kanaka Maoli and Micronesian Solidarity." Lā Hoʻi Hoʻi Ea
panel, 26 July 2021, on Zoom, 6–7:30 P.M.

Trask, Haunani-Kay. "Sons." In *Light in the Crevice Never Seen*, 55–56. Corvallis,
OR: Calyx Books, 1999.

"Trouble the Water Pt. 1—Kimberly & Scott Roberts." YouTube, uploaded by
ReelBlack, 1 Oct. 2008, www.youtube.com/watch?v=NRd7tucADbk.

True, Jacqui. *The Political Economy of Violence against Women*. Oxford: Oxford
University Press, 2012.

"12 Steps to Changing Yourself and the World with Activist Patrisse Cullors."
Reform the Funk, 19 Dec. 2021. www.reformthefunk.com/features/12-steps-to
-changing-yourself-and-the-world-with-activist-patrisse-cullors.

University of Hawai'i at Hilo. *Final Environmental Impact Statement: Thirty Meter Telescope Project*, vol. 1. Hilo, 8 May 2010. dlnr.hawaii.gov/occl/files/2013/08/2010 -05-08-HA-FEIS-Thirty-Meter-Telescope-Vol1.pdf.

"U. of I. Right to Reject Prof's Hate Speech." *Chicago Tribune*, 11 Sept. 2014. www .chicagotribune.com/opinion/editorials/ct-salaita-u-of-i-professor-hate-speech-edit -0911-20140911-story.html.

US Campaign for the Academic and Cultural Boycott of Israel. Accessed 29 Sept. 2021. usacbi.org/about/.

"U.S. Relations with Syria: Bilateral Relations with Syria." U.S. Department of State, 20 Jan. 2021. www.state.gov/u-s-relations-with-syria/.

Verduzco, Gabriel. "Decolonial Love Is Possible." Student paper for English 482 ("Colonial Love / Decolonial Love"), University of Hawai'i, 10 May 2022.

Vincent, Isabel. "Inside Co-founder Patrisse Khan-Cullors' Million-Dollar Real Estate Buying Binge." *New York Post*, 10 April 2021. nypost.com/2021/04/10/inside -blm-co-founder-patrisse-khan-cullors-real-estate-buying-binge/.

Voice of Witness. "Vision Plan." Voice of Witness (website). Accessed 18 Sept. 2021. voiceofwitness.org/wp-content/uploads/2008/06/Voice-of-Witness-VISION -PLAN.pdf.

Volpp, Leti. "The Citizen and the Terrorist." *UCLA Law Review* 49, no. 5 (2002): 1575–600.

Warren, Calvin. *Ontological Terror*. Durham, NC: Duke University Press, 2018.

"Weaponizing Anti-Semitism: IHRA and the End of the Palestine Exception." USACBI Webinar. USACBI.org, 6 April 2021. usacbi.org/2021/04/video -weaponizing-anti-semitism-ihra-and-the-end-of-the-palestine-exception-usacbi -webinar/.

Weheliye, Alexander G. *Habeas Viscus: Racializing Assemblages, Biopolitics, and Black Feminist Theories of the Human*. Durham, NC: Duke University Press, 2014.

West, Cornel. "Ta-Nehisi Coates Is the Neoliberal Face of the Black Freedom Struggle." *The Guardian*, 17 Dec. 2017. www.theguardian.com/commentisfree /2017/dec/17/ta-nehisi-coates-neoliberal-black-struggle-cornel-west.

Whitlock, Gillian. "Post-ing Lives." *Biography* 35, no. 1 (2012): v–xvi.

Wilderson, Frank B., III. *Afropessimism*. New York: Liveright, 2020.

———. "Afro-Pessimism & the End of Redemption." *Occupied Times*, 30 March 2016. theoccupiedtimes.org/?p=14236.

———. "An Afropessimist on the Year since George Floyd Was Murdered." *The Nation*, 27 May 2021. www.thenation.com/article/society/george-floyd -afropessimism/.

———. "I am Frank Wilderson AMA." Reddit, 2016. Accessed 13 Sept. 2021. www .reddit.com/r/Debate/comments/5al9pl/i_am_frank_wilderson_ama/.

———. "'We're Trying to Destroy the World': Anti-Blackness & Police Violence after Ferguson: An Interview with Frank B. Wilderson III." *Ill Will Editions*, 2015. Accessed 13 Sept. 2021. illwilleditions.noblogs.org/files/2015/09/Wilderson-We-Are -Trying-to-Destroy-the-World-PRINT.pdf.

Wolfe, Patrick. "Settler Colonialism and the Elimination of the Native." *Journal of Genocide Research* 8, no. 4 (2006): 387–409.

———. *Traces of History: Elementary Structures of Race*. London: Verso, 2016.

Woods, Clyde, guest ed. "In the Wake of Katrina: New Paradigms and Social Movements." Special issue, *American Quarterly* 61, no. 3 (2009).

Wortham, Jenna. "How a New Wave of Black Activists Changed the Conversation." *New York Times*, 28 Aug. 2020. www.nytimes.com/2020/08/25/magazine/black-visions-collective.html.

Wright, Richard. "Between the World and Me." *Black Star News*, 16 Feb. 2020. www.blackstarnews.com/education/education/richard-wright-%E2%80%9Cbetween-the-world-and-me%E2%80%9D.html.

Wrigley-Field, Elizabeth. "Life Years Lost to Police Encounters in the United States." *Socius: Sociological Research for a Dynamic World* 6, 6 Aug. 2020. journals.sagepub.com/doi/pdf/10.1177/2378023120948718.

Wurth, Julie. "Kennedy: We Did the Right Thing." *News-Gazette*, 19 Sept. 2014. www.news-gazette.com/news/kennedy-we-did-the-right-thing/article_fddoc2b6-6787-50f7-ab47-cb25380365af.html.

Wynter, Sylvia. "No Humans Involved: An Open Letter to My Colleagues." *Forum N.H.I. Knowledge for the 21st Century* 1, no. 1 (Fall 1994): 42–73.

———. "Unsettling the Coloniality of Being/Power/Truth/Freedom: Towards the Human, After Man, Its Overrepresentation—An Argument." *CR: The New Centennial Review* 3, no. 3 (Fall 2003): 257–337.

Wynter, Sylvia, and Katherine McKittrick. "Unparalleled Catastrophe for Our Species? Or, to Give Humanness a Different Future: Conversations." In *Sylvia Wynter: On Being Human as Praxis*, edited by Katherine McKittrick, 9–89. Durham, NC: Duke University Press, 2015.

Yablonka, Hanna. *The State of Israel vs. Adolf Eichmann*. Translated by Ora Cummings with David Herman. New York: Schocken Books, 2004.

Yamashiro, Aiko. ""Some Baby Steps toward a Decolonial Love Story." *Ke Kaʻupu Hehi ʻAle* (blog), 11 May 2015. hehiale.com/2015/05/11/some-baby-steps-toward-a-decolonial-love-story/.

Yes! Editors. *The Black Lives Issue, Yes! Magazine*, 26 Aug. 2020. www.yesmagazine.org/issue/black-lives/2020/08/26/black-lives-matter-founders.

Yglesias, Matthew. "The Jones Act, the Obscure 1920 Shipping Regulation Strangling Puerto Rico, Explained." *Vox*, 9 Oct. 2017. www.vox.com/policy-and-politics/2017/9/27/16373484/jones-act-puerto-rico.

Yingling, Charlton, and Tyler Parry. "The Canine Terror." *Jacobin*, 19 May 2016. www.jacobinmag.com/2016/05/dogs-bloodhounds-slavery-police-brutality-racism/.

Yost, Brian. "The Voices of Others: Dave Eggers and New Directions for Testimony Narrative and Cosmopolitan Literary Collaborations." *Ariel* 42, no. 1 (2011): 149–70.

Zacharek, Stephanie. "A Shivery, Understated Tension Runs through Fruitvale Station." *Village Voice*, 20 July 2013. www.villagevoice.com/2013/07/10/a-shivery-understated-tension-runs-through-fruitvale-station/.

Zahzah, Omar. "Digital Apartheid: Palestinians Being Silenced on Social Media." *Aljazeera*, 13 May 2021. www.aljazeera.com/opinions/2021/5/13/social-media -companies-are-trying-to-silence-palestinian-voices.

Zeitgeist Films. "Trouble the Water." Accessed 18 Sept. 2021. zeitgeistfilms.com/film /troublethewater.

Zertal, Idith. *Israel's Holocaust and the Politics of Nationhood*. Translated by Chaya Galai. New ed. Cambridge: Cambridge University Press, 2010.

Žižek, Slavoj. "The Subject Supposed to Loot and Rape: Reality and Fantasy in New Orleans." *In These Times*, 20 Oct. 2005.

Index

Italic page numbers refer to figures.

bin Laden, Osama, 130
Biography (journal), 9, 156, 206–7, 237n1, 241n7
biopolitics, 15
Birzeit University (BZU), 180
Black kinship, 72; in *Fruitvale Station*, 79, 82–84; in *When They Call You a Terrorist*, 26, 109–43
Black Lives Matter (BLM), 1, 8–9, 27, 177, 189, 191, 199, 203, 220–21, 224, 227, 237n1, 240n1, 241n7, 244nn3–6, 245nn7–9; and abolitionism, 28, 69, 74–75, 110, 113–17, 138–39, 142, 158, 229; and Afro-pessimism, 75, 96, 242n17; and *Between the World and Me*, 25–26, 71, 75, 88–104, 109, 242n17; and breath/breathing, 26, 72–73, 89, 109, 112, 115–16, 119, 122, 126–28, 132, 244n23; and citizenship, 26, 71–72, 75, 77, 81, 85–88, 95, 115–19, 128–30, 134–36; fighting antiblackness, 26, 68, 70–77, 84, 86, 89, 96, 99–101, 114–15, 119–20, 124–28, 242n17; and *Fruitvale Station*, 25, 70, 75–88, 103, 109, 242n12; and Hurricane Katrina, 59, 67, 241n5; and intersectionality, 23, 69, 90, 110, 116–17, 134, 137, 242n17; solidarity with Palestinians, 74, 104–6, 131–32; and *When They Call You a Terrorist*, 26, 109–43, 229
#BlackLivesMatter (hashtag), 70, 76, 122, 137. *See also* Black Lives Matter (BLM)
Black Lives Matter and Immigration Syllabi, 203
Black Lives Matter Atlanta, 138
Black Lives Matter–Canada, 115, 141, 245n8
Black Lives Matter Global Network Foundation (BLMGNF), 114–15, 119, 141–42, 244n4, 244n6, 245n8
Black Lives Matter–Los Angeles, 139
Black Panther (film), 73, 242n12
Black Panther (superhero), 73, 95, 141, 241n8, 242n16
Black Panther: A Nation under Our Feet (comic), 73
Black Panther Party, 74, 135–36, 141, 220, 242n12
Black radical tradition, 74, 104, 119–20, 126, 133
Black studies, 9, 12, 14–16, 18
Blackwater, 51

Black Youth Project 100 (BYP100), 122, 132, 138, 141
Bland, Sandra, 87
#BLM (hashtag). *See* #BlackLivesMatter (hashtag); *see also* Black Lives Matter (BLM)
BLM and Immigration Syllabi. *See* Black Lives Matter and Immigration Syllabi
Bloom, Harold, 18
#BlueLivesMatter, 74
Boggs, Grace Lee, 131
Boggs, James Lee, 131
Boone, Steven, 77
Born Hustler, 62, 67, 240n20
Bouie, Jamelle, 59
Boullata, Issa J., 248n10
Boycott, Divestment and Sanctions (BDS) campaign, 8, 23, 28, 189, 229, 235, 252n31; activism against, 153–57, 176, 247n5, 247n8; and Black Lives Matter, 74, 104, 131–32; and Steven Salaita's firing, 27, 144–83. *See also* US Campaign for the Academic and Cultural Boycott of Israel (USACBI)
Bradshaw, Peter, 77
Brady, Nicolas, 15, 237n3
breath/breathing, 1, 3, 11, 28; and Black Lives Matter, 26, 72–73, 89, 109, 112, 115–16, 119, 122, 126–28, 132, 244n23; denial of, 10; and Mauna Kea protectors, 189, 191, 210, 231–35; and police violence, 68, 72–73, 112, 244n23. *See also* ea
Breathe Act, 128
Bronner v. Duggan et al., 247n6
Brooks, Gwendolyn, 137
brown, adrienne maree, 10, 199, 215
Brown, Cherrell, 132
Brown, Elaine, 133
Brown, Marie Alohalani, 195, 216
Brown, Michael, 26, 68, 71–73, 77, 87, 92, 131, 242n11
Brown, Wendy, 11, 13
BTS, 114
BTS ARMY, 114
Bush, Barbara, 34–37
Bush, George H. W., 34–35, 54
Bush, George W., 38–41, 44, 49, 53–54, 56–57, 63
Butler, Judith, 11, 13, 154
Butler University, 155
Byrd, Jodi, 204

Cynthia G. Franklin is Professor of English at the University of Hawaiʻi. She coedits the journal *Biography* and is author of *Academic Lives: Memoir, Cultural Theory, and the University Today* (2009), as well as *Writing Women's Communities: The Politics and Poetics of Multi-Genre Anthologies* (1994).

www.ingramcontent.com/pod-product-compliance
Lightning Source LLC
Chambersburg PA
CBHW032101040426
42336CB00040B/633